THE
JOHANNINE
LITERATURE

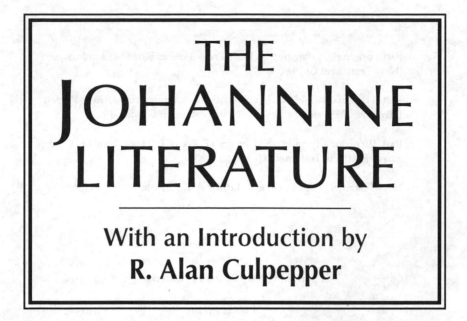

THE
JOHANNINE
LITERATURE

With an Introduction by
R. Alan Culpepper

Barnabas Lindars, Ruth B. Edwards
& John M. Court

Sheffield
Academic Press

Part I originally published by JSOT Press 1990 as Barnabas Lindars, *John* (New Testament Guides, 4)

Part II originally published by Sheffield Academic Press 1996 as Ruth B. Edwards, *The Johannine Epistles* (New Testament Guides, 19)

Part III originally published by JSOT Press 1994 as John M. Court, *Revelation* (New Testament Guides, 20)

New Testament Guides General Editor A.T. Lincoln

Published by
Sheffield Academic Press Ltd
Mansion House
19 Kingfield Road
Sheffield S11 9AS
England

Typeset by Sheffield Academic Press
and
Printed on acid-free paper in Great Britain
by Bell & Bain Ltd
Thornliebank, Glasgow

British Library Cataloguing in Publication Data

A catalogue record for this book is available
from the British Library

ISBN 1-84127-081-4

CONTENTS

Part III

REVELATION
John M. Court

ABBREVIATIONS

AB	Anchor Bible
ANTC	Abingdon New Testament Commentaries
Bib	*Biblica*
BJRL	*Bulletin of the John Rylands University Library of Manchester*
BNTC	Black's New Testament Commentaries
BTB	*Biblical Theology Bulletin*
CBQ	*Catholic Biblical Quarterly*
EKKNT	Evangelisch-Katholischer Kommentar zum Neuen Testament
FRLANT	Forschungen zur Religion und Literatur des Alten und Neuen Testaments
HNT	Handbuch zum Neuen Testament
HTKNT	Herders theologischer Kommentar zum Neuen Testament
IBC	Interpretation Biblical Commentary
IBT	Interpreting Biblical Texts
ICC	International Critical Commentary
ISBE	Geoffrey Bromiley (ed.), *The International Standard Bible Encyclopedia* (4 vols.; Grand Rapids: Eerdmans, rev. edn, 1979–88)
JBL	*Journal of Biblical Literature*
JEH	*Journal of Ecclesiastical History*
JETS	*Journal of the Evangelical Theological Society*
JSNT	*Journal for the Study of the New Testament*
JTS	*Journal of Theological Studies*
MNTC	Moffatt NT Commentary
NCB	New Century Bible
NHL	Nag Hammadi Library
NICNT	New International Commentary on the New Testament
NIGTC	The New International Greek Testament Commentary
NovT	*Novum Testamentum*
NRSV	New Revised Standard Version
NTS	*New Testament Studies*
REB	Revised English Bible
SNTSMS	Society for New Testament Studies Monograph Series
TDNT	Gerhard Kittel and Gerhard Friedrich (eds.), *Theological Dictionary of the New Testament* (trans. Geoffrey W. Bromiley; 10 vols.; Grand Rapids: Eerdmans, 1964–)
WBC	Word Biblical Commentary
WUNT	Wissenschaftliche Untersuchungen zum Neuen Testament
ZNW	*Zeitschrift für die neutestamentliche Wissenschaft*
ZTK	*Zeitschrift für Theologie und Kirche*

AN INTRODUCTION TO THE JOHANNINE WRITINGS

R. Alan Culpepper

SETI is the 'search for extra terrestrial intelligence'. Radio waves from deep space are intercepted and analyzed for evidence of meaningful patterns. Suppose that someday a radio telescope records a 'communication' that might begin with numbers, then progressively more complicated mathematics, then a brief pictorial glossary, a grammar with numbered sections, and finally a text that could be deciphered using the glossary and grammar. We would analyze this communication from another world from every conceivable approach. What does it tell us about life in this world 'above'? Who are its authors? What is their understanding of life? What gives their life meaning, and although we will never see them, given the separation of time and distance, what might they teach us?

The Johannine Corpus

In many respects the Johannine writings are like a communication received from a distant time and place, another world that is both like and unlike ours in surprising ways. The Johannine writings, whose common attribution to the apostle John is evidence that their similarities were recognized by the church early on, are a collection of five writings: a gospel, three letters, and an apocalypse. Of course, we are not the first to read and ponder these writings. They are among the most influential writings of Christianity and Western civilization. They have profoundly influenced religious thought, Christian theology, religious art, and English literature. The Gospel's characterization of Jesus as 'the Word' opened the Christian message to new understandings and eventually shaped the doctrine of the Trinity. John 3.16 has become a basic credo of the Christian faith, and the 'new command', 'that you love one another as I have loved you' (Jn 13.34), is the foundation of Christian ethics. The stories of Jesus turning water to wine, talking with Nicodemus at night and the Samaritan woman at the well, healing the man born blind, raising Lazarus, and washing the disciples' feet are so widely known that most people would be surprised to learn these stories occur only in John. Similarly, John's vision of the throne and the sea of glass and the new Jerusalem shape our images of heaven, just as his descriptions of the bowls of wrath, Armageddon, and the Millennium have inspired terror, awe, and hope in every generation.

The purpose of this volume is to lead the reader deeper into the peculiar visions and voices of these writings, so that the reader may enter the Johannine writings more discerningly and with even greater appreciation of their beauty and timeless descriptions of life long ago, life 'from above', and life as it is and can be now. In order to decipher these writings, one must understand their peculiar forms, tune one's ear to their language, and explore the world from which they come. This essay offers an introduction to the study of the Johannine writings, and each of the three parts that follow explore the Gospel, the Letters, and the Apocalypse of John in greater detail.

Genre

One of the first questions we ask of a writing, whether we are aware of it or not, and whether it is a letter from a friend, a magazine article, or a legal document, is 'What kind of writing is this?' The answer to this question tells us something about how to read the document and what to expect as we read. A gospel is 'sui generis'; it is a new genre unto itself. It owes a great deal to ancient biographies, some of which were used in the cults of heroes or immortals, and some of which were used in school traditions to relate the life and teachings of the founder and to trace the line of succession. The Gospel of John is clearly a gospel, and is more like the other three New Testament gospels than any other writings, including the apocryphal gospels, but it is also noticeably different. It has therefore been called the 'spiritual gospel' and a 'maverick gospel'. It is more abstract in language and thought, more overtly theological, and contains more discourse material than the other gospels. Differences in respect to content, language, imagery, chronology, geography, and theology are all evident upon close examination.

Similar observations can be made about the letters and the Apocalypse. The letters, while each different, are so similar that they are generally viewed as the work of one author, who identifies himself as the 'elder' at the beginning of each of the two shorter letters. On the other hand, each is peculiar. 2 and 3 John follow the form of ancient letters, though 2 John is addressed either literally or metaphorically to 'the elect lady and her children', while 3 John is addressed to a named individual, Gaius. Both letters close with hopes of a personal visit and greetings. The elder sends greetings from 'the children of your elect sister' at the end of 2 John and greetings from 'the friends' at the end of 3 John. By contrast, 1 John reflects so little of the form of an ancient letter that interpreters have at times searched for other terms to describe it: a circular letter, tract, manifesto, homily, or encheiridion (see below Edwards, 'The Johannine Epistles', Chapter 3 §1). 1 John lacks both an epistolary opening and greetings in closing. Instead, it opens with a prologue that bears some resemblance to the prologue of the Gospel, rather than an epistolary address. Appeals to the readers as 'my little children' (2.1), 'beloved' (2.7; 4.1, 7, 11), 'little children' (2.12, 28; 3.18; 4.4; 5.21), 'fathers' (2.13, 14), 'young men' (2.13, 14), 'children' (2.14, 18), and 'brothers' (3.13) reflect the close relationship between author and readers or hearers, whatever the form of the writing.

Similar anomalies are evident in the form of Revelation. Just as John is clearly a gospel, though different from any other gospel in its form, so Revelation is clearly an apocalypse (Rev. 1.1), though again different from any other. Like other apocalypses, it features a tour of the heavens, revelations of coming events, numerology, animal symbolism, a deterministic view of history, and the promise of judgment of the wicked and vindication for the righteous. On the other hand, it has both an outer frame appropriate for an apocalypse (Rev. 1.1-3) and an inner frame appropriate for a letter (Rev. 1.4-8). John identifies himself as the author, the seven churches that are in Asia as the recipients, and adds a typical (Pauline?) blessing, 'Grace to you and peace' (Rev. 1.4). John then introduces the setting of his revelation, the letters to the seven churches, and the vision that follows ('I, John, your brother...' 1.9).[1] At the end, an epilogue and benediction close the narrative ('I, John, am the one who heard and saw these things' 22.8) and offer blessings and warnings appropriate for the ending of an apocalypse (22.18-20) and greetings to the saints appropriate for the ending of an epistle (22.21).

What emerges from this preliminary survey of the forms of the Johannine writings is that they are identifiable as biblical writings in that they resemble and make use of the forms of other biblical writings (gospel, letter, apocalypse), but the authors are not bound by these conventions. One might say that the Johannine writers were

---

1.   See David L. Barr, *Tales of the End: A Narrative Commentary on the Book of Revelation* (Santa Rosa: Polebridge Press, 1998), pp. 25-34.

incapable of coloring in the lines. More accurately, they knew the established forms but blended and adapted them for their own creative purposes. This evidence of creative license should caution us as later readers to be careful about making assumptions about what these writings 'must' be saying or how they say it.

Authorship: The Early Witnesses

The question of how these five writings are related to one another leads naturally to questions about authorship. We have already noted that, different as they are, the five are all attributed by tradition to the apostle John. On the other hand, while the author of Revelation identifies himself as 'John', he does not claim to be an apostle, and the other four writings are anonymous. The Gospel refers to its author as the 'beloved disciple' (Jn 21.24-25), and the author of 2 and 3 John identifies himself as 'the elder'. Are all five writings the work of one man, the apostle John or a teacher and theologian in Asia Minor late in the first century by the same name? Or were the Gospel and Letters written by one author and Revelation by another? Or were there multiple authors: sources, an evangelist, and one or more editors for the Gospel; one or two different authors for 1 John and the shorter letters; and a separate author and perhaps redactor for Revelation? Both the history of tradition and the internal evidence of the writings themselves bear on these questions.

The story of the reception and the growth of traditions about the origins of the Johannine writings begins faintly, with possible echoes or allusions to them in writings that date from the early part of the second century. Little can be established from these possible allusions. Nothing remains of the works of Papias (c. 130 CE) except in fragments and quotations by Irenaeus, Eusebius, and other writers. In one notoriously obscure quotation Papias refers to the testimony of both John the apostle and 'the presbyter John'.[2] Whether Papias knew the Gospel of John and Revelation is debatable. In his zeal to establish a chain of testimony to the apostolic authorship of the Gospel, Irenaeus mistakenly claims that Papias had been a hearer of the apostle John. Eusebius, who rejected Revelation, records that Papias 'used quotations from the first epistle of John'.[3]

Polycarp apparently knew 1 Jn 4.2-3, 2 John 7, or both, because his

---

2.   Eusebius, *Hist. Eccles.* 3.39.3-4; see R. Alan Culpepper, *John the Son of Zebedee: The Life of a Legend* (Columbia, SC: University of South Carolina Press, 1994), pp. 109-12.

3.   Eusebius, *Hist. Eccles.* 3.39.17; see Culpepper, *John the Son of Zebedee*, p. 92.

Epistle to the Philippians (c. 140 CE) contains an echo of these verses: 'For everyone who does not confess Jesus Christ has come in the flesh is an anti-christ'.[4] Justin Martyr (d. c. 165 CE), who lived in Ephesus before he moved to Rome, offers further tantalizing and perplexing data. Justin quotes Rev. 20.4-5, attributing it to 'a certain man with us, whose name was John, one of the apostles of Christ'.[5] Justin may also refer to Jn 3.3, but the reference is debated. His silence about the other Johannine writings, especially the Gospel, is surprising. He does not quote from the Gospel of John, says nothing about its apostolic origin, and does not connect it with Ephesus. Still, he is the first to identify the Seer of Revelation with the apostle John.

By contrast, the Gospel of John was quoted and used extensively by the Valentinian Gnostics in Rome. Ptolemy, one of Valentinus's early students, wrote a commentary on the prologue of the Gospel, and Heracleon wrote the first commentary on John about 170 CE. The growing use of the Gospel in orthodox circles can be traced in the practice of the Quartodecimans. Following Polycarp, who followed the Johannine chronology, they claimed that Easter should always be celebrated on the 14th day of the Jewish month of Nisan, the same day as Passover. Other allusions to John can be seen in the teachings of the Montanists, and in Tatian's use of the Gospel in his harmony of the four Gospels, called the Diatessaron. The first orthodox writer to identify the fourth evangelist as John, presumably the apostle John, is Theophilus of Antioch (168–181 or 188 CE).[6]

Irenaeus (c. 130–200) was the first to make the case for the apostolic authorship of the Johannine writings, and his view rapidly became the accepted tradition. It is noteworthy that widespread use of the Gospel preceded the development of the argument for its apostolic authorship. Once the Gospel came into common use, and in order to secure its place among the orthodox writings, Irenaeus had to show that it was written by an apostle. He did so by claiming that the Gospel was written by the apostle John, in Ephesus, and that the apostle lived there to an advanced age: 'Afterwards, John the disciple of the Lord, who also had leaned upon His breast, did himself publish a Gospel during his residence at Ephesus in Asia.'[7] There is no place in Irenaeus's understanding of the authorship of the Johannine writings for John the Elder, the otherwise unknown figure mentioned by

4.   Polycarp, *Phil.* 7.1.
5.   Justin Martyr, *Dialogue with Trypho* 81.
6.   Theophilus, *Ad Autolycum* 2.22.
7.   Irenaeus, *Adv. Haer.* 3.1.1.

Papias. Irenaeus identified the Beloved Disciple as the apostle John, and elsewhere speaks of the author of 1 and 2 John and Revelation as 'John, the Lord's disciple'.[8] For this understanding, Irenaeus may have drawn upon the writings of Papias. If so, he stands four steps from the apostle: Irenaeus, Papias, travelers who followed the elders, the elders, and finally the apostles.[9]

In another passage, Irenaeus recalls hearing Polycarp as a youth, as Polycarp told of his association with the apostle John,[10] but Irenaeus does not report that Polycarp taught that the apostle John was the author of the Fourth Gospel, the Epistles, or Revelation. It is hard to draw firm conclusions about the tradition prior to Irenaeus. Irenaeus's testimony is credible but not certain, substantial but open to suspicion at key points. He at least created the synthesis of tradition in favor of the apostolic authorship and therefore the orthodoxy of the Johannine writings: the apostle John, who was also the Beloved Disciple of the Gospel, the elder of the Epistles, and the Seer of the Apocalypse, lived in Ephesus to an old age and wrote the Gospel and Letters there and the Apocalypse on the island of Patmos. Irenaeus's synthesis became the church's tradition.

With Irenaeus, the battle for the fourfold Gospel was won. The authority of the Gospel as Scripture was never again in question, and the attribution of the Johannine writings to the apostle became the accepted tradition. The Bodmer Papyrus $\mathfrak{P}^{66}$, which dates about 200 CE is the earliest manuscript to contain the superscription 'Gospel according to John. $\mathfrak{P}^{75}$ (early third century) contains the same superscription.

Although the apostolic authorship of the five Johannine writings was widely accepted and no doubt led to the acceptance of the five writings as Scripture, there were occasional skeptics and critics, even in the early centuries. In Rome, Gaius (c. 170–80 CE), a presbyter and noted orthodox scholar and an opponent of Montanism, rejected both the Gospel of John and Revelation and denied the apostolic authorship of both writings. In support of his opposition to the Gospel, he noted its historical discrepancies and differences from the other gospels.

In Alexandria, the place of the Epistles and Revelation seems to have been in some doubt. Clement (?—c. 215) knew 2 John and

---

8.   Irenaeus, *Adv. Haer*. 1.16.3.
9.   Culpepper, *John the Son of Zebedee*, p. 110.
10.   Irenaeus, *Adv. Haer*. 3.3.4; Eusebius, *Hist. Eccles*. 5.20.5-7.

attributed it to the apostle.[11] Origen, on the other hand, is vague about the number of the epistles and comments that 'not all say that these are genuine'.[12] Dionysius (200–65 CE), a pupil of Origen who later became head of the Alexandrian School, was the first to raise critical arguments against the apostolic authorship of Revelation. He noted that others before him had rejected and impugned the book. Dionysius, however, allowed that Revelation was written by a 'holy and inspired person' named John, but maintained that this John was not the author of the Gospel and the Epistles because they contain no similar identification of their author and because of the difference in the character of Revelation and differences in language and style.[13] In this regard, Dionysius's arguments sound remarkably modern.

Debate over the place of Revelation continued into the fourth century. Eusebius (260–340 CE), whose history of the church preserves many traditions that would otherwise be lost to us, comments: 'Of the writings of John in addition to the gospel the first of his epistles has been accepted without controversy by ancients and moderns alike but the other two are disputed, and as to the Revelation there have been many advocates of either opinion up to the present.'[14] Eusebius himself attributed Revelation to John the elder rather than to the apostle. Others rejected the book and attributed it to the heretic Cerinthus.[15] When Eusebius lists those books that are recognized as Scripture and those that are 'spurious' or 'not genuine', he includes Revelation in both lists, and lists 2 and 3 John among the 'disputed books'.[16] Citing Papias, Jerome, the greatest biblical scholar of the fourth century, argued that the two shorter epistles were written by John the elder.[17] Elsewhere, however, Jerome attributes the Letters to the apostle John.[18] In spite of these continuing debates, the place of the Johannine writings in the life of the church was secure. Bishop Athanasius listed all the books of the New Testament in order and none others in his Easter letter of 367 CE, and thereafter the list was adopted by the Councils of Hippo (393 CE) and Carthage (397 CE). In

---

11. Clement of Alexandria, *Fragments from Cassiodorus* 4.

12. Origen, *Exposition on the Gospel According to John* 5.3.

13. Dionysius, quoted in Eusebius, *Hist. Eccles.* 7.25.1-2, and *Hist. Eccles.* 7.25.6-27.

14. Eusebius, *Hist. Eccles.* 3.24.17-18.

15. Eusebius, *Hist. Eccles.* 7.25.2.

16. Eusebius, *Hist. Eccles.* 3.24.17, 3.25.2-3.

17. Jerome, *Lives of Illustrious Men* 18.

18. Jerome, *Letters* 53.8 (J. Migne, *Patrologia latina* 22.548), cited by R.E. Brown, *The Epistles of John* (AB, 30; Garden City, NY: Doubleday, 1982), p. 11.

the Eastern church, however, the Diatessaron continued to be used, and Revelation was slow in gaining full acceptance.

Text

The texts of the Johannine writings have come down to us by separate traditions. No manuscript contains only the five Johannine writings, and the earliest copies of the Johannine writings are preserved in different manuscripts. None of the 'original manuscripts' of any of the New Testament writings has survived, so scholars must reconstruct the earliest readings from the available manuscripts. Fortunately, the textual traditions are well represented, at least from the fourth century on.

The earliest text of the Gospel of John is $\mathfrak{P}^{52}$ (Manchester, John Rylands Library, P. Ryl. Gr. 457), which contains the text of Jn 18.31-33 and 18.37-38. This fragment was discovered in Egypt and published in 1935. Because it is generally dated about 125, it is widely regarded as the earliest fragment of the New Testament. Some scholars, however, believe that a date of 150–75 is more accurate.[19] In addition to $\mathfrak{P}^{52}$, 16 other papyri contain parts of the text of the Gospel. $\mathfrak{P}^{75}$ agrees closely with Vaticanus (B), and $\mathfrak{P}^{66}$, the earliest text of the four gospels (about 200 CE), stands between Vaticanus (B) and Sinaiticus (ℵ). Although there were already variations in the texts by 200, when these two papyri agree they provide strong evidence for the text they represent.

The Epistles are more weakly represented in the textual tradition. The principal witnesses for the Johannine Epistles are the great fourth-century codexes Vaticanus (B) and Sinaiticus (ℵ), as well as Alexandrinus (A), Ephraimi (C), and $\mathfrak{P}^{74}$. The Trinitarian reference in 1 Jn 5.7-8, or 'Johannine Comma' as it has been called, does not appear in any Greek manuscript before 1400 CE. It first appears in Latin manuscripts that come from North Africa and Spain, beginning in the fourth century, so it is evidently a gloss motivated by the Trinitarian debates of the fourth and fifth centuries.

The text of Revelation is preserved in six papyrus fragments, eleven uncials (i.e., manuscripts written in capital letters; only three of which contain a complete text of Revelation), and 292 minuscules (i.e., manuscripts written in cursive script).[20] The earliest fragment of

19. See Culpepper, *John the Son of Zebedee*, p. 108.
20. David E. Aune, *Revelation 1–5* (WBC, 52; Dallas: Word, 1997), pp. cxxxvi-cxl.

Revelation is $\mathfrak{P}^{98}$, which may date from the late second century and contains Rev. 1.13-20. $\mathfrak{P}^{47}$, late third century, contains Rev. 9.10–17.2 and agrees closely with the most important uncials: $\aleph$, A, C, and P.

If these writings come from the same author, community, or provenance, they have come to us through different ecclesiastical traditions, their canonical status was judged variously in the early centuries, and they are preserved in different manuscripts with different textual traditions.

Language and Style

The style of each of the Johannine writings bears a familial resemblance to that of the other writings in this corpus. Generally, they are all written in a relatively simple and Semitic Greek style. It has often been suggested that the author(s) of the Gospel and Revelation thought in Aramaic but wrote in Greek. On the other hand, evidence of translation of the Greek texts from a Semitic original is generally unconvincing.

The style of the Gospel is relatively uniform, making it difficult to show that proposed sources differ in style from the rest of the Gospel.[21] The Gospel of John is also noted for its overuse of key terms, its fondness for double meanings, and its apparently pointless stylistic variations. The Gospel uses a relatively limited vocabulary, only 1,011 different words, only 112 of which occur only once in the New Testament.[22] Since there are 15,416 words in the Gospel, the vocabulary is only 6.5 percent of the total words, which is almost the lowest in the New Testament. The Gospel uses particles frequently (esp. *alla* and *oun*, 'but' and 'then'). Among the Gospels, John makes the least use of the adversative construction *men...de*, which never occurs in the Johannine Epistles or Revelation. Both John and Revelation differ from general New Testament usage in the degree of their preference for *dia* with the accusative ('because of') over *dia* with the genitive ('through'). The Gospel and Letters of John display a striking fondness for the conjunction *hina* ('in order that', 'so that'), using the term

---

21. See Eduard Schweizer, *Ego Eimi* (FRLANT NS 38; Göttingen: Vandenhoeck & Ruprecht, 1939); Eugen Ruckstuhl, *Die literarische Einheit des Johannesevangeliums* (Studies Friburgensia NS 3; Freiburg in der Schweiz: Paulusverlag, 1951); and Robert T. Fortna, *The Gospel of Signs: A Reconstruction of the Narrative Source Underlying the Fourth Gospel* (SNTSMS, 11; Cambridge: Cambridge University Press, 1970).

22. James Hope Moulton, *A Grammar of New Testament Greek. IV. Style*, by Nigel Turner (Edinburgh: T. & T. Clark, 1976), p. 76.

relatively more frequently than any other books of the New Testament.

The style of the Epistles has been worked over thoroughly in the debate regarding their common authorship with the Gospel. A.E. Brooke compiled impressive lists of the phrases common to the Gospel and the Letters, re-examined a list of 50 peculiarities of the style of the Epistles, and compiled lists of the Greek words that occur in the Epistles and those that occur in the Gospel but not in the Epistles.[23] C.H. Dodd used the differences in style to argue for a difference in authorship between the Gospel and the Epistles, pointing in particular to the fact that the Epistles use a more limited vocabulary of prepositions, adverbial particles, conjunctive particles, and compound verbs and different idiomatic expressions.[24] Dodd's arguments were carefully and critically reviewed by W.F. Howard, W.G. Wilson, and A.P. Salom, who weakened the force of Dodd's arguments by pointing out that the differences in length, genre, content, and setting could account for the differences in style rather than different authors.[25] In her discussion of the Greek style of 1 John later in this volume, Ruth Edwards notes the author's fondness for 'if' clauses, antitheses, test formulas, short sentences, and excessive use of 'and'. Among the significant Gospel themes that do not occur in the Epistles are: salvation and destruction, Scripture, glory, sending, seeking, above and below, and judgment.[26]

The book of Revelation uses a Greek vocabulary of only 916 words, 128 of which do not occur elsewhere in the New Testament. Since there are 9834 words in the Nestle text of Revelation, the vocabulary is 9.0 percent of the total words. Like the Gospel, the style of Revelation is marked by Aramaisms and Hebraisms. Redundancies, parataxis, and the influence of Hebrew idioms and expressions (such as the frequency of the preposition *enopion*, 'before', which suggests the influence of the Hebrew *liphne*) are common. Unlike the Gospel, however, the syntax of Revelation is so distinctive that commentators

23. A.E. Brooke, *A Critical and Exegetical Commentary on the Johannine Epistles* (ICC; Edinburgh: T. & T. Clark, 1912), pp. i-xix, 229-42.

24. C.H. Dodd, 'The First Epistle of John and the Fourth Gospel', *BJRL* 21 (1937), pp. 129-56.

25. W.F. Howard, 'The Common Authorship of the Johannine Gospel and Epistles', *JTS* 48 (1947), pp. 12-25; W.G. Wilson, 'An Examination of the Linguistic Evidence Adduced against the Unity of the First Epistle of John and the Fourth Gospel', *JTS* 49 (1948), pp. 147-56; A.P. Salom, 'Some Aspects of the Grammatical Style of 1 John', *JBL* 74 (1955), pp. 96-102.

26. I. Howard Marshall, *The Epistles of John* (Grand Rapids: Wm B. Eerdmans, 1978), p. 33.

have had to write a grammar of the book in order to handle its peculiar style.[27] Solecisms, i.e., deviations from standard grammar, abound: gender discrepancies (masculine for feminine or neuter, feminine for masculine or neuter, etc.), and misuse of cases (nominative for accusative, genitive for dative, etc.). The extent to which these are due to the influence of Aramaic or Hebrew native thought patterns, sources, translation errors, deliberate efforts to convey a meaning, or errors that would have been removed by more careful editing is debated. Some of the differences in vocabulary between the Gospel and Revelation are difficult to explain if they come from the same author: 'lamb' (*arnion*: John once, Rev. 29 times; *amnos*: John twice, Rev. never), 'Jerusalem' (*Ierousalem*: John never, Rev. twice; *Ierosolyma*: John 12 times, Rev. never).

Use of the Old Testament

The use of the Old Testament offers another revealing point of comparison for appraising the relationships among the Johannine writings. The Gospel reflects thorough familiarity with the Old Testament and makes facile use of it, even though it quotes the Old Testament only infrequently: 17 to 20 times. The following list reflects the 17 passages printed in italics in the Nestle 26th edition of *Novum Testamentum Graece* (Stuttgart: Deutsche Bibelstirtung, 1979) and the three additional passages cited by C.K. Barrett[28] as quotations or adaptations of Old Testament references:

John	1.23	Isa. 40.3
	1.51	Gen. 28.12
	2.17	Ps. 68(69).10
	6.31	Exod. 16.14-15; Ps. 77(78).24-25
	[7.42	Ps. 88(89).4-5; Mic. 5.1(2)]
	[10.16	Ezek. 34.23; 37.24]
	10.34	Ps. 81(82).6
	12.13	Ps. 117(118).25-26
	12.15	Zech. 9.9
	12.27	Ps. 6.3; 41(42).7

27. See R.H. Charles, *A Critical and Exegetical Commentary on the Revelation of St. John*, I (ICC; Edinburgh: T. & T. Clark, 1920), pp. cxvii-clix; and David E. Aune, *Revelation 1–5* (WBC, 52; Dallas: Word, 1997), pp. clx-ccvii.

28. *The Gospel According to St. John* (Philadelphia: Westminster Press, 2nd edn, 1978), pp. 28-29.

        12.38   Isa. 53.1
        12.40   Isa. 6.10
        13.18   Ps. 40(41).10
        15.25   Ps. 34(35).19; 68(69).5
        19.24   Ps. 21(22).19
    [19.28-29. Ps. 68(69).22]
        19.36   Exod. 12.10, 46; Num. 9.12; Ps. 33(34).21
        19.37   Zech. 12.10

This list is revealing in several respects. First, the uncertainty regarding precisely what reference is being cited reflects the degree to which some of the references have been adapted, and the brevity of the citations in question. The references in brackets are not printed in italics in the Nestle text. Second, it is apparent that John frequently uses texts that were used by other New Testament writers, which suggests that they have come to him in Christian traditions or testimonia collections. Third, many of the citations are christological in their focus. The distribution is interesting: Genesis one citation, Exodus two; Numbers one, Psalms thirteen, Isaiah three, Ezekiel two; Micah one, Zechariah two. Fourth, the citations are clustered, with five of them occurring in chapter 12 and four at the climax of the passion narrative. It is also significant that the citations generally appear in the narrative rather than in the discourse material.

Significant as the quotations are, the extent of John's knowledge and use of the Old Testament can hardly be gauged by a survey of the explicit citations. Such a survey does not expose the influence of the Wisdom tradition on John's Christology, the manner in which Jesus is depicted as a fulfillment of the role of Moses, the Old Testament background of John's use of the term 'Son of Man', the influence of Isaiah on the 'I am' sayings, or the way in which John has drawn on Old Testament imagery in the discourses on the sheep and the shepherd in John 10 and the vine and the branches in John 15. The question of the texts that John used is still debated. In places John's citations conform to the Greek Septuagint, but in other places John may cite a Hebrew text, adapt the text for his purposes, or quote from memory. Some of the quotations may also have come to the evangelist in his sources. Regardless, the thought of the Gospel is deeply rooted in the Scriptures of Israel and grows naturally from them.

Like the Pastoral Epistles, the Johannine Epistles do not quote the Hebrew Scriptures or make explicit use of them. The two shorter letters do not refer to the Scriptures—due in large measure no doubt to their brevity and subject matter. More surprising is the lack of appeal to the Scriptures in 1 John. The only biblical reference is to 'Cain who was from the evil one and murdered his brother' (3.12). On the other hand, the Epistles breathe the same atmosphere as the Hebrew Scriptures. Jeremiah's description of the new covenant (Jer. 31.33-34) is essential for 1 Jn 2.3-11 and much of the rest of 1 John (see below). Moreover, 1 John elevates keeping the commandments as a requirement for abiding in fellowship with God. The essential nature of God is described in 1 John in terms drawn from the Scriptures: light, righteousness, and love. The concept of truth that is so carefully defined in 1 John and the role that is ascribed to the Spirit are again an extension of the treatment they receive in the Hebrew Scriptures. Therefore, while the Johannine Epistles do not quote the Scriptures, one must be careful not to give too much weight to this silence.[29]

A similar caution is required in evaluating the Apocalypse's use of Scripture. The book of Revelation never employs a formula of fulfillment or explicitly cites the Scriptures, but Old Testament words, phrases, images, and allusions appear throughout the book. The Nestle text prints portions of the following verses in italics (signifying a quotation):

Revelation	1.7	Dan. 7.13; Zech. 12.10; Gen. 12.3; 28.14
	2.27	Ps. 2.8, 9
	4.8	Isa. 6.3; Amos 3.13
	6.16	Hosea 10.8
	7.16	Isa. 49.10
	7.17	Isa. 25.8
	11.11	Ezek. 37.5, 10
	14.5	Zeph. 3.13; Isa. 53.9

Revelation	1.7	Dan. 7.13; Zech. 12.10; Gen. 12.3; 28.14
	15.3	Ps. 111.2; 139.14; Amos 3.13; 4.13; Deut. 32.4; Ps. 145.17; Jer. 10.7
	15.4	Jer. 10.7; Ps. 86.9; Isa. 2.2; Jer. 16.19
	19.15	Ps. 2.9
	20.9	2 Kings 1.10, 12
	21.4	Isa. 25.8
	21.7	2 Sam. 7.14; Ezek. 11.20

---

29. This paragraph is adapted from my essay on '1-2-3 John' in Gerhard Krodel (ed.), *The General Letters* (Minneapolis: Fortress Press, 1995), pp. 132-33.

Again, however, this list hardly tells the whole story. The index of the Nestle text lists 635 Old Testament references in the book of Revelation.[30] The author of Revelation is so steeped in Scripture that he uses its language to describe his visions. He draws heavily on the prophetic texts and shows that the Christ event is the fulfillment Israel's prophets. Because the references are brief and allusive it is difficult to say much about the basis of the seer's knowledge of the Scriptures. References to most of the books of the Old Testament are evident, as is dependence on the Hebrew as well as the Septuagint.[31]

As we have seen, the principal Johannine writings (excluding the two shorter epistles) are steeped in the language of the Hebrew Scriptures even though they seldom quote them. Quotations are noticeably absent from 1 John and the discourses in the Gospel, and Revelation uses allusions, images, and terms drawn from the Scriptures rather than actual quotations. Still the relationship between the Gospel's and Revelation's use of Scripture is not sufficiently close in technique or text to provide evidence of a common origin.

Thought

The similarities and differences among the Johannine writings are probably most striking in the area of their thought or theology. Common to all the writings, recognizing the limitations of 3 John especially, are their pervasive dualism and to lesser extents their concerns with Christology and fulfillment. The sections on the Gospel, Letters, and Revelation that follow in this volume explore the thought of the writings in more detail. Here we can only draw attention to the relationships among them in respect to dualism, Christology, and fulfillment.

Dualism is a form of thought, or a worldview, that divides reality sharply into two spheres, one good and one evil. Dualism can be cosmological (heaven and earth, above and below), temporal (this age and the age to come, already and not yet), or soteriological (lost and saved, children of darkness and children of light, dead and alive). It can be absolute (two eternal powers, one good and one evil) or it can be limited (one God, that which is of God and that which is not of God). The Johannine writings are overtly dualistic, but in different

---

30. Nestle, *Novum Testamentum Graece*, 26th edn, pp. 739-74.

31. For a full, recent discussion of these issues, see G.K. Biele, *John's Use of the Old Testament in Revelation* (JSNTSup, 166; Sheffield: Sheffield Academic Press, 1998).

ways. They espouse a dualistic worldview in which there is one sovereign God, but a sharp conflict between all that is of God and all that is opposed to God. Human beings therefore stand in one camp or the other. A whole series of terms and images reinforce this dualism: above and below, true and false, love and hate, good and evil, life and death, light and darkness, Christ and the devil, and so forth. Because the terms have either a positive or a negative value, related terms can be used almost interchangeably: 'In him was life, and the life was the light of all people' (Jn 1.4).

The dualism of the Gospel is primarily concerned with reception of that which is true and authentic and rejection of that which is false. Jesus, the Christ, the Son of God, reveals all that the Father has given to him: life and light. The characters in the Gospel then reflect and represent various responses to this revelation—the various forms and stages of belief and unbelief. The more typical Jewish and early Christian dualism of that which is and that which is yet to come is transformed in John's 'realized eschatology' into that which is from above and that which is 'from below'. Jesus is 'from above'; those who are 'from below' or 'of this world' cannot believe unless they are 'born from above'. In turn, those who believe, who are born 'again' or 'from above' (Greek: *anothen*), have 'crossed from death into life'. Vestiges of the traditional, temporal dualism remain, especially in references to 'the last day' (6.39, 40, 44, 54).

In 1 John the dualism and the language in which it is expressed is especially close to that of the farewell discourse in John 13–17. It places the community of believers over against the world. The world (here meaning all that is opposed to God) opposes them because they are of God:

> If the world hates you, be aware that it hated me before it hated you (John 15.18).
> Do not love the world or the things in the world. The love of the Father is not in those who love the world (1 John 2.15).

Those who remain faithful do what is true (1.6), 'walk in the light' (1 Jn 1.7), love the brothers and sisters in the community (2.10), remain with them (2.19), and confess the Son (2.23). Those who are not walk in darkness (1.6), lie (1.6), hate their brothers and sisters (2.9), go out from them (2.19), and deny that Jesus is the Christ (2.22). Some of the same dualistic language is present in the shorter epistles also: 'whom I love in the truth' (2 Jn 1), 'your children walking in the truth' (2 Jn 4), but 'many deceivers have gone out into the world, those who do not confess that Jesus has come in the flesh; any such person is the deceiver and the antichrist' (2 Jn 7). Johannine dualism reinforces community solidarity: 'the truth…abides in us and will be with us forever' (2 Jn 2), but 'do not receive into the house or welcome anyone who comes to you and does not bring this teaching' (2 Jn 10). This principle may explain Diotrephes' refusal to receive Demetrius and others who are sent by the elder in 3 John. Gaius, however, 'walks in the truth' (3 Jn 3) because he receives those who are sent by the elder. They are 'co-workers with the truth' (3 Jn 8), but Diotrephes is 'spreading false charges' (3 Jn 10). Therefore, the elder admonishes Gaius: 'do not imitate what is evil but imitate what is good. Whoever does good is from God; whoever does evil has not seen God' (3 Jn 11).

The dualism of Revelation takes a somewhat different form and is expressed in different terms. The dualism of above and below sets the stage for the seer's vision in which he is taken up into heaven and shown what is about to take place on the earth (4.1). The predominant dualities, however, relate to the opposition between the false powers of earthly (Roman) authority and the true power of Christ. Christ is the lamb who was slain (5.6), while the emperor (probably Nero or Domitian) is portrayed as the beast with a mortal wound (13.1-3). The great dragon (Satan) is thrown down to earth, where it pursues the woman who gives birth to a male child (13.13). The faithful worship the lamb (5.8, 12), while those who are deceived worship the beast (13.4). In the end, the great harlot (Rome) who had received power from the dragon (Satan) is overthrown, and those who worshiped the beast are destroyed by terrible plagues. On the other hand, those who refused to worship the beast are conquerors 'by the blood of the lamb and by the word of their testimony, for they did not cling to life even in the face of death' (12.11). The faithful, who are now dreadfully persecuted, will be rewarded with life in the heavenly city, the new Jerusalem, whose glory is described in the closing chapters of the book. Revelation, therefore, is steeped in dualism, but its dualism is played in a different key.

Christology, not dualism, is the real focus of each of the Johannine writings. Dualism is merely the conceptual context in which Christology and the appeal to respond to Christ in faith are developed. In the Gospel, the prologue sets forth the community's understanding of Christ as the fulfillment of Wisdom, or the Word incarnate. He is greater than John the Baptist, and he is the one of whom Moses spoke. As the Logos, Jesus' words reveal the Father, and his works demonstrate his continuing sovereignty over nature (changing water to wine, multiplying loaves, walking on water, healing the sick, and raising the dead). Jesus therefore fulfills the Torah of Moses, the words of the prophets, the Scriptures, and the feasts of the Jews in Jerusalem. He can say 'I am', echoing the revelation of the divine name to Moses. Jesus is the Son of God, whose words and works—and ultimately his death—glorify the Father. He is 'the lamb of God that takes away the sin of the world (1.29, 36), so, fittingly, he dies on the day of preparation for the Passover. He is also the Son of Man who fulfills the Jewish hopes for the future. Already, the judgment is taking place (Jn 3.19), and the dead are being raised (5.24-29). The Gospel is breathtaking, dizzying, in the brilliance and innovation of its Christology.

The Letters, by contrast, seem more concerned with stopping the progress of continuing innovation. Their emphasis is on what the community has heard and received 'from the beginning' (1 Jn 1.1; 2.7, 13, 14, 24; 3.11; 2 Jn 5, 6). The 'new command' is an old command that they have had from the beginning, to love one another (1 Jn 2.7). The language of Father–Son still predominates, confirming that the Epistles are closely related to the Gospel, but the emphasis tilts toward concern with the character of God, who is light (1.5), righteousness (2.29), and love (4.7). One must confess that Jesus is the Christ, the Son (2.23-24), but a new concern surfaces. One must confess 'that Jesus Christ has come in the flesh' (4.2; 2 Jn 7). One ought, therefore, to 'abide in the teaching of Christ' and not 'go beyond it' (2 Jn 9).

The Gospel's recurring emphasis on fulfillment is noticeably muted in the Letters. 1 John 1.4 and 2 John 12 speak of their joy being fulfilled, but there is no appeal to the fulfillment of Scripture or the traditions and hopes of Israel. Nevertheless, the Scriptures are still the foundation on which the elder's thought is based. Very likely, Jeremiah's vision of the new covenant in Jeremiah 31 lies behind the elder's claims, especially in 1 John 1 and 2.

> I will put my law within them, and I will write it on their hearts; and I will be their God, and they shall be my people. No longer shall they teach one another, or say to each other, 'know the Lord', for they shall all know me, from the least of them to the greatest, says the Lord; for I will forgive their iniquity, and remember their sin no more. (Jer. 31.33-34 NRSV).

In 1 Jn 1.9 the elder assures the community that if they confess their sins, God 'is faithful and just' and will forgive their sins. If one says, 'I have come to know him', but does not obey his commandments, that one is a liar (1 Jn 2.4). The elder writes to the little children, the fathers, and the young people, 'because you know him' (1 Jn 2.12-14). They have received God's anointing, 'so you do not need anyone to

teach you' (1 Jn 2.27). All of these elements echo Jeremiah 31 and suggest that the elder understands that the promise of a new covenant
has been fulfilled in them.

The Christology of Revelation emphasizes fulfillment in two
respects. Christ is the one in whom the hopes of Israel are fulfilled
and the one in whom all history will culminate. Like other apocalyptic
writings, Revelation uses animal imagery. Jesus is the Lion of the tribe
of Judah (Gen. 49.9), the Root of David (Isa. 11.1, 10). He is also the
lamb that was slain (Rev. 5.5-6), but as we have seen Revelation uses
arnion here, whereas Jn 1.29, 36, which declares that Jesus is 'the lamb
of God that takes away the sin of the world', uses *amnos*. The relationship between the two writings, even at this point, is not clear. Scholars
debate whether the Gospel identifies Jesus as the Paschal lamb (which
was not a sacrificial offering), the suffering servant, or the apocalyptic
lamb that crushes the evil powers (Rev. 17.14). Some blending of the
first two actually seems more likely than the latter.[32] In the end, the
faithful are invited to 'the marriage supper of the lamb' (Rev. 19.9),
which celebrates the lamb's victory over the kings of the earth and
their captains and their horses. Fulfillment of Scripture is presumed
throughout, but never explicitly affirmed. The verb 'fulfill' (*pleroō*)
occurs only twice (Rev. 3.2; 6.11), and never in reference to the
Scriptures. While there are many references to writing and writings in
Revelation, 'the Scriptures' are never mentioned and never quoted
explicitly or with a formula of fulfillment.

Neither the Letters nor the Apocalypse matches the richness and
creativity of the Gospel's Christology, and neither do they emphasize
fulfillment in the way the Gospel does. At the same time, the points of
contact, such as they are, are between the Gospel and the Letters, and
the Gospel and Revelation. The Letters speak of Jesus primarily as
Christ and Son. Revelation depicts Jesus primarily by means of the
image of the lamb. Once again, therefore, the Johannine writings
reveal differences as striking as their similarities. The Revelation of
John in particular seems only tangentially related to the other Johannine writings.

The independence of Revelation in language and style, genre, and
thought suggests that it is not written by the same author or authors
as the other Johannine writings. It may come from the same general
milieu, but it is probably best to think in terms of a Johannine school

32. For a full discussion of these alternatives, see Barrett, *John*, pp. 176-77; Raymond E. Brown, *The Gospel According to John* (AB, 29; Garden City, NY: Doubleday,
1966), pp. 58-63.

gathered around the Beloved Disciple: the evangelist, the elder, and loosely connected with this school, John the Seer.[33]

An Invitation to Read Further

Reading and studying the Johannine writings can be a source of immense pleasure, intellectual stimulation, and spiritual nurture. The Gospel and Revelation, especially, are powerful and moving master-pieces of literary art. The questions about their origin, social setting, and function lead one into a fascinating exercise in reconstructing and imaginatively entering into one of the major streams or trajectories of early Christianity. At the same time, the Johannine writings are both profound and prophetic. They explore the significance of the Incarnation from a post-Easter perspective. They raise timeless questions about the meaning of life, the relationship of time and eternity, this world and the world 'above', the movement of history toward a purposeful end, and what it means to live in fellowship with God in a fallen world. Each of the three sections that follows leads the reader further into the mysteries and rewards of these five writings, so similar and so different.

33. For a full discussion of the legends about the apostle John, the authorship of the Johannine writings, and the Johannine school, see Culpepper, *John the Son of Zebedee*.

Part I

JOHN
Barnabas Lindars, SSF

COMMENTARIES ON JOHN

Commentaries on the Gospel of John are legion. The reader is advised to buy one good commentary, and to work through the Gospel with it systematically. The following short selection gives commentaries which either do not require knowledge of Greek on the part of the reader or can be used without difficulty by those who have no knowledge of Greek:

G.R. Beasley-Murray, *John* (WBC; Waco: Word, 1987). A good all-round commentary with helpful summary explanation sections following the more detailed analyses.

R.E. Brown, *The Gospel According to John* (AC; 2 vols.; Garden City, NY: Doubleday, 1966–70). One of the major commentaries of the twentieth century with full bibliographies and appendices on key themes and issues.

D.A. Carson, *The Gospel According to John* (Pillar Commentary; Grand Rapids: Eerdmans, 1991). The best of the more conservative commentaries.

B. Lindars, *The Gospel of John* (New Century Bible; London: Oliphants, 1972). Comprehensive yet concise and accessible to non-specialist readers.

F.J. Moloney, *The Gospel of John* (Sacra Pagina; Collegeville, MN: Liturgical Press, 1998).

G.R. O'Day, *The Gospel of John* (New Interpreter's Bible, 493-875; Nashville: Abingdon Press, 1995). Pays particular attention to literary and theological issues and contains helpful reflection sections for preachers and teachers.

R. Schnackenburg, *The Gospel According to St. John* (ET; 3 vols.; New Herders Theological Commentary on the New Testament; vols. I–II New York: Seabury, 1980; vol. III, New York: Crossroad, 1982). Long, but highly recommended for balanced discussion of major issues and for its theological insights.

The following require knowledge of Greek:

C.K. Barrett, *The Gospel According to St John* (Philadelphia: Westminster, 2nd edn, 1978). Very good on issues of text and language and one of the few commentaries that argues for and works with the view that John knew and used the Synoptic gospels.

R. Bultmann, *The Gospel of John* (ET; Philadelphia: Westminster, 1971). Has exercised profound influence on modern study of John. Not easy to use because of its reordering of the text but always worth the effort because of its theological interpretation and insights.

Among still useful older commentaries are:

E.C. Hoskyns, *The Fourth Gospel* (ed. F.N. Davey; London: Faber & Faber, 2nd edn, 1947). Shows a strong grasp of theological issues.

B.F. Westcott, *The Gospel According to St. John* (London: John Murray, 2nd edn, 1882). A classic from the nineteenth century that is both conservative and imaginative.

Chapter One

ORIENTATION

A Gospel of Surprises

If the Gospel of John had been the only account we possessed of the life of Jesus, we might still be fascinated and intrigued by it, and we might even wonder whether it could possibly be true. But the problems which it presents would not be so complex and difficult as they become when it is read as the last of four Gospels, all purporting to describe the same thing. To read John straight after the others cannot fail to reveal vast differences. John starts with a philosophical statement (1.1-18), which has no counterpart in the Synoptic Gospels. Then comes the witness of John the Baptist (1.19-34). This may suggest a move into familiar territory, in spite of the very different presentation from the Synoptic parallels. But this hope is quickly shattered by the call of the first disciples (1.35-51), which has virtually nothing in common with the Synoptic accounts (e.g. Mk 1.16-20; Lk. 5.1-11), and indeed seems irreconcilable with them. This problem of the relation to the Synoptic Gospels continues through to the end.

At the same time a reading of John shows also differences of style. After the first two chapters, and the surprise caused by discovering the Cleansing of the Temple (2.13-22) before the ministry of Jesus has even begun, instead of near the end, the narrative ceases to be episodic and gives way to long discourses and debates of Jesus in Jerusalem, which are completely different from the Synoptic Gospels. The difference extends beyond the literary form to the effect which is produced. Here Jesus emerges as a remote personality, almost wholly taken up with the subject of his personal authority in relation to God. The story of Jesus has been shifted onto a different plane with a new centre of interest.

Though John's picture of Jesus has important points of contact with the earlier tradition, there is a very pronounced change of emphasis. Jesus' awareness of an intimate relation with God, whom he addresses as 'Father' (e.g. Mt. 11.25-27), becomes in John an insistent theme.

Jesus constantly calls himself 'the Son' in a way that implies christo-logical significance, equivalent to the less frequent designations 'Son of God' and 'Son of Man'. There is a similar change in the claim of Jesus that he has been 'sent' by God. In the Synoptic Gospels the idea refers to Jesus' prophetic vocation (e.g. Mt. 10.40), like the prophets of old or John the Baptist, who was also 'sent' according to Jn 1.6. But the idea is applied to Jesus in John in a more fundamental sense. John gives a distinct impression that Jesus is a heavenly emissary from God, who has been sent down to earth and then returns after his work on earth is done (cf. Jn 17.1-5). As Wayne Meeks has pointed out in a celebrated article, this raises not only the problem of the pre-existence of Jesus, but also the question whether John is indebted to a myth of a descending and ascending heavenly emissary, and if so where it comes from. Evidently John's understanding of the person and work of Jesus differs from the Synoptic tradition.

This different understanding in its turn raises further problems, which can be grouped under the headings of history, reception and influence.

History in John

It is already clear that there is a disconcerting lack of agreement between John and the Synoptics on matters of history. Further exam-ples can easily be found. Many attempts have been made to harmo-nize these discrepancies. It has even been suggested that Jesus did his dramatic action of cleansing the Temple twice over. Such a suggestion is surely a counsel of despair.

This is only one level of the historical problem. A deeper question is posed by the presentation of Jesus himself. The Gospel of John has played an immensely important part in the formulation of Christian doctrine, because of the statements which Jesus makes about himself, suggesting that he is the Son of God in a unique sense. From such statements Christian tradition has asserted that Jesus is the incarnate Son of God, both human and divine. We may well ask how far this represents what the evangelist intended to convey? The question warns us to be on our guard against presupposing too easily that the christological statements in John mean exactly the same as the later definitions.

But behind that there is the more disturbing question whether Jesus actually said the things that are attributed to him in the Fourth Gospel. Has the later construction of Christian doctrine been built on claims attributed to Jesus which he never made at all, and might well have repudiated if he had known about them? It is this kind of question which makes the problem of the historical value of the Gospel so acute.

Questions of this kind are not merely historical questions. They raise the whole problem of hermeneutics, that is, the proper way to understand the Fourth Gospel and its meaning for today. If Jesus in the Fourth Gospel poses the question of his identity to his opponents, it is inevitable that the Gospel puts the same question to the readers, and still does so today.

Reception

Most scholars agree that ch. 21 is an appendix to the Gospel. The original ending came at 20.30-31, in which the readers are addressed directly, and the purpose of the Gospel, to enable faith in Jesus as Christ and Son of God, is expressly stated. So the evangelist has an audience in mind for whom this unique account of Jesus may be expected to be meaningful. One reason, then, for the differences from the Synoptics is likely to be the special character of the people for whom it was written.

Consequently these differences can be used to determine the nature of the expected readership. At the very least, the Prologue suggests that the readers include people who would wish to relate the Gospel's claims concerning Jesus to a philosophical account of the nature of God and cosmology. This could imply a Greek or Gnostic readership. But it will also turn out that the disputes of Jesus in Jerusalem, which form the bulk of chs. 3–12, are concerned with issues between Christians and Jews opposed to them at the time when relations between church and synagogue had reached breaking-point. This suggests that the readers are actually involved in such disputes.

Considerations of this kind have led to various proposals concerning the identity of the readership. The important point is that the Gospel has been written in such a way as to speak to their condition. It is thus possible to identify broadly various groups to whom this might apply, such as Jewish Christians, Gentile Christians, Jews in Palestine or the Diaspora, proto-Gnostics and pagan Greeks. They are people, each with their own traditions and ideology, with whom it may be supposed that John has 'relations' (to use a happily neutral word suggested by Beasley-Murray).

Influences

The idea that the evangelist writes for some or all of these groups pre-supposes that John is familiar with their religious concepts and knows how to make the gospel message meaningful to their situation. Some scholars would go further and try to prove that John was actually indebted to the ideology of such a group. This was the assumption of the History-of-Religions school, and is especially associated with the interpretation of Rudolf Bultmann. It is the kind of suggestion that can be very upsetting to modern readers, who feel that their confidence in the Fourth Gospel as a genuinely Christian book and an authentic record of Jesus is being undermined. It is thus all the more important to make a determined effort to discover the truth about John by careful and objective study, and to be ready to approach all these questions with an open mind.

Many Dimensions

The Gospel of John is deceptively simple in style and vocabulary. But it also has a mysterious quality, suggesting hidden depths. The reader is alerted at the outset that the story of Jesus is the crucial manifestation of a cosmic struggle between light and darkness (1.5). Thus the story operates at two levels, and the facts which are described also have symbolic meaning in relation to the theology of John. The historic circumstances of Jesus in his time are the stage on which the ultimate cosmic drama is played out. Jesus' victory (16.33) is not just a personal triumph, but the act in which the light finally overcomes the darkness and God's plan of salvation for all humanity is achieved.

At the same time there is another dimension. Though the readers are rarely addressed directly (but cf. 20.31), the Gospel challenges them to a decision all the way through. The Fourth Gospel is not episodic, like the Synoptics, but carefully planned with a series of set pieces, each leading up to a dramatic climax. The presentation is controlled by the skillful use of dialogue, or dramatic monologue, to engage the readers on the side of Jesus and to confront them personally with the decision which is set before Jesus' audience in the play. John's writing has perennial power, and challenges the modern reader still.

False Expectations

These preliminary considerations have given some idea of the scope of study of John. But a word of warning is desirable about the danger of approaching John with false expectations. In the first place, the multi-dimensional character of the Gospel obviously precludes the idea that it is a straight historical record of what actually happened and what Jesus actually said in his ministry. It is a mistake to suppose that there was any direct reporting of Jesus in his earthly life. The Synoptic Gospels are based on a variety of traditions, some oral and some written, which embodied the memories of people who knew Jesus, and evolved over a long period. Similarly John is dependent on the work of predecessors, and it should not be assumed that the underlying materials were substantially different from those used by the Synoptic writers.

It may be urged that this judgment does not allow for the claim within the Gospel itself that it was written by an eyewitness, described as 'the disciple whom Jesus loved' (21.20, 24). More will have to be said about this later. For the moment it must simply be asserted that, even if some element of eyewitness testimony has been incorporated in the Gospel, it does not have the status of a contemporary report of what was seen or heard. In so far as personal memories were available, they were memories of events long since past, which had inevitably been affected to some extent by later reflection in the light of the rise of Christianity. Moreover the evangelist used them creatively to produce a multi-dimensional and highly dramatic presentation of the tradition, in which all were adapted for the aim in view.

This also means that the hope of using the Fourth Gospel to decide whether, as a matter of history, Jesus made a personal claim to divinity as the Son of God must be abandoned. Though John certainly used items from the tradition of the sayings of Jesus, the major discourses in which such claims are made are more like the speeches in a play, in which the author expresses a considered understanding of the function and meaning of the characters. The Gospel of John is far too complex for a simplistic view of its historical value to be plausible.

Another false expectation arises from the philosophical and spiritual aspects of the Gospel. Some people wrongly suppose that John is a treatise on the life of prayer. It is true that those who wish to explore the ways of contemplative prayer will find much food for thought in John. Indeed, John's spirituality, expressed in terms of a mutual indwelling of God and Jesus and the disciples (14.18-24), is most valuable for those who read the Gospel with the aim of deepening their spiritual life. But it was not written as a guide to prayer. Its value for this purpose operates at a deeper level of apprehension of its message.

Finally, John is not a resource-book for dealing with moral questions. Good and evil are treated in terms of truth and falsehood, and sin is usually a matter of refusal to put faith in Jesus. The only moral virtue is the love command (13.34-35; 15.1-17), but that does in a sense embrace all the others. But there is no extended treatment of moral issues in John.

The Jews in John

One particular matter, which affects the whole tone of the Gospel, and presents a difficult problem for many modern readers, must be settled at the outset. This is the strange way in which the opponents of Jesus are constantly referred to simply as 'the Jews'. It is strange, because of course Jesus and his friends are Jews too. There are various ways of explaining this, but, whatever the reason, the effect has been extremely unfortunate. It lays John wide open to the charge of anti-Semitism. This is so undesirable in a sacred book, which is treasured as the revelation of the love of God for all people, that serious thought needs to be given to the question whether new translations should seek a way round this, just as the problem of sexist language has to be faced by modern translators. In both cases what is at stake is not the true meaning of the text, but the impact of a literal translation on a highly sensitive area of modern consciousness. One can get around it to some extent by substituting 'the Jerusalem authorities' for 'the Jews', as this is what is usually meant. But this is not sufficient to cope with the vicious tone of 8.31-47, in which the descendants of Abraham are referred to *en bloc* as sons of the devil. And of course Jesus is the speaker. We may well ask if Jesus spoke of his own people in this way. Was he an anti-Semite? Some people would take the Gospel of John as evidence that he was.

Here, then, is an issue which demands patient and objective study on the part of every modern reader. It is not enough to try to remove the problem by means of a technicality, such as the suggestion that 'the Jews' means the inhabitants of the province of Judea in contrast with the Galileans. Nor can we distinguish between the ruling classes who opposed Jesus as 'the Jews', and the common people who accepted him, because the designation has the effect of fatally blurring this distinction.

On the other hand there is not the least reason to suppose that the evangelist wishes to encourage anti-Semitism. John's intentions are clarified by the somewhat bitter editorial observation in 12.42-43. The context shows that the real issue is the failure of the first Christians to convert the majority of their fellow Jews. It was the cause of much pain and heart-searching among the earliest Christians, who wondered how it could be fitted into God's plan of salvation. An answer was found in the prophecy of Isa. 6.9-10, which tells of the disobedience of the people, who are deaf to God's message. This is quoted several times in the New Testament (cf. Mt. 13.14-15; Acts 28.26-27), and appears here in the present context in Jn 12.40. John's comment in 12.42 has been recognized, especially since the work of J.L. Martyn, as a retrojection of the situation in John's own time (perhaps 85–90 CE). By this time relations between Christians (especially Jewish Christians) and the majority of Jews had reached breaking point. There was mutual hostility, and it is not possible to exonerate either side. The subsequent history, when the Christians gained power, is a shaming story for Christians, and it is this subsequent experience which has defined the idea of anti-Semitism ever afterwards. John shows the beginning of this sad state of affairs, but the issue in the Gospel is not whether one is a Jew or not, but whether one is a believer. In fact 'the Jews' in John means 'the unbelieving Jews', no more and no less, and the application of this to the Jerusalem authorities reflects the situation referred to in 12.42-43.

Inclusive Language

John's presentation of Jesus has been deeply influenced by the tradition of Jesus' own spirituality, which is exemplified in the Lord's Prayer and is expressed in his characteristic address to God as *Abba*, which means Father. John not only retains this in prayers of Jesus (11.41; 12.27-28; 17.1, 5, 11, 25), but also makes extensive use of the correlation 'Father' and 'Son' in the discourses when Jesus is speaking of his relation to God throughout the Gospel. This feature of John is deeply meaningful and helpful to many readers, but it must be recognized that the use of specifically masculine concepts can also be hurtful and alienating.

Obviously the Gospel cannot be rewritten to remove the language of Father and Son without doing violence to its literary form. But readers who are sensitive to this issue may like to substitute in their own minds the correlation 'Parent and Offspring', or 'Parent and Child'. This can be justified from the Prologue of the Gospel (1.1-18).

Here John sets out the philosophical basis of the relationship between God and Jesus in terms of the incarnation of the Word of God. The use of Word (*logos*)to denote the coeternal Offspring of God replaces Wisdom in the literary models which lie behind the Prologue (Prov. 8.22-31; Ecclus 24; Wis. 7.22–8.1). Wisdom (Hebrew *hokmah*, Greek *sophia*) is a feminine word, and so is often personified as a woman. John had to avoid this because of the incarnation of the Offspring in the man Jesus. At this point a parenthesis in v. 14 is important, though often misunderstood on account of faulty translation. 'The Word became flesh', says John, 'and we saw his glory, *glory as of an only son of a father.*' This is an analogy, and the usual translation 'glory as of the only Son from the Father' (RSV) is incorrect. 'Glory' here virtually means 'reflection'. Thus Jesus reflects the glory of God as a son reflects the aspect of a father on account of family likeness, and of course that is true of parent and offspring without regard to sex. It is thus clear that the Father and Son language in John is always a matter of analogy. John knows that, when one passes from analogy to direct language about God, one passes to a realm of understanding where sexual differentiation is transcended.

FURTHER READING

The most perceptive overview and discussion of the main issues in the interpretation of the Gospel of John in the modern era until the early 1980s are to be found in J. Ashton, *Understanding the Fourth Gospel* (Oxford: Clarendon Press, 1991), especially pp. 9-117. Professor Felix Just of Loyola Marymount University maintains a useful website on the Johannine literature and bibliographical resources at http://clawww.lmu.edu/faculty/fjust/John.htm.

The article by Wayne Meeks referred to in this chapter is 'The Man from Heaven in Johannine Sectarianism' and can be found in J. Ashton (ed.), *The Interpretation of John* (London: SPCK, 1986), pp. 147-73, while the work of J.L. Martyn is *History and Theology in the Fourth Gospel* (Nashville: Abingdon Press, 2nd edn, 1979).

A valuable recent collection of essays on a variety of interpretative issues surrounding this Gospel is R.A. Culpepper and C.C. Black (eds.), *Exploring the Gospel of John* (Louisville, KY: Westminster John Knox Press, 1996).

Chapter Two

THE EVANGELIST AND THE GOSPEL

Who Was the Author?

Our study of the question of the Jews in John has shown that it is necessary to take into account conditions towards the end of the first century, when the strained relations between church and synagogue were near to disruption. This at once indicates that, in spite of attempts to assign John to an earlier date, a date fairly late in the century is required. This does not conflict with the traditional date for John, because that was always put in the nineties, even though the evangelist was identified with the apostle John and regarded as an eyewitness of what is recorded in the Gospel. Assuming that the apostle is also to be identified with the 'Elder' of the Johannine Epistles (2 Jn 1; 3 Jn 1), an appealing picture can be gained of the evangelist as a very old man, who addresses his readers as 'little children' (e.g. 1 Jn 2.1). This picture remains the most widely accepted popular opinion concerning the authorship of the Fourth Gospel.

However, it is already clear that the Gospel of John is far too complex to be considered merely an old man's reminiscences. If the late date is accepted, the length of time available allows for the formation and reworking of traditions over a long period before the actual writing of the Gospel. One possibility is that the apostle John was the *originator* of the special traditions which lie behind the Fourth Gospel, and these were preserved and developed in the Johannine church until someone else wove them into the finished form of the Gospel.

The important point here is not whether the apostle John was the originator of the special traditions, but the fact that, whatever their provenance, it is the evangelist who comes at the *end* of the process who is the real author of the Fourth Gospel. This person may have had access to some accurate traditions, derived from an eye-witness, but the Gospel shows that it was never intended to be a simple historical account of the life of Jesus, as we have already seen.

Of course it does have to be recognized that John constantly makes claims concerning the truth, but this refers to the message, not to a special source of information. On the other hand there is a definite statement about authorship in the Appendix (21.24), which cannot be simply brushed aside. We shall therefore look carefully at the evidence about authorship before considering the way in which the task of writing the Gospel has been approached. This will introduce the factors which have gone into the making of the Gospel, in which the relationship between the underlying tradition and the creative handling of it by the evangelist can be put into perspective.

John

We start from the fact that the Fourth Gospel has always been known as the Gospel according to John, and this goes with the traditional view that the evangelist was the apostle John. Although this tradition continues to have supporters among modern scholars, the majority cling to it only in the most tenuous form, or abandon it altogether. It is thus important to see the reasons why the traditional identification is regarded by most scholars as untenable.

The name John does not actually occur in reference to an apostle in the Gospel at all. In 1.37-40 we hear of an unnamed disciple. But even if he is identified with the evangelist, as some have supposed, it is unlikely that John son of Zebedee is intended, because the context makes no room for his brother James. In the Appendix (21.2) the two sons of Zebedee are mentioned in a group of seven disciples, but they are not named individually. But two others of the seven are not named at all, so there are really four disciples with whom the writer might be identified, and it is arbitrary to decide that he is John. The matter is complicated further by the fact that one of these four is referred to in v. 7 as 'the disciple whom Jesus loved'. The Beloved Disciple has already appeared at 13.23; 19.26; 20.2, and although he is traditionally identified with John, in fact his identity is never disclosed. It seems, then, that the author is deliberately hiding the identity of the Beloved Disciple, and it must be judged unlikely that one of the sons of Zebedee is meant in 21.2 rather than one of those left unnamed.

The strongest external evidence in favour of the identification with John is the statement of Clement of Alexandria, preserved in Eusebius (*Hist. Eccles.* 6.14.7), written about 180 CE. 'Last of all John, perceiving that the external facts had been made plain in the Gospels, being urged by his friends and inspired by the Spirit, composed a spiritual gospel.' But we know from Irenaeus (*Adv. Haer.* 1.8.5) that the Gnostic

Ptolemaeus had before this already composed a commentary on the Prologue of the Gospel, which he attributed to 'John, the disciple of the Lord'. Thus the Beloved Disciple is assumed (on the strength of 21.24) to be the author of the Gospel, and he has already been identified with the apostle John. The reason for this identification in the middle of the second century is obvious. By this time apostolic authorship was becoming an essential criterion for acceptance. We should also note that in the quotation from Clement above, Clement is concerned to explain the *late* appearance of the Fourth Gospel, which did not become widely known until long after the general diffusion of the Synoptic Gospels. So the conditions were laid down for the long-standing tradition that the Gospel was written by an apostle some 60 years after the events which it describes, thus making an exceptional combination of a late date and a claim to eye-witness reporting. But the identification of this person with the apostle John may well have arisen simply as a means of claiming apostolic authorship for a work that was actually anonymous.

For this reason it is really a mistake to look for *other* people called John who might have written the Gospel, or for that matter to look for anyone else in the New Testament, though numerous suggestions have been proposed along these lines. What is more important is to decide whether the editorial note in 21.24 is correct in identifying the evangelist with the Beloved Disciple. This at least might save the claim to eye-witness testimony, even if the evangelist's name has been lost beyond recall.

The Beloved Disciple

Doubt about the identity of the Beloved Disciple does not automatically exclude the view that he was a real person, actually present on the occasions where he is mentioned (13.23; 19.26; 20.2; 21.7, 20-23; possibly also 1.35; 18.15; 19.35). But apart from the editorial note in 21.24, there is no indication in the text that he was the author of the Gospel as we know it. Many scholars today dismiss 21.24 as a false deduction. Manifestly the purpose of the note is to legitimate the Gospel, and this ties up with its late diffusion and difficulty in gaining acceptance in orthodox Christian circles.

However, the information in 21.24 can be accepted as broadly true if the Beloved Disciple is identified with the founder of the Johannine tradition. Though Bultmann denied that the Beloved Disciple was ever intended to be more than a fictitious, ideal figure, in the last 40 years there has been a growing critical consensus that he is a real historical person, whose testimony lies behind the Fourth Gospel. On this view full weight is given to the fact that the Gospel shows signs of being the end-product of a long literary process, in which the core information has been worked up by successive hands, forming a distinctive 'Johannine school'. If this is correct, it can be reasonably claimed that the Beloved Disciple is the source of the special information in the Gospel and the inspiration of the 'school' of which he was the founder.

The Beloved Disciple on this view constitutes a precious link between the actual history of Jesus and the formation of the Gospel. But he is not responsible for its final form and cannot be identified with the evangelist. This leaves open the question of eye-witness reporting, for the extent to which that has survived in the final form is impossible to determine.

In spite of this growing consensus, I find myself siding with Bultmann on this issue on literary grounds. To me the Beloved Disciple is a creation of the evangelist in order to serve a specific function. He is one of the Twelve, who at crucial moments gives expression to the evangelist's own views. He represents true discipleship, understanding the necessity of the death of Jesus when all others fail. He is thus a foil to Peter, who in spite of being the acknowledged leader failed by denying Jesus three times. Thus the Beloved Disciple is in one sense the evangelist, because he embodies the evangelist's own faith. But in another sense he is one with whom the reader should identify, for the whole purpose of the Gospel is to convey the same understanding to every reader. Once we see the function of the Beloved Disciple in this way, a new dimension opens up in the study of John, the literary dimension of rhetorical effect and reader-response, which is just as important for understanding the Gospel as the question of its historical value.

On this view the Beloved Disciple is an ambiguous and intriguing personality, and it would not be surprising if the Johannine church thought he must be the evangelist making a veiled self-reference. One purpose of the appendix (21.1-23) might be to deal with this suggestion. If so, v. 23 refuses to divulge his identity and throws it back to the readers to look to their own discipleship. For of course the Beloved Disciple is *both* the evangelist *and* the readers from a functional point of view. However, it seems that some still thought that he was literally the evangelist, and this idea is embodied in the editorial note of v. 24, and in the end prevailed.

The Function of the Beloved Disciple

When we turn to the actual passages in which the Beloved Disciple is mentioned, we are at once faced with the problem of John's use of historical tradition.

First we note that John does not mention any of the three occasions when the sons of Zebedee and Peter were taken aside by Jesus according to the Synoptic tradition (cf. Mk 5.37; 9.2; 14.33). This would be extraordinary if the Beloved Disciple were really John the apostle. The Beloved Disciple, however, is first marked out in John's account of the Last Supper (13.21-30). This is a passage which clearly has a close relation to the Synoptic tradition. In the Synoptics Jesus prophesies that one of the disciples will betray him (Mt. 26.21 = Mk 14.18). John reproduces almost exactly the same words as Mark (13.21). Mark gives no indication who the traitor might be, in spite of recording the anxious questioning of the Twelve. Matthew, however, changes this to a question by Judas alone, who thereby incriminates himself. In John this feature is built up in a highly dramatic way. The questioning becomes a signal by Peter to the Beloved Disciple to find out, as he is close to the breast of Jesus. So the Beloved Disciple alone is privileged to understand what Jesus is doing.

It is clear that in this brilliant presentation of the tradition, which is remarkable for its dramatic irony, John is writing for the benefit of the readers. The aim is to teach the true meaning of discipleship. The Beloved Disciple is present, close to Jesus, but there is only the briefest whispered conversation, and otherwise he is a silent spectator. Unlike Peter, he does not loudly assert his willingness to follow Jesus to death—but neither does he deny him three times. Thus the function of the Beloved Disciple is only to express understanding of Jesus, and that is what the evangelist hopes to achieve in the readers.

This functional purpose of the character of the Beloved Disciple favors the suggestion that John has added him into the story of the Last Supper, which is based on older traditions which made no mention of him. The same thing happens in the second episode (19.25-27), where the mother of Jesus is assumed to be one of the women at the cross (cf. Mt. 27.56; Mk 15.40) and the Beloved Disciple, who actually becomes her new son, is a newcomer to the tradition. The Beloved Disciple enters the story again in 20.2-10, when he runs with Peter to see the empty tomb. It is he who draws the correct conclusion from what they see, and believes in the resurrection. As before, there is a Synoptic parallel, in which the Beloved Disciple does not figure at all. This is Lk. 24.12, which is unfamiliar to many modern readers because it has been banished to the footnotes in several modern translations (e.g. RSV, NEB, REB) on text-critical grounds. But even if it is not original in Luke, it is still likely to be a tradition about Peter which did not include the Beloved Disciple, rather than a gloss derived from John.

Finally the Beloved Disciple features once more in the Appendix, 21.1-23. The basic story is the miraculous catch of fish, which again has a parallel in Luke, but in connection with the original call of the first disciples (Lk. 5.1-11). In John 21 the motif of discipleship is also the chief issue. As we have seen, John (like Luke) mentions Peter and the sons of Zebedee, but it is probable that the Beloved Disciple is one of two others left unnamed, so that his identity is not disclosed. Once more he functions as one who can recognize the risen Lord without full physical sight (vv. 4, 7). The final point in the story is that, whereas Peter is reinstated as a disciple of Jesus (vv. 15-17), even to the extent of matching his death (vv. 18-19, cf. 13.37), the Beloved Disciple will continue to follow Jesus until he comes again—precisely because he is the model for every reader (vv. 20-23).

Fact and Fiction in John

By suggesting that the Beloved Disciple has been added into the underlying source on each occasion when he appears, we have opened up the whole question of the relationship between fact and fiction in John. To many people these are mutually exclusive alternatives. Either John's life of Jesus is historical, and should be accepted as it stands, or it is fictitious, and therefore a worthless forgery. Modern scholarship of all shades of opinion seeks to find a middle way between these two extremes. Some scholars veer to the side of fact, others to the side of considerable creativity on the part of the evangelist. But even on a maximalist view of historicity, room must be left for some degree of author's license. John uses a highly dramatic style of presentation. The treatment of the theme of questioning about the traitor in 13.21-30 is perhaps the most stunning example. A historical play, like Shakespeare's *Richard II*, is not judged to be true or false by its accuracy of detail, which cannot possibly be reproduced on the stage, but by its success in conveying the real issues and the character of the leading personalities. It must also be pointed out that the Synoptic writers also use author's license in their own ways. Where Matthew and Mark overlap, either Matthew has drastically reduced Mark or Mark has expanded Matthew (cf. Mt. 8.28-34 = Mk 5.1-20, where Mark is more than twice the length of Matthew). John is therefore not alone in exercising freedom in writing up the gospel traditions. But John's aims are more complex and the method involves a greater degree of creativity.

If the evangelist was not an eye-witness of the events, dependence on sources was inescapable. These were not plentiful, and suffered distortion with the passage of time. John did not have a private pipe-line of authentic tradition, but had to use the same kind of sources as the Synoptic writers. These must be understood before we can go further in assessing the special quality of the Gospel of John.

Sources for the Life of Jesus

All four Gospels should be regarded primarily as biographies of Jesus, but all four have a definite theological aim. The modern approach to biography was unknown in the ancient world, and the evangelists' concept of their task is quite similar to Suetonius's *Lives of the Caesars*. To take Mark as an example, there is a clear theological aim, which corresponds with the primitive preaching. Jesus proclaimed the kingdom of God, was crucified, and was raised by God to be exalted as the Messiah of the coming kingdom. So Mark shows Jesus preaching the kingdom, and eventually crucified, and the Gospel ends with the announcement of the resurrection (Mk 16.1-8). At the same time the theme of Jesus' identity runs through Mark, reaching a minor climax with Peter's confession at Caesarea Philippi halfway through the Gospel (Mk 8.27-30), and a final climax with the confession of the centurion immediately after Jesus' death on the cross (Mk 15.39). In fact this theological structure of Mark has a certain similarity to that of John.

Mark achieved his aim mainly by the arrangement of material and editorial linkages, but without radical rewriting of the sources. These were largely anecdotes, and there are signs that some of them had already been put together in short collections, e.g. Mk 2.1–3.6; 4.1-34. Similarly it is widely held that Matthew and Luke made use of a collection of the teachings of Jesus (the so-called Q document). But such collections do not amount to strictly historical records. By the time that the Gospels were written the materials for a proper life of Jesus did not exist. No contemporary records were kept, and no one thought about writing a life of him until it was almost too late. For the most part Mark had to make do with an assortment of traditions, consisting of memories of Jesus which had been repeated orally without any control of accuracy before being committed to writing. Form-critical study of these traditions has shown that they owe their survival to their practical use in the community for the instruction of new members and similar purposes. Thus these traditions were repeated because of their social function, but this would be likely to lead to some degree of distortion to make them relevant.

Nevertheless, it would be absurd to claim that the truth about Jesus was totally lost in this process. The anecdotes and collected sayings of Jesus crystallize the impression of him and his message as he was remembered. What we have in the Synoptic Gospels is three 'identi-kit' portraits of Jesus, each differing to some extent on account of the outlook of the evangelist, but all recognizably the same person, even though none is a photograph taken from life.

John's picture of Jesus, however, is different. This could be due to the use of independent traditions, not known to the other evangelists, but it might also be due to far greater use of author's license, resulting in a more individual portrait, possibly further removed from histori-cal accuracy. Which is it likely to be?

John and the Synoptic Tradition

To answer this question we must look at the extent to which John and the Synoptics are in agreement. First, we can distinguish between anecdotes and discourses. The anecdotes (e.g. healing miracles) are usually very similar to the Synoptic material, even though they may have important variations in detail. The discourses, on the other hand, are entirely different. They are reasoned arguments on such subjects as the divine authority of Jesus himself, quite unlike the Synoptic sermons of Jesus (Mt. 5–7; Lk. 6), his tirade against the scribes and Pharisees (Mt. 23) or the apocalyptic discourse (Mk 13). The difference can be seen very clearly in John 5. Here a Synoptic-type healing story (vv. 1-9, including an almost identical verbal parallel with Mk 2.11 in v. 8), is followed by a dialogue with the Jerusalem authorities (vv. 10-18). This prepares the ground for a long monologue of Jesus on his authority, which has no Synoptic links (vv. 19-47).

Secondly, there are sayings of Jesus in a proverbial style which have close parallels in the Synoptic tradition. Some of these are put together in short sequences (notably 4.35-38; 12.24-26; 13.16-20). Oth-ers are scattered through the discourses (e.g. 3.3, 5; 8.51), often with the opening 'Amen, amen, I say to you', as in the Synoptic Gospels (e.g. Mt. 18.3, which may be an independent version of the saying in Jn 3.3, 5).

Thirdly, John's passion narrative (chs. 18–19) has a general resem-blance to the Synoptic passion narratives, in spite of many differences of detail.

Various theories have been proposed to account for these similarities and differences. It can be argued that John is directly dependent on one or more of the Synoptic Gospels in the places where there is close verbal agreement. But it is never a simple relationship. For instance, John's account of the Feeding of the Multitude is followed by the Walking on Water (6.1-21), as in Mk 6.32-52, and there are many features in common with Mark. But some details of vocabulary are closer to the parallel narrative in Matthew. Also, there are links with the second feeding in Mk 8.1-10 and with other sea episodes, such as Mk 4.35-41. Thus it is not just a matter of following one of the Synoptic accounts. It could be the case that John had a general familiarity with all the Synoptic accounts, which became merged in the retelling. There must be many preachers who have done this.

An alternative view, which has been gaining ground in recent study, is based on the assumption that many traditions about Jesus were transmitted through more than one channel. This can indeed be seen within Mark, for the two feeding miracles in Mark 6 and 8 are surely variant versions of the same event. The advantage of this view is that it explains why John's use of traditions parallel to the Synoptic Gospels is so patchy, and it also accounts for further material of similar type (e.g. the Marriage at Cana, 2.1-10).

In the passion narrative (Jn 18–19) and some of the events leading up to it (11.47–12.17) it is possible to trace a closer connection with Mark, but this may be due to the fact that the main outline of the passion narrative was relatively fixed before it was reproduced by Mark, because it was retold each year in the Christian Passover. Moreover there are features in John which have close links with the special material in Luke. Here again opinion is divided whether John used Luke or had access to Luke's source. A glimpse at one of these passages will show the complexity of the relationship between John and the Synoptics and the difficulty of reaching a definitive conclusion.

John and the Anointing of Jesus

The story of the Raising of Lazarus (11.1-44) is set in the household of Mary and Martha at Bethany, very near to Jerusalem. Then in 12.1-8 their home is the place where Jesus is anointed by a woman during a meal. This corresponds with Mk 14.3-9, but there the house is the home of Simon the leper, and the woman is not named. Here, however, Mary attends to Jesus while Martha serves the meal, just as in the entirely separate story of the two sisters in Lk. 10.38-42, which is set in an unnamed village, presumably in Galilee, long before Jesus goes up to Jerusalem. Moreover, whereas the woman in Mark anoints Jesus' head, Mary in John anoints his feet, and wipes them with her hair. This links with another Galilean episode, Lk. 7.36-50, in which a Pharisee entertains Jesus to a meal, and an unnamed woman washes his feet with her tears and wipes them with her hair, before anointing them as an additional act. This woman is traditionally identified with Mary Magdalene (mentioned two verses later in Lk. 8.2), but John does not seem to be aware of this, in spite of naming her Mary.

How are these links to be explained? In my view, the simplest solution is that John's basis was the Bethany story as it is found in Mk 14.3-9. This was already associated with the passion narrative in the tradition because of the reference to the burial of Jesus (Mk 14.8, cf. John 12.7). But John took the *setting* from the story of Martha and Mary, with the detail that 'Martha served' (cf. Lk. 10.40). Also the anointing of the *feet* of Jesus and wiping with hair reflect the other story in Luke (using the same words as Lk. 7.38). But these connections become simpler when we observe that Luke's *source* at Lk. 7.38 probably did not include anointing at all, but simply had washing the feet with tears and wiping with hair. Luke has added the motif of anointing from the Bethany story, which he omits from the passion narrative, though it is clear that he knows that anointing should apply to the head rather than the feet (Lk. 7.46). If, then, John was dependent on Luke's source rather than Luke as such, the way was open to *substitute* the anointing of the feet of Jesus instead of washing them. Thus John uses the Bethany story, but takes the motif of the feet from Luke's source, whereas Luke reproduces the source, but adds the motif of anointing from the Bethany story. Moreover, if John had the story in an independent source, it is likely that it contained the other story of Mary and Martha in close proximity to it. This explains how John has been able to use this as the setting, and also why John does not make the identification with Mary Magdalene, because the source did not contain Lk. 8.1-3.

Before we leave this example, we must ask why John chose to take the one detail of the feet from the Galilean story. When we compare John's anointing story with the account of the Last Supper in ch. 13, it at once becomes apparent that there are subtle links between them, which prepare the reader for the issues at stake. The apparently pointless detail that 'Martha served' now falls into place. It prepares for Jesus' teaching on service in 13.12-17. Similarly, Mary's washing of Jesus' feet with ointment prepares for Jesus' washing of the disciples' feet in vv. 4-11. Moreover, the reference to Jesus' burial relates the tradition to his death. Jesus' washing of the disciples' feet is an act of service which signifies cleansing in a deeper sense, the total cleansing which is effected by the saving death of Jesus and appropriated in baptism (briefly and allusively indicated in Jesus' answer to Peter in 13.10).

One more dramatic link is provided by the disciples' complaint that the expensive ointment should have been sold for the poor. In John it is Judas who makes this complaint, and the point is underlined with the information (not known from any other source) that Judas was the treasurer and used to pilfer the common fund (12.4-6). This information is taken up and used with great skill in 13.28-29. Here the disciples think that Judas' departure from the Supper is to give money to the poor. In fact it is, as only the Beloved Disciple (and the reader!) knows, to betray Jesus to death.

John's Use of Sources

The example of the anointing story has illustrated several features of John's use of sources, even if we cannot be certain whether it is based on the Synoptic Gospels as we know them or on the kind of sources underlying them. First, it shows that sources of this type certainly lie behind the Fourth Gospel. Secondly, the use of elements drawn from several different stories to make a composite picture can be observed elsewhere, and must be regarded as a feature of John's compositional technique. Thus the healing of a paralyzed man at the pool of Bethesda (or Beth-zatha) in 5.1-9 also seems to have three components: a Jerusalem healing story in 5.1-7, unknown from the Synoptic tradition; the conclusion in v. 8, expressed in words from the famous story of the man let down through the roof of a house in Capernaum (Mk 2.11); an additional note in v. 9 that this was done on the sabbath, introduced for the sake of the dialogue in vv. 10-18.

A third feature of John's use of sources is the freedom exercised in adapting them. This may seem reprehensible at first sight, but a little thought shows that it is inevitable. John's methods are no worse than what we find in Matthew, where the man with a legion in Mk 5.1-20 has become *two* men in Mt. 8.28-34. This sort of thing falls within the bounds of an author's license.

Fourthly, the subtle relationship between the anointing story and John's Last Supper account shows the care and deliberation of the evangelist. The irony of the presentation is intended to make the reader think of the deeper issues—in this case the meaning of discipleship in the light of the sacrificial death of Jesus, which is set off by the contrast of Judas. Hence full recognition must be accorded to the evangelist as a creative writer, who should not be dissolved into a mass of hands in a 'school' which produced the Fourth Gospel over a long period. Previous layers of the Johannine tradition are either sources comparable to those which lie behind the Synoptic Gospels, or earlier workings of the evangelist, in which these features of style were developed and perfected.

The Signs Source

In his great commentary on John, Bultmann took up the suggestion of Faure that the miracle stories in John were drawn from a special source, which can be referred to as the Signs Source. The numbering of the first two signs (2.11 and 4.54) seemed to support this theory, though both verses contain obviously Johannine elements. Basically the suggestion is harmless enough, as such a collection is comparable to the series in Mk 2.1–3.6. But Bultmann sought to prove that the source had a distinct theological tendency to which the evangelist was opposed, in spite of making use of the source almost intact. This was a popular presentation of Jesus as a miracle worker, developed in a Hellenistic milieu to make him out to be a divinity. In a Hellenistic setting, where popular pagan religion was influenced by Greek ideas, such a person would be regarded as a *theios anēr* ('divine man'), i.e. one in whom divine powers were at work, who might be raised to the company of the gods at his death; or he might even be considered to be one of the gods visiting the world in human likeness (cf. Acts 13.11). In John it was claimed that a distinction could be made between *sēmeia*, 'signs', identified with the miracles interpreted in the light of this unsatisfactory christology, and *erga*, 'works', identified with the miracles understood as the saving acts of God. Thus the people tend to evince an inadequate faith in Jesus in response to his signs (cf. 2.22; 3.2), but Jesus challenges them to perceive them as the 'works' of God in order to reach genuine faith (e.g. 5.20; 10.37-38). This theory was elaborated by Fortna (1970), who attempted to reconstruct a 'Signs Gospel', including a passion narrative, as the major narrative source behind the Fourth Gospel.

This theory is open to several objections. In the first place, the semi-pagan Christology attributed to the source is unknown in the New Testament. It is really most improbable that the evangelist would engage in polemic with the source at the same time as reproducing it almost word for word. In fact this impression is really a feature of John's dialogue technique, whereby a person is made to misunderstand an initial statement of Jesus in order to evoke a further defini-

tion at a deeper level of meaning. The classic examples are
Nicodemus in 3.4, 9 and the Samaritan woman in 4.11, 15. Examples
involving miracles are the dialogues of chs. 5 and 9. Fortna, in a recent
revision of his work (1989), has abandoned the idea of a 'divine man'
Christology. In his view the source had an orthodox doctrine of Jesus
as the Messiah, but it was simplistic and needed to be greatly elaborated to serve the evangelist's purpose.

Secondly, the word *sēmeion* cannot be used as a source criterion. It
occurs more frequently in John's editorial writing than in the material
attributed to the source, and it does not carry a pejorative sense, so
that the contrast with *ergon* cannot be maintained. The *signs* are
intended to produce faith (20.30-31) so that the people may accept
Jesus as the one who does the *works* of God which are the eschatological acts of salvation (5.20-23).

Thirdly, the attempt to reconstruct the source out of the text of the
Gospel grievously underestimates the extent of John's reworking of
sources, and fails to establish convincing criteria for deciding what
belongs to the source. Even though John may not have made direct
use of the Synoptic Gospels, the proper starting-point for source analysis must always be the passages which have parallels with them,
where John's handling of such traditions can be most easily seen.

The Discourse Source

The discourses of John, on the other hand, present a sharp contrast
with all the known sources for the life of Jesus, and thus require a
different explanation. Here again Bultmann proposed a Revelation-
Discourse Source. In this case his proposal was far more radical, for
he argued that it was the work of a proto-Gnostic sect, adapted to
apply to Jesus.

As the name implies, the source was held to be a collection of revelations given by a Revealer from heaven. These conveyed the secret
knowledge (*gnōsis*) whereby mortal human beings could be freed
from the imprisonment of earthly existence and ascend in spirit to the
divine life, following the ascent of the Revealer himself. This 'savior-
myth' belonged to the teaching of a pre-Christian Gnostic sect, which
Bultmann identified with the ancient sect of the Mandeans, still surviving in Iran. Their system is based on a radical dualism, the aim
being to escape from the realm of darkness into the divine light. Their
religious titles preserve the Aramaic language of their origins, and so
point to Syria as their first home. The writings of the sect show hostility to Jesus, but give honor to John the Baptist, who is identified with

the heavenly deliverer (Enosh-Uthra). It remains uncertain, however, whether the Baptist is an original feature. But Bultmann saw this as the key to the connection with Christian origins (for the Baptist sect cf. Acts 18.25; 19.1-7). Thus John took over a Gnostic document, in which the Baptist was the Revealer, and applied it to Jesus. The document was composed in Semitic poetic style comparable to the Wisdom literature. This can be seen in the Prologue and in numerous discourse passages elsewhere (e.g. 3.31-36).

For the subject matter of the document Bultmann compared the non-canonical *Odes of Solomon*, which are second-century poems on themes of divine truth, which survive in a Syriac version. But they are not necessarily the product of a Gnostic sect, and the similarities with John are more likely to be due to dependence on John than the other way round. However, the more recent discovery of Gnostic writings from Nag Hammadi has provided much better models, and shows that a document of the kind proposed by Bultmann is by no means impossible.

Nevertheless, the Johannine discourses are not primarily concerned with this kind of spirituality, but with presenting Jesus in person as the object of faith. This was recognized by Bultmann, who argued that John radically altered the character of the document, just as in the case of the Signs Source. The alteration here consisted in making the secret knowledge the revelation of the identity of Jesus himself. Those who believe in Jesus are enabled to enjoy eternal life. They thus already possess the future benefits which belong to the coming age in the thought of earliest Christianity. Thus the source, with its timeless and mystical concept of salvation, enabled John to break through the eschatological frame of the primitive kerygma (proclamation), producing a 'realized eschatology', i.e. the idea of present realization of what properly belongs to the future (cf. 5.25). At the time when the Gospel was written the delay of the parousia, or Second Coming, of Jesus was causing a crisis of confidence in the church's message. John's discourses supply the necessary reinterpretation of the message to show its permanent value, regardless of the passage of time. In adapting the source the evangelist was careful to retain the centrality of the preaching of the cross in the kerygma (which of course the source did not contain), so that the necessity of the death of Jesus is presented as an essential aspect of the meaning of faith in him (cf. 3.14-16; 8.28-29).

As before, it must be questioned whether a source of this kind is a necessary hypothesis. In any case, the source cannot be separated from the rest of the Gospel on grounds of style. The very considerable

adaptation which would be required to make such a source suitable
for John's purpose suggests that a better explanation would be to
regard the postulated document not as a source but as a model.

But if it is models that we are looking for, there are other possibilities which are nearer to the beginnings of Christianity in a Jewish setting. The Prologue is most likely to be modelled on Jewish Wisdom
poems, as we have seen. Again, the discourse on the Bread of Life in
6.32-58 is based on the Old Testament story of the manna in the
wilderness in Exodus 16, and John expressly attributes it to teaching
given by Jesus in the synagogue at Capernaum (6.59). This suggests
that the model is the synagogue homily or sermon, in which the liturgical lessons or Scripture readings are expounded, such as we find in
the Jewish *midrash*. As it is only the Prologue which appears to have
literary models behind it, it is reasonable to suppose that the rest of
the discourses are based on the evangelist's own homilies delivered in
the Johannine church.

The Homilies of John

The observation that the discourses of John are modelled on homilies
brings them back into the mainstream of Christian life, and so makes
them seem less strange as the work of the evangelist. Moreover, this
theory greatly eases the problem of understanding the relationship
between the discourses. For, in spite of some cross-referencing, the
discourses tend to be complete in themselves. This view has been
espoused by a number of modern commentators, notably R.E. Brown.
He argued that the homilies stem from the work of the Beloved Disciple (assumed to be the founder of the Johannine tradition), which was
taken up and used by the evangelist. But in my opinion it is a mistake
to distinguish between the author of the homilies and the evangelist.
It is much better to think of the homilies as the evangelist's own
preaching, in which the technique was worked out. On this view the
homilies are best regarded as the evangelist's first drafts, incorporated
with varying degrees of alteration into the larger work.

The homiletic theory thus explains the unique feature of the discourses, but we still have to ask what sources were available for them
in the first place. Here the analogy of a modern preacher may help. A
preacher may start from a passage of Scripture, taking a text from it as
the opening of the sermon, and then build up the sermon as an exposition and application of it. John does not begin with a passage of the
Hebrew Scriptures, but with an item from the tradition of the sayings
of Jesus. A glance at the opening verses of the discourses will show

that a saying from the tradition is the starting-point far more than is commonly realized.

Some of the discourses begin with a narrative from the tradition (e.g. 5.1-9; 6.1-21), which serves the same purpose as a passage from Scripture. When this happens, John inserts dialogue to make the transition to the discourse (cf. 5.10-18; 6.22-30). But the discourse itself, based on a homily, has its own saying from the tradition, which we can regard as the text of the sermon. Thus the discourse with Nicodemus starts with a saying (3.3, 5), which has already been shown to be a traditional saying of Jesus (cf. Mt. 18.3; Mk 10.15). It provides the motif of origination from God, which is the theme of the whole discourse (cf. vv. 6, 31). Similarly in 5.19 Dodd detected a parable from the tradition, which he called the Parable of the Apprenticed Son. This opens up the theme of the authority of Jesus, who does 'nothing on my own authority' (v. 30). In the Bread of Life discourse Jesus' opening treatment of the topic in 6.32-34 contains a reminiscence of the Lord's Prayer (the response of the people in v. 34 echoes 'Give us this day our daily bread'). In 8.12 'I am the light of the world' has a Synoptic counterpart in Mt. 5.14, and introduces the theme of witness. In 8.31-38 a new discourse begins with a dialogue which includes another parable by Dodd, the Slave and the Son in v. 36. The Good Shepherd allegory of 10.7-18 is similarly based on the Parable of Sheep and Shepherd in 10.15.

Other sayings from the tradition occur at strategic points in the discourses, notably the eucharistic words of Jesus (cf. Mk 14.22-25) in 6.52-56 and a version of Mk 9.1 in 8.51, 52. Though they have been adapted for their present context in every case, they are sufficiently close to sayings which have survived in the Synoptic tradition to be recognized as source material.

If each discourse is basically a sermon expounding a text, we should not expect the main body of it to be derived from a source, as Bultmann supposed. It is altogether probable that it is the evangelist's own composition. John works like a playwright, who invents dialogue and speeches to convey the message of the play through the medium of drama. There is risk in this procedure, because it blurs the distinction between history and interpretation. Moreover, John's method seems to be a step on the way to what happened in the second century, when Gnostic teachers used the device of secret teaching by the risen Jesus as a vehicle for their own views. The justification of this procedure in John's case is the integrity with which the fundamental issues of Christian faith are exposed.

The Making of the Gospel

If the raw materials of the Gospel consisted of existing homilies and an assortment of other items from the tradition, it is not difficult to imagine the evangelist at work in making them into a coherent whole. It therefore comes as something of a surprise to find that there are various abrupt changes of theme and contradictions of time and place, which suggest a more complex process. Various suggestions have been made.

Bultmann's view, as we have seen, takes the Gospel to be based on three major sources, signs, discourses and passion narrative. He also postulated that the discourses had been disarranged through accidental displacement of sheets of the autograph. In his view a later editor, whom he called the Ecclesiastical Redactor, reassembled them in the wrong order, and at the same time showed his real aim of making John's teaching conform more closely with Christian orthodoxy by inserting various corrections. By these insertions he countered the timelessness of the teaching by bringing in references to the coming judgment in a literal way (e.g. 5.25-29). He also added allusions to the sacraments ('water' in 3.5 to make an allusion to baptism, and the eucharist in 6.51b-58), which the evangelist, having a wholly spiritual theology, would have disapproved. It must be said that most scholars find these suggestions arbitrary and unconvincing.

Brown, supporting the homiletic view, thought of the evangelist's work as the making of a consistent narrative on the basis of homilies, but accounted for the breaks of continuity by assuming that a later editor inserted further material which the evangelist had omitted. This explains some degree of overlap, e.g. 3.31-36 can be regarded as an alternative version of 3.16-21, and 6.51-58 repeats the substance of 6.35-50.

The possibility that the Gospel has been supplemented after the completion of the main composition should be accepted, because it gives the best explanation of some glaring difficulties. It is, in fact, almost universally recognized that ch. 21 has been added by a later editor after the original conclusion in 20.30-31, presumably after the death of the evangelist.

But it is also possible that the evangelist had already supplemented the Gospel with additional material, so as to incorporate further homilies which would reinforce the value of it. This theory solves several difficulties. One obvious example is ch. 6 on the Bread of Life. This is a self-contained piece, but it breaks the continuity between chs.

5 and 7, so that many commentators have argued that the chapter is misplaced and ought to follow ch. 4. But reasons can be found to suggest that it was deliberately placed after ch. 5. For instance, seeing that the Bread of Life discourse is based on the manna story in Exodus 16, it makes a superb example of the claim of Jesus in 5.46 that Moses 'wrote of me'. As interpolation is a more natural editorial procedure than accidental displacement, which is really quite hard to visualize, the theory that ch. 6 has been added in a second edition of the Gospel is worth serious consideration. Similarly, the ending of 14.31, 'Rise, let us go hence', should obviously be followed by the walk to Gethsemane, but this does not happen until 18.1. Chapters 15 and 16, which go over some of the same themes as ch. 14, and the Prayer of Jesus in ch. 17 evince anxiety for the future safety of the disciples and the unity of the community, and so could be additional pieces in the light of new dangers.

Other possible changes in the second edition are the addition of the Prologue (1.1-18), which has had the original opening of the Gospel about the Baptist dovetailed into it (1.6-8), and the insertion of the Raising of Lazarus (11.1-44), which has replaced the Cleansing of the Temple (now moved to 2.13-22) as the immediate cause of the plot to arrest Jesus in 11.47-53 (cf. Mk 11.15-18). These changes have a theological interest. The Prologue provides the rational basis of the Christology of John, which is presupposed throughout the Gospel, and (if it is indeed an addition for the second edition) was added precisely to clarify this. The Raising of Lazarus is a superbly dramatic presentation of Jesus as the lord of life and death before the account of his own death and resurrection in the narrative which follows.

The Woman taken in Adultery (7.53–8.11), which is an excerpt from a lost gospel, came into the text of John as late as the third century, and is not found in the best manuscripts.

The Style of John

One reason for insisting on the decisive role of the evangelist as the real author of the Gospel, including material introduced in a second edition, is the homogeneous style and vocabulary. This cuts across the division of sources proposed by Bultmann. A large number of typical features are present in all three divisions. Some of these are less frequent in material of Synoptic type (the signs and the passion narrative), and this encouraged Fortna to reconstruct his Signs Gospel out of this material. But this is a mistake, because specifically non-Johannine features are never sufficient to make possible reconstruction of the source in anything but the most fragmentary form.

The only way to appreciate John's style is to read the Gospel atten-
tively, preferably in the original Greek. John's Greek is simple and
straightforward. Because of its repetitiveness it is easy for beginners
to grasp. Contrary to expectation, John does not use long philosophical words. Verbs are preferred to abstract nouns. The readers are constantly summoned to 'believe into' (*pisteuein eis*) Jesus, which means
to entrust themselves to him, but the word for 'faith' (*pistis*) never
occurs at all. Synonyms are used without discrimination (notably
pempein and *apostellein* 'to send' and *agapān* and *philein* 'to love'). It is
thus possible that Greek was not John's first language, which might
well have been Aramaic if the Gospel originated in Syria.

However, these features are not enough to guarantee a single
author, for there seems to be a common style in the writings of the
Johannine community. The three Epistles of John are not necessarily
the work of the same writer, but they are remarkably similar in style.
There is nonetheless an important difference. The authentic work of
the evangelist shows a flair for dramatic presentation and depth of
theological penetration which are lacking in the Epistles. Thus it is
correct to speak of a characteristic style of the Johannine community,
which the evangelist also shares. But the evangelist is marked out
from the rest by individuality and creative ability, which color the
Gospel from end to end.

John's distinctive style appears in the organization and presentation
of the material. In looking at the passages dealing with the Beloved
Disciple we have seen how an item from the tradition is built up into
a highly dramatic episode. Another striking example is the Raising of
Lazarus in ch. 11, in which a whole series of delaying tactics holds
back the climax, which at last comes as a sudden revelation to everyone present.

Similarly, the discourses are steadily built up to a climax. The subject is announced, often using a saying from the tradition, as we have
seen. If the dialogue form is used, the speaker may misunderstand
Jesus, as in the case of Nicodemus in 3.1-10. This gives the cue for
Jesus to redefine his statement, so as to take the subject to a deeper
level. Another technique, which often appears in monologues, is for
the evangelist or Jesus to make a sweeping statement, and then to
limit its application by making a further statement which modifies it,
e.g. 1.11-12; 8.15-16.

In all such cases it is the characters in the story who are ignorant of
what Jesus means or of what he is leading up to. The readers are not
in doubt, for they know from the first chapter who Jesus is, and so can

always guess what the climax will be. This is deliberate, as it is not John's purpose to mystify the readers, but to engage their attention, so that they may be confirmed in their faith and equipped to defend it against the opponents of the church.

For this reason John is not really interested in the characters of the story except as foils to Jesus. The tendency is to use them functionally to represent different responses. We have already seen the important function of the Beloved Disciple, who typifies the evangelist's own mind and is the true follower of Jesus with whom every reader should identify. Peter's role is dictated by the tradition, which includes his confession of faith (John's version of this is in 6.69) and his three denials in the passion narrative. He thus stands for loyalty without full understanding. Thomas, as everyone knows, represents doubt about the resurrection. Andrew and Philip are missionaries. John the Baptist has the special function of witness to Jesus as the Son of God.

The character of Jesus himself in John's presentation is affected by features of the theology and style of the Gospel. Jesus is always in complete control. He knows what he will do, so that his request for information is really a test (6.6). He has insight into the characters of others (2.25; 4.16-19). In debate with his opponents he can appear petulant, especially in the discourse of 8.31-58. A more tender side to Jesus appears in the discourses on discipleship, especially when he speaks of his relationship with God in terms of loving union (14.18-24). This is most likely to be a reflection of the evangelist's own ideals.

The conclusion is inevitable that John writes at a time when the living memory of Jesus is fading, and so the portrait of Jesus is becoming more stereotyped and shaped by dogmatic considerations. The picture in the Fourth Gospel needs to be corrected by the less consciously contrived indications furnished by the Synoptic tradition. But it has its own intrinsic value, because it expresses deep thought about the meaning of Jesus by a person of outstanding ability at a creative stage in early Christianity.

Summary

In this chapter we have looked at the main problems surrounding the identity of the evangelist. It has been necessary to throw doubt on the traditional identification with the Beloved Disciple and the apostle John. But it has also been shown that there is no final consensus of scholars on this issue.

It has also appeared unsafe to presuppose that any of the Gospel is based on direct eye-witness reporting. This led to a discussion of the function of the Beloved Disciple from the point of view of the literary character of the Gospel and the evangelist's aims. It also demanded an appraisal of the available sources and their relation to the traditions in the Synoptic Gospels. It was observed that some scholars hold that John made direct use of one or more of the Synoptic Gospels. Other source theories were also reviewed.

Next the composition of the Gospel was considered. The advantage of the homiletic theory, espoused by a number of recent commentators, was shown to be in providing a credible explanation of the discourses, which are a special feature of John. Though they are only marginally related to the sayings tradition, we saw that in nearly every case a saying of Jesus from the tradition is the 'text' of the sermon, so that it is permissible to regard them as expositions of the teaching of Jesus in relation to the special issues confronting the Johannine church.

The homiletic theory assumes that the discourses are largely based on sermons delivered over a period of time. It was also suggested that some were composed later than the original edition of the Gospel and added to it subsequently. Many theories assume that the source materials were worked up into preliminary drafts, and some think of alternative drafts which have both found there way into the finished Gospel. If the number and variety of theories of this kind is held to count against them all, it must at least be recognized that the Gospel raises real problems of composition which cannot be solved by glossing over them.

Such questions can be disheartening to the student who is new to the serious study of John, but in fact frank recognition of them and their implications for understanding the Gospel in its setting can help to give a much greater awareness of the achievement of the evangelist. Further help can be gained by looking at the historical circumstances of the Gospel and the world of thought to which it belongs. This will be the subject of the next chapter.

FURTHER READING

The problem of the authorship of the Fourth Gospel is dealt with in the introductions to the standard commentaries. M. Hengel puts this problem into relation with the history of the composition of all the Johannine literature in *The Johannine Question* (Philadelphia: Trinity Press International, 1989).

A recent attempt to deal with fact and fiction in John's Gospel is that of D. Tovey, *Narrative Art and Act in the Fourth Gospel* (Sheffield: Sheffield Academic Press, 1997).

Bultmann's theory of sources was examined in detail by D.M. Smith in *The Composition and Order of the Fourth Gospel: Bultmann's Literary Theory* (New Haven: Yale University Press, 1965).

The major advocate of the Signs Source is R.T. Fortna in two works—*The Gospel of Signs: A Reconstruction of the Narrative Source Underlying the Fourth Gospel* (SNTSMS, 11; Cambridge: Cambridge University Press, 1970; rev. edn, 1990) and *The Fourth Gospel and its Predecessor: From Narrative Source to Present Gospel* (Philadelphia: Fortress Press, 1989). His hypothesis is disputed by G. van Belle, *The Signs Source in the Fourth Gospel: Historical Survey and Critical Evaluation of the Semeia Hypothesis* (Leuven: Peeters, 1994).

A classic treatment of the view that John is independent of the Synoptics if found in C.H. Dodd, *Historical Tradition in the Fourth Gospel* (Cambridge: Cambridge University Press, 1963). Complementary studies of John's use of tradition are provided by B. Lindars, *Behind the Fourth Gospel* (London: SPCK, 1971) and J.D.G. Dunn, 'John and the Oral Gospel Tradition in H. Wansborough (ed.), *Jesus and the Oral Gospel Tradition* (Sheffield: JSOT Press, 1991), pp. 351-79. There has been a recent resurgence of the view that John knew and used the Synoptics, a resurgence evidenced in particular by the essays in A. Denaux (ed.), *John and the Synoptics* (Louvain: Louvain University Press, 1992). For a judicious assessment of the history of scholarship on this issue, see D.M. Smith, *John Among the Gospels: The Relationship in Twentieth Century Research* (Minneapolis: Fortress Press, 1992).

R.A. Culpepper, *Anatomy of the Fourth Gospel* (Philadelphia: Fortress Press, 1983) has helpful discussions of the speech patterns and the characterization in this Gospel. M. Casey, *Is John's Gospel True?* (New York: Routledge, 1996), pp. 80-97 discusses the Gospel's style and vocabulary and the question of Aramaic influence on its language.

Chapter Three

THE READERS OF THE GOSPEL

The World of John

The idea that the Gospel of John is based on the evangelist's own homilies draws attention to the nature of the audience. But it presupposes that the Gospel was written for internal consumption in the Johannine church, whereas the closing words of 20.30-31 express an evangelistic aim. But these aims are not mutually exclusive, for the Gospel could have been written both to confirm the faith of the members of the church and to appeal to interested enquirers like Nicodemus (cf. 3.2; 7.50; 19.39). To understand the Gospel properly we need to know not only what sort of people comprised the Johannine church, but also the range of the wider audience to which it might be addressed. We shall also need to know how the Johannine Christians relate to other strands of Christianity in the first century.

There are two main avenues of research in this area. One method is to compare the Gospel with the thought of the various social and religious groups of the ancient world, noting any particular points of contact with their writings. This may help to determine what kind of people belong to the orbit of John. The other method is to search the Gospel for references to contemporary conditions. We have already seen something of this sort in the evangelist's comment on leading Jews who did not dare to commit themselves to Christian faith (12.42-43). This is an important clue to the milieu of the Gospel and the date when it was written.

Hellenistic Thought

We begin with the first of these two methods, because it has had priority in the history of the interpretation of John. As we have seen, the Gospel was first appreciated in Gnostic circles, and subsequently gained recognition in the mainstream of Christianity only very slowly. The Gnostic sects posed a threat to Christianity in the second century, because they were basically non-Christian groups which adopted

Christian ideas into their teachings and claimed to possess the truth of salvation. But they are only one element in the Hellenistic world of New Testament times. Greek culture and language had spread throughout the eastern Mediterranean as a result of the conquests of Alexander the Great, including Palestine, where Greek was regularly used by the upper classes and required for diplomacy and commerce. Thus Jews, like the other peoples of the region, were necessarily affected by the wider influence of Greek philosophy and by the spread of various cults at this time. Such influence has been observed in the Jewish Wisdom literature, especially in the personification of Wisdom as a woman in Proverbs 1–9 and in Ecclesiasticus 24, which may have been developed as a counterblast to the Isis cult, and also in Wis. 7.22–8.1, which shows signs of Stoic philosophy.

1. Gnosticism is concerned with the revelation of divine knowledge to enable the soul to achieve union with the divine. As it rests on a dualist philosophy, the process of salvation requires release of the immortal soul from the prison of the body in order to ascend to the divine life. In some of the Gnostic systems the secret knowledge which solves this problem is itself the means of escape. Such knowledge might be imparted by a revealer from heaven (the savior-myth), but this is not found in all systems. The origins of Gnosticism are probably to be traced to Hellenistic groups on the fringe of Judaism, which came into existence before they seized the Christian teaching as support for their views. A central interest was to work out the required cosmology by interpreting the Jewish creation accounts in the light of Platonist philosophy. John's Prologue was sure to attract them.

2. However, attempts to combine the creation accounts with Greek philosophy were already being made within orthodox Judaism by Philo, the Jew of Alexandria (c. 20 BCE–50 CE). His work can be compared to the aims of the Gnostics, because he interpreted all the Jewish regulations of the Law, which he faithfully observed, as helps to maintaining the intellectual raising of the mind to God. He conceived this as the union of the human mind with the wisdom or rational ordering of reality which belongs to God. To express this idea he borrowed the use of *logos* (properly, 'word') from Stoic philosophy, so that the *logos* of the human mind seeks harmony with the *logos* of God. The similarity of this to the Jewish Wisdom tradition extends also to the tendency to personification, so that Philo can think of God's *logos* as his offspring and image, and call it his son.

Clearly there is a certain parallel here to John's Prologue, and some scholars have thought that John was indebted to Philo. However, John shows no tendency to reproduce other aspects of Philo's enormously complex and wide-ranging thought. In particular, Philo achieved his intellectual interpretation of the Law by allegorizing the details in terms of virtues and vices, following the lead given by an earlier Alexandrian Jewish writing, *The Letter of Aristeas*. There is nothing remotely resembling this in John. The common ground between Philo and John is to be found in the Jewish Wisdom literature.

3. Another almost contemporary expression of Hellenistic religious thought is contained in the Hermetic literature, generally dated in its present form to the second century CE. In these writings Hermes Trismegistos (really a new version of the Egyptian god Thoth) is the agent of rebirth through whom humans, corrupted by lust, may be conformed to the image of the archetypal Man and so achieve the vision of God. The idea of rebirth comes into Jn 3.1-8, but it is entirely unnecessary to regard the evangelist's treatment of this subject as dependent on this literature.

4. If any of these currents of thought are relevant to John, it must be concluded that the Johannine church belongs to the fringe of Christianity in the New Testament period. We are already aware that a confrontation with Judaism seems to be an ineradicable feature of the scene. A highly syncretistic milieu, in which both Jews and Christians are in contact with proto-Gnostic groups is not unthinkable. But the essentially Jewish basis of the thought of the Fourth Gospel is shown by the roots of so many of the ideas in the Old Testament. The Prologue, which shows no direct traces of Greek philosophy, is sufficiently accounted for by the Wisdom passages, and does not need the Gnostic myth of the descent of a savior figure. The other aspect of this myth, i.e. his return (ascent) to heaven, is really part of John's *Christian* heritage, for Jesus' exaltation is an essential feature of the primitive proclamation (cf. Acts 2.36).

On the other hand, our previous study of the discourses may suggest a different kind of contact with the thought represented by these groups. The evangelist is not concerned with the release of the soul from the prison of the body, but with eternal life as an experience. This takes us back to the model of Philo as an intellectual and speculative Jew. It suggests that the true relationship between the Fourth Gospel and the Hellenistic world is to be sought in a Hellenistic-Jewish group, which is not unorthodox, but has an intellectual approach to the ancestral religion and an interest in philosophical speculation to undergird it. If that is the kind of Jewish group which is in dialogue with the Johannine church, it is likely that the church includes converts from this group in its ranks.

Qumran Thought

The idea that John was indebted to Greek thought owes its currency to the impression given by the Prologue, and was promoted in modern times by scholars who had had a classical education. In spite of some dissentient voices, this view predominated in Johannine studies until the discovery of the Dead Sea Scrolls at Qumran in 1947 opened up new understanding of Judaism in New Testament times. Here were the writings of Jews, fanatically devoted to the Law, who nevertheless had a range of ideas which makes them very different from Judaism as known from the rabbinic tradition. They had vivid expectations of the coming intervention of God to conquer the forces of evil and to set up the messianic kingdom, similar to the ideas of the apocalyptic literature of the time. But they also had a spirituality based on a moral dualism of the struggle of good and evil to gain the mastery of the human soul. Having also a highly developed angelology, they thought of warring spiritual forces, headed by the Angel of Light (also called the Spirit of Truth) and the Angel of Darkness (also called the Spirit of Falsehood). Thus the great eschatological battle is fought out at the individual level in every person.

The similarities between this and certain features of John are obvious. Though the Holy Spirit is never referred to as an angel, the same title is used (the Spirit of Truth, 14.17; 15.25; 16.13), and the chief function of the Holy Spirit is to reveal the truth. John also characterizes the devil as a dealer in falsehood (8.44). The opposition of light and darkness and the tendency to speak of good and evil in terms of truth and falsehood are both features of John which reflect Qumran. Moreover, the Qumran community appears to be a sectarian body, regarding itself as possessing the monopoly of religious truth, and in this way invites comparison with the Johannine church, which is widely recognized to be sectarian in type. Its common meal for those initiated into full membership includes the blessing of bread and wine, similar to the Christian eucharist. It has also been suggested that the Johannine Christians may have observed the Qumran calendar of feasts, which differed from that of the main body of Judaism, as this might explain why John makes the Last Supper the day before the Passover in contrast with the Synoptic tradition.

Initial enthusiasm overstressed the importance of these similarities. There are also very substantial differences, notably the Qumran devotion to the Law and the pride of place given to the Zadokite priesthood. It is now recognized that the points in common with Qumran were not peculiar to the sect (probably the Essenes), but characteristic of Judaism more widely at this time. Hence the lasting effect of the discovery of the Scrolls is not to range John alongside Qumran, but to give decisive support to the Jewish character of John and the Johannine church.

Qumran and the Date of John

A further consequence of the discovery of the Scrolls was that one of the obstacles to an early dating for John was removed. If the decisive influence on John was contact with Greek thought, a late date when the church was establishing itself in the Gentile world seemed to be required. But now the leading ideas of John could already be found in Jewish writings before the rise of the Christian era. This led to attempts to date John much earlier than had ever been suggested, even by conservative scholars. The chief protagonist was J.A.T. Robinson, whose ideas received their fullest treatment in his magisterial book *The Priority of John* (1985).

Various factors contributed to this conclusion. It was noted that John's topography of the Holy Land was correct. John also knows Jewish customs. Moreover, John has traditions not found in the Synoptic Gospels, which appear to be based on good information. We hear of a baptizing mission on the part of Jesus in 3.22 and 4.1-3, and all the events of chs. 1–3 take place in Judea, which suggests an early phase of Jesus' ministry of which the Synoptic Gospels know nothing. We have already seen that John must have used traditions comparable to the Synoptics but independent of them. This possibility was investigated by Dodd in *Historical Tradition in the Fourth Gospel* (1963). Where there are parallels with the Synoptics (e.g. the cleansing of the Temple), it is arguable that John preserves the more reliable version. So, also, John's timing of this incident at the very beginning of Jesus' ministry (2.13-22) instead of at the end might be correct.

The argument so far could lead to the conclusion that John had better sources than the Synoptic writers, but that would not necessarily imply an early date for the writing of the Gospel. That, however, became more possible in the light of the evidence from Qumran for John's world of thought. Thus the evangelist's presentation of the traditions need not be regarded as any later than the date of the Synoptic Gospels, and could even be earlier. So Robinson took the final logical step and proposed that John was a redactor of primitive traditions which were superior to the Synoptic sources, making the Fourth Gospel the most reliable of all. Robinson recognized that the Gospel is the end product of a process, and did not claim that it was completed before the Synoptics, so that the 'priority' of John rests in its greater historical worth. But arguing along these lines, Robinson in the end found himself driven to the traditional position that the Beloved Disciple was to be identified with the apostle John, who was the direct source of the information reproduced by the evangelist.

Although many readers were delighted by this conservative conclusion on the part of a scholar considered to be a radical, it has not won agreement from the majority of scholars, and is unlikely to do so. Our study of the making of the Gospel in the last chapter has pointed to literary factors that are totally neglected by Robinson. Though the use of independent strands of tradition has been fully recognized, it has been necessary to recognize the vast scale of rewriting by the evangelist. It is only by denying outright John's characteristic irony that Robinson can claim that the high priest's prophecy of the destruction of Temple and nation in 11.48-52 carries no allusion to the actual events of 70 CE. Further points will be considered in the next sections.

The Jews and the Pharisees

It has long been held that a date after the Jewish War is required because of John's references to the Jewish classes and parties. In spite of the good information about the Holy Land already referred to, in this matter there does seem to be an anachronism.

In the first place the most frequent designation is simply 'the Jews'. This occurs 48 times, but some cases (e.g. 'the king of the Jews' as a title for Jesus 6 times in the passion narrative) can be discounted. Elsewhere it is used without discrimination to mean the Jewish people, the inhabitants of Judea, the people of Jerusalem, and the Jewish authorities in Jerusalem. In 6.41, 52, which is set in Galilee, it is not clear whether the Jews are the same as the crowd (6.22, 24) or a different audience, who might be the officials of the synagogue at Capernaum (6.59). The effect of this blanket use of the term is to differentiate Jesus from his own people in a way that is not found in the Synoptic Gospels and is not really credible in the historical life of Jesus.

Secondly, the Pharisees are mentioned 16 times, but the usage in John can scarcely be regarded as correct for the period before the Jewish War. The Pharisees were predominantly a lay movement working for the improvement of piety and observance of the Law among the common people. They did, however, have members in high places, including the Sanhedrin, so that when John refers to 'the

chief priests and the Pharisees' (7.45; 11.47, 57; 18.3) and 'the authorities and the Pharisees' (7.48), that is not incorrect. Josephus, the Jewish historian, who belonged to the ruling class and unwillingly
commanded the Jewish forces in Galilee during the Jewish War, had
himself joined the Pharisees as a young man. But because of their non-
involvement the Pharisees were not considered dangerous when the
war was over, so they were available to fill the vacuum of leadership
of the chastened and dispirited people. Thus the Pharisees became the
leading Jews after 70 CE, and it is from their tradition that rabbinic
Judaism has developed. In the Synoptic Gospels the Pharisees
function as we should expect them to do in the lifetime of Jesus. His
conflict with them is about the application of the Law, so they are
often mentioned alongside the scribes. But in John the scribes are
never mentioned. The Pharisees are not clearly differentiated from
'the Jews' in the sense of the Jewish authorities. The conclusion that
the usage in John reflects the situation when the Pharisees became the
real leaders after the disaster of the Jewish War is hard to resist.

Thirdly, the Sadducees also are never mentioned in John. They
were the ruling Jewish party. The high priest's family and most of the
members of the Sanhedrin were Sadducees. Their decision to yield to
the pressure of the Zealots and to make war on Rome in 66 CE proved
to be their downfall, and after 70 CE they ceased to exist. John's failure
to use the name does not necessarily imply ignorance of it, because (as
in the Synoptic Gospels) 'the chief priests' (i.e. the members of the
high-priestly families who sat in the Sanhedrin) was usually more
appropriate. But John never refers to the chief priests without also
mentioning the Pharisees, and this is surely significant in the light of
what has been said above.

Church and Synagogue

John shares with the Synoptic Gospels the tradition of opposition to
Jesus on the part of Pharisees and other authorities. But apart from
the breaking of the sabbath (5.10; 9.14), which is clearly based on this
tradition, the issues in the Fourth Gospel are completely different. As
the subject of the discourses is usually an aspect of Christology, it has
often been held that the scenario in which Jesus is in dispute with the
Jews is an artificial use of the traditions to provide a setting for a doctrinal debate which really belongs within Hellenistic Christianity.
Largely as a result of the work of J.L. Martyn, however, it is now
widely accepted that the discourses are concerned with the actual
issues of the church and synagogue debate at the time when the

Gospel was written. This point must be taken in conjunction with the threat of excommunication from the synagogue (9.22; 16.2), and the information in 12.42 about would-be believers who dare not commit themselves. Just as Jesus in his historic ministry was often on trial on account of the criticisms of the scribes and Pharisees, and eventually was tried by the highest authorities, so the Johannine Christians are on trial, and may have to face deprivation and even martyrdom. We do not have to postulate a late date for opposition as such. Mark's 'Little Apocalypse' already warns that 'you will be beaten in synagogues' (Mk 13.9). Thus it is not the threat of persecution which points to a later date, but the issues which are at stake.

Once we take the discourses as evidence for the Jewish and Christian debate, we can see immediately that the centre of interest has shifted to aspects of christology which were not at issue in the earlier period. It appears from 9.22 that 'the Jews had already agreed that if any one should confess him to be Christ, he was to be put out of the synagogue'. This is widely held to reflect the situation towards the end of the century.

The Jews after the fall of Jerusalem were saved from despair by the efforts of the Pharisees, who made themselves into a new Sanhedrin at Javneh. They issued directives on the keeping of the Law in home and synagogue, and encouraged patience and submission to the will of God. Christians were disapproved, because they did not keep the Law and thereby 'led the people astray'. This is the complaint against Jesus in Jn 7.12, but it exactly corresponds with the traditional rabbinic statement preserved in *b. Sanhedrin* 43a that Jesus was 'to be stoned, because he practised magic and enticed and led Israel astray'. The full passage makes it clear that 'to be stoned' simply means to suffer the death penalty, because it goes on to say that Jesus 'was hanged (i.e. crucified) on the Preparation of the Passover'. This again tallies with the threat of stoning in Jn 8.59; 10.31, 39; 11.8, and also with the Johannine timing of the crucifixion. Thus John is here in touch with hostile traditions which became standard Jewish polemic after the breach between church and synagogue.

The final break is generally identified with the decision of the rabbis at Javneh to include a curse against 'the Nazarenes and the Minim' in the *Amidah*, or Eighteen Benedictions, recited as a sort of creed by all worshipers in the synagogue at the opening of the sabbath service. The twelfth benediction thanks God for keeping Israel safe from her accursed enemies, with an obvious allusion to the Romans. The additional words add the Nazarenes (Christians) and Minim (heretics) to these enemies. The new clause effectively excluded Christians from synagogue worship, as they could not recite the words without cursing themselves. The date of this addition is uncertain, but generally held to be about 85–90 CE. John's references to excommunication in 9.22; 12.42; 16.2 may well have some connection with this move on the part of the rabbis. In any case it is sufficient to observe that during this period relations between church and synagogue were strained to breaking-point.

The Law in John

A final indication of a fairly late date for John is to be found in the references to the Law in the discourses. It has been suggested above that the Johannine church was in dialogue with a group of Hellenistic Jews who had an interest in the philosophical and spiritual aspects of their religion, rather like the situation of Philo. If that is the case, it is probable that John's church was recruited from this group, and this may help to explain the ambiguous relationship between them. But for our present purpose the point of interest is the spirituality of the Law to be found in this kind of group.

We usually think of the Law as a set of rules that have to be observed to maintain a person's good standing with God. It is more difficult to think of it as the focus of personal religion. But this is what it became for many Jews of the Second Temple period, and so it has continued to the present day. The spirituality of the Law tends to make it a mediator between God and his covenant people, because it conveys his good will and care for them and provides the means for their response. This function of the Law can be put on a philosophical footing if it is correlated with the Wisdom tradition. In the earliest relevant passage, Prov. 8.22-31, Wisdom is God's partner in creation, rejoicing in all that comes into being, and especially 'delighting in the sons of men'. So the readers are invited to receive Wisdom, for they thereby gain the key to a truly fulfilled life and receive the favor of God. In this passage the Law is not mentioned, but it does come in when this passage is rewritten by Ben Sira in Ecclesiasticus 24. For in this presentation of it the Law is identified as the highest expression of God's Wisdom.

To put this into perspective we must note that Ben Sira was a conservative, aiming to preserve the best of the national heritage of Judaism. Writing about 200–180 BCE, he was opposed to those who sought the ways of God through dreams and visions, and that means the apocalyptic movement which belongs to this period. He also distrusted the appeal to Greek philosophy, which was characteristic of the Sadducees and educated classes. Against both tendencies Ben Sira insisted that the knowledge of God and the understanding of reality were available in the Law, which embodies the whole Wisdom of God. So in Ecclus 24.1-12 Wisdom is not only God's agent in creation, but also dwells among God's people, making her earthly home in Jerusalem and the Temple itself. Then in v. 23 it is stated that all her riches (recounted in vv. 13-22) 'are the book of the covenant of the Most High God, the law which Moses commanded us'. From it streams abundant Wisdom, described in the following verses in terms of the rivers of Paradise. Thus the Law is the true embodiment of the Wisdom of God.

This description has numerous points of contact with the Prologue of John, so much so that it must be regarded as the greatest single literary influence behind it. But here, instead of the Law, the fullest expression of God is in Jesus, the Word made flesh. This contrast is stated explicitly: 'The law was given through Moses; grace and truth came through Jesus Christ' (1.17). John also shares the rabbinic opposition to the attempts of visionaries to gain access to the heavenly secrets (cf. 1.18; 3.13; 5.37). Thus John's Christology is worked out against a spirituality in which the Law has cosmic status as the means of salvation. It is reasonable to conclude that a Wisdom theology of this kind was a central feature of the Jewish group which was in such sharp debate with the Johannine church.

It is thus not surprising to find, as we shall see later, that in the christological discourses of John 3–10 the Law is an important factor in nearly every case. For instance in the Bread of Life discourse there is a further allusion to Ecclesiasticus 24, for in 6.35 Jesus echoes the words of Wisdom in Ecclus 24.21. Thus the opponents of John claim that the Law is the true spiritual nourishment. John counters this by asserting that Jesus is the real bread from heaven. The significance of this debate for the date of John will be clarified in the next two sections.

The Use of the Gospel in Debate

We have seen earlier that the discourses are a unique feature of the Fourth Gospel, which differentiates it from the Synoptics. We can now see that they carry the evangelist's treatment of the great issues of Christology in the debate with the synagogue. But this raises the question why John used the form of a gospel to deal with it. A more detailed look at the discourses will show that John set out to anchor the argument in the Jesus tradition by building the discourses on crucial sayings of Jesus from the available sources. Thus the Christian claims about Jesus, especially the advanced Christology of the Johannine church, could be shown to be consistent with the tradition. This would effectively answer the objection that the Christian claims go far beyond the commonly remembered impressions of Jesus himself. Moreover, it would give assurance to the Christians themselves that their faith was soundly based in the Jesus tradition.

It is for this reason that a saying from the tradition can be detected at the start of most of the discourses. In our consideration of the discourses as homilies in the last chapter it was suggested that this is comparable to the 'text' of a sermon. Now we can see that it is the warrant for the argument which is to follow in the rest of the discourse. This point can be illustrated from the discourse with Nicodemus in John 3.

In our previous consideration of this discourse we observed that it began with a saying from the Jesus tradition which lays down the principle that a birth from above is necessary for salvation (3.3, 5). It follows from this that the revelation of divine truth must also come from above. The conclusion will be that Jesus himself, as the one who brings the divine revelation, must also have come from above in some sense (vv. 31-36). But it is now clear that, for the purpose of the debate with the unbelieving Jews, the Jewish claim that the revelation is already available in the Law must also be taken into account. This is done in 3.10-15. Here Jesus upbraids Nicodemus for being a 'teacher of Israel', who nevertheless does not have access to the truth which is necessary for salvation. No earthly person can ascend to heaven to get hold of this saving knowledge (v. 13). Very few modern readers can pick up the Old Testament allusion in this verse, but it would have been obvious to the members of the Johannine church and their Jewish rivals. It is a reference to Deut. 30.11-14, where the people's fear that God's commandment might be too hard to discover, and might even require someone to go up to heaven to fetch it, is refuted on the grounds that it is available to all in the Law. For John the truth of God is fully accessible only in Jesus, and not only in Jesus as 'a teacher come from God' (v. 2), but in Jesus who was lifted up on the cross (vv. 14-15). We shall see the importance of this aspect of John's argument later. For our present purpose it is enough to recognize that the implied reference to the Law at this point confirms our observation of the pattern of the Johannine discourses: a saying from the Jesus tradition enunciates a spiritual principle. This is then shown to be inadequately catered for by the Law. Finally, Jesus is shown, by contrast, to be the true agent of God to provide what is needed to achieve salvation.

This example enables us to see that the discourses reflect real disputes with the synagogue. The conflict situation of the earlier tradition is now far more acute, and the readers can be expected to look to the Gospel to strengthen their confidence in their position. The great attention given to the theme of discipleship in chs. 13–17 shows real anxiety about the future position of the disciples, in ways that reflect the ordeal that the readers themselves are passing through.

The Johannine Sect

The matters in debate between church and synagogue differed as time went on, and in John we can see traces of all the issues that were raised. In the Synoptic tradition the issue at stake is practice. There can be no doubt that this was an important point of conflict between Jesus and the scribes and Pharisees. Jesus apparently is lax in regard to the practice of the sabbath and the rules of purity laid down in the Law and promoted by the Pharisees. John makes use of the sabbath issue in 5.9-16; 7.15-24; 9.14-16.

At the same time, from the earliest days the debate was focused on the question of Jesus' messiahship. John shows awareness of several disputed points on this issue in ch. 7, but the real centre of the debate for the Johannine church was the advanced Christology which is presented in the Fourth Gospel itself, and shows Jesus as the replacement of the Law in theology and spirituality. This touches the crucial question of monotheism, which, it is claimed, is breached by John's Christology (cf. 5.18; 10.33). In the eyes of the Jews the Johannine Christians were leading the people astray (7.12), and were even guilty of blasphemy (10.33).

The sharpness of the debate in John suggests that the Johannine church is a beleaguered sect, alienated from the local society, intensely loyal internally, but hostile to those outside. The command to love one another (13.34) gives a splendid example, but it does not extend to the opponents. Those who are within are the children of God (1.12), but the opponents are the children of the devil, who is the father of lies (8.39-47). The polarization of categories into truth and falsehood, which we have seen to be a feature in common with the Qumran sect, applies also to their relationship with the Jewish community, who may well have shared the same attitudes. For their opponents are evidently threatened by them and are taking drastic steps to curb their influence (15.18–16.4).

The sectarian character of the Johannine church is thus due to social pressures. Christianity started as a movement within Judaism, but gradually Christians and Jews became bitterly opposed to one another. The Johannine church is a particularly acute example of this, and it is reasonable to suggest that pressures of this kind have played a part in the development of some of the distinctive facets of John's theology.

Other Christians

The sectarian character of the Johannine church has also been attributed by modern scholars to its relationship with other Christian groups. The theory of Bultmann that John depended on a proto-Gnostic source led to the conclusion that the Johannine church adhered to a Christianized version of the saviour-myth which marked it off from mainstream Christendom. On this basis it is possible to read the Gospel as a sort of code, in which 'the Jews' are really the main body of Christians, who bitterly oppose the Johannine sect.

Starting from similar considerations, but without adopting Bultmann's theory, R.E. Brown attempted to work out the relationship with other Christian groups in his influential book *The Community of the Beloved Disciple* (1979). Brown takes the Beloved Disciple seriously as the founder of the Johannine tradition. In spite of the complex process which lies behind the finished Gospel, the evangelist was able to reproduce this tradition with considerable fidelity. Thus the Beloved Disciple represents Johannine Christianity in the Gospel. Other characters represent other groups. John the Baptist represents a Baptist group from which the Christians need to distance themselves. The Samaritan woman in ch. 4 represents Samaritan converts to Christianity (cf. Acts 8.5-25). This agrees with the view of Cullmann, who argues that Samaritans were a crucially important element in what he calls the Johannine circle.

The most daring feature of Brown's reconstruction is the claim that Peter in the Fourth Gospel represents mainstream, catholic Christendom over against the sectarianism of the Johannine church. Peter's position as the leader of the Twelve is acknowledged in John, but he is upstaged by the Beloved Disciple. However, this is not Brown's primary point, but rather the special character of John's Christology. John shows an advance on the rest of the New Testament in giving the strongest statement of the divinity of Jesus and the clearest expression of his pre-existence. Within the Fourth Gospel itself Peter's confession of faith (6.69) stops short at saying that Jesus is 'the Holy

One of God'. It is often held that the Johannine insistence on the flesh—that the Word became flesh (1.14)—is aimed at correcting a contemporary tendency to Docetism, i.e. the doctrine that Jesus only *seemed* to be human and only *seemed* to die on the cross, which is generally regarded as the earliest of the christological heresies of the second century. But if this is a necessary correction, it merely highlights the fact that in general John's own Christology only too easily encourages this kind of misunderstanding, because of the distance which is placed between Jesus and the rest of mortals and the insistence that salvation, as God's gift, can come only from one who is divine.

Thus, at a time when the church was expanding in the Hellenistic world with very little central control, it is not surprising to find differences of doctrinal emphasis and the beginnings of conflict over heresies. At such a time the Johannine church might well present the appearance of an eccentric group, unwilling to be identified with the main body of Christians on account of profound disagreement on matters of doctrine. Although I find it hard to accept the idea that the character of Peter in the Fourth Gospel has anything to do with this kind of ecclesiastical situation, the possibility that the Johannine church stood apart from the main body should not he denied.

The Johannine Epistles

The dangers inherent in the Christology of John become apparent in the Johannine Epistles. Brown argues that they were not written by the evangelist, but by a devoted supporter, the 'Elder', after the evangelist's death. The three letters are all addressed to an urgent situation within the Johannine church. Precisely what the evangelist had feared when composing the prayer of Jesus in John 17 has come about. The members of the church are splitting into factions. The Elder is identified with one side in the dispute, and his purpose is to resist the dissident group. He denounces them and warns the readers against them.

The point at issue is that the dissidents 'deny that Jesus is the Christ' (1 Jn 2.22). They do not confess 'that Jesus Christ has come in the flesh' (1 Jn 4.2-3, cf. 2 Jn 7). Brown interprets this to mean that they separate 'Jesus' (the human Jesus) from 'the Christ' (the divinity of Jesus). In their view only his divinity matters. The result is that they think of salvation in terms of union with his divinity. They think that this union gives to them a sinless existence, and so they refuse to acknowledge their own sin or the need for atonement through the death of Jesus (1 Jn 1.8–2.6).

The most arresting feature of Brown's interpretation is his contention that in this acrimonious debate *both* sides claimed the support of the Gospel in support of their views. The ambiguity of the Johannine Christology lends itself to opposite impressions simply by emphasis on one aspect to the exclusion of the other. The position of the dissidents shows the tendency towards Gnosticism, with its world-denying dualism and its concept of salvation as knowledge brought down from the heavenly sphere. Brown suggests that the Johannine group of churches (more than one centre is indicated by 2 and 3 Jn) did not survive the disruption, because it has left no trace in the known groups of the second century. The dissidents, then, are likely to have been swallowed up in one of the Gnostic sects, while the rest were absorbed in the great church.

Brown's reconstruction is not definitive, but is the best on offer. The information at our disposal is too scanty to allow certainty. One further factor still needs to be mentioned. Whereas the Gospel is preoccupied with the conflict between the church and the unbelieving Jews, there is not a trace of this in the three epistles. The reason may well be that the worsening situation attested by the Gospel (especially if 15.18–16.4 was added in a second edition) has reached the point of no return. By this time the life of the Johannine church is totally separate from its former Jewish contact. In that case, it may even have moved to a new location.

The Home of the Johannine Church

Tradition connects John with Ephesus. But this may be due to the identification of the evangelist with the John who wrote Revelation, whose connection with Ephesus is certain. Apart from this identification, which cannot be sustained, there seems to be no firm ground for locating the Gospel and Epistles at Ephesus. However, the possibility should not be excluded, because it satisfies some of the factors which need to be taken into account.

   a.   Though there is no direct link between the Gospel and Revelation, they have images in common, especially the Lamb of God (Jn 1.29, 36; Rev. 5.6 and often) and the water of life (Jn 4.14; 7.37-38; Rev. 22.1, 17).

b. Ignatius of Antioch is our first witness to Docetism, and his letters, written at Ephesus, have echoes of Johannine diction, though he does not know the Gospel.

c. Many sects existed at Ephesus, so that it makes a suitable setting for John's contact with Hellenistic groups and other non-Christian influences.

d. There was a large Jewish community in Ephesus (cf. Acts 18.19, 24-28; 19.8-20) and a small Baptist group (Acts 19.1-7).

A possible alternative would be Syria. Ignatius was bishop of Antioch, the capital city of the province. The *Odes of Solomon*, which are poems that reflect Johannine language and ideas, are probably Syrian in origin. If the theory of influence from the proto-Gnostic group which lies behind the Mandeans is correct, that would also indicate Syria as the point of contact.

John's reliable knowledge of Galilee and Jerusalem have persuaded some scholars that the Gospel has its origin in Palestine, but it is unlikely that the Johannine church was located there, especially if a date for the Gospel around 85–90 CE is accepted. It may be right, however, to accept connections with all three places, and assume that the community moved under pressure of circumstances from Palestine first to Syria and eventually to Ephesus. Wherever the Gospel was written, the distinctive style and diction of both Gospel and Epistles suggest a closely knit community with a tradition of its own, which would be resistant to radical change in spite of moving into new regions.

Summary

John's Gospel was written by a Christian for Christians, and the largest single influence on the evangelist was the Christian tradition. But the unique features of the Gospel demand recognition of the special circumstances which brought it into being. Aspects of the Gospel which appear to relate it to Hellenistic thought have suggested that it is a fresh presentation of the Christian message in terms of Greek thought. Thus Greek thought would have been the major influence behind the Gospel and indicate the intended readership. A similar claim for background and milieu have been made for links with proto-Gnosticism. In fact, the Hellenistic aspects of the Fourth Gospel are sufficiently accounted for in Jewish Hellenistic sources.

That the Gospel is more centrally based in Jewish thought has now become clear from the evidence of the Dead Sea Scrolls, which have furnished remarkable parallels to the Fourth Gospel. The discovery of the Scrolls also opened up the possibility of a much earlier date for the Gospel than had previously been suggested either by tradition or by critical scholarship. A crucial issue in discussion of this question is John's references to the Pharisees. Though the argument is not conclusive, on balance John's references best suit the situation of the ascendancy of the Pharisees after the Jewish War, and can be taken to reflect the readers' experience of Judaism at that time.

The Fourth Gospel was shown to reflect some of the accusations which became a standard part of the later Jewish polemic against Christians. It was also observed that references to the threat of excommunication from the synagogue best suit the conditions which led up to the situation of extreme estrangement in the last decade of the first century.

The next step was to determine the main issue between the Johannine church and the Jewish community. This was shown to be the attitude to the Law, not just in matters of practice, but especially in theology and spirituality. The basis was found in the Wisdom tradition, in which the Law is the embodiment of Wisdom. John claims that the divine Wisdom is most fully embodied in Jesus, who is the true revelation of God and agent of eternal life. In presenting this Christology in the discourses, John starts from a saying of Jesus from the tradition. This gives the basic principle which lies behind the christological conclusion, and the contrast with the Law is referred to, at least by implication, in the course of the argument.

The sectarian character of the Johannine church was then attributed to the acute situation of conflict in which it was placed. It also appeared probable that the church stood apart from the mainstream of Christendom, exhibiting tendencies in Christology which some would view with alarm. Though it is impossible to be sure how far the views of other Christian groups are represented in the different personalities of the Fourth Gospel, Brown's analysis of the connection between the Gospel and the subsequent disintegration of the Johannine church has much in its favor.

Brown wrote *The Community of the Beloved Disciple* with one eye on the divided state of Christendom in modern times. The history of the Johannine church shows conflict on two fronts, with the unbelieving Jews and with warring factions within. Its sectarian character is shown by the high esteem given to the love command as a feature of the in-group, which apparently does not apply to relations with those outside the group. John was alive to this danger, and strove to prevent it. John's own understanding of the gospel message rises above sectarianism to embrace all humanity. The argument that Jesus replaces the Law as the agency of salvation is no mere polemic, but a heartfelt statement that the bounds of a nationalist faith have been broken and salvation is open to all.

FURTHER READING

C.H. Dodd in *The Interpretation of the Fourth Gospel* (Cambridge: Cambridge University Press, 1953), surveyed possible backgrounds of thought, suggesting particular affinities with Philo and the Hermetic literature. He did not take into account the Dead Sea Scrolls. On the latter's relationship to this Gospel, see J.H. Charlesworth (ed.), *John and Qumran* (London: Geoffrey Chapman, 1972) and Charlesworth's own later views in 'The Dead Sea Scrolls and the Gospel according to John', in R.A. Culpepper and C.C. Black (eds.), *Exploring the Gospel of John* (Louisville, KY: Westminster John Knox Press, 1996), pp. 65-97.

The Gnostic text that has closest resemblances to John's Gospel is the Nag Hammadi tractate known as The Trimorphic Protennoia. See the discussion of Y. Jansenns, 'The Trimorphic Protennoia and the Fourth Gospel', in A.H.B. Logan and A.J.M. Wedderburn (eds.), *The New Testament and Gnosis: Essays in Honour of R.McL. Wilson* (Edinburgh: T. & T. Clark, 1983), pp. 229-44 and C.A. Evans, 'On the Prologue of John and the *Trimorphic Protennoia*', NTS 27 (1980–81), pp. 395-401.

The case for an early date for John's Gospel was argued by J.A.T. Robinson, *The Priority of John* (London: SCM Press, 1985). His work is severely criticized by M. Casey in *Is John's Gospel True?* (New York: Routledge, 1996), especially pp. 199-217. Casey also returns a negative verdict on the historical value of John. J.L. Martyn, *History and Theology in the Fourth Gospel* (Nashville: Abingdon, 2nd edn, 1979) relates the date of the Gospel to the tensions and hostilities between church and synagogue at the end of the first century CE, while R.E. Brown, *The Community of the Beloved Disciple* (New York: Paulist Press, 1979) attempts to reconstruct the history of a Johannine Christianity marked by these and other conflicts. For a careful argument for the genesis of the Gospel within a family quarrel between Jewish Christians and other Jews, see J. Ashton, *Understanding the Fourth Gospel* (Oxford: Clarendon Press, 1991), especially pp. 121-98.

Chapter Four

UNDERSTANDING JOHN

Asking the Right Questions

The Gospel of John is not just a biography, but a theological interpretation of Jesus to promote faith. It has survived the situation of conflict in which it was written, and the subsequent demise of the Johannine community, to become one of the most highly valued books of the Bible. It may be claimed that the Fourth Gospel can be read with profit without the paraphernalia of scholarship, and of course this is true up to a point. But our study of the complex questions relating to the author and the readers in the last two chapters have shown that factual matters and understanding are inextricably intertwined. We have already had to trespass on the territory which now lies before us, as we approach the theology of the Fourth Gospel and its meaning for today.

The task of understanding will be eased if the right questions are put to the text. In the first chapter it was pointed out that people often approach John with the wrong expectations. It is obvious that the author's purpose needs to be appreciated first in tackling any book. We have not only looked into this in the case of John, but also seen how this purpose is achieved through the skillful construction of both narrative and discourse in relation to the needs of the Johannine church.

Seeing that the purpose of John is to promote belief in order that the readers may have 'life', we can see at once that one reason why the Fourth Gospel differs radically from the Synoptic Gospels is that it is addressed to people whose concept of what constitutes salvation differs from that of the mainstream of earliest Christianity. This, then, is the best point from which to begin our investigation. Salvation is the end to which the whole presentation of the Gospel is directed, and it controls the structure of the evangelist's theology. And, of course, it is the real issue in the debate with the opponents of the Johannine church.

The Concept of Salvation

The chief clue to the distinctive character of John's concept of salvation is the use of 'life' or 'eternal life' instead of 'the kingdom of God' or 'the kingdom of heaven'. Only in 3.3, 5 is 'the kingdom of God' used, and that, as we have seen, is a version of a traditional saying of Jesus (cf. Mt. 18.3; Mk 10.15). When the idea is taken up in the discourse which it introduces, it becomes 'eternal life' (3.15, 16, 36). It is the reason for God's action in Christ, unforgettably expressed in the 'miniature gospel' of 3.16: 'For God so loved the world that he gave his only Son, that whoever believes in him should not perish but have eternal life.'

It seems, then, that the evangelist and the readers are not vitally interested in the notion of the kingdom of God, even though it was frequently on the lips of Jesus himself. To understand this change we must look first at the phrase in the teaching of Jesus and earliest Christianity. It properly denotes the rule of God, and in certain contexts it can even be a substitute-word for God himself (thus 'the kingdom of heaven is at hand' can mean 'God is near', referring to his eschatological coming). The preaching of Jesus is specially concerned with preparing his audience for the coming of the kingdom in this sense, as a future event which is expected imminently. His moral teaching is set in the context of a testing confrontation with God. In readiness for this he turns attention to the springs of action in the heart. At the same time he proclaims that the coming action of God will prove to be the arrival of blessing for the poor and despised. Thus salvation consists in surviving the coming ordeal and enjoying the eschatological kingdom of God that lies beyond it.

This teaching of Jesus is in line with widespread hopes and expectations in his time. Both the Dead Sea Scrolls and the contemporary apocalyptic literature presuppose that the present time is the last generation before the final act of God to set up the everlasting kingdom. It is possible to distinguish between a popular political concept, which expresses the hope of liberation from the Roman power and the setting up of the messianic kingdom on earth, and a more esoteric transcendental concept, which looks for a cataclysmic intervention by God and the start of a new age, indeed a new creation, in which God will reign supreme. As a prophet and visionary, Jesus most likely held a view comparable to the second scheme rather than the first (which would make him politically dangerous). But his audience evidently cherished hopes of the first kind, and this explains why he was reticent about making a messianic claim, though in the end this was the charge on which he was convicted and crucified.

This concept of salvation is thus a practical matter. It is a coming state of blessedness, in which all will observe the high morality which befits God's kingdom. It does not necessarily entail abrogation of the Jewish Law, but rather a state in which that will be perfectly fulfilled. The famous prophecy of the new covenant in Jer. 31.31-34 (perhaps referred to by Jesus himself at the Last Supper, Mk 14.24; 1 Cor. 11.25), exactly expresses this. Jesus expects this new state of affairs to be ushered in by God himself on the coming great day, and not to be brought about by human intervention.

Realized Eschatology

This concept of salvation was naturally reaffirmed by the primitive Christian community. The only new factor was that Jesus was proclaimed to be risen and exalted as the Messiah in heaven, where he is ready to act as God's agent in the inauguration of the everlasting kingdom.

The idea of a future divine act is generally referred to as 'consistent eschatology', in the sense that statements concerning the future are logically consistent and really refer to the future. But some aspects of Jesus' teaching suggest that the future conditions are already available (cf. Mt. 12.28; Lk. 17.21). How far such sayings mean that the future is already realized in the present (realized eschatology) is disputed. He may have meant only that anticipations of the conditions which belong to the future are already apparent, and these reinforce the claim that the coming kingdom is near.

The apostolic proclamation, however, inevitably introduced a new dimension. Jesus, exalted and enthroned at the right hand of God, already has his rightful position in the future kingdom. So now the idea of salvation has two poles. The kingdom in the full sense still belongs to the future, but it is present in so far as Jesus is acknowledged as Lord. So the conditions of the future already operate in the life of the church under his heavenly lordship.

This interim period before God's final act was not expected to last long. Paul (Rom. 13.11-12; 1 Cor. 7.29) and the author of Hebrews (10.25, 37) still expect the end imminently. But as time passed and still Jesus' coming (the parousia) did not take place, it became necessary to settle for indefinite delay. In fact, the key to coping with the problem was already available in the concept of the present lordship of Jesus. If people die before the parousia, that does not mean that they lose their share in the coming kingdom, for their souls go to a place of waiting (Rev. 6.9-11) close to Jesus (Phil. 1.23), whether the time be long or short (1 Thess. 4.13-17).

This view of the programme of salvation is not strictly realized eschatology, because it does not imply that the future is wholly swallowed up in the present. It is much more an anticipated eschatology, and its crucial feature is the dynamic concept of salvation now, but not yet. Christians live in the conditions of the coming age, but at the same time look forward to the consummation when Jesus will come in glory as God's agent for the general resurrection and the judgment.

Life and Eternal Life in John

How, then, are we to understand John's concept of salvation against this background? It is often claimed that the evangelist teaches a realized eschatology in the strict sense, rejecting the idea of a future divine act. Bultmann's existential interpretation of the Gospel sees life as 'authentic existence', which results from the act of faith in Jesus (cf. 3.15-16). But this excludes Johannine expressions of consistent eschatology (e.g. 5.25-29), which Bultmann had to attribute to a subsequent Ecclesiastical Redactor. But the matter is not so simple as this, for consistent eschatology is basic to the argument of passages that Bultmann does accept. Thus the discourse of 5.19-47 uses a parable from the tradition (v. 19) to argue that God's Son is his agent for the eschatological acts of the general resurrection (v. 21) and the judgment (v. 22), and therefore should receive the same honor as the Father (v. 23). As the Son is identified with Jesus, faith in him makes available now the state of salvation that is due to follow these acts (v. 24). He does not say that these acts will not happen at all.

It is reasonable to conclude from this and other passages that the Fourth Gospel has the same dynamic concept of 'now, but not yet' as we can already see in Paul. Eternal life means life that belongs to the coming age (*ha-'olam ha-ba* in rabbinic sources). The Hebrew *'olam* means 'lasting state', and so can refer either to eternity or to an epoch of time. The phrase can thus be used as a substitute for the kingdom of God, placing the emphasis not on his rule, but on his eternity. The Greek translation *aiōn* tends to emphasize the notion of eternity still further. There is an instructive example in Mk 10.30, where Jesus promises rich rewards in this life 'and in the age (*aiōn*) that is coming eternal (*aiōnios*) life'.

John's preference for this expression shows a decisive shift away from the future reference, but without denying it altogether, as we have seen. But John is more concerned with the present experience of life in the rich sense suggested by 10.10. This life is eternal in as much as it belongs also to the coming age, and so lasts on without ending. Salvation is thus the possession of such life both now and eternally.

Thus John's concept of salvation does not dissolve the future entirely in a timeless present, and to that extent it is in line with the mainstream Christian tradition. We must assume that what appears to be a more timeless way of speaking is used because it is more meaningful to evangelist and readers alike, and also to the Jews with whom they are in dialogue. They are people who do not need liberation from poverty and political oppression, but from false ideas about the attainment of eternal life.

A New Dimension

With this concept of salvation in mind, we can see that the theology of John is chiefly concerned with showing how Jesus is the effective agent of salvation for all who will believe in him. In the Fourth Gospel, as we have seen, this function of Jesus is contrasted with the Law, which the opponents claim is the true means of life. But in John's view believing in Jesus introduces a new dimension, which cannot be found in the Law. This is perhaps best expressed in modern terms as the category of personal relationship.

This is really the distinguishing feature of the teaching of Jesus, and explains his conflict with the scribes and Pharisees. Without in any way denying the Law, Jesus made the state of the heart the decisive factor rather than the letter of the Law. In prayer he encouraged a simple directness, exemplified in his own address to God as 'Father', without honorific titles. The idea of the coming of God, usually depicted in horrific terms in contemporary apocalyptic, becomes something to be welcomed. No one need fear the judgment of God except those who obdurately refuse to open their hearts to receive him.

After the resurrection this aspect of Jesus' teaching was maintained by a strong sense of fellowship with him in his glory. Baptism into the name of Jesus meant initiation into the company of those who confessed him as Messiah and Lord. From a very early date, perhaps from the beginning, Christians began to invoke him as their heavenly leader, using the formula *marana tha*: 'Our Lord, come!' (1 Cor. 16.22, cf. Rev. 22.20). The sense of fellowship with Jesus made it possible to follow his own simple approach to God, addressing him as 'Abba, Father' (Rom. 8.15; Gal. 4.6).

This sense of personal fellowship with Jesus, and through him with God, is also a feature of John. It is especially represented in 14.18-24, where Jesus speaks of his future relationship with the disciples. Here there are two overlapping unities, of the Father with Jesus and of Jesus with the disciples (v. 20).

The chief phrase used to express this relationship in John is to 'believe in (literally, "into") Jesus'. This means to entrust oneself to Jesus, fully accepting what he proclaims himself to be. The phrase is unusual, but it does occur 8 times elsewhere in the New Testament besides the 36 cases in the Gospel of John and 3 cases in 1 John. It is not found in the Septuagint or in secular Greek. Evidently it is not confined to the evangelist, but should rather be seen as characteristic diction of the Johannine church.

The phrase is important for the theology of the Fourth Gospel, because it can be used only with a personal object. It would be unthinkable to 'believe into' the Law. It makes of Jesus a personal mediator between the believer and God, whereas the Law, however much it is a testimony to the grace of God (1.16), is essentially an impersonal instrument.

On the other hand, those whose spirituality is centred on the Law as the embodiment of the Wisdom of God, obviously find in it great riches (cf. Ecclus 24.25-34), and will not easily be convinced that the gospel of Jesus has more to offer. Moreover, if the teaching of Jesus led to conflict with the Pharisees, Christian teaching about Jesus also leads to conflict, because it seems to lead the people astray by downgrading the Law, and the position accorded to Jesus almost makes of him a second god, which would be blasphemy (5.18; 7.12; 10.33). The theology, however, which John sets forth in the Prologue and the discourses of the Gospel has an answer to both these points. The dimension of personality turns out to be crucial.

The Prologue

The Prologue (1.1-18) has been the subject of an immense number of studies. It has been claimed to be a pre-Johannine Semitic poem, and many attempts have been made to reconstruct what might have been its original form. From a literary point of view there is much to be said for two basic observations: it is a distinct composition in the style of Semitic Wisdom poems, even if not actually written as poetry, and the intruded verses in prose on John the Baptist (vv. 6-8, 15) have been meshed into it in the course of its incorporation into the Gospel. However, there is no compelling reason to regard it as older than the

Gospel, or as composed by a different hand. In my view, it was added as part of the second edition to give the rationale of the Christology which is everywhere assumed in the Gospel, though not elsewhere stated in philosophical terms. As a composition in the style of the Wisdom poems, it need not be regarded as based on any more specific model. It has already been pointed out that it has its closest parallel in Ecclesiasticus 24.

The crucial point in the Prologue is v. 14: 'And the Word became flesh'. This is the first clear statement of the incarnation, which became a fundamental doctrine of Christianity, but has been the subject of immense controversy. Obviously this cannot be followed up here, and we must be content with trying to answer two questions: where did the evangelist get the idea from, and what does it actually mean?

The first question cannot be answered by those who look for the origin of John's ideas in Greek or Gnostic sources. Greek religion knows of gods who appear as human beings (cf. Acts 14.11-12) and of supermen who are raised to the company of the gods (as in the emperor cult), but not of a divine being who actually becomes human and mortal. Gnostic dualism, totally separating the divine from the human, cannot entertain the notion of incarnation. It is the Wisdom tradition of Hellenistic Judaism which offers the best solution, as nearly all modern scholars agree. This can be traced in the New Testament through Paul (1 Cor. 1.30), the 'Colossian hymn', Col. 1.15-20 (possibly post-Pauline), and the opening verses of Hebrews (1.1-4), in which Wisdom as God's Son is his agent in creation and active in Jesus in the work of redemption.

John's statement that the Word became flesh is only marginally different from this. Instead of saying that the Word/Wisdom/Son of God was active in Jesus, John says that it was embodied (became flesh) in Jesus. I believe that this slight difference arises from the use of the Ecclesiasticus poem. There the Wisdom of God is embodied in the Law; it *is* the Law (Ecclus 24.23). John agrees up to a point; but the fullness of God's self-revelation is available only in Jesus (v. 18). It thus seems likely that the inspiration for the groundbreaking claim in v. 14 is the Ecclesiasticus poem, which has been the catalyst of a new dimension of Christology as a result of John's preoccupation with claims concerning the Law.

With regard to the second question, we have to bear in mind the Semitic tendency to personify abstracts. Wisdom is *God's* wisdom, an attribute of God. It is by *his* skill that the world was made. When this property of God is personified, it is usually personified as a woman, because the word for wisdom is feminine in both Hebrew and Greek. But the same idea can be expressed by referring to the Word of God as his agent in creation (cf. Ps. 33.6). This gives a masculine alternative (Greek *logos*), which also lends itself to personification, so that in Philo God's Word is even referred to as his 'firstborn son' (*Agr.* 51), without any suggestion of a 'second god'. But when, as in the Fourth Gospel (and already in Colossians and Hebrews), God's Wisdom/Word/Son is said to be active in the person of Jesus, or even incarnate in him, the way is open for a subtle shift from the *metaphorical* language of personification to the *metaphysical* concept of personal relations within God himself, such as John has attempted to set out in vv. 1-2 of the Prologue. John's position becomes clearer when we see how it relates to the contrast with the Law. If the Law is the embodiment of God's Wisdom, it can be said to have been with him as an idea in his mind from the beginning, before it 'became incarnate' in its written form as given to Moses on Mount Sinai. In fact rabbinic tradition asserts that the Law is one of seven pre-existent things in this way. So also Jesus, as the embodiment of God's eternal Word, is the pre-existent Son of God.

It is important to realize that John's concept of the pre-existence of Jesus carries no implication that he is anything less than fully and truly human. Though the living memory of Jesus was disappearing by the time that the Gospel was written, the anchorage in the record of Jesus as a man of recent history is unquestioned, and his death is real, and would be inexplicable without his real humanity. It may seem extraordinary for John to make Jesus speak of his relationship with God before the foundation of the world (17.5, 24) and claim that 'Before Abraham was, I am' (8.58), but the whole point of the Prologue is to explain how this could be so.

Nevertheless, the concept of incarnation is so daring that it is not at all surprising that the Jewish opponents sensed here a threat to monotheism. However, it must be made clear that John's doctrine of incarnation did not *start* the accusation that the Christians were treating Jesus as God (5.18; 10.33). In fact, quite the opposite is the case, because the Prologue is an attempt to provide a rational explanation of existing Christian practice so as to show that the complaint is unfounded. What started it was the claim that, having been exalted to God's right hand as the Messiah, Jesus was worthy of equal honor (5.23), and the offending practice was the custom of invoking Jesus in that position, which we can see in the *marana tha* prayer (1 Cor. 16.22). This is the step, taken in the earliest days of Christianity but unprecedented in Judaism, which set Christianity on its unique course.

Incarnation

The basic historic fact is that Jesus was a man who died by crucifixion under the governorship of Pontius Pilate. We shall see later that it is this fact which in John's view proves that Jesus is the Son of God. But there is no suggestion in the Fourth Gospel that, because he is the Son of God, he did not really die. In so far as Jesus is represented as aware that he will rise from the dead, this is because Jesus knows God's plan of redemption and so has faith that his death will be abundantly fruitful (11.54; 12.24). When Jesus performs miracles, these are human acts done by divine inspiration, like the miracles of Elijah or Elisha. But at the same time they are 'works of God' (5.36), because they signify God's saving plan to bring healing and eternal life to all humanity. Similarly, Jesus' remarkable insight into people's minds is a human characteristic, and the woman of Samaria is correct in drawing the conclusion that Jesus must be a prophet (4.19). Such power of insight would be considered normal in a prophet.

Hence it is entirely wrong to separate acts of Jesus which proceed from his divine nature and acts which proceed from his human nature, as was done by some of the Church Fathers in interpreting the Fourth Gospel. All his acts are fully human, but in and through them there is the Word of God, declaring their meaning for salvation. In this sense they are all divine acts at the same time. The pre-existent Son/Wisdom/Word of God, who perpetually communes with God, being in the bosom of the Father (1.18), does his communing in and through Jesus, and so Jesus always does what is pleasing to the Father (8.29).

The Old Testament in John

Before we leave the Prologue we must note the allusions to other parts of the Old Testament. The opening verses have an obvious relation to Gen. 1.1-4, which is clearly intentional. Much more important are the allusions to the giving of the Law to Moses in vv. 14-18. In saying 'we have beheld his glory' (v. 14), the evangelist knows that the readers are sure to think of Moses' request to God in Exod. 33.18: 'Show me your glory.' The glory which the eye of faith perceives in Jesus as the incarnate Word is 'full of grace and truth'. These words are based on God's self-revelation to Moses as the Lord 'abounding in steadfast love and faithfulness' (Exod. 34.6). Later Jewish tradition insisted that this was not direct sight of God (v. 18, cf. 5.37). For John, only Jesus makes God fully known, and this the Law could never do.

However, John has a positive attitude to the Law from the point of view of its prophetic value. This carries forward the conviction of earliest Christianity that all the scriptures of the Old Testament are prophetic of the plan of salvation. Matthew frequently inserts proof-texts with the formula 'that what was spoken by the prophet might be fulfilled' (e.g. Mt. 4.13). Significantly John uses an almost identical formula (e.g. 12.38) and has some of the very same texts. Thus there is a debt in the Fourth Gospel to the use of Scripture in debate with Jews, which was common to all branches of the primitive church from the earliest times.

The chief sources of texts quoted in this way are the Prophets and Psalms. This is characteristic not only of earliest Christianity, but also of the Scrolls, which use similar techniques of quotation, including some of the same texts, in relation to the Qumran Sect itself. The theory is that in the Scriptures God has made known in advance the programme of the end time, which is now on the brink of fulfillment.

This concept of fulfillment is not confined to specific quotations from Scripture, but pervades most of the scriptural allusions throughout the Gospel. This applies to the references to Moses in the Prologue which we have just seen. The revelation of God in Jesus as the incarnate Word is not only better than the revelation to Moses in the Law, it is also the fulfillment of that earlier revelation in the order of redemption.

Jesus' Qualifications

The main discourses which follow in chs. 3–10 are concerned with Jesus' qualifications for his function as the agent of God's final act of redemption, and give an idea of the way in which he performs it.

The *Nicodemus discourse of ch. 3* makes the basic point that the act of salvation depends on the initiative of God, and therefore the agent of salvation himself must originate from God. As God's agent to fulfill his own plan of salvation he was God's Son given to the world (3.16). The giving of God's Son surpasses the gift of the Law, because that did not make accessible the image and glory of God, as has been done in Jesus (3.13). Only of him can it be said that 'The Father loves the Son, and has given all things into his hand' (3.35). What, then, does Jesus convey which is not available in the Law? The answer is not simply that, as a person, he conveys the knowledge of God in personal terms, but that in his humanity he was lifted up on the cross

(3.14). This point will prove to have decisive importance in later chapters.

The discourse with the Samaritan woman in ch. 4 presupposes that Jesus is the agent of salvation, but expresses it in different terms. The water of life is of course a metaphor used in the Wisdom tradition, and is applied in Ecclesiasticus 24 to the inexhaustible supply of Wisdom which is available in the Law. Though the Samaritans were really Jews and kept the Law according to their own customs, John uses them to represent the wider world. In particular John takes up the Samaritan concept of the Messiah, which is more the expectation of the true teacher. Jesus, as the mediator of the living water of the divine Wisdom, is qualified to be the fulfillment of Samaritan hopes, and by implication those of the whole world (4.42). Though the point is not brought to the surface, the discourse suggests that another reason why Jesus surpasses the Law is the universality of the gospel.

In the discourse of ch. 5 the point at issue is the authority of Jesus to override the law of the sabbath. The argument turns on the fact that Jesus' act of healing on the sabbath is a model of the eschatological acts which he is destined to perform. Indeed, through such acts the future condition of eternal life is already accessible to believers (5.21-24). Jesus' authority is grounded in the fact that his acts are always done in accordance with the instructions of his Father (5.19). Thus he does not rely on human authorization, or even on the witness of John the Baptist (5.36). There is witness to his authority, however, in the Scriptures, because they are prophetic of the eschatological age, and in the Law itself Moses wrote of Jesus in this sense (5.46).

The Bread of Life discourse of ch. 6 clearly builds on the Wisdom theme of the nourishment of the soul. The argument is based on the manna miracle of Exodus 16. In John's milieu the Wisdom which the manna typifies is contained in the Law. This explains the reference to teaching in v. 45, quoting a passage of Isaiah in which the metaphor of abundant spiritual food is also present (Isa. 54.11–55.5). Of course Jesus surpasses the Law in this respect. The proof of this is his saving death, subtly referred to in vv. 53-58 by means of the eucharistic tradition of Jesus' body and blood, for the eucharist is the ceremony in which the saving death of Jesus is proclaimed (1 Cor. 11.26). Though denied by some scholars, the whole discourse has eucharistic overtones from start to finish. The Christian eucharist provides spiritual as well as physical nourishment because it is the celebration of Jesus' *death*, and that is what makes him the true bread in a way that the Law can never be.

The episodic discourse of 7.1–8.30 combines the theme of the necessity

of Jesus' death with the question whether he has the proper creden-
tials for messiahship. It is implied that he does have them, but his
death is more important. The death is referred to cryptically in the
idea of 'going away' (7.32-36; 8.14, 21-22), but becomes explicit in the
reference to lifting up in the saying of 8.28. The Law is adduced in
7.15-24 and in 8.12-20, which takes up the theme of witness from ch. 5.
Jesus, still refusing to accept human witness, declares that the legal
requirement for two witnesses to support a case is met by the agreement between himself and the Father. This at last opens the way to
understanding the importance of the crucifixion, because the cross
demonstrates the unity between Jesus and the Father (8.29).

The short and sharp discourse of 8.31-59 presents Jesus' opponents as
children of the devil by contrast with Jesus' own affiliation to God.
The point of this contrast appears in a saying from the Jesus tradition
in 8.51, 52 (cf. Mk 9.1). As God's Son, Jesus can give eternal life,
because he has life in himself, for indeed he is pre-existent (v. 58).
Though the Law is not mentioned, it is clear that the Jews, who have
the Law and rely on their descent from Abraham as the covenant
people (8.39), do not have the capacity to give life which is claimed by
Jesus, and which will be demonstrated in his death and resurrection.

The story of the Man Born Blind in ch. 9 is really preparatory to the
climax in the next chapter, contrasting the sight which Jesus gives (in
fact, creates) with the spiritual blindness of the Pharisees. In *the Allegory of the Shepherd in 10.1-18* Jesus is contrasted with all predecessors
(v. 8), and then proclaims himself the Good Shepherd who gives his
life for the sheep. This is the point which was made at the end of the
discourse in 8.28-29, and it enables John to heighten the emotional
force of the climax in 10.22-30, where Jesus' saving action for the sake
of the 'sheep' is the final proof that he and the Father are one (v. 30).
Thus Jesus' unique relationship with God is stated in the simplest
possible terms. To the protest of 'blasphemy' he makes recourse once
more to the Scriptures ('your law', v. 34), making what many readers
feel to be a dubious debating-point. But the real point is that, by perceiving the true meaning of Jesus' 'works', i.e. his whole earthly ministry, the opponents 'may know and understand that the Father is in
me and I am in the Father' (10.38). That is his real qualification, and
that is how he is able to effect salvation.

The Death of Jesus

The death of Jesus thus turns out to be the decisive factor of the whole
argument, just as it is the climax of the narrative structure of the

Gospel as a whole. This point needs to be made strongly, because the Fourth Gospel is so often thought of as the gospel of the incarnation that the death of Jesus tends to be neglected. But in our consideration of the incarnation above, it was pointed out that for John it is the death of Jesus that is the real proof that he is the pre-existent Son of God.

The starting-point is the voluntary character of Jesus' death. John rightly saw that, though Jesus was condemned to death, it was in one sense entirely voluntary, because he could have saved himself by retracting his message. Jesus lays down his life of his own accord, and the power to take it up again (i.e. the resurrection) simply follows on from the power to lay it down (10.18). The two acts are really two sides of a single coin, as we shall see in a moment. Jesus says, 'For this reason the Father loves me' (10.17), because his acceptance of death is his freely willed choice to obey the charge given by the Father. In giving his life for the sheep he demonstrates not just his own pastoral care, but the Father's own will for the salvation of all people (10.29). This makes it plain for all to see that he is at one with the Father (10.30).

John places great emphasis on the demonstrative aspect of the cross (cf. 8.28). The reason is given in 3.14, where the idea of lifting up the Son of Man is first introduced. Many scholars detect a double meaning in the idea of 'lifting up'. Literally it refers to the cross, but theologically it refers to the exaltation of Jesus to heaven. If this is correct, it probably entails a reference to Isa. 52.13, the introduction to the prophecy of the Suffering Servant, which tells of his exaltation after his humiliation even to death (the same Greek word is used for 'lifted up'). It is then exaltation in the eyes of the world. The world can see the exaltation of Jesus in the crucifixion, not because of a juggling with the meaning of a word, but because what is actually seen in that horrifying event is the ultimate demonstration of his moral union with the Father, which *also* issues in his exaltation to God's right hand (hence 'glorified' is used instead of lifted up in 12.23; 13.31).

The death of Jesus is at the same time the supreme moral victory in the flesh. Jesus' personal wishes and his natural shrinking from death are totally subordinated to the will of God (12.27-30). Thus in his person the devil's grip on humanity is broken. The victory over 'the prince of this world' is won (12.31). This historic event is therefore at the same time the cosmic victory which is needed to usher in the eschatological age.

John also carries forward the traditional interpretation of Jesus' death as an atonement sacrifice which belongs to earliest Christianity (cf. 1 Cor. 15.3), and which is accepted in the Johannine church (1 Jn 2.2). It is referred to in the testimony of John the Baptist (1.29, 35). Jesus gives his life *for* the life of the world (6.51), *for* the sheep (10.11, 15), *for* his friends (15.13).

Atonement is not stressed in the Fourth Gospel, however, because the essential point for the argument is the concept of Jesus' union with the Father. This is demonstrated in the cross, and once this is grasped by the believer, the way is opened to enter into personal relationship with God through Jesus. The death of Jesus is what 'draws' people to believe in him (12.32), and believing in him is precisely the personal relationship in which salvation is experienced. Thus the cross is the high point of the revelation of God's love, and his love is what effects salvation.

The Son of Man

Each time John uses the 'lifting up' theme Jesus refers to himself as the Son of Man. This title is used by Jesus frequently in the Synoptic Gospels. The exact meaning of the phrase in the sayings of Jesus has been the subject of endless controversy. This can be touched on here only briefly, and we shall have to be content with trying to understand the use in John, and especially why it is so prominent in connection with the cross.

'Son of Man' occurs in the Gospels only in sayings attributed to Jesus, or in reference to them. It is never used as a title for Jesus in Christology outside the Gospels, except in Acts 7.56 (which may be modelled on a gospel saying). 'Son of man' in Aramaic just means a man or a human being, or it may be used collectively for people. The three occurrences outside the Gospels and Acts have this meaning, all in biblical quotations (Heb. 2.6 = Ps. 8.4; Rev. 1.13 and 14.14 = Dan. 7.13). So when Jesus used it as an impersonal reference to himself, it would seem obvious that it should mean 'a man like me' (cf. Mt. 8.20 = Lk. 9.58).

Unfortunately the matter is complicated because of the interpretation of Dan. 7.13. In Daniel's vision power is given to 'one like a son of man', i.e. a human figure, after all the beasts (that is, enemies of the Jews) have been brought into subjection. In Jewish interpretation in New Testament times this man-like figure is identified with the Messiah. For this reason it is widely held to be a messianic title. Synoptic sayings attributed to Jesus which speak of his future glory often combine the designation Son of Man with clear allusions to Dan. 7.13 (e.g. Mt. 24.30). But the question of whether Jesus himself intended to make a messianic claim when he used this phrase as a title, or whether all the relevant sayings which suggest this are inauthentic, remains hotly disputed.

For our present purpose it is sufficient to notice two things. First, even if many sayings are inauthentic, enough are so well embedded in the tradition that Jesus' use of Son of Man to refer to himself in some sense can be safely regarded as a genuine characteristic of his style. John has picked it up from the sayings tradition. Secondly, in the Synoptic tradition the phrase is used in Jesus' predictions of the passion (e.g. Mk 8.31). Here again it is disputed whether this means 'the Messiah must suffer' or 'I must suffer' or (ironically) 'a man must suffer', meaning oneself.

The use in the Fourth Gospel is certainly a matter of adopting the phrase as a style-feature, and closer examination of all the occurrences suggests that they are modelled primarily on the passion predictions. It has been argued by Smalley that they are all based on traditional sayings, but this is difficult to prove. The connection with the passion predictions can be seen in 3.14, where John's word 'must' is reminiscent of Mk 8.31, and this connection can be followed through in 8.28; 12.23, 34; 13.31, all referring to the lifting up or glorification of the Son of Man. In the light of our study of the death of Jesus in the Fourth Gospel, it is altogether probable that the phrase is used in these examples not as a messianic title but precisely because the death is a *human* act. It is the supreme moment in the human life of Jesus when his union with the Father is demonstrated.

This provides the key to understanding the other Son of Man sayings in John. The phrase is not a title, but functional. Thus the programmatic statement of 1.51 tells of a future occasion when heaven will be joined to earth, 'the angels of God ascending and descending upon the Son of Man'. It is a human event in which heavenly glory will be revealed. This must surely be the crucifixion. 3.13 tells of the revelatory function of the Son of Man, and this is immediately elucidated in the reference to the cross in 3.14. If this functional use of the Son of Man is borne in mind, it becomes apparent that the Fourth Gospel has a specialized use of the phrase, which is closely integrated into the Johannine theology. It refers to the human death of Jesus, which is the earthly point of revelation of his divine glory.

The 'I am' Sayings

In the climactic saying of 8.28 Jesus not only mentions the lifting up of the Son of Man, but also asserts that as a result of it 'you will know that I am he'. The phrase 'I am he' is literally 'I am' (*egō eimi*). It is one of a number of 'I am' sayings, which are nearly always quite striking in their context and constantly attract the attention of readers of the Gospel. It is often claimed that they have special importance in the structure of John's theology, but two reasons suggest that they should not be given undue weight.

In the first place they are very unevenly distributed, and do not usually form the climax of an argument. Obviously an 'I am' saying is a statement of who Jesus is, and the identity of Jesus is the great topic of *all* the discourses. But in most of the discourses to try to give these sayings climactic significance only leads to distortion of the argument and obscures their real function.

Secondly, as Bultmann showed, the logical status of the 'I am' sayings is variable. Usually it is a recognition-formula, answering the question of what something is. Thus in 6.35, 41, 48, 51 'I am the bread of life' explains what the bread under discussion is: it is Jesus himself. But it also carries with it the overtones of a qualificatory-formula, answering the question 'what are you?' For by identifying the bread as himself, Jesus shows that he is himself the nourishment of the soul that the bread signifies. The same applies to 8.12; 10.7, 9, 11, 14; 14.6; 15.1, 5. 11.25 ('I am the resurrection and the life') is similar, but in this case it is the climax of the argument, because it constitutes the challenge to faith.

A different logic is required by 6.21, where *egō eimi* has no predicate, and so must be translated 'It is I'. This is a recognition-formula without the qualificatory aspect. In fact it is a direct quotation from the tradition (corresponding to Mk 6.50 exactly).

We are left with the six absolute uses of *egō eimi* in 8.24, 28, 58; 13.19; 18.5, 6. Apart from 8.58, these must also be translated 'I am he'. It is generally recognized that in 8.21-29 the discourse has allusions to the prophecy of Isa. 43.10-13. Here God declares himself to be the only Savior, and the people are his witnesses so that all 'may know and believe and understand that I am he' (*egō eimi* in the Greek version). In other words he means 'I am the Savior'. The same is true in Jn 8.24, 28, which form the climax of the discourse. Jesus points to himself as the agent of salvation. This also applies to 13.19.

There is, however, a further complicating factor. In Isa. 43.10, 13 God says 'I am he', and, although the words in the Hebrew are different, there is a real possibility that this is an allusion to God's revelation of his name in Exod. 3.14, 'I am who I am' (Greek version *egō eimi ho ōn*). What about Jesus in 8.24, 28? Is he claiming for himself the name of God? But this cannot be the proper meaning of the text here, which requires to be understood as 'I am he (i.e. the agent of salvation)', as we have just seen. The most that can be said is that John might have wished, by this choice of words and allusion to Isaiah, to suggest also that Jesus is the visible representative of God who bears this name.

But what about 8.58? Here there is an electrifying effect caused by the juxtaposition of past and timeless present tenses: 'Before Abraham was born, I am', i.e. exist. In fact this could be translated 'I am he' as before, meaning in this case 'I am the one who gives life' (cf. 8.51). But on the usual interpretation, which contrasts the birth of Abraham at a point in time with the timeless existence of Jesus as God's Son from eternity, the saying in its context means that Jesus can give life, because he has life in himself, being eternally existent. Even so, the text does not require a reference to Exod. 3.14, which again could be no more than an additional allusion, and cannot be proved to be John's intention.

Finally the *egō eimi* comes very impressively in the account of the arrest of Jesus in 18.5-8. In v. 5 Jesus simply identifies himself as the one whom the soldiers are seeking. But then, by a striking example of the evangelist's dramatic skill, this is repeated in v. 6 with a comment on the effect of Jesus' words: 'When he said to them, "I am he", they drew back and fell to the ground'. This surely is the effect of a theophany! But it still must be translated 'I am he' (as also in v. 8), though it perhaps carries the sense 'I am the agent of salvation', as in 8.28. The arrest begins the process of the act of salvation in which Jesus is revealed as the agent of salvation (13.19), and the aim of these verses is to show Jesus as in complete control of his destiny.

It remains true that the 'I am' sayings in John always make a great impression on readers of the Gospel, increasing the sense of the numinous and strange personality of Jesus. But for understanding John, it is necessary to be on guard against reading too much into them. In particular, it is a mistake to single them out as a basis for analyzing the Christology of John. In so far as they carry an allusion to Exod. 3.14, this is no more than what has been said in the Prologue in 1.14, 18, which provides a far better basis for understanding what the evangelist means.

The Resurrection

Jesus says 'I am he', and he means the Son of Man, who is lifted up on the cross, and whose crucifixion is also his glorification. This is the proper starting-point for understanding John's treatment of the resurrection. The cross is central to the evangelist's theology of salvation, because it is the earthly act in which Jesus' glory as the Son of God is revealed and made accessible through the response of faith. The resurrection of Jesus is his transformation from death to glory, anticipating the transformation which all believers will share in the general resurrection (5.24-25; 11.21-27). The resurrection *stories* in chs. 20 and 21 are subordinate to this teaching as testimony. These stories all have a basis in the tradition, as we have already seen in considering the sources of the Gospel. But in each case John has built up the episode around a particular character in order to make a theological point, the necessity of believing in the risen Jesus without sight or touch.

From what we have seen of the evangelist's aims and methods, we should be ready to accept that none of these stories is a factual account of what actually happened. They are a careful reworking of stories which are themselves popular expressions of the proclamation of the resurrection, and have their own problems from the point of view of historical criticism. The earliest written evidence for the resurrection, however, is not the stories in the Gospels, but the statement quoted by Paul in 1 Cor. 15.3-7, which lists a series of appearances of Jesus, beginning with Peter. These verses begin with the important comment that 'Christ died for our sins according to the scriptures', which refers to the atoning death of Jesus and its foreshadowing in Scripture (Isa. 53 and other passages), which we have already considered. Then in v. 4 we are told that 'he was raised on the third day according to the scriptures'. This has important links with the Fourth Gospel, which show that John's teaching on the resurrection is anchored in the earliest tradition.

In the first place the idea of the third day, or three days, comes into the teaching of Jesus in two significant passages which link up with John. The first is Lk. 13.32-33, in which Jesus speaks of his death as 'going away' (cf. Jn 7.33-36; 8.21-22), and uses the idea of three days idiomatically to represent a short space of time. This refers to the time required for him to complete his mission, which he is determined to continue in spite of the danger to his life. John applies this idea, using the phrase 'a little while', to the interval between Jesus' death and subsequent vindication (14.19; 16.16-19).

The other saying is Jesus' claim to be able to destroy the Temple and build another in three days (Mk 14.58). Jesus probably did not mean it literally, but used it as a vivid way of expressing his absolute certainty of the vindication of his message of renewal in an incredibly short time. The saying is used as a taunt by the hostile crowd at the cross (Mk 15.29-30), which ironically applies it to his death and resurrection. John actually puts the saying into the mouth of Jesus himself in the account of the cleansing of the Temple, which may well be its proper context (2.20). In the next verse it is said explicitly that it does not really mean the destruction and rebuilding of the Temple (impossible at the time when John was writing), but 'the Temple of his body' (v. 21).

In the second place the very same context refers to scriptural prophecy. Jesus' resurrection was 'according to the scriptures' (1 Cor. 15.4), and Jn 2.22 also points to the agreement of the words of Jesus with Scripture. This verse is a valuable vignette of the earliest Christian theology. For John tells us that the disciples remembered Jesus' words after his resurrection and discovered their true meaning by elucidating them in the light of Scripture. Reflection by the disciples after the resurrection is mentioned again in the account of the triumphal entry in 12.16, drawing attention to the agreement of memory and Scripture.

Thus the resurrection for the evangelist is a theological datum, quite apart from the resurrection stories. When we look again at the teaching on the passion with this fact before us, it becomes clear that the resurrection has colored John's whole approach. Jesus will not only give his life, but 'take it again' (10.17). The lifting up of the Son of Man becomes his glorification (12.23; 13.31). His death will be immensely fruitful (11.52; 12.24). Though he dies, the disciples will see him again, though not in the way that the world sees (14.19-33). This is not a reference to resurrection appearances in a literal sense, but (as the context makes completely clear) the mutual indwelling of Jesus and the disciples which will be established permanently through the faith-relationship. The same idea is expanded in 16.16-24, promising a joyful relationship between the disciples and Jesus in glory.

The Paraclete

In the debates between Jesus and the unbelieving Jews, the evangelist has set out to show that Jesus surpasses the Law. But the Law remains always available, whereas Jesus has died and been withdrawn from view until his coming at the parousia. However the teaching on the resurrection has claimed that his withdrawal is to be seen in a positive light as the means of establishing a permanent relationship with him in glory. Clearly it is necessary to say something more about this relationship, if the argument is to be complete. This is the context of John's special teaching on the Holy Spirit.

The Spirit of God in the Old Testament is, like the Wisdom of God, an attribute of God himself, denoting his energy and creative power. It can be personified as a divine force, energizing the great heroes and inspiring the prophets. In a society which thinks of angels and lesser spirits there is a tendency to make God's Spirit also a subordinate being of this kind. In Qumran, with its highly developed angelology, the Spirit of Truth is an angel opposed to the Spirit of Falsehood, who is the devil. In the Synoptic tradition Jesus has to distinguish his claim to be inspired by the Spirit of God from popular demonology (Mt. 12.24-32). The designation Holy Spirit (extremely rare in the Old Testament) came into currency in New Testament times to distinguish the Spirit of God from other spirits.

The Fourth Gospel has little use for angelology or demonology, but does reflect the Qumran type of dualism, with the devil as 'the father of lies' (8.44). But although the expression 'the Spirit of Truth' is used (14.17; 15.26; 16.13), this does not refer to a subordinate spirit, but to the Holy Spirit as the power of God himself. John's special interest is the inspiration of Christians who live in fellowship with the exalted Jesus. Here again we can see a basis in the tradition. The picture of earliest Christianity in Acts shows that the gifts of the Spirit and the powers of the age to come are already available. Paul explains that, sharing in the sonship of Jesus as God's children, Christians have the constant help of the Spirit (Rom. 8.12-17, 26-27). The way in which John makes this point in 7.37-39 is disconcerting, because it seems to imply that the Holy Spirit was not available at all (or did not even exist) before Jesus was glorified. But what it really means is that this *function* of the Spirit was not available before the completion of Jesus' saving work.

It is in connection with this function that Jesus can be said to be the giver of the Holy Spirit. This is expounded in the discourses at the Last Supper (14.16–17, 26; 15.26–16.15). Here it is shown that the Spirit will be the helper of the disciples when they are persecuted for their faith. The idea is enlarged further to include all the work of carrying forward the mission of Jesus. There is a literary debt to the tradition here (cf. Mt. 10.17-25, and the table of parallels in Brown, p. 694). This is where the unusual designation Paraclete (*paraklētos*) comes in, which is variously translated 'advocate', 'comforter', 'counsellor' or 'helper'. The legal sense of advocate is probably basic in view of the function of the Spirit in the tradition (cf. Mt. 10.19-20), but John uses the word more broadly here. The point in John is that the Spirit is *another* Paraclete (14.16), to act as helper to the disciples in place of Jesus himself.

John's talk about the Paraclete has a strongly personal coloring. Precisely because the continuing relationship with Jesus in glory is a personal relationship, the power which he gives to them, which is the power of God, can be no less personal. There is no suggestion in John that the Spirit is an impersonal divine power that can be manipulated by a person whose heart is estranged from God.

Just as John's doctrine of incarnation had immense influence on the subsequent development of Christology, so also the teaching on the Paraclete decisively affected the Christian idea of the Holy Spirit as a *person* within the Godhead, thus laying the foundation for the doctrine of the Trinity. But for John it is not a matter of a metaphysical theory, but of Christian experience which all believers can share.

Summary

John writes for people, whether friend or foe, whose idea of salvation in the religious quest is best expressed with the words 'life' or 'eternal life'. In interpreting the gospel message in this way, the evangelist does not teach a realized eschatology in which the future is wholly absorbed in the present. The point is that the conditions of the future are available now, anticipating the future consummation, which still remains a valid concept in its own right. It was also observed that this is an intellectual rather than a political understanding of salvation. This probably reflects the social milieu of the readers.

Cutting across the social divide, the teaching of Jesus, Paul and John conveys a new dimension in the religious thought of the time, which is best expressed today as an enhancement of the idea of personal relationship. So for John the essential means of grasping salvation is to 'believe into' Jesus, which implies much more than intellectual assent to propositions about him. This is contrasted throughout the Gospel with a contemporary Jewish concept of the Law as the embodiment of the divine Wisdom and the means of eternal life.

Thus the Gospel is concerned with the qualifications of Jesus to be regarded as the means or agent of eternal life. In the Prologue and the discourses Jesus' capacity to achieve this purpose is contrasted with that of the Law, and he is found to have all the right qualifications. In addition to this contrast, John also builds on the contemporary conviction that the Scriptures are prophetic, revealing in advance God's plan of salvation, which is now in process of actualization.

The Prologue shows both contrast and fulfillment in that, like the Law, Jesus is the embodiment of the pre-existent Wisdom/Word/Son of God, but surpasses and fulfills it. Reflecting the glory of God (like an only son of a father), he is the only real theophany of God, who is essentially beyond human sight.

The discourses attend to various aspects of salvation. It gradually becomes clear that the decisive difference between Jesus and the Law is the mutual indwelling of Jesus and the Father, and this is demonstrated supremely in his voluntary acceptance of the cross. So the death of Jesus is the climax of his revelation of the Father. It is at the same time the ultimate moral victory in which 'the prince of this world' is overcome. John's presentation of the death of Jesus in the passion narrative tones down the horror of crucifixion, emphasizing the fulfillment of Scripture, and Jesus' final word is 'It is finished' (*tetelestai*, 19.30). The saving work of God is thus accomplished.

In connection with the passion it was shown that John uses the designation 'Son of Man' to refer to Jesus as the agent of a human act which reveals the divine glory. This human act is his death on the cross, which is both a literal 'lifting up' and at the same time his glorification. This provides the clue to John's idea of the resurrection, which is the new relationship with God established as a result of Jesus' death.

In the interval before the parousia Christians have the help of the Holy Spirit, the Paraclete. Though the teaching on the Holy Spirit in the Fourth Gospel is well in line with that of the New Testament in general, the insistence on the personal character of the Spirit is an important new emphasis, which has had profound consequences for Christian doctrine.

FURTHER READING

The treatment of the theology of the Fourth Gospel in R. Bultmann, *Theology of the New Testament*, II (New York: Scribner, 1955), has many penetrating insights. The more straightforward account of the Gospel's theology in G.E. Ladd, *A Theology of the New Testament* (Grand Rapids: Eerdmans, rev. edn, 1993), pp. 248-344, remains helpful, as does R. Kysar, *John, The Maverick Gospel* (Louisville, KY: Westminster John Knox Press, rev. edn, 1993). D.M. Smith, *The Theology of the Gospel of John* (Cambridge: Cambridge University Press, 1995) provides an excellent concise discussion.

There are significant discussions on particular issues mentioned in this chapter. On Christology, see U. Schnelle, *Anti-Docetic Christology in the Gospel of John* (Minneapolis: Fortress Press, 1992) and P.N. Anderson, *The Christology of the Fourth Gospel: Its Unity and Disunity in the Light of John 6* (Valley Forge, PA: Trinity Press International, 1996). On the law, see S. Pancaro, *The Law in the Fourth Gospel* (Leiden: E.J. Brill, 1975) and on the Old Testament in John, see M.J.J. Menken, *OT Quotations in the Fourth Gospel: Studies in Textual Form* (Kampen: Kok Pharos, 1996).

On the death of Jesus, see M.C. de Boer, *Johannine Perspectives on the Death of Jesus* (Kampen: Kok Pharos, 1996). On the Son of Man, see D. Burkett, *The Son of Man in the Gospel of John* (Sheffield: JSOT Press, 1991). On the 'I am' Sayings, see D.M. Ball, *'I Am' in John's Gospel: Literary Function, Background and Theological Implications* (Sheffield: Sheffield Academic Press, 1996). On the resurrection, see A.T. Lincoln, ' "I Am the Resurrection and the Life": The Resurrection Message of the Fourth Gospel', in R.N. Longenecker (ed.), *Life in the Face of Death: The Resurrection Message of the New Testament* (Grand Rapids: Eerdmans, 1998), pp. 122-44. On the Spirit, see G.M. Burge, *The Anointed Community. The Holy Spirit in the Johannine Tradition* (Grand Rapids: Eerdmans, 1987).

Chapter Five

APPLICATION

'The Spiritual Gospel'

The study of the Fourth Gospel needs to he done in depth in order to gain a true understanding of John. In the process preconceived ideas are challenged and have to be discarded, and new and unsuspected features of John's thought begin to emerge.

For most new students the first problem is to come to terms with the problem of historicity. John's narratives and dialogues are so vivid and circumstantial that at first sight they compel acceptance as eye-witness accounts. It takes time to realize that they were never intended to be historical reports. Too great a concern with historical problems is counter-productive, because it leads away from the more important task of understanding what John has to say.

It soon becomes apparent that the purpose of the Gospel could not have been achieved if it had been another volume of the same type as the Synoptic Gospels. The Church Fathers sensed this, and that is why Clement of Alexandria referred to it as 'the spiritual gospel'. The aim is to promote belief in Jesus as the Christ and Son of God so that 'you may have life in his name' (20.31). The words 'in his name' briefly point to the personal relationship of mutual indwelling between Jesus and the disciples which is an essential teaching of the Gospel. The idea of 'life' as the object of the religious quest replaces the traditional preference for the kingdom of God, in accordance with the aspirations of the readers, whether Christians or unbelievers.

Thus the Gospel is concerned with historical tradition only in so far as it helps this spiritual purpose. Two other factors have dictated the form of the whole Gospel and set the parameters for the evangelist's approach. First, to promote Christian faith in a milieu which was very different from that of the earliest church, it was necessary to show that the Christian claims about Jesus were anchored in the original tradition. Secondly, John must counter the claim that 'life' is available in the Law, and answer accusations that the Christian position is 'leading the people astray' by detaching them from the Law and amounts to 'blasphemy' in the status accorded to Jesus.

These two factors tend to create a tension between historical tradition and the current needs of theology. John solves it by making the tradition the starting-point for the theological construction. This explains the pattern of the discourses, which usually start with a traditional saying of Jesus providing the theological principle which is then worked out to a christological conclusion. However, apart from such individual sayings, the discourses must be the free composition of the evangelist, because they are concerned with aspects of Christology which were simply not an issue previously.

Fundamentals of Faith

When we consider, however, the factors which account for the large element of creative writing in the Gospel, the biggest surprise is to find that the theology is far closer to the mainstream of early Christian teaching than appears at first sight. Most people are so dazzled by the Prologue that they assume that the Gospel is a new philosophizing interpretation of Christian faith all through. However, we have seen that the Prologue differs from the rest of the Gospel from a literary point of view, being deliberately modelled on the Wisdom poems. Its function is to give the rational basis of the positions which are taken for granted in the rest of the Gospel. In fact, the point of the Prologue is to explain the crucial position of Jesus as the agent of universal salvation. This means that it supports the mainstream teaching about Jesus and his work of redemption.

John fully accepts the fact that the historic life and death of Jesus are indispensable. The outline of Jesus' ministry is used as the vehicle of the theology. The death of Jesus is given great prominence, because it is the key to the whole doctrine of salvation. Resurrection stories are retold, not only to complete the traditional pattern but also to point to the new relationship with God in the era of salvation. These items are presented in the light of the traditional concept of God's predetermined plan. John, in common both with contemporary strands of Judaism and the earliest Christian preaching, holds that the plan of salvation has been revealed in advance in the prophetic Scriptures, and is now in process of actualization. It is fulfilled in the person of Jesus, and those who believe in him already experience the eternal life which belongs to the Last Day.

Where the Gospel seems most vulnerable, and in danger of losing grip on the traditional teaching, is in the handling of the divinity and humanity of Jesus himself. It is often felt that the Fourth Gospel suppresses the humanity of Jesus to such a degree that it becomes negligible from the point of view of salvation. In considering the Johannine church we have seen that it is very likely that this was actually how some of the members understood John. In modern times Käsemann has argued in *The Testament of Jesus* (1968) that the evangelist was in fact a docetist, regarding Jesus as a divine visitant, and using the tradition of his death merely as a means of expressing a spiritual truth.

However, the preceding pages should have persuaded readers that John accepts the full humanity of Jesus as historically true and theologically indispensable. Jesus has constant communion with God, and is himself the embodiment of God's Word/Wisdom/Son. Thus he is correctly referred to as the Son of God. But all his acts are human acts in which the Father's will is accomplished. The death of Jesus is the climax of these acts, and it is real. It is easy to describe John's account of Jesus in terms of a myth of the descent of a redeemer, who reveals the way of salvation and then returns to heaven whence he came. Quite apart from the fact that none of the myths of antiquity is exactly like this, for John the whole point is that in the case of Jesus this is no myth, but what was actually happening in his human life.

The Second Step

To see how to move beyond understanding to application, it may be helpful to compare an approach to the parables of Jesus which has come to be known as the New Hermeneutic. The basic observation is that the parables are not merely illustrative stories, but are stories which are effective in themselves. They perform the function of changing the hearers' perception of reality. Starting from conventional presuppositions, the story leads to a new perspective. A language-event has taken place, and the hearers will never see the matter in the old way again.

Bearing this observation in mind, we need to ask why the parables fail to make a similar impact on readers today. The reason is that our world-view and our presuppositions are so different from those of the original hearers. We thus have to think ourselves into the position of the original hearers as far as possible, so as to feel the parable's impact, before attempting to see what kind of application of it would be valid today. A well-known example is the parable of the Pharisee and the Tax-collector (Lk. 18.9-14). This fails to make its impact on modern readers, because we automatically identify ourselves with the tax-collector rather than the Pharisee, especially as we have inherited a false stereotype of the Pharisees as hypocrites. But the original hearers would have despised the tax-collector, making himself rich through extortion in the service of the hated Romans, and would have looked up to the Pharisee as an exemplary religious leader. It is in that setting that the parable would be a language-event to the hearers, changing their perception of God's scale of values.

Seeing the parable in these terms, however, is only the first step. For the hermeneutical process to be complete, the second step must be taken of applying this kind of fresh understanding to comparable circumstances today, in which our own ideas and interests may be presented with equally challenging observation.

Applying this method on a large scale to the Fourth Gospel, we can now see that the whole of Chapter 4 on 'Understanding John' was an extended example of the first step of thinking ourselves into the situation of the original readers. Placing ourselves alongside them, we listened to the Gospel as those whose concept of salvation is eternal life. We ranged ourselves alongside some who found the focus of their religion in the Law. But at the same time we were pulled by the whole presentation of the Gospel to side with the Christian readers, for whom Jesus is the focus of religion. The nature of eternal life, as presented by John, turned out to be a personal relationship with God mediated by Jesus' historic death and subsequent endless life, and made available through the faith-relationship with him.

The element of new realization, which makes of the Gospel a language-event when it is read as far as possible through the eyes of the original readers, is John's treatment of the cross. In the crucifixion, which extinguishes Jesus' power to save himself, the climax of God's love in giving his Son is reached (3.16), and the union of the human Jesus and the divine Father is revealed (10.30). The lifting up of the Son of Man on the cross is also his glorification (13.31). It is the moment when God's plan of salvation is accomplished (19.30). The eye of faith can see this in the moment of human tragedy, and enter into fellowship with the one who so died.

The second step is to recognize that the historic events which lie behind the Fourth Gospel, and which are interpreted in this way by John, have symbolic value for the interpretation of life as it is experienced now. The Fourth Gospel has an existential dimension, because it is concerned with the problem of existence. For a modern reading the concept of 'life' as the goal of salvation might need revision. But it will stand for the deepest aspirations of every individual reader. The notion of an inadequate means of achieving these aspirations (represented in the Gospel by the Law) will correspond with the reader's own barriers to reality in facing fundamental issues through clinging on to anything less than the naked truth. The cross in John's presentation is not so much the shock to one's cherished certainties through the impact of inexplicable suffering, as the test of integrity in facing reality to the farthest limit. The sense of desertion is discovered to be union, and the moral victory over evil is won.

Integration

Some help in detailed application of the Fourth Gospel along these lines may be gained from current trends in literary criticism. Structural analysis, which has been developed in connection with narrative, can be applied to particular sequences of the Gospel, including the arguments of the discourses. The method exposes the dynamics of the narrative, showing how the author sets out the aim and the steps whereby that aim is achieved. By shearing off the visual details, the basic structures are exposed, which can then be seen to correspond with universal aspects of human experience.

Allied to this is the method of deconstruction, which aims to purge from the text the presuppositions which are brought to it by the assumptions of the reader. There is currently fashionable a 'hermeneutics of suspicion', which suspects any reading of a text which presupposes an orthodoxy or a stereotype as a key to interpretation. This is, however, a two-edged weapon. In seeking to remove the harm done to a text by the reader's unexamined presuppositions, the interpreter may impose fresh presuppositions which are equally misleading.

It is evident that work of this kind still belongs to the first step, which is the understanding of the text in itself. However, the second step is not to be regarded as a separate activity, undertaken after all the work of understanding John has been completed. It is rather a fresh reading of the Gospel with full self-awareness. Having laboured to understand John through detailed critical study, and aware of one's own concept of salvation, one's own meaning of 'life', and one's own false substitutes for the truth, it is possible to read through the Gospel with intelligent appreciation, not being side-tracked into the wrong questions (such as the historical problems), but seeing it all objectively as John's presentation of Jesus, and at the same time being subjectively aware of it as speaking to one's own understanding of existence. In this way objective study and present application are integrated into a single whole. The objective side is seen to be indispensable to understanding. It is not thrown aside as a fruitless and frustrating exercise. On the contrary, it opens up the true riches of the Fourth Gospel and enables one to make them one's own.

FURTHER READING

The understanding of John in the first five centuries CE is outlined by M.F. Wiles, *The Spiritual Gospel* (Cambridge: Cambridge University Press, 1960), and also discussed by T.E. Pollard, *Johannine Christology and the Early Church* (Cambridge: Cambridge University Press, 1970).

There has been a wealth of recent literary studies of John, many of which treat the role of the reader. Among such studies are R.A. Culpepper, *Anatomy of the Fourth Gospel* (Philadelphia: Fortress Press, 1983); J.L. Staley, *The Print's First Kiss: A Rhetorical Investigation of the Implied Reader in the Fourth Gospel* (Atlanta: Scholars Press, 1988); M. Davies, *Rhetoric and Reference in the Fourth Gospel* (Sheffield: JSOT Press, 1992); M.W.G. Stibbe, *John as Storyteller: Narrative Criticism and the Fourth Gospel* (Cambridge: Cambridge University Press, 1992) and *John's Gospel* (New York: Routledge, 1994); C.R. Koester, *Symbolism in the Fourth Gospel* (Minneapolis: Fortress Press, 1995); J.L. Staley, *Reading with a Passion: Rhetoric, Autobiography, and the American West in the Gospel of John* (New York: Continuum, 1995); F.F. Segovia (ed.), *'What is John?' Readers and Readings of the Fourth Gospel* (Atlanta: Scholars Press, 1996).

A helpful reading of John that challenges its interpretation in terms of individual salvation and highlights its political implications is D. Rensberger, *Johannine Faith and Liberating Community* (Philadelphia: Westminster Press, 1988). Among feminist readings of John are those by S. Schneiders in 'Women in the Fourth Gospel and the Role of Women in the Contemporary Church', *BTB* 12 (1982), pp. 35-45 and 'A Feminist Reading of John 4:1-42', in *idem*, *The Revelatory Text* (San Francisco: HarperCollins, 1991), pp. 180-99. An excellent reflective reading of John in the light of the perennial human issues of love and death can be found in P.W. Gooch, *Reflections on Jesus and Socrates* (New Haven: Yale University Press, 1996), pp. 230-305.

Part II

THE JOHANNINE EPISTLES
Ruth B. Edwards

COMMENTARIES AND GENERAL WORKS ON 1–3 JOHN

Commentaries are surprisingly numerous. The following are recommended for introductory study and can be readily used by those with no knowledge of Greek. Commentaries in this list will be cited below by author's name, with date only.

R.A. Culpepper, *The Gospel and Letters of John* (IBT; Nashville: Abingdon Press, 1998). Succinct; includes discussion of wider issues.

C.H. Dodd, *The Johannine Epistles* (MNTC; London: Hodder & Stoughton, 1946). A seminal work.

K. Grayston, *The Johannine Epistles* (NCB; London: Marshall, Morgan & Scott; Grand Rapids: Eerdmans, 1984). Lively and stimulating.

J.L. Houlden, *The Johannine Epistles* (BNTC; London: A. & C. Black, 1973). Terse and scholarly.

J. Lieu, *The Second and Third Epistles of John* (Edinburgh: T. & T. Clarke, 1986). A detailed study of the two shorter epistles.

W. Loader, *The Johannine Epistles* (Epworth Commentary; London: Epworth Press, 1992). Brief, simple and lively.

I.H. Marshall, *The Epistles of John* (NICNT; Grand Rapids: Eerdmans, 1978). Quite detailed and balanced.

P. Perkins, *The Johannine Epistles* (New Testament Message, 21; Wilmington, DE: Glazier, 1979). Readable introduction.

D. Rensberger, *1 John, 2 John, 3 John* (ANTC; Nashville: Abingdon Press, 1997). Clear and lively.

D.M. Smith, *First, Second, and Third John* (IBC; Louisville: John Knox Press, 1991). Reflective; discusses the Common Lectionary's use of 1 John.

J.R.W. Stott, *The Epistles of John* (Leicester: Inter-Varsity Press, 1964). Still helpful.

The following contain detailed discussion of critical issues:

A.E. Brooke, *The Johannine Epistles* (ICC; Edinburgh: T. & T. Clark, 1912). Still useful.

R.E. Brown, *The Epistles of John* (AB, 30; Garden City, NY: Doubleday, 1982). Major scholarly work, very thorough with full bibliographies.

R. Bultmann, *The Johannine Epistles* (ET; Hermeneia; Philadelphia: Fortress Press, 1973). While not his best work, contains insightful material.

R. Schnackenburg, *The Johannine Epistles* (ET; HTKNT, 13.3; Tunbridge Wells: Burns & Oates, 1992). Full, scholarly, balanced and readable.

S.S. Smalley, *1, 2, 3 John* (WBC, 51; Waco, TX: Word Books, 1984). Careful study; good bibliography.

G. Strecker, *The Johannine Letters* (ET; Hermeneia; Minneapolis: Fortress Press, 1996). Thorough and scholarly.

B.F. Westcott, *The Epistles of St John* (London: Macmillan, 4th edn, 1902). Especially useful on language and exegesis.

Commentaries in foreign languages:

H.-J. Klauck, *Der Erste Johannesbrief* (EKKNT, 33.1; Zürich: Benziger/Neukirchener, 1991). Thorough German scholarship.
F. Vouga, *Die Johannesbriefe* (HNT 15:3; Tübingen: Mohr Siebeck, 1990). Stimulating work with unusual ideas.

Basic books and articles:

R.E. Brown, *The Community of the Beloved Disciple* (New York: Paulist Press, 1979).
—*An Introduction to the New Testament* (AB Reference Library; New York: Doubleday, 1997).
R. Bultmann, *Theology of the New Testament*, II (ET; London: SCM Press, 1955).
J.H. Charlesworth (ed.), *John and Qumran* (London: Chapman, 1972). Reissued as *John and the Dead Sea Scrolls* (New York: Crossroad, 1990).
L.T. Johnson, *The Writings of the New Testament: An Interpretation* (London: SCM, rev. edn, 1999).
J.-D. Kaestli, J.-M. Poffet and J. Zumstein (eds.), *La communauté johannique et son histoire* (Geneva: Labor et Fides, 1990).
W.G. Kümmel, *The Theology of the New Testament* (ET; London: SCM Press, 1973).
—*Introduction to the New Testament* (ET; London: SCM Press, 1975).
J. Lieu, *The Theology of the Johannine Epistles* (Cambridge: Cambridge University Press, 1991).
I.H. Marshall, 'Johannine Theology' and 'John, Epistles of', in *ISBE*, II (Grand Rapids: Eerdmans, 1982), pp. 1081-98.
G. Vermes, *The Complete Dead Sea Scrolls in English* (London: Penguin, 1998; also New York: Allen Lane, 1997).

Chapter One

WHY STUDY THE JOHANNINE EPISTLES?

1. *A Group of Enigmatic Writings*

The three epistles of John occupy only five or six pages of an English
Bible, yet they are among the most intriguing writings of the New
Testament. Were they written by one person or more? In what sort of
community did they originate, and what situation are they addressing? What is the background to their thought? How do they relate to
the Gospel of John? What is their theological message, and does it
have any relevance to the modern world? These are some of the issues
which will be considered in this part of the book.

2. *The Apostle of Love?*

Saint Jerome relates an anecdote about the Apostle John: when he
grew old and infirm his disciples used to carry him into church where
he repeated again and again, 'Little children, love one another'. When
asked why he always said the same words, he replied, 'Because it is
the Lord's command. When only this is done, it is enough.' Love is
certainly a prominent theme in the Johannine writings. John's Gospel
cites Jesus' new commandment 'love one another' (Jn 13.34; 15.12, 17)
three times. 1 John repeatedly stresses the need to love: 'Little children, let us love, not in word or speech, but in truth and action' (3.18);
'Beloved, let us love one another, for love is from God' (4.7; cf. 4.16
etc.). The theme reappears in 2–3 John. It may indeed have been the
Epistles, rather than the Gospel, which Jerome had in mind when he
recorded his famous anecdote.

Yet sensitive readers have noticed a tension between the message of
love and some of the attitudes displayed. In John's Gospel the Evangelist's apparent hostility to 'the Jews' causes concern. In 1 John the
problem is more with the author's attitude to those whom he calls
'antichrists' and 'deceivers' (2.18, 26). He never identifies them, but he
alludes to them indirectly in polemical statements like 'Who is the liar

but the one who denies that Jesus is the Christ?' (2.22). Other passages seem to refer to opponents' unsatisfactory conduct, for example, 'Whoever says, "I know him", but does not obey his commandments, is a liar' (2.4). 2 John similarly uses the terms 'deceiver' and 'Antichrist' of opponents (v. 7). Readers are warned not to receive into their house anyone who does not bring the correct teaching. Is it really showing Christian love to disparage opponents in this way, isolating them from the community? Is not dialogue more constructive than abuse?

3. *Light and Darkness*

The reason for the apparent gap between the splendid Johannine teaching on love and the stern condemnation of those who do not share the same understanding of the faith lies in belief in an absolute distinction between truth and falsehood. For the Johannine author(s) these are exact opposites, totally incompatible with one another. They are as different as light and darkness—a frequent metaphor in these writings. At the start of 1 John the author proclaims: 'This is the message which we have heard from him and announce to you, that God is light and in him there is no darkness at all' (1.5). He also speaks of 'walking in the light' and 'walking in the darkness'. These polarized opposites—light/darkness, truth/falsehood, good/evil, 'of the world'/'not of the world', Christ/Antichrist, God/Devil, life/death—reveal a dualistic world-view in which everything is seen as black or white. There are no half-truths, no shades of grey. As Bultmann (1955) among others has stressed, this 'dualism' is characteristic of the whole Johannine corpus. There are parallels to this mode of thought in the Qumran texts (Dead Sea Scrolls), in other Jewish and New Testament writings, and in Gnosticism, which we shall be exploring later. A dualistic framework also undergirds Revelation, though the light/darkness imagery is not so strong there.

Pedagogically these opposites are important. In an urgent situation, if you want to persuade someone to do what is right or to believe what you hold to be true, it is no use hedging your views round with numerous qualifications. You need to be clear-cut and decisive. This is exactly what the author of 1 John is. He knows what he believes to be right and true, and he states it clearly and decisively. But such confident attitudes can also cause problems.

4. *Them and Us*

One problem is that such attitudes tend to polarize people as well as ideas. Groups and individuals are categorized as 'true believers' or 'heretics'. You are either 'in' or 'out'. In recent years scholars such as R.E. Brown and W.A. Meeks have criticized the Johannine writings as 'sectarian'. A key verse is 1 Jn 2.19, 'They went out from us, but they were not of us; for if they had been of us, they would have remained with us.' These dissidents are condemned as belonging to 'the world' and contrasted with those of orthodox faith: 'What they say is of the world, and the world listens to them. We are of God; whoever knows God listens to us' (4.6). In other words, 'We are right, and they are wrong.'

This raises a further question about the Johannine concept of love. Is it a *universal* love, or only for those within the accepted circle? Judaism taught the need to love one's 'neighbour' (usually understood as 'fellow Jew'). It was considered acceptable to hate one's enemies (e.g. Ps. 139.21-22). By contrast Jesus, according to the Synoptics, taught love of enemies and redefined the meaning of 'neighbour' to include even Samaritans. When in John's Gospel Jesus commands his followers to love 'one another', many scholars see this as narrowing the love command to believers. In 1 John Jesus' teaching on love also seems to be restricted. It is expressed in terms of loving *tous adelphous* (literally, 'the brothers'), which the NRSV renders inclusively as 'brothers and sisters' and the REB as 'fellow-Christians'. But who are these 'brothers'? Are they all humanity, or just Christians? Or only one group within those who would claim to be Christian? And does the author really intend 'brothers' to include 'women'?

For many readers the seemingly negative attitude to the world also raises difficulties. 1 John warns, 'Do not love the world or the things in the world' (2.16). Are we not meant to love God's good creation? The problem is that the Johannine writings use the term *ho kosmos* ('the world') with more than one meaning. In John's Gospel it is sometimes used quite positively in the sense of the created order, which is loved by God (Jn 3.16); but it is also used of people in opposition to God, who are seen as belonging to 'this world', and not having 'eternal life'. Sometimes these two different meanings are used in the same sentence: 'He was in the world, and the world was made through him; yet the world did not know him' (Jn 1.10). The danger with this ambivalent usage is that all too easily the phrase 'the world' can be taken as implying that God's creation is evil, or that material things in general are bad (as happened in Gnosticism). In 1–3 John the problem is even more acute than in John's Gospel, as positive uses of 'the world' are almost lacking, and teaching is given which might readily foster negative attitudes to God's material gifts: 'The love of the Father is not in those who love the world; for all that is in the world—the desire of the flesh, the desire of the eyes, the boastfulness of life—comes not from the Father but from the world' (1 Jn 2.16-17). This world is said to be passing away, whereas those who do God's will live for ever. Here we are close to the concepts of those Jewish thinkers who sharply contrasted this 'world' or 'age' (Hebrew *ha*ᶜ*olam hazzeh* has both meanings) with the 'world' or 'age' to come. Taken to an extreme these ways of thought lead to intolerance, an 'other-worldly' withdrawal from society, and rigorous asceticism. But can they also have more positive effects?

5. *Right Behaviour and Right Belief*

How does one decide who are 'inside' the community and who are not? Two criteria appear to be used, one ethical, the other doctrinal.

(a) The ethical criterion concerns love and right behaviour. 'Whoever says "I am in the light", while hating a "brother", is still in darkness' (1 Jn 2.9); 'Everyone who hates their "brother" is a murderer' (3.15). In contrast, those who refuse to love 'the world' are acceptable. Similarly, 'anyone who does what is right is righteous', while 'anyone who commits sin is a child of the devil' (3.7-8). Sometimes these twin ethical criteria of love and right conduct are combined in a single affirmation: 'The children of God and the children of the devil are revealed in this way: all who do not do what is right are not from God, nor are those who do not love their "brothers" ' (3.10). 3 John sets out similar tests: 'Whoever does good is from God: whoever does evil has not seen God' (3 Jn 11). But who defines 'what is right'? And what about those who sometimes do right, and sometimes wrong? Or those who love most of the time, but sometimes fall short?

(b) The second test is right belief: 'Every spirit that confesses Jesus Christ come in the flesh is from God, and every spirit that does not confess Jesus is not from God' (4.2; cf. 2.22; 4.15; 5.1). Similarly 2 John 7 states that those who do not confess Jesus Christ coming in the flesh are 'the deceiver and the Antichrist'. Precisely what is meant by these phrases about 'confessing' Jesus Christ? Several of the statements are ambiguous in the Greek and many different solutions have been put forward as to the identity of the 'deceivers'. But even if we knew exactly who they were, it would still be difficult to apply such teaching today. With our imperfect knowledge of God, who can define what is truth and what is falsehood? Testing by confession of 'the truth' leads all too easily into the perils of heresy-hunting. At the same time, in a world which has experienced Nazism, apartheid, and many other kinds of religious and ethnic oppression, one is acutely aware of the wickedness perpetrated by those who substitute evil for good in their sense of values. Surely we can look to the Bible for guidance concerning truth and falsehood?

6. Do Believers Sin?

In defining any dogmatic belief it is difficult to ensure that one's statements are both logical and unambiguous—a point to which compilers of ecumenical 'Agreed Statements' would readily assent. All too often what we say is misunderstood by someone who reads or hears it without sharing our presuppositions or immediate concerns. Such problems become even more acute with a hortatory text designed to inculcate certain attitudes or effect a particular form of conduct. What may seem perfectly clear and logical to the author(s), may not seem so to the readers. This is especially true if the reader is distanced from the original text by time, space, or culture, as we are from the Johannine Epistles.

These contain theological tensions and ambiguities which pose difficulties for the modern reader eager to discover their true meaning. A particular problem concerns 1 John's teaching on sin. In the first two chapters the author clearly envisages the possibility that those to whom he is writing are capable of sinning: 'If anyone sins, we have an advocate with the Father, Jesus Christ the righteous' (2.1). Yet he goes on to say, 'Nobody who abides in him sins; nobody who sins has seen or known him' (3.6). The first part of this sentence might possibly be taken to mean that when Christians sin, they break their fellowship with Christ. But the second part clearly states that those who sin have *never* known Christ. The logical conundrum in reconciling this with the statement 'If we say we have no sin, we deceive ourselves' (1.8) is made even more difficult by the following verses: 'Everyone who commits sin is from the devil…*nobody born from God commits sin*' (3.8-9). Quite apart from the tension with earlier statements, this stands against the evidence of Christian experience. Is the author confused? Is he uncritically combining different sources? Can the words bear another meaning? Or is the apparent contradiction to be explained by the writer's rhetorical purpose? These and other theological questions will be discussed later, but meanwhile we need to consider a method for pursuing this enquiry.

7. Methodology

Since Bultmann—if not before—scholars have been aware that there is no such thing as 'presuppositionless exegesis'. We are all children of our time, products of particular social and educational systems, and are influenced, whether we recognize it or not, by our upbringing, our intellectual and religious convictions (or non-convictions), and possibly adherence to, or rebellion against, a particular denominational background. While we can never divorce ourselves from these factors—indeed many would hold it is wrong to try to do so—we need to be aware of them and to have a conscious methodology in studying a text.

Through the centuries there have been many different approaches to the interpretation of the Johannine Epistles. In the Church Fathers one finds them used for controversial, doctrinal and devotional purposes. For example, Irenaeus uses 1–2 John's denunciations of 'antichrists' to encourage true belief and the forsaking of 'false' teaching. Clement of Alexandria and Tertullian use 1 Jn 5.16-17 to discuss different kinds of sin. Augustine draws freely on 1 John to promote the ideal of Christian love; Cyprian to urge ethical conduct. From the earliest citations we find the Johannines (especially 1 John) treated as Scripture. It is assumed that the writings are inspired and their teachings to be adopted. Some Fathers show an awareness of what we would call critical issues. Dionysius of Alexandria is famous for separating the authorship of John's Gospel and the Apocalypse; Jerome reports the view that 2–3 John are by an 'Elder' rather than John the Evangelist. But the Fathers were mostly concerned with dogmatic issues, and with encouraging Church members to live holy lives.

In patristic writing 1–3 John tend to be overshadowed by the Gospel of John, envisaged as the work of a preacher of sublime truth who soared up to heaven like an eagle (so Augustine). But there was a source of concern: John's Gospel was very early adopted by Gnostics like Ptolemaeus and Valentinus, who built up elaborate systems drawing on the syncretistic thought of Greece and the East, couching their ideas in language quite close to that of the Gospel. This led to suspicions about its orthodoxy, and sometimes 1 John was used by orthodox Fathers to defend it.

In the mediaeval and Reformation periods the Johannines seem again to have been mostly used for devotional, dogmatic, and controversial purposes. It is not until post-Enlightenment times that one finds the first serious critical scholarship, especially in Germany. It is beyond our scope to discuss the development of modern scholarship, but it is probably fair to say that until around the 1970s the main concerns were with historical, theological and literary-critical issues. What is the genre of 1–3 John? Can one identify written sources? Did the same author write John's Gospel and the Epistles? Are there differences in language, style and theology between these writings? Who are the 'opponents' of 1 and 2 John? What ecclesiastical situation do the Johannines presuppose? There has, for example, been considerable interest in Germany over the question of *Frühkatholizismus* (early Catholicism), and whether the presbyter of 2–3 John is a bishop. From the 1950s to the 1970s there was also an especially strong interest in 'Biblical Theology'—an attempt to bring the Bible's doctrinal and ethical teaching into a coherent pattern. Scholars focused on the 'theology' of individual authors or groups of writings, e.g. the Pauline letters; the Johannine writings. Sometimes Revelation was considered alongside John's Gospel and 1–3 John; more often it was treated separately. Most scholars treated the theology of the Johannine Gospel and Epistles as a unity, including Kümmel, Guthrie, Bultmann and Marshall—to name a few notable figures. An outstanding exception was Dodd, who as early as the 1930s had argued for separate authorship of these writings on theological as well as linguistic grounds.

Those who practised such historical-critical scholarship might be 'liberals' or 'conservatives', and they differed widely in their conclusions. But their methods were basically the same. More recently, scholarship has begun to separate even further the various Johannine writings. Judith Lieu in *The Theology of the Johannine Epistles* (1991) argues that they must be allowed in speak in their own right rather than under the shadow of the Gospel; both she and Kenneth Grayston have suggested that more than one author may be involved in the composition of 1–3 John.

New methods and issues have also emerged. Following the work of scholars like Malherbe, Theissen and Meeks, there has been a surge of interest in the social background of the Epistles. In *The Community of the Beloved Disciple* (1979), followed by his massive commentary on the Johannines (1982), Raymond Brown has put forward an elaborate conjectural history of the community which he believes to lie behind both Gospel and Epistles, and the loves and hates of its members. Particularly in North America, but also in Britain, there has been a lively interest in the question of whether this community was a 'sect'.

The Johannines' teaching on Christology and love, once piously accepted at its face value, has come in for much criticism.

Partly as a reaction against the negative and 'atomizing' character of some historical-critical scholarship, recent decades have seen the rise of new types of criticism in which practitioners have sought to look at the biblical writings holistically, and to be more aware of their functions as 'text'. Scholars such as H.-J. Klauck, F. Vouga, and D.F. Watson are now applying 'rhetorical criticism' to the Johannines, and D. Neufeld has recently published an analysis of 1 John based on speech-act theory (1994). Structuralist, post-structuralist, and semiotic interpretative methods have not yet hit our texts, though these and other modern 'criticisms' are being applied to John's Gospel. Side by side with these new approaches, study by traditional methods is continued by both conservative and radical scholars. Thus Johannine studies are in a creative state of flux.

8. *Approach of this Study*

The basic approach of the current study is historical-critical. It considers such issues as sources, authorship, literary unity, style, genre and milieu as objectively as possible. At the same time, starting with the shorter Epistles, it seeks to understand the Johannines as literary wholes, with an awareness of their rhetorical purpose and their effects on readers and hearers. Rather than treating the Epistles in their canonical order, the study will begin with 3 and 2 John. I do this because their form and contents are relatively straightforward and easy to grasp, and I treat 3 John first, since I believe that it was written before 2 John. After this we turn to the most challenging Epistle, namely 1 John, which raises a bigger range of interesting ideas.

A special focus will be the Johannines' theological content—for it is as *theological* writings, rather than as 'great literature', that most modern readers study these texts. We shall therefore need to evaluate their teachings and presuppositions in such key areas as Christology and ethics. The aim is to let the Epistles speak in their own right, without positing any particular relation to John's Gospel. But inevitably comparisons must be drawn with other books of the New Testament, not only because parts of 1 John, in particular, cannot be understood without some reference to them, but also because such comparisons are valuable in their own right. It will also be helpful to refer to the Johannines' wider background in the Hebrew Bible and contemporary Jewish and Graeco-Roman writings.

In all this readers should bear in mind that 1–3 John, like the rest of the New Testament, are written in Greek. Many students suppose their language is easy, since their range of vocabulary and grammatical constructions is small; in fact, the Greek of 1 John is in many places ambiguous and obscure. Most translations—and even some commentaries—gloss over the difficulties. In the present study it is possible to discuss only a few of the controversial passages, but it is hoped that readers will be stimulated to explore further their detailed exegesis for themselves.

Finally, I hope to share with readers my own commitment to the Christian faith, and the belief that we can learn something of value from these writings, though one should not accept their message uncritically. In the final chapter I shall attempt to assess something of their strengths and weaknesses, and discover some message for the world today.

FURTHER READING

Composition and authorship:

Introductions to commentaries by Brown (1982), Dodd (1946), Houlden (1973), Marshall (1978).

D. Guthrie, *New Testament Introduction* (Leicester: Apollos; Downers Grove, IL: InterVarsity Press, 4th edn, 1990), esp. pp. 858-900.

W.G. Kümmel, *Introduction to the New Testament*, II (ET; London: SCM Press, 1975).

Theology:

R. Bultmann, *Theology of the New Testament*, II (ET; London: SCM Press, 1955).

W.G. Kümmel, *The Theology of the New Testament* (ET; London: SCM Press, 1973).

I.H. Marshall, 'Johannine Theology' and 'John, Epistles of', in *ISBE*, II (Grand Rapids: Eerdmans, 1982), pp. 1081-98..

J. Lieu, *The Theology of the Johannine Epistles* (Cambridge: Cambridge University Press, 1991).

Community and sectarianism:

R.E. Brown, *The Community of the Beloved Disciple* (New York: Paulist Press, 1979).

B.S. Childs, *The New Testament as Canon* (London: SCM Press, 1984), pp. 482-85.

Rhetorical criticism:

H.-J. Klauck, 'Zur rhetorischen Analyse der Johannesbriefe', ZNW 81 (1990), pp. 205-24.

D. Neufeld, *Reconceiving Texts as Speech Acts: An Analysis of 1 John* (Leiden: E.J. Brill, 1994). -

F. Vouga, 'La réception de la théologie johannique dans les épîtres', in J.-D. Kaestli, J.-M. Poffet and J. Zumslein (eds.), *La communauté johannique et son histoire* (Geneva: Labor et Fides, 1990), pp. 283-302.

D.F. Watson and A.J. Hauser, *Rhetorical Criticism of the Bible* (Leiden: E.J. Brill, 1994).

Chapter Two

2 AND 3 JOHN: FORM, STYLE AND CONTENT

1. *Types of Letter in the Ancient World*

The Graeco-Roman world knew many different kinds of epistolary writing. There were short philosophical treatises in the form of letters, like the Epistles of Epicurus; fictional letters written as creative literary exercises; official letters reporting on events or asking for advice; pastoral and ecclesiastical letters, like those of Paul in the New Testament and Ignatius and Polycarp in the Apostolic Fathers. And there were private letters, sometimes quite literary, like Cicero's letters to his friends, sometimes informal and almost illiterate, like the thousands of letters on papyri dealing with business matters and domestic affairs. It is helpful to have these different categories in mind in considering the literary form of 1–3 John.

The private letters are most relevant to 2 and 3 John. Many of these take a regular form: (a) greeting in the third person singular; (b) a wish for good health for the recipient; (c) main body, often containing a request; (d) sometimes a reference to a possible meeting; (e) final greetings and wishes for good health. The following is a typical example:

> Dromon to Zenon greetings. We give thanks to all the gods if you are in good health yourself and everything else is in good order. We too are well, and in accordance with your instructions I am taking every care that no one troubles your people. When you are well enough to sail up (the Nile), order one of your people to buy a measure of Attic honey; for I need it for my eyes by order of the god. Keep well (PCairo Zen. 59426, third century BCE).

2. *The Form, Style and Content of 3 John*

3 John begins with a greeting in the third person, 'The Elder to the beloved Gaius' (v. 1), followed by a wish for good health and expression of pleasure (vv. 2-4). Next the author praises Gaius and requests him to send some 'brothers' on their way worthily of God. The author

refers to a previous letter (as commonly in such correspondence); mentions a man called Diotrephes who is causing problems, and promises a visit to sort things out. He commends a certain Demetrius, expresses his hope of seeing Gaius in person, wishes him peace, and sends greetings from friends.

Of all the writings in the New Testament, 3 John conforms most closely to the pattern of a private letter such as the papyrus example just cited. It is short—only 185 words—shorter than any of Paul's letters, but about the same length as some of Cicero's shorter letters. It would fit comfortably on to a single sheet of papyrus. It is concerned with a specific problem. It may well have been conveyed to Gaius by the Demetrius who is so warmly commended (cf. 1 Pet. 5.12, commending its bearer Silvanus; also Cicero, *Ad Fam*. 1.3).

At the same time there are some peculiarities: (a) the author's name is not given, but only his title, 'the Elder'. This may indicate that he is writing in his capacity of a church leader, rather than purely personally. (b) The regular word for 'greetings' (*chairein*) is missing from the opening salutation. The omission of a word for greeting is not uncommon in Aramaic letters, but very rare in Greek ones. (c) The health wish takes an unusual form: the author prays that Gaius is keeping in good physical health, as he is well in his *psychē* (life, spirit or soul). This makes a distinction between Gaius's bodily and spiritual health. (d) There are a few peculiar turns of expression in the Greek. (e) Instead of the usual 'keep well' at the end of the letter, it has 'peace'. This corresponds to the Jewish greeting *shalom*, extremely common in Aramaic letters. Other Semitic turns of expression include 'walk' in the sense of 'behave' (v. 3) and 'mouth to mouth' for 'face to face' (v. 14).

The letter uses many phrases familiar from secular letters, for example, 'I was very pleased', 'you will do well' (often associated with a request). It also contains some specifically Jewish-Christian vocabulary: 'the congregation' (*ecclēsia*), 'gentiles', 'fellow workers', 'children' (for the addressees), 'the Name', and 'brothers' in the sense of a religious community. In places the phraseology is reminiscent of John's Gospel and 1 John, for example, the references to 'seeing God' and being 'of God' (v. 11; cf. Jn 1.18; 1 Jn 4.4, etc.) and the themes of 'witness' (5 times), 'truth' (6 times) and 'love' (6 times)—a remarkable number of occurrences for such a short letter. Note especially v. 12b, 'and you know that our witness is true' (cf. Jn 21.24); 'the friends' (v. 15; cf. Jn 15.14-15). It is possible that the Elder, as pastor, is deliberately echoing Jesus' words from the Johannine tradition. The striking personification of truth in v. 12 may recall Jn 15.26-27 (the spirit of truth as witness). 'Peace' as a greeting reminds us of Jesus' greeting in Jn 20.19, 26, though it could be just a Christian form of the regular Jewish greeting (cf. Paul's usage).

The main business of the letter, as Malherbe (1977) has argued, is *hospitality*. In the ancient world where inns were few and unreliable most travellers used private hospitality. Sometimes people entertained complete strangers (cf. Abraham's proverbial welcoming of angels). Those who shared religious beliefs often gave hospitality to one another, but there was always a risk of being imposed on. It is evident from 3 John that travelling brothers whom Gaius (a common Latin name) had not known personally had visited him, and taken back good reports to the Elder. The Elder warmly commends Gaius for his generosity to strangers who came 'in the Name', since they had been able to rely entirely on Christian hospitality without taking anything from pagans. He urges him to continue such action, so that they may become 'fellow workers with the truth'. The motivation is theological rather than personal.

Next the Elder deals with the inhospitable Diotrephes. He complains that Diotrephes 'is hungry for power' (literally, 'likes the pre-eminence'); he does not receive the Elder, and he talks nonsense about him. Not content with that, Diotrephes has declined to receive the 'brothers' and has expelled them. There has been much debate about Diotrephes' ecclesial role. Some have thought that he was an early monarchic bishop, either 'orthodox' or 'heretical'. But if Diotrephes is a bishop, why is the Elder interfering in his area of jurisdiction? Is there not a danger of reading into this text later forms of church government?

The nature of the Elder's dispute with Diotrephes has also been much debated. There seems no reason to view it as doctrinal: no doctrinal issues are mentioned. Some believe that the issue is *authority*, understanding *ouk epidechetai* in v. 9 as 'does not accept our authority' and *ekballō* ('expel') and *kōlyō* ('hinder') in v. 10 in the technical ecclesiastical sense of 'excommunicate' and 'forbid'. But *epidechetai* can mean just 'receive hospitably' (cf. v. 10), and the other words are more plausibly understood as 'decline' to receive someone in one's house and 'not permit' other members of a house church to do so. Nor does the verb *phlyareō* ('talk nonsense') mean 'bring charges against', but rather 'gossip maliciously' (cf. 1 Tim. 5.13). The dispute, then, seems to be about church hospitality rather than doctrine or authority. We are dealing with a pastoral and moral, rather than ecclesiastical, issue (so Stott 1964).

What of the Elder's own status? There is no hint that he is an apostle; but if he is only a local church leader, why does he write so authoritatively to a member of another congregation? Perhaps he is relying on greater seniority in the faith, or presuming on his personal relationship to Diotrephes and Gaius. We note the references to mutual friends, the promise of a visit, and the implication that Gaius is one of his 'children' or protégés. Whatever the circumstances, the Elder is in a position to commend, censure and exhort: Gaius is praised for his Christian behaviour and his hospitality; Diotrephes is held up as a model of how *not* to behave. In all this 3 John follows a common pattern of rhetoric designed to earn goodwill, assign praise and blame, and affect the behaviour of others (cf. Watson, 'A Rhetorical Analysis of 3 John: A Study in Epistolory Rhetoric' [1989]). The author's generous attitude over hospitality to fellow Christians is remarkable. No conditions are laid down; no limits on length of stay (contrast the *Didache*); no doctrinal safeguards. Even strangers should be received who come 'for the sake of the Name'. One is reminded of Jesus' teaching: 'Freely you have received; freely give' (Mt. 10.8).

3. 2 John: Opening Address and the 'Elect Lady'

2 John follows the same structure as 3 John. There is a greeting from the Elder to the recipients (vv. 1-3), a reference to his joy (v. 4), and a request (v. 5), leading to the main business—a warning against 'deceivers' (vv. 6-11). The author expresses a wish to visit the recipients, and sends greetings (vv. 12-13). There are, however, differences. The letter is not addressed to a named man, but to an 'elect lady and her children' (we shall return to this enigmatic greeting later).

The prescript contains other unusual features. Instead of the simple health wish, we have an elaborate 'ecclesiastical' greeting, 'There will be with us grace, mercy, peace, from Father God and from Jesus Christ, the Son of the Father, in truth and love'. The form is similar to the specifically Christian greetings in other New Testament letters where *charis* ('grace') is substituted for secular *chairein* ('rejoice'). 'Peace' also occurs in other New Testament letters, taken over from Jewish greetings; 'mercy' is less common (but note 1 Tim. 1.2; 2 Tim. 1.2; Jude 2). There are, however, peculiarities in the Elder's formulation. (a) He does not identify himself by name (cf. 3 John); (b) the formal greeting comes in a separate sentence from the opening address; (c) it is a statement rather than a wish (contrast 1–2 Peter, Paul and the Apostolic Fathers). It looks as if v. 3 has been awkwardly added to a simpler greeting. Observe also the curious juxtaposition of favourite Johannine vocabulary—'love', 'truth', 'abide' (vv. 1-2)—with untypical vocabulary (v. 3), notably 'grace' (in John's Gospel, only in the Prologue, never in 1 John), 'mercy' (not elsewhere in Johannine literature), the un-Johannine 'Father God' (lacking the article with 'God' and the modifier 'our'), and the peculiar, quasi-liturgical, description of Jesus as 'the Son of the Father'. Yet v. 3 also uses typical Johannine vocabulary in the phrase 'in truth and love', tacked on to the Pauline-style greeting. The most probable explanation is that the author himself added this rather grand 'apostolic' greeting to give his letter more theological weight and to emphasize the concepts of truth and love so dear to him.

We turn now to the problem of the 'elect lady' (*eklektē kyria*, with no word for 'the'). There is no exact parallel to this designation in biblical or secular Greek. Most modern commentators suppose the phrase is used metaphorically for a church. In the Hebrew Bible, Jerusalem or Zion is often personified as a woman; sometimes Israel is pictured as God's bride—imagery occasionally picked up in the New Testament (cf. Rev. 21.2; Eph. 5.25-28). In the *Shepherd of Hermas*, a second-century CE allegorical writing, the Church appears as a woman in a vision and is addressed by the author as *kyria* (V.I.5). But there are major differences between these images and 2 John's. In Revelation, Ephesians and *Hermas* it is the new Jerusalem or the church *as a whole* which is personified, not one congregation. Yet if the 'elect lady' of v. 1 is the whole church, who is her 'elect sister' in v. 13?

Examples of a local church personified as a woman are not frequent: several commentators cite 2 Cor. 11.2, Tertullian, *Ad Martyras* 1.1 and 1 Pet. 5.13 in this connection. But the first two authors make it abundantly clear that they are writing figuratively: Paul wishes to present the Corinthian Christians to Christ 'like a pure virgin'; Tertullian (writing in North Africa c. 200 CE) speaks of 'lady mother *church*' (*domina mater ecclesia*) providing from her bountiful breasts for prisoners. In neither case is the word *eklektē* used. 1 Peter 5.13 provides the closest parallel in *hē en Babylōni syneklektē* 'the co-elect (woman) in Babylon'. It is usually assumed that *syneklektē* here means the church at Rome; but it is possible that it refers to an individual woman (so Bigg 1910).

Could *eklektē kyria* in 2 John 1 also be taken in its more natural sense of a real woman? Four possible interpretations have been put forward: (a) *Kyria* might be a proper name, and *eklektē* an adjective (ancient Greek did not use capitals to indicate proper nouns); (b) *kyria* might be an adjective and *Eklektē* a proper name; (c) both *Kyria* and *Eklektē* might be proper names; (d) perhaps neither is a proper name. Each hypothesis will be briefly considered in turn.

(a) *Kyria*, meaning 'mistress', 'lady' (cf. Aramaic 'Martha') is found as a personal name in both inscriptions and papyri; *eklektē*, meaning 'chosen', or 'elect' (of God) is an appropriate epithet for a Christian leader (cf. Rom. 16.13, Rufus, the elect in the Lord; Ignatius, *Phil.* 11.1, Rheus Agathopous, an elect man). It has been objected that one might expect the definite article with *eklektē*. We can reply that this letter is not written in fully idiomatic Greek, having other linguistic peculiarities (cf. the occurrence of 'Father' both with and without the article in v. 3); if *eklektē kyria* means 'the church' the absence of the article is also odd.

(b) In favour of *kyria* as a common noun is its frequent appearance in the papyri as a polite and affectionate form of address to an older woman (cf. P. Oxy 744, 'to Berous my lady', etc). Against this has been argued the absence of 'my' with *Kyria* and lack of evidence for *Eklektē* as a personal name in contemporary papyri (so Brown 1982, p. 653). Indeed, Findlay alleged that '*Eklektē* occurs nowhere else in Greek...as a proper name' (1909: 23). One may reply that 'my' is not always found with *kyria* in the papyri, and although the name *Eklektē* has not so far been found in the papyri, it is attested in Greek inscriptions, along with a parallel male name *Eklektos* (known also in literary sources). We may mention also a series of inscriptions of imperial date from Rome with the woman's name *Eclecte* or *Eglecte* (c. 7 times). Although the inscriptions are in Latin, the form of this name is Greek. The idea that *Eklektē* might be a personal name also receives some support from Clement of Alexandria, who thought that 2 John was written to 'a certain Babylonian woman called Electa' (according to the *Adumbrationes*, a Latin translation of his *Hypotyposes*).

A problem often raised with understanding *Eklektē* as a proper name is its reappearance at v. 13. Mention of two women with the same name in such a short letter might seem improbable, but the ancient world had a smaller range of women's names than we do (cf. all the New Testament Marys). The woman in v. 13 need not be a blood sister; she may equally well be a Christian sister, herself a church leader. Alternatively *eklektē* in v. 13 could be the adjective 'elect'. It might seem awkward to use the same Greek word both as a proper name and as an adjective within 13 verses, but ancient writers were not so sensitive to such grammatical distinctions as modern ones; the repetition of *eklektē* in v. 13 must deliberately echo v. 1, and it is likely the two women shared a common role. Incidentally, the final greetings are not from the 'elect sister' herself, but from her children. If this is a real woman, she must be either deceased or at least not present with the writer. In either case it is hard to believe she is a church.

(c) The idea that both *Kyria* and *Eklektē* might be proper names is described by Westcott (1902) as 'very strange', but such double names are common in the ancient world, and *Eclecte* occurs combined with other personal names in the Roman inscriptions mentioned.

(d) The case for the 'elect lady' as a real woman does not stand or fall on taking *Kyria* or *Eklektē* (or both) as a proper name. 'Chosen lady' could equally well be a sobriquet (or nickname), like the Gospel of John's 'disciple whom Jesus loved', for someone whom the author, for whatever reason, did not wish to name directly. One sometimes suspects that a reason why the 'elect lady' has been so rarely taken as an individual is reluctance to assume that a woman could have led a church. But female church leaders are attested elsewhere in the New Testament: we note particularly 'Nympha and the church at her house' (Col. 4.15) and Phoebe, minister or deacon of the church at Cenchreae (Rom. 16.1). Thus our *eklektē kyria* may well have hosted or led a local congregation; 'her children', to whom the letter is also addressed, were probably not her physical children, but rather members of her house church. Thus the letter is still written to a church even if the 'elect lady' is taken to be an individual.

4. 2 John: Main Body

What is the basic purport of 2 John? The Elder says that he loves the 'elect lady and her children' in truth (using the same phraseology as 3 Jn 1). He says that not only he loves them, but so do 'all who know the truth', because of 'the truth that abides in us'. The linking of love and truth is striking. The phrase '*all* who know the truth' is either hyperbole (cf. Rom. 1.8, when Paul says that the faith of the Roman Christians is talked of over the *whole* world), or, more probably, an exclusive claim to know the truth on behalf of the author and his community. Next the Elder rejoices that he has found some of the lady's children walking in the truth. Functionally, this sentence, like the opening one, is a *captatio benevolentiae*, to win the goodwill of the recipients (cf. 3 Jn 3). But the tone may be less warm than in 3 John if only some of the lady's children walk in the truth.

The Elder then moves on to his main agenda, marked by a repeated address to the 'lady' (*kyria*)—vocatives are common in the papyri at this point—and the typical verb *erōtaō*, 'ask'. But instead of the usual request for a favour, we have an exhortation to mutual love. The author assures the lady that he is not writing 'a new commandment, but one which we had from the beginning' (the vocabulary is Johannine: cf. *entolē*, 'commandment', 14 times in 1 Jn; 11 times John's Gospel). But the sentence is phrased awkwardly: one would expect a second person verb, 'I request you, lady, that you...', not a first person plural ('we'). One would also expect a specific request rather than theological exhortation. The phraseology seems to be modelled on 1 John, where the author writes, 'This is the commandment which we had from the beginning that we love one another' (3.11) and 'Beloved, I do not write a new commandment to you, but an old commandment which you had from the beginning' (2.7). 'From the beginning' is a favourite phrase of 1 John (8 times) and is indicative of the author's harking back to the foundations of Christianity.

Next, the Elder defines love: 'This is love, that we walk according to his commandments' (v. 6a). The structure, 'This is x', followed by a 'that' clause, or another noun, is a favourite in 1 John (e.g. 1.5; 3.11; cf. Jn 15.12; 17.3). The remarkable point is that love is defined entirely in terms of keeping God's (or Christ's) command—a thought found also in 1 John. Another definition follows, exactly parallel in syntax: 'This is the command, as you heard from the beginning, that you walk in it' (v. 6b). Note again the characteristic phrase 'from the beginning', harking back to origins. It is ambiguous whether 'in it' (a feminine pronoun in the Greek) refers to the 'commandment' or 'love', or even to 'truth'. But it makes little difference to the sense. The phrase seems rather repetitive, but it serves to stress the significance the author attaches to love, truth and obedience.

He now speaks of some who have presumably failed in these areas—deceivers who 'have gone out into the world' (another Johannine phrase: cf. 1 Jn 4.1)—who does not confess Jesus Christ 'coming in the flesh'. These deceivers are defined (vv. 7-8) as 'the deceiver and the Antichrist' (using the same formula, 'this is...', in spite of the plural antecedent). The vocabulary is Johannine, including the use of 'confess' with a personal object (cf. Jn 9.22; 1 Jn 2.23, etc.), 'Antichrist' (unique to the Johannine writings in the New Testament: cf. 1 Jn 2.18, 22; 4.3), and reference to Jesus 'coming in the flesh' (cf. 1 Jn 4.2). The 'deceiver' reminds us of 'those who deceive you' in 1 Jn 2.26 (cf. Rev. 12.9; also 1 Tim. 4.1). The content also is very close to the thought of 1 John, where we have the same idea that those who do not make the right christological confession are God's archetypal spiritual enemy. The seriousness of such an allegation should not be underestimated. But who are guilty of this terrible act? They may be the same group as are denounced in 1 John for denying Jesus' incarnation (assuming that is the meaning of 2 John's ambiguous phrase here: see Chapter 8 §3).

The author also warns his addressees to be on their guard that they do not lose what has been achieved. For everyone who 'goes ahead' (*proagō*) and does not abide in Christ's teaching does not 'have' the Father or the Son. This is the only place in the New Testament where *proagō* (an un-Johannine word) is used in a metaphorical sense. It is evident that the author is a conservative Christian, nervous of 'progressives' who (in his view) go beyond the basic teaching of (or about) Jesus. His is not the spirit of intellectual enquiry or innovative theology, but rather of faithfulness to what he has received. So serious does he deem departing from this tradition that he forbids the elect lady and her children greet them or give them hospitality, because to do so would be to share in their evil deeds. This is a far cry from the generous, condition-free hospitality of 3 John. Either the situation has drastically changed, or we are dealing with a different author.

So we reach the end of the letter. The author says that having many other things to write, he does not wish to use paper and ink; he would rather speak personally to his addressees, 'so that our joy may be full'. The sentence parallels the end of 3 John, though there the author says 'pen and ink'. References to writing materials are exceedingly rare at the end of papyrus letters. This raises the possibility of a direct imitation of 3 John by 2 John, as is also suggested by the complicated syntax in v. 12. The 'extreme joy' at the prospect of a meeting seems out of place in a letter sparked by a doctrinal crisis. The phrase is virtually identical to the one used more appropriately in the opening of 1 John. Is this another sign that 2 John is imitative?

5. *Conclusion*

We conclude that, while there is no reason doubt that 3 John is a genuine private letter, 2 John is more problematic. Though clearly in letter form, it has more specifically 'Christian' features, including the lengthy prescript. It has a less engaging and less direct style than 3 John, and is obscure in places. Bultmann and others have suggested that it might be an artificial compilation in imitation of 3 John. If so, its purpose would be to claim the authority of the 'Elder' (presumably a well-known figure) to refute 'heresy'. We know that 1 and 2 John were used for this purpose in the patristic church, just as 3 John was used to urge bishops to be hospitable. But the conjecture lacks proof. An alternative might be to see it still as secondary to 3 John, but a genuine letter by a church leader who was also a presbyter ('elder'). A third alternative is to regard the letters as the work of one man, but to explain the differences in style as due to their having different purposes. The lack of clarity might arise from old age, or from the fact that the author was not a native Greek speaker. Both letters contain Semitizing vocabulary, and 2 John also shows features of Semitic syntax (esp. v. 2, where a participial clause with the verb 'abiding' is resolved into a main clause with an indicative verb). All this may have some bearing on authorship, which will be the theme of Chapter 4.

FURTHER READING

Commentaries by Brown (1982), Bultmann (1973), Lieu (1986), Schnackenburg (1992), Stott (1964), Strecker (1996).

On form and style:

R.W. Funk, 'The Form and Structure of II and III John', *JBL* 86 (1967), pp. 424-30.

D.F. Watson, 'A Rhetorical Analysis of 2 John according to Greco-Roman Convention', *NTS* 35 (1989), pp. 104-30.

—'A Rhetorical Analysis of 3 John: A Study in Epistolary Rhetoric', *CBQ* 51 (1989), pp. 479-501.

J.L. White, 'The Greek Documentary Letter Tradition Third Century BCE to Third Century CE', in J.L. White (ed.), *Studies in Ancient Letter Writing. Semeia* 22 for 1981 (Chico: Scholars Press, 1982), pp. 89-106.

On the church situation:

A.J. Malherbe, 'The Inhospitality of Diotrephes', in J. Jervell and W.A. Meeks (eds.), *God's Christ and his People* (FS Dahl; Oslo: Universitetsforlaget, 1977), pp. 222-32.

E. Schweizer, *Church Order in the New Testament* (ET; London: SCM Press, 1961).

For the 'Elect Lady' as probably a personification:

Commentaries by Brown (1982), Grayston (1984), Marshall (1978), Schnackenburg (1992), Westcott (1902).

G.G. Findlay, *Fellowship in the Life Eternal* (London: Hodder & Stoughton, 1909).

For the 'Elect Lady' (or her sister) as probably an individual woman:

C. Bigg, The Epistles of St. Peter and St. Jude (ICC; Edinburgh: T. & T. Clark, 1910), esp. p. 197 on the 'elect sister'.

L. Morris, in D.A. Carson, R.T. France *et al.* (eds.), *New Bible Commentary: 21st Century Edition* (London: Inter-Varsity Press, 1995), p. 1271.

D.R. Pape, *God and Woman* (Oxford: Mowbray, 1977), p. 206.

D. Guthrie, *New Testament Introduction* (Leicester: Apollos; Downers Grove, IL: InterVarsity Press, 4th edn., 1990), p. 889.

Chapter Three

1 JOHN: FORM, STYLE, SOURCES AND BACKGROUND

1. *Literary Form*

The literary form of 1 John is an enigma. The Church Fathers refer to it as a 'letter', as do modern translations. But it lacks opening address, final greetings, and other marks of a letter such as personal references. Some scholars have tried to get round this by suggesting that it is a *literary* letter. But even literary letters and religious or philosophical treatises in epistolary form contain greetings (cf. Epicurus's *Letter to Menoeceus*; the *Letter of Aristeas*; the gnostic *Treatise on the Resurrection*).

F.O. Francis, in a much cited article (1970), defended the epistolary character of 1 John, observing that not all papyrus letters have closing greetings. He claimed a parallel to 1 John's opening in a letter cited in Josephus (*Ant.* 11.123-24) and noted 1 John's reference to prayer (5.14-17), arguing that prayer is 'an established element in the epistolary close in the NT epistles' (p. 125). But his arguments are unconvincing. The supposed parallel in Josephus to the 'double opening statement' of 1 Jn 1.1-3 is weak, and in any case the Josephus also contains the traditional epistolary greeting with *chairein*. 1 John does not *end* with prayer, but restates old themes in new language, finishing with a warning against idols. Moreover, there are big differences between the idiosyncratic material on prayer in 1 John and the closing Pauline benedictions cited as parallels. More recently F. Vouga (1990) has defended 1 John's status as a letter, but his theory likewise founders on the absence of opening greetings and epistolary ending (not obviated by calling 5.13 a 'final benediction').

So what are the alternatives? Dodd and others have suggested that 1 John might be a circular letter, intended for a number of local churches. But once again the absence of greetings provides a major obstacle. If 1 John were intended for several congregations, one would expect this to be made explicit (cf. Col. 4.16; Rev. 1.4–3.1). Others see 1 John as a tract addressed to the church at large (so Houlden 1973). This would be compatible with the author's address to his recipients as 'beloved', 'brothers' and 'little children'—terms used by an established teacher to those viewed as pupils. The problem here is that 1 John refers to a specific doctrinal crisis and even to specific (unnamed) individuals. The difficulties are compounded by the fact that those who designate 1 John a 'tract' (or 'tracrate') use the term in a bewildering range of senses. Some appear to regard it as a kind of general 'manifesto', suitable for all Christians (so Kümmel 1975, p. 437); others see it as denoting a homily or pastoral address to a specific audience (so Marshall 1978, p. 14). Smalley (1984) describes 1 John as a 'paper' in the modern sense, thus leaving the ancient genre unsolved. Deissmann (1910) identified 1 John as a 'diatribe' (a form of ethical discourse especially favoured by Cynics and Stoics). Though it lacks the biting wit of some diatribes, it shows affinities with the more gentle paraenesis of the philosopher Epictetus. Grayston (1984) has suggested that 1 John is an encheiridion, that is, an instruction book for disciples for applying a master's teaching. These proposals will be considered later.

The problem of genre is not unique to 1 John in the New Testament. The letter of James also lacks an epistolary ending, and it too has been identified as a 'diatribe' or paraenesis. Hebrews has valedictory greetings, but like 1 John no opening greetings. Possibly an original epistolary greeting for 1 John has been lost, or rather replaced by the formal prooemium. Conceivably some final greetings have also been removed when an original letter was adapted for a wider purpose. Before reaching any conclusions on form we need to look in more detail at 1 John's structure and style.

2. *The Structure of 1 John*

It is difficult to discern a logical structure in 1 John. Writing in 1912, Brooke went so far as to say that any attempt to analyse the Epistle should be abandoned as useless (1912, p. xxxii). This has not prevented numerous scholars seeking to discover an overarching plan. In an influential article T. Häring proposed alternating ethical and christological themes, culminating in the tying of the two together in 4.7–5.12; but this does not solve all the problems (see Schnackenburg [1992], p. 12 and Strecker [1996], p. xliii). Brown (1982, p. 764) tabulates 42 sample attempts, dividing the text into two, three or seven parts (the most favoured divisions) plus the Prooemium and, in some cases, an Appendix. Vouga (1990) offers a fresh analysis based on ancient rhetorical and epistolary theory, but his study forces the text unnaturally into classical patterns and some of his subdivisions are quite unconvincing (e.g. the idea that the whole of 1.5–2.17 is a *captatio benevolentiae*).

The following analysis is offered as guide to aid the reader, without any claim that it represents the author's intention:

A. PROOEMIUM or formal opening (1.1-4)
B. MAIN BODY:
    1. Theme of light and darkness: walking in the light as a sign
      of fellowship with God (1.5–2.11)
    2. Admonitions and warning against love of the world (2.12-17)
    3. The 'last hour' and true confession or denial of Christ (2.18-27)
    4. The children of God and the children of the devil (2.28–3.24)
    5. The two kinds of spirits (4.1-6)
    6. The nature and the demands of love (4.7-21)
    7. Victory and testimony (5.1-12)
C. CONCLUSION:
    Purpose of writing, postscripts and re-affirmations (5.13-21).

In fact, all the sections overlap in content with others. 1 John's structure has aptly been described as spiraliform: it moves from one subject to another by association of ideas, and then returns to a subject already discussed. Thus the author's thoughts on any particular subject, such as love, or sin, or spiritual birth, are not grouped systematically, but have to be culled from different parts of the writing. One is tempted to compare 1 John to a rather rambling sermon, but the writer does have a definite persuasive purpose in mind and seems to have composed in this way because he believed it was likely to gain conviction.

3. *The Greek Style of 1 John*

Houlden writes: 'The impression the writer of 1J gives is of tenacious and inflexible insistence on a small number of points which he hammers again and again' (1973, p. 3). 1 John is certainly noted for its distinctive style with a limited vocabulary and a small range of grammatical constructions, which are used repeatedly. Many of these features are apparent even in translation, and we cite a few striking examples. The author is fond of 'if-clauses' where the second part of the sentence is not the logical outcome of the first; for example, 'If we accept human testimony, God's testimony is greater' (5.9), where the author means, 'If we accept human testimony, much more ought we to accept God's, since it is superior'. He loves general statements of the type, 'Anyone who does x is…' (e.g. 2.4). He makes much use of antitheses: contrasts are continually drawn between those who love their 'brothers' and those who hate them; those who 'do' the truth and those who do not. He likes using demonstratives to look forward to what he is about to say: 'And this is the message which we have heard...' (1.5, etc; cf. 2 Jn 6), or to look back: 'And this is the spirit of the antichrist' (4.3). He also uses demonstratives to give a 'test formula': 'By this we know...' (e.g. 3.19). Rather confusingly, this 'test formula' can refer either to what has preceded or to what follows (e.g. 2.3 and 2.5); sometimes it is ambiguous. The author favours short sentences and parataxis, rather than involved periods with subordinate clauses (the Prooemium is an exception). A characteristic feature of 1 John is its limited range of conjunctions or linking particles, with excessive use of 'and'.

This last feature may be due to a Semitic background, since in Hebrew the conjunction 'and' serves a great variety of functions. Other possible Semitic features are the use of 'everyone...not' for 'nobody'; hanging nouns, pronouns and participles, and the partitive use of 'out of', for example, 4.13, literally, 'he has given us out of his Spirit', when he means 'he has given us (a share of) his Spirit'. We may also mention the phrases 'doing the truth' (1.6), 'believing in the Name' (3.23), and 'shutting up one's bowels' in the sense of refusing to have compassion (3.17).

But some recent scholars have suggested that all three Johannines are constructed according to the elaborate rules of Graeco-Roman rhetoric. Thus Watson has argued that 1 John's repetitions are deliberately designed to make his message more effective. Far from being boring, 'the highly repetitive and emphatic nature of 1 John is one of its striking, yet unappreciated features' (1993, p. 99). He offers as an example 1 Jn 2.12-14—a strange passage consisting of six solemn admonitions addressed in turn to 'children', 'fathers', and 'young men'. Each group is addressed twice, with a change of tense in the verb. Scholars have puzzled whether these are people of different age-groups or different stages of Christian development, or whether, by a kind of poetic licence, they might be addressed to all believers as they develop in maturity in their Christian life. Some commentators have even suggested that we have two drafts of the same material.

Watson (1989) proposes that this is an example of the rhetorical figures of *distributio, conduplicatio* and *expolitio* ('distribution', 'reduplication', 'polishing'). In v. 12 the author addresses the whole group as 'children'; next he addresses two sub-groups, 'fathers' and 'young men' (*distributio*). Then he repeats his admonitions with an elegant variation in the word for 'children' and a change of tense (*conduplicatio*). He also varies his reasons for addressing the groups (*expolitio*).

The whole passage, Watson claims, is formally a *digressio* (digression), which serves an emotional function in praising the audience and creating goodwill after the author's initial establishment of his premises and refutation of opponents. But similar repetitions occur regularly in the Hebrew Bible (e.g. Ps. 148.12), and one wonders whether much is gained by offering such sophisticated names to this obscure passage. Classical rhetoric hardly seems to be the key to 1 John's style.

4. *Written or Oral Sources?*

Other scholars have sought to explain 1 John's peculiar structure and syntax by theories of sources. In 1907 E. von Dobschütz isolated four pairs of antithetical statements in 1 Jn 2.28–3.12 which he suggested were derived from a Hellenistic source which had been expanded with hortatory material. Bultmann went further. In a long article in the *Festgabe für Adolf Jülicher* (1927) he identified 26 antithetical pairs (or triplets), which he believed came from a 'gnostic' environment. Bultmann, like Dobschütz, argued that the main source (*Vorlage* or *Grundschrift*) has been split up by the author of 1 John and interspersed with homiletic or hortatory material. Bultmann's theory has been strongly criticized by Brown. Apart from questions over the proposed gnostic background, the chief problem is why, if the author had a coherent source before him, did he break it up so unsatisfactorily and scatter the antithetical sayings? Similar problems arise with the theory of W. Nauck, who in *Die Tradition und der Charakter des ersten Johannesbriefes* (1957) argued that the postulated 'source' was composed by the author of 1 John himself. But who would mutilate their own work in this way? There are also many uncertainties as to what was in the original *Vorlage*, and what is redaction.

In 1966 J.C. O'Neill argued that 1 John incorporates twelve poetic admonitions from a Jewish source. But this postulated source is too hypothetical to win credence, and, besides some odd interpretations, the theory involves excising phrases to provide the poetic structures. Both Nauck and O'Neill have done a service in highlighting 1 John's *Jewish* background. They had the advantage, not available to Dobschütz and Bultmann (in his original article), of the newly published Dead Sea Scrolls with all that they have to contribute to our understanding of first-century Judaism.

If the specific source theories of these authors have not won many adherents, the distinctions they made between different kinds of material in 1 John have been widely accepted. Two main types have been identified: (a) didactic or apodeictic, that is, quasi-credal state-ments of common belief, and (b) hortatory or homiletic material. But sometimes the author seems to shift from one type of statement to the other, and it is not always clear to which category some sentences belong. Grayston (1984) therefore suggests that 1 John has more than one author—a group of Christian leaders who composed an initial agreed statement (1.1–2.11), and a main writer who used and expanded this statement. Others see the variations in style as due to a single author's dual purpose: first, to state Christian truth and correct error; and second, to encourage his community (so Schnackenburg [1992]). The case for multiple authorship or specific identifiable sources has not been proved; nevertheless, it remains probable that our present text does incorporate material from a variety of sources.

In an important study O.A. Piper (1947) drew attention to the extent to which the author draws on common tradition shared between him-self and his readers, for example, the love command. Terms like 'antichrist', 'chrism' and 'God's seed' are introduced without explana-tion, presuming that the readers are familiar with them. There are fre-quent references to 'what you know' or 'what you have heard from the beginning', as well as direct professions of faith (e.g. 4.2). Piper reckons that there are at least 30 passages where reference to a com-mon faith is certain, as well as around 20 other possible examples. He argues that the author is drawing on his own oral teaching. Piper does not preclude the idea of some pre-formed material (e.g. 1.6-10 with its 'hymnic' structure), but he strongly argues that there is no *written* source; only *oral* materials lie behind the text. Similar ideas were put forward by Dodd (1946), who believed that the author is drawing on the church's basic *kerygma* or tradition, though he cites it in a 'gnosticizing' and 'Johannine' form. The idea of an oral tradition behind 1 John, either in the author's own preaching or in the church's *catechesis*, has much to commend it. But how far does the teaching of 1 John conform to mainstream Christian tradition? Many scholars have postulated Hellenistic-Gnostic affinities.

5. *The Background of 1 John*

In the 1930s Dodd suggested that Gnosticism formed an important element in the background to 1 John. He took as an example 'This is the message we heard from him, "God is light" ' (1.5). The author speaks as if he is giving his audience a well-known axiom. But where in the Gospels, Dodd asks, do we find the sentiment 'God is light'? It occurs in a Hellenistic pagan writing from Egypt—the *Hermetic Cor-*

pus (*CH* 1.6) where the god Poimandres declares, 'I am that light, Nous your God' (*Nous*, i.e. 'Mind', 'Intelligence', 'Reason'). Similar thoughts are found in Philo, a Jewish first-century writer much influenced by Greek philosophy: 'God is light…and not only light but the archetype of every other light' (*Somn.* 1.75). The *Hermetic Corpus* lays stress on knowledge of God as the source of salvation, and on ideas of 'seeing' God mystically, of rebirth, and of being identified with God. Dodd also cited parallels to 1 John's striking use of *sperma*, 'seed', and *chrisma*, 'anointing' in Gnosticism (1937: 147-53).

The discovery of a library of Coptic gnostic texts in 1945 confirmed Dodd's hunch that the concepts of divine 'seed' and 'anointing' are thoroughly at home in Gnosticism. The *Gospel of Philip* knows 'chrism' as a 'mystery' alongside baptism and eucharist. Couched in typically obscure language the text states: 'It is from water and fire and light that the son of the bridal chamber came into being. The fire is the chrism, the light is the fire' (2.3, NHL 140). Other texts which speak of a spiritual chrism include the *Pistis Sophia* and the *Gospel of Truth*; the latter mentions also 'the light which is perfect and filled with the seed of the Father' (1.3, NHL 49). The idea of divine seed impregnating Silence, who gave birth to *Nous*, is attested as 'gnostic' by Irenaeus in his *Refutation of Heresies* (*Adv. Haer.* 1.1.1 and 1.11.1). It is not surprising that a number of scholars today, including most notably Vouga (1988), see Gnosticism as an important factor in 1 John's background.

At first sight the parallels between 1 John and the Nag Hammadi texts are impressive: but when one examines the material in its fuller context, one is struck by the real differences between their theology and 1 John's. The whole thought-system presupposed by Valentinian Gnosticism is vast and complex, and quite alien to 1 John's. Nearly all the texts are later than any plausible date for 1 John: the *Pistis Sophia* and *Gospel of Truth*, for example, are probably second century CE, the *Gospel of Philip* probably later third century CE. Rather than being a source for Johannine thought, these texts were likely influenced by it. Is there any other possible source nearer to hand?

The metaphor of God as light is found already in the Hebrew Bible (e.g. Ps. 27.1; 36.9), though without 1 John's sharp light–dark dichotomy and underlying dualism. Closer parallels are provided by the Dead Sea Scrolls (first discovered in 1947). These are the writings of a Jewish group who separated themselves from their fellow Jews to live a life of asceticism, prayer and community at Qumran, by the Dead Sea. They date from before 70 CE. The most striking parallels to 1 John cluster in the *Manual of Discipline* or *Community Rule* (1QS), which makes continual contrasts between good and evil, light and dark, truth and falsehood. This text divides humanity into two camps, the 'sons of light' and the 'sons of darkness'. God has appointed two spirits for them, the 'Spirit of Truth' and the 'Spirit of Falsehood' (or 'Injustice'). 'Those born of truth spring from a fountain of light, but those born of injustice spring from a source of darkness. All the children of righteousness are ruled by the Prince of Light and walk in the ways of light, but all the children of injustice are ruled by the Angel of Darkness and walk in the ways of darkness. The Angel of Darkness leads all the children of righteousness astray...' (1 QS III.18-22, trans. Vermes [1998]). One is immediately reminded of 1 John's references to the 'Spirit of Truth' and the 'Spirit of Error' (4.6), and of its dualistic framework generally. The similarities of thought are not confined to 1 John, but extend also to the Gospel of John (cf. Brown in Stendahl 1958).

In both the Qumran texts and 1 John the dualism is moral and eschatological rather than absolute, as in Zoroastrianism (where good and evil contend as equal powers). God is in control; indeed in Johannine theology victory has already been won (1 Jn 5.4; cf. Jn 16.33). Qumran dualism also differs from the dualism of developed Gnosticism in that God, not a demiurge, is creator, and creation is good.

The Qumran texts stress the unity or 'community' (Heb. *yaḥad*) of their members; we may compare the *koinōnia*, or fellowship, of 1 John. They emphasize the need for confession of sin, witness, enlightenment from God, and the cleansing work of the Spirit of Truth (1 QS IV). All these features have parallels in the Johannine corpus. The Qumran covenanters are taught to love their 'brothers' as themselves and to succour the poor, needy and strangers (CD VI.20-21). 'Brothers' here means members of the community. A particularly interesting parallel concerns the Covenanters' use of the term 'idols'. Any member who 'walking among the idols of his heart...sets up before himself his stumbling-block of sin so that he may backslide' is cursed (1 QS II.11-12, trans. Vermes [1998]). It has been plausibly suggested that the strange final warning of 1 Jn 5.21 refers not to pagan images, but to these 'idols of the heart'—sinful thoughts which lead to backsliding and ultimately apostasy.

In studying the Johannine literature and the Scrolls one observes many other similarities of language and thought; but there are also significant differences. The Qumran texts contain no parallel to 1 John's 'chrism' and 'seed', or the concept of being 'born of God'. They frequently refer to the Covenant, never explicitly mentioned in 1 John. They await a future messiah (or messiahs), whereas the Johannines affirm that the messiah has already come. The Qumran community is hierarchically organized with strict rules and penalties for misconduct, whereas the Johannine community seems informally structured. Qumran piety is centred round the Jewish Law and its correct interpretation, whereas Johannine faith focuses on Jesus as Son of God and messiah. On the other hand, we must remember that a large range of texts survive from Qumran reflecting the life of the community—rule books, hymns, prayers, florilegia and exegetical works—whereas for the community believed to lie behind 1 John we have very limited evidence.

Some scholars (e.g. J.H. Charlesworth [1972]) have been so impressed at the parallels between Johannine and Qumran thought that they believe the Johannine writer(s) may have been directly influenced by Qumran. But most are more cautious. Brown believes that the Scrolls provide better parallels to Johannine thought than Hellenistic-Gnostic texts cited by Dodd and Bultmann, but at the same time he argues they cannot be seen as a direct source for John's thought (in Charlesworth 1972, p. 7).

We may sum up by saying that the Scrolls illuminate a Palestinian-Jewish background to 1 John, but they form only part of its milieu. 1 John clearly owes much to the Hebrew Bible, and there are also parallels in Gnosticism and extra-biblical Jewish literature. *The Testaments of the Twelve Patriarchs* have an ethical earnestness strongly reminiscent of 1 John: they stress the importance of love (e.g. *T. Benj.* 3). They too speak of the Spirit of Truth and the Spirit of Error, and the forensic role of the former (*T. Jud.* 20). But there are problems in using these texts as a source for Johannine thought because of possible Christian editing. The Qumran texts by contrast not only predate the Johannines but are also free from Christian interference. Thus they are especially significant. The Johannine writings are not unique in the New Testament in showing affinities with Qumran thought: light/darkness dualism is found in other New Testament texts (e.g. Ephesians).

This leads us to an important point. We have so far concentrated on potential backgrounds in Jewish and Hellenistic-Gnostic thought, but we should never forget the Johannines' debt to basic Christian tradition. Dodd himself drew attention to phrases and ideas which 1 John shares with the *kerygma* of the Synoptic Gospels, especially Matthew (1946, pp. xxxviii-xxxix). More significant, perhaps, is the possible debt of 1 John to the Gospel of John (discussed further in Chapter 4 §4). The interesting question of the relation of 1 John's thought to that of the remaining New Testament writings (e.g. Paul, James, 1 Peter) is rarely touched on, though we shall return to it in Chapter 9 (esp. §§2-3).

6. Conclusions

1 John has a loose structure and a distinctive style. It is not a letter in the normal sense of the term, and its designation as such by the Church Fathers may be because there was no other clear category in which to place it. Nor is it a 'tract', in the sense that the writings of the Hermetic Corpus or the Nag Hammadi Library are tracts. It contains homiletic material, but is clearly more than a written sermon. In its hortatory sections, it shows affinities with Testamentary literature, but it is neither a 'testament' nor a philosophical treatise masquerading as a letter. It has striking parallels in the Qumran *Manual of Discipline*, but is less legal and prescriptive than this rule-book. Nevertheless, it may have been designed for use in a particular Christian community.

Suggestions for written sources (Bultmann, Nauck, O'Neill) have not proved convincing. The memorable, rhythmic, antithetical style and frequent repetitions suggest the inclusion of material designed for oral delivery and perhaps memorization. An intriguing hypothesis is that of Grayston that it might have been intended as an encheiridion or handbook. Ancient examples of this genre (not discussed by Grayston) are Epictetus's *Encheiridion*, summarizing the ethical teaching of his *Diatribes* or *Discourses* (which also survive) and Augustine's *Enchiridion*, which he made himself as a summary of his teaching. If 1 John were a summary of the oral teaching of a great master, perhaps originally a native Semitic speaker, this could explain its hortatory tone, its loose structure and ambiguities, its repetitions and even its occasional references to a specific situation (retained because of their wider applicability). However, we have to ask how widely known in the Jewish world was the specific genre of the *encheiridion*? Whatever its literary form, 1 John is geared to the needs of readers who share the author's basic religious presuppositions and commitment. Its primary purpose seems to be to keep them on the right course in their journey of faith.

FURTHER READING

Genre, structure and style:

Commentaries by Brown (1982), Dodd (1946), Grayston (1984), Houlden (1973), Perkins (1979), Rensberger (1997), Schnackenburg (1992), Smalley (1984).

A. Deissmann, *Light from the Ancient East* (ET; London: Hodder & Stoughton, 1910, esp. p. 242). Same view in 4th rev. edn. (ET; London: Hodder & Stoughton,

1927 and Grand Rapids, MI: Baker Book House, 1978). See esp. p. 244.

C.H. Dodd, 'The First Epistle of John and the Forth Gospel', *BJRL* 21 (1937), pp. 129-56.

F.O. Francis, 'The Form and Function of the Opening and Closing Paragraphs of James and 1 John', *ZNW* 61 (1970), pp. 110-26.

W.G. Kümmel, *Introduction to the New Testament* (ET; London: SCM Press, 1975).

J.C. Thomas, 'The Literary Structure of 1 John', *NovT* 40 (1998), pp. 369-81.

F. Vouga, 'La réception de la théologie johannique dans les épîtres', in J.-D. Kaestli, J.-M. Poffet and J. Zumstein (eds.), *La communauté johannique et son histoire* (Geneva: Labor et Fides, 1990), pp. 283-302, esp. pp. 258-88.

Rhetorical analysis:

H.-J. Klauck, 'Zur rhetorischen Analyse der Johannesbriefe', *ZNW* 81 (1990), pp. 205-24.

F. Vouga, 'La réception de la théologie johannique dans les épîtres', in J.-D. Kaestli, J.-M. Poffet and J. Zumstein (eds.), *La communauté johannique et son histoire* (Geneva: Labor et Fides, 1990), pp. 283-302, esp. pp. 287-91.

D.F. Watson, '1 John 2:12-14 as *Distributio, Conduplicatio, and Expolitio*: A Rhetorical Understanding', *JSNT* 35 (1989), pp. 97-110.

—'Amplification Techniques in 1 John: The Interaction of Rhetorical Style and Invention', *JSNT* 51 (1993), pp. 99-123.

Sources:

Commentaries by Brown (1982; esp. pp. 760-61 on Bultmann's reconstucted source), Marshall (1978; esp. p. 30 on Nauck).

R. Bultmann, 'Analyse des ersten Johannesbriefes', in R. Bultmann and H. Freiterr van Soden (eds.), *Festgabe für Adolf Jülicher zum 70. Geburstag* (Tübingen: J.C.B. Mohr [Paul Siebeck], 1927), pp. 138-58. Reprinted in E. Dinkler (ed.), *Exegetica: Aufsätze zur Erforschung des Neuen Testaments* (Tübingen: J.C.B. Mohr [Paul Siebeck], 1967), pp. 105-23.

W. Nauck, *Die Tradition und der Charakter des ersten Johannesbriefes* (WUNT 3; Tübingen: Mohr Siebeck, 1957).

J.C. O'Neill, *The Puzzle of 1 John* (London: SPCK, 1966).

O.A. Piper, '1 John and the Didache of the Primitive Church', *JBL* 66 (1947), pp. 437-51.

E. von Dobschütz, 'Johanneische Studien I', *ZNW* 8 (1907), pp. 1-8.

Background:

J.H. Charlesworth, 'A Critical Comparison of the Dualism in 1QS 2:13-4:26 and the Dualism Contained in the Gospel of John', in J.H. Charlesworth (ed.), *John and Qumran* (London: Chapman, 1972), pp. 76106, esp. pp. 101-104. Reissued as *John and the Dead Sea Scrolls* (New York: Crossroad, 1990).

—*The Old Testament Pseudepigrapha*. I. *Apocalyptic Literature and Testaments* (London: Darton, Longman & Todd, 1983). For *Testaments of the Twelve Patriarchs*).

C.H. Dodd, 'The First Epistle of John and the Fourth Gospel', *BJRL* 21 (1937), pp. 129-56.

F. García Martínez, *The Dead Sea Scrolls Translated: The Qumran Texts in English* (Leiden: E.J. Brill; ET, Grand Rapids: Eerdmans, 2nd edn, 1996).

J.M. Robinson (ed.), *The Nag Hammadi Library* (San Francisco: Harper & Row, 1977).

K. Stendahl (ed.), *The Scrolls and the New Testament* (London: SCM Press, 1958), esp. ch. 12.

G. Vermes, *The Complete Dead Sea Scrolls in English* (London: Penguin, 1998; New York: Allen Lane, 1997).

F. Vouga, 'The Johannine School: A Gnostic Tradition in Primitive Christianity?', *Bib* 69 (1988), pp. 371-85.

Relation to the Gospel of John:

Commentaries by Brooke (1912; esp. pp. i-xxvii—with much citation in Greek), Brown (1982; esp. pp. 32-35 with chart II, pp. 757-59), Culpepper (1998), Grayston (1984; esp pp. 12-14), Schnackenburg (1992; esp. pp. 32-39); Smith (1991, esp. pp. 26-30); Strecker (1996, esp. pp. xxxv-xlii).

Chapter Four

WHO WROTE THE JOHANNINES AND WHEN?

1. *Patristic Evidence*

The question 'who wrote the Johannines?' cannot be separated from
that of the authorship of the Gospel of John and Revelation. From the
fourth century CE all these writings were ascribed in the manuscripts
to 'John'. The fact that no further identification is given suggests that
the most famous New Testament John is intended, namely John, the
son of Zebedee. It is likely that these titles are older than their first
attestation; indeed there are hints that the chief 'Johannine' writings
were attributed to the Apostle as early as c. 200 CE.

The evidence is complex, and for the views of some early witnesses
we have to depend on summaries in later sources, which may not be
reliable. The situation is complicated by the fact that John is a common name, and even when 'John' is further defined as 'the disciple of
the Lord', one still cannot be sure that the Apostle is intended. Moreover, legend-making was rife in the early patristic period, as can be
seen from the various apocryphal Acts, and there was a strong desire
to attribute as many writings as possible to apostolic figures. With
these cautions in mind we review the patristic evidence.

An early witness is Irenaeus of Lyons (died c. 200), who more than
once refers to 'John, the Lord's disciple', who 'reclined on his breast',
whom he takes to be the author of the Gospel of John, Revelation, and
1 John. He may not have been the first to do so: the Gnostic Ptolemaeus, whom Irenaeus quotes, ascribed at least the Gospel Prologue
to 'John', and the orthodox Father Theophilus of Antioch (? c. 180)
quotes from the Gospel of John as by 'John' (though he does not identify him as an apostle). Irenaeus clearly attests developed traditions
about this John: he believed that he wrote his Gospel after the other
three in his old age, and he associates it with Ephesus where, he says,
John lived into the reign of Trajan (98–117). Irenaeus also quotes from
what we now call 1 and 2 John, but he treats these as a single letter.

Another important witness is the Muratorian Canon. This list of

New Testament writings is generally believed to have been composed at Rome c. 190–200 (though some favour an Eastern origin and a fourth-century date). This ascribes the Gospel, *two* Epistles and the Apocalypse to 'John', and quotes the opening of 1 John in defence of the Gospel of John, assuming its author to be an eye-witness. This text seems to be reacting against doubts concerning the orthodoxy of the Gospel of John, possibly because it was so much used by Gnostics. Clement of Alexandria (c. 150–215) quotes from the 'greater Epistle of John' (presumably 1 John), and Tertullian (c. 160–225) ascribes 1 John, the Gospel and the Apocalypse to the Apostle John. Other writers from the third to fifth centuries echo similar views.

Based on this patristic evidence a seemingly attractive hypothesis has been put forward that John, the son of Zebedee—one of Jesus' original twelve apostles—in later life migrated from Palestine to Ephesus, had a spell of exile on Patmos (where he wrote the Apocalypse), returning to Ephesus, where he composed the Gospel and 1–3 John. Polycrates, bishop of Ephesus (c. 189–98) says that 'John' died at Ephesus; his tomb was shown there in antiquity (Culpepper 1994, chs. 4–6; Brown 1966, 1982).

But will this hypothesis stand up to close examination? The New Testament gives no hint that the Apostle John ever went to Ephesus. Mk 10.39 predicts the martyrdom of the two sons of Zebedee: James, we know, was martyred early and there was a tradition (incompatible with Irenaeus's testimony) that John also died young (see Barrett 1978: 103, citing Papias and other authorities). Moreover, only Revelation out of all the New Testament 'Johannine' writings actually claims to be by someone called John, and even this gives no hint that its author was an apostle. It has been strongly argued (Gunther 1980) that its author was an Asian prophet, who erroneously got identified, first with John the son of Zebedee, and later with the author of the Gospel of John and the Johannine Epistles. The Gospel of John and 1 John are both strictly anonymous; 2–3 John's claim to be written by a 'presbyter' will be discussed later.

Sometimes it is alleged that Irenaeus's testimony is of great value since in his youth he lived in Asia Minor and knew Polycarp, bishop of Smyrna, who reputedly knew John the Apostle. But it must be noted that Polycarp himself never attributes the authorship of the Gospel of John or 1–3 John to the son of Zebedee. Ignatius (who wrote to the Ephesians and other churches in Asia) is also silent on this, and says nothing about any connection between John and Ephesus.

The status of 2 and 3 John is especially doubtful. These letters were omitted from the Syriac text of the New Testament until the fifth to sixth centuries, which strongly suggests that apostolic authorship was not attributed to them. None of the writers we have earlier cited mentions 3 John, and some refer to just one letter by John. The great biblical scholar Origen (c. 185–254) doubted the authenticity of 2 and 3 John. Eusebius admits that their canonicity was disputed. Although Jerome (c. 342–420) himself believed that all three Johannine letters were by the Apostle, he too attests the belief that 2 and 3 John were by a different author, whom he calls 'John the Presbyter'. The idea of two men called John, both living at Ephesus, is found in a number of other authors (Lieu 1986, ch. 1), and some scholars have conjectured that the Epistles and Gospel were written by this second John (cf. Hengel 1989; Bauckham 1993). Others, however, dispute his very existence.

All this suggests that the patristic testimony concerning 'apostolic' authorship of 1–3 John should be regarded with reservation, and that we must take also careful account of the internal evidence.

2. *Internal Evidence*

2 and 3 John claim to be written by a presbyter or 'elder', a term probably denoting ecclesiastical office. It is unlikely an apostle would so designate himself, especially if he were seeking to assert his authority in matters of hospitality or doctrine. This means that if 1 John is by the same author as 2–3 John, it is unlikely to be by an apostle. Recently, however, the common authorship of 1–3 John has been strongly challenged. Several eminent scholars believe that 2–3 John were written by a different author from 1 John, and some even separate the authorship of the two shorter letters. A good case has been made for regarding 2 John as dependent on both 1 John and 3 John, but this is compatible with either common authorship for 2–3 John (so Grayston 1984) or separate authorship (so Bultmann 1973). In neither case do we get much help over the authorship of 1 John. The canonical history of the letters sheds little light on the problem, except to show that 2 and 3 John are not a 'pair of inseparable twins' (the phrase is Judith Lieu's, 1986, p. 50).

The presence of Semitic turns of expression in all three Johannines points to an author of Jewish origin (Schnackenburg 1992, pp. 8-93; cf. Brown 1982, p. 24). This would be compatible with authorship by John the Apostle, but does not demand it. It has sometimes been argued that the apparent claim to eye-witness in 1 Jn 1.1-4 points to apostolic authorship. But there were other eye-witnesses besides the son of Zebedee! In any case, in spite of the emphatic verbs of perception, these verses are more plausibly read as a claim to continuity with apostolic tradition (cf. Loader 1992, p. 4). The case for John the son of Zebedee as the author of 1 John has to rest on a threefold identification: (a) the epistolary writer(s) with the author of John's Gospel; (b) the Gospel author with the 'beloved disciple'; (c) the 'beloved disciple' with the son of Zebedee—all assumptions which must be discussed.

3. 1 John and the Gospel of John

Was 1 John written by the same person as the Gospel of John? The style and thought of the two writings are so similar that numerous scholars have argued that the same man must have composed both (see Guthrie 1970, pp. 876-81; Marshall 1978, 1982, pp. 1096-97). Yet as early as the nineteenth century H.J. Holzmann pointed out differences in both theology and style. His arguments were taken up and amplified by Dodd (1937). In spite of various attempts (e.g. by Brooke 1912, Howard 1947 and Wilson 1948) to demonstrate a single mind behind these two texts, the idea of separate authorship has grown in popularity, and is today favoured by such scholars as Grayston, Houlden, Lieu and, more hesitatingly, Schnackenburg. The evidence is highly complex. On the one hand 1 John and the Gospel have a large stock of similar vocabulary and turns of expression, and a common fund of distinctive theological ideas. On the other hand, there are subtle differences of style (e.g. in the use of particles, prepositions and participles). There are also different nuances in theology (e.g. over the atonement, parousia, Spirit). One problem in reaching a conclusion is knowing how much allowance to make for possible variations within the style of a single author and for developments of thought in response to a fresh situation. Also John's Gospel and 1 John belong to different genres, the gospel-form being essentially narrative and epistles hortatory.

This last difference is not so great as one might suppose, since John's Gospel contains much theological discourse similar in style to the hortatory material of 1 John. In fact, one of the most interesting stylistic observations that have been made is that 1 John stands especially close to the more reflective parts of the Gospel of John, notably John 15–17 (cf. Brown 1982, esp. pp. 108-109). This raises a fresh question. Is the Gospel itself a literary unity? Numerous scholars have pointed out *aporiae* or awkward transitions suggesting seams between traditions or, possibly, different sources. It is widely believed that the Fourth Gospel had a long literary development, and went through more than one edition (so Brown 1966–70; Lindars 1972; Schnackenburg 1968–82). Chapters 13–17 are among the material frequently attributed to the Gospel's (hypothetical) second edition. Could it be that the author of 1 John was a reviser or editor of the Gospel? Such a hypothesis is difficult either to prove or to refute.

We now turn to the enigma of the 'beloved disciple'. This figure appears only in the Gospel of John's passion and resurrection narrative (13.23; 19.26-27; 20.2-10; 21.7, 20-23). He is portrayed as specially close to Jesus, being present at the Last Supper and the crucifixion. Chapter 21 (probably an appendix) appears to identify him as author: 'This is the disciple who is bearing witness to these things, and who has written these things; and we know that his witness is true' (21.24). While some scholars suppose that 'these things' refers only to the resurrection appearance just described, it is much more plausible that the phrase is intended to denote the whole Gospel. In other words the author(s) of Jn 21.24 are promoting 'the disciple whom Jesus loved' as the authority behind John's Gospel. He is its 'ideal' author (so Bauckham 1993).

But who wrote this verse? The use of the first person plural suggests a group. It has been plausibly suggested that it alludes to a Johannine school, circle or community, gathered round their leader the 'beloved disciple' (so Culpepper 1975; Cullmann 1976; Brown 1979). 'School', 'circle' and 'community' are not exact synonyms: 'school' implies a more formal structure like an ancient philosophical school, 'circle' a more loosely organized group, and 'community' a body of people sharing a common social and religious life. John's Gospel never reveals the identity of this 'beloved disciple'. He appears to be one of the seven fishermen listed in Jn 21.2; he *could* have been one of the sons of Zebedee mentioned there, but he could equally have been one of the unnamed disciples. Some identify him with the Apostle John; some with the 'Elder' John (Hengel [1989] supposes that he reflects both at once). Others have argued that he must be regarded as strictly anonymous—an otherwise unknown early Christian leader (so Cullmann 1976). Bultmann (1971, p. 484) saw him as a purely ideal figure. While dogmatism is out of place, the most likely conclusion is that he was a real person known to those in his own circle, who played a significant role in putting the Gospel into its present form. The internal evidence is insufficient to substantiate the patristic identification of him with either John, the son of Zebedee, or the shadowy 'John the Elder'. Whether or not this figure is identical with the author(s) of 1–3 John is doubtful. The idea of a Johannine community with a distinctive theology and style, and more than one theological writer, remains the best explanation of both the similarities and dissimilarities of the Johannine corpus.

4. *The Date of the Johannines*

Any attempt to date 1–3 John is fraught with difficulty because of the lack of objective criteria. There are no allusions to datable events (e.g. the accession of a Roman emperor), or to datable individuals. None of the persons named—Gaius, Demetrius, Diotrephes—is known from other sources (the first two are very common names in the Roman Empire, and attempts to identify them with other New Testament figures of the same name have been unsuccessful). Nor are allusions to church order much help in dating. If Diotrephes (or the Elder) were an emerging monarchic bishop, then this might point to a date late in the first century, contemporary with 1 *Clement* and possibly the Pastoral Epistles, or even as late as Ignatius (c. 110–140), that great enthusiast for the episcopate! But, as was seen in Chapter 2, a much more informal church order seems likely. Even this does not help much, since informal patterns seem to have continued alongside more structured ministries for many years. References to travelling missionaries occur in such chronologically diverse contexts as Paul's genuine letters, the Gospels of Matthew and Luke, and the *Didache* (? c. 90–120).

It might be supposed that the references to false teachers could aid dating. But scholars are unable to reach agreement on the identity of the opponents, opinions varying between Jews, Cerinthians, Docetists and Gnostics (cf. below, Chapter 5). Even if one of these groups could be securely identified as the 'opponents', a wide range of dates would still be possible.

The securest evidence for dating 1 John comes from external sources, notably citations in patristic writings. According to Eusebius the 'former Epistle of John' was used by Papias (? c. 130 CE). There are a number of possible echoes in Ignatius, Barnabas, Justin Martyr, Hermas and the *Epistle to Diognetus* (all probably second century CE). It is not certain whether 1 John was known to Polycarp (early second century). In his *Epistle to the Philippians*, in language very similar to 1 Jn 4.2-3 and 2 John 7, he writes: 'Everyone who does not confess that Jesus Christ has come in the flesh is an Antichrist; and whoever does not confess the witness of the cross is of the devil' (*Phil.* 7.1). While some scholars have argued that he is drawing on a common stock of vocabulary and ideas, it seems more probable that these words are dependent on 1 or 2 John (or both). All this suggests that 1 John was known in patristic circles in the *first half* of the second century. Earlier than this we cannot go with any confidence, since the alleged echoes in *1 Clement* are too doubtful to be of any use. The patristic citations, of course, provide only an *ante quem*: the Johannines might have been newly written when cited, or much older.

Could it be that 1–3 John were actually written before the Gospel of John? It has been argued that they present a more primitive *Christology*: for example, Jn 1.14 boldly identifies Jesus with the Logos, whereas 1 Jn 1.1 speaks more indirectly of 'the word of life'—and does so ambiguously, so that one cannot tell whether it is talking about Jesus personally or the gospel message. The Epistles, it has been argued, also presuppose a more primitive *soteriology*: they speak crudely of the blood of Jesus washing away sin (1 Jn 1.7), whereas the Gospel uses more subtle imagery (cf. Jn 19.34). 1 John expects an imminent parousia (e.g. 2.18), while the Gospel works mostly with a sophisticated 'realized' eschatology. 1 John seems to refer to the Spirit impersonally as an 'unction' (2.27), whereas the Gospel (or at least Jn 14–16) has a more developed doctrine of a personal Holy Spirit. All this evidence could point to a chronological priority of 1 John, as has been eloquently argued by Grayston (1984).

On the other hand theological simplicity does not necessarily mean chronological priority. The evidence is also consistent with the view that these Epistles represent a rearguard action by a conservative Christian, who has been distressed at the way some 'progressive' thinkers have taken certain Johannine concepts to extremes. His references to those who do not accept Jesus as the 'Christ come in the flesh' have been taken as polemic against 'docetic' thinkers who had concluded from the Gospel's affirmation of Jesus' divinity that he was not truly human. Similarly, the allusion to Jesus' blood washing away sin could be seen as a response to those who thought of his death merely as an example. But 1 John's Christology is by no means 'low': Jesus and the Father are frequently treated on an equal footing, and in many sentences it is ambiguous to which of these the author refers; at least one text may attribute divinity to Jesus (5.20). 1 John also contains several passages which *may* echo the Gospel, notably 2.7; 3.14 and 3.15 (cf. Jn 13.34; 5.24; 8.44). All this is consistent with the view that 1 John was written *after* the Gospel of John, as has been argued by many recent scholars, including Houlden (1973), Brown (1982), Marshall (1978) and Smalley (1984).

While no certainty is possible, the balance of the evidence favours the idea that 1 John was written after at least a first edition of the Gospel of John (so Schnackenburg 1992). But one cannot preclude that parts of the Gospel (e.g. the Prologue and ch. 21) were composed after

1 John was written. With that we shall have to be content. It should also be noted that the dating of the Gospel is itself controversial. While some scholars have supported an early date, most experts favour one late in the first century, after the split between Christianity and Judaism (c. 85–100 CE). The idea that 1 John was written to *accompany* the Gospel or as an explicit refutation of misunderstandings of it seems unlikely in view of the shortage of clear citations from it.

As for 2–3 John, the evidence is even more scanty. Some see the reference to a previous letter in 3 John 10 as an allusion to 2 John; more probably it refers to a lost letter. The fact that 3 John is written in a very simple style does not mean that it *must* be early. It seems plausible on literary grounds that 2 John is dependent on 3 John, but we have to admit no certainty is possible.

5. *Conclusions*

The results of this investigation have proved rather meagre. We do not know *who* wrote 1–3 John nor *when* they were written, nor even *in what order* they were written. It is still possible to argue for a common authorship of 1–3 John and the Gospel of John by John, the son of Zebedee, though this now seems unlikely. Little is gained from postulating Papias's 'Elder' John as author. 1 John might have been written before or after the Gospel, or between two editions of the Gospel, though a date after its main composition seems most likely. A plausible order for the Epistles is 3 John, 1 John, 2 John, but alternatives are possible. 1–3 John might be by one, two, or even three different authors. As for an absolute date, the Gospel and at least 1–2 John seem to be known to patristic writers by the second century CE; a date towards the end of the first century seems quite plausible. Whatever the chronology, the Gospel and all three Epistles are clearly related. The hypothesis of a Johannine 'school' or 'community' centred round the 'beloved disciple' has much to commend it.

FURTHER READING

Introductions to commentaries on 1–3 John by Brooke (1912), Brown (1982), Grayston (1984), Houlden (1973), Loader (1992), Marshall (1978), Schnackenburg (1992), Smalley (1984), Strecker (1996).

C.K. Barrett, *The Gospel According to St. John* (London: SPCK; Philadelphia: Westminster Press, 2nd edn, 1978), esp. pp. 59-62, 100-144.

R. Bauckham, 'The Beloved Disciple as Ideal Author', *JSNT* 49 (1993), pp. 21-44.

R.E. Brown, *The Gospel According to John* (AB, 29, 29A; 2 vols., Garden City, NY: Doubleday, 1966–70, esp. Introduction, section VII.

—*The Community of the Beloved Disciple* (New York: Paulist Press, 1979).

—An Introduction to the New Testament (AB Reference Library; New York: Doubleday, 1997).

R. Bultmann, *The Gospel of John: A Commentary* (ET; Oxford: Basil Blackwell, 1971).

—*The Johannine Epistles* (ET; Hermeneia; Philadelphia: Fortress, 1973).

O. Cullmann, *The Johannine Circle* (ET; London: SCM Press, 1976).

R.A. Culpepper, *The Johannine School* (Missoula, MT: Scholars Press, 1975).

—*John, the Son of Zebedee* (Columbia: University of South Carolina Press, 1994).

J.J. Gunther, 'Early Identifications of the Authorship of the Johannine Writings', *JEH* 31 (1980), pp. 407-27.

D. Guthrie, *New Testament Introduction* (Leicester: Apollos; Downers Grove, IL: InterVarsity Press, 4th edn, 1990), pp. 858-900.

M. Hengel, *The Johannine Question* (ET; London: SCM Press; Philadelphia: Trinity Press International, 1989).

L.T. Johnson, *The Writers of the New Testament: An Interpretation* (London: SCM Press, rev. edn, 1999), esp. pp. 561-62.

J. Lieu, *The Second and Third Epistles of John* (Edinburgh: T. & T. Clark, 1986).

B. Lindars, *The Gospel of John* (NCB; London: Oliphants, MMS, 1972), esp. pp. 50-51

I.H. Marshall, 'Johannine Theology' and 'John, Epistles of', *ISBE*, II (1982), pp. 1081-98.

R. Schnackenburg, *The Gospel According to St. John* (HTKNT, 4.1; 3 vols.; ET; London: Burns & Oats; New York: Seabury, 1968–82).

On style and language:

C.H. Dodd, 'The First Epistle of John and the Fourth Gospel', *BJRL* 21 (1937), pp. 129-56.

W.F. Howard, 'The Common Authorship of the Johannine Gospel and Epistles', *JTS* 48 (1947), pp. 12-25.

W.G. Wilson, 'An Examination of the Linguistic Evidence Adduced against the Unity of Authorship of the First Epistle of John and the Fourth Gospel', *JTS* 49 (1948), pp. 147-56.

Chapter Five

CHRISTOLOGY AND THE 'OPPONENTS'

1. *Introduction*

1 John was especially valued in antiquity for its 'orthodox' Christology. Yet curiously it contains no systematic exposition of doctrine: doctrinal beliefs are assumed rather than argued. The author deals with them as they arise, in no discernible order, but as suits his rhetorical purpose. Many scholars have seen this purpose as polemical—to attack false teachers or dissidents. R.A. Whitacre (1982) sees 1 John as continuing, at a different level, a polemical stance found already in the Gospel. P. Bonnard goes so far as to call all three Johannines 'fundamentally polemical from beginning to end' (1983: 14). Numerous attempts have been made to identify the 'opponents' in question: charismatics, Jews, Cerinthians, Docetists, and Gnostics have all been suggested. Scholars have assiduously sought to delineate their errant ethics and Christology by careful analysis of the text; some have postulated more than one group of adversaries. Elaborate hypotheses have been put forward about the history of the Johannine community and the fate of the various groups. The present chapter challenges the view that the primary purpose of the Johannines was polemical, and seeks a more positive understanding of their Christology.

2. *Methodology*

In the search for 'opponents' interest has naturally centred on 1 John, the longest of the three Epistles, with the fullest ethical and christological content. Attention has already been drawn (above Chapter 3 §3) to the author's fondness for certain kinds of conditional ('if') clauses and general statements of the type, 'anyone who does x is y'. These have regularly been interpreted as polemical in character. Thus when the author writes, 'If we say that we have fellowship with him and walk in the darkness we are liars' (1.6), it is assumed he is 'getting at' a group who claim a special fellowship with God. Similarly the state-

ments, 'The one who says "I know him" and does not keep his commandments is a liar' (2.4), and 'Nobody who remains in him sins' (3.6)
and 'Everyone who hates his "brother" is a murderer' (3.15), are taken
to refer to these adversaries who claim to 'know' God and be sinless,
while blatantly breaking God's law and hating their fellow Christians.
The fullest reconstructions of opponents' views made on these lines
are by Brown (1982, pp. 762-63) and Painter (1986).

The problem with the method is that it fails to allow sufficiently for
the author's vigorous and idiosyncratic 'upfront' style. He loves antithesis: 'If we say that we have no sin, we deceive ourselves and the
truth is not in us. If we confess our sins, he is faithful and just to
forgive us our sins and cleanse us from all unrighteousness' (1.8-9).
Those who see this as polemic fail to take the 'we' seriously. Rather
than attacking a specific group of 'opponents' who claim to be sinless,
the author is warning his own community that they must not make
this claim. Moreover, it is usually assumed that 1 John's distinctive
vocabulary is drawn from the 'opponents', notably such terms as
koinōnia, 'fellowship', *chrisma*, 'unction' and *sperma*, 'seed' (of God).
Hence Painter suggests that the 'opponents' are perfectionist charismatics, who claim a special fellowship with God and a divine anointing which preserves them from sin. It is true that the words
'fellowship' and 'unction' are not found in the Gospel of John, nor is
'seed' with reference to God, but there is no reason why, if 1 John is
by a different author, he should not use different vocabulary; even if
the two texts are by the same man, not enough of his writing survives
to enable us with confidence to say that certain vocabulary *must* have
come from an outside source. The author nowhere attributes to *opponents* claims to have 'community' or spiritual 'anointing'; rather he
reassures his readers that this is what they themselves have (cf. 1.3;
2.20, 26). The idea that 1 John, in its ethical teaching, is attacking a
group of charismatic 'pneumatics' who profess to be sinless is ill-
founded. It is the author's own community for whom he claims special guidance from the Holy Spirit (cf. Jn 16.13).

3. *Christological Confessions and Controversies*

What of our author's christological statements? These first appear in
1 Jn 2.18-25, when he announces that it is the 'last hour' and adduces
as evidence that the expected 'Antichrist' has come in those who deny
Christ. He writes: 'Who is the liar but the one denying that Jesus is the
Christ? This is the Antichrist, the one denying the Father and the Son'
(2.22). It is clear from the context that he is speaking of a specific

group of Johannine Christians who have seceded from the community but who, he claims, never really belonged to it (2.19). 2 John also
seems to refer to specific opponents when it says, 'Many deceivers
have gone out into the world, who do not confess Jesus Christ coming
in the flesh. This is the deceiver and the Antichrist' (v. 7). It is unclear
whether these are the same group as in 1 John or a different one.
Many scholars interpret the reference to their 'going out into the
world' as referring to missionary activity; they also see 2 John 9 as
alluding indirectly to them: 'Anyone who goes ahead and does not
remain in Christ's teaching does not possess God'.

Another likely polemical passage in 1 John is that which speaks of
testing the spirits: 'By this you know the Spirit of God: every spirit
which confesses Jesus Christ having come in the flesh is from God.
And every spirit which does not confess Jesus is not from God' (4.2-3).
This statement too is in the context of a warning against the Antichrist.
It is reasonable to suppose that specific people are in mind. The
author's designation of them as 'false prophets' (4.1) as well as 'antichrists' suggest they were church leaders whose christological teaching he sees as erroneous. But it should be noted that he does not state
their teaching and then refute it with arguments; rather he discredits
his opponents by the use of pejorative language ('false prophets';
'antichrists').

The affirmation (5.6) that Jesus came by both water and blood is
also probably polemical. The author's strong insistence that Jesus did
not come by water alone, but by blood must be aimed at someone, or
some group, who denied this. We note the claim that it is the Spirit
which bears witness, and the Spirit is truth. 1 John also contains a
number of shorter christological affirmations, including the statements 'everyone who trusts that Jesus is the Christ is born from God'
(5.1); 'whoever confesses that Jesus is the Son of God, God remains in
that person, and that person in God' (4.15); and 'we have seen and
bear witness that the Father has sent the Son, the Saviour of the
world' (4.14). It is not so certain that these are polemical, since they
could also be read as positive teaching, seeking to strengthen readers
in the faith. The same applies to 1 John's final christological statement
in 5.20 (to be discussed below, §5).

4. *Attempts at Identifying the 'Opponents'*

Apart from 'charismatics', four main groups of 'opponents' have been
suggested. These overlap with one another in a quite complicated
way, but we shall try to deal with them as concisely as possible.

Jews and Jewish Christians

Early this century A. Wurm proposed that 1 John's opponents were Jews who denied Jesus' messiahship, a hypothesis revived by O'Neill (1966). In support of this may be cited the reference to those who deny that Jesus is the Christ (2.22), where the Greek could mean 'those who deny that the messiah is Jesus', and the positive affirmation that Jesus is the Son of God (4.15), where 'Son of God' could be a messianic title. But it is most unlikely that practising religious Jews would have been members, or former members, of a fully Christian community, as the 'opponents' must be. Nor can the 'opponents' be 'judaizers', that is, Jewish Christians seeking to maintain their former practices, for there is no polemic against the Law, or circumcision, or other observances, such as one finds in other New Testament Epistles. The author's polemic is christological. We should therefore be looking for a group who fail to adopt what the author would see as an 'orthodox' *interpretation* of Jesus' sonship and messiahship. We therefore turn to some groups criticized in the early church as having 'unorthodox' Christologies.

Cerinthians

Cerinthus was a well-known Gnostic teacher (c. 100 CE), denounced by the second-century Church Fathers as a heretic. Eusebius cites from Irenaeus a story about Cerinthus and John. The two were in a bath-house at Ephesus. As soon as John knew that Cerinthus was there, he ran out for fear that the building might collapse as a divine punishment for Cerinthus's heresy (Irenaeus, *Adv. Haer.* 3.3.4). This apocryphal anecdote (a similar story is told about the gnostic Basilides and John) presupposes that John and Cerinthus are theologically opposed. Irenaeus and Jerome assume that the Gospel of John was written against Cerinthus, who is said to have believed that 'Christ' descended on a purely human Jesus at his baptism, making him divine, and departed from him at death. It has been suggested that the confession that Jesus has come *in the flesh* may be intended to affirm Jesus' true incarnation, as opposed to the idea that he only became Christ at his baptism. Supporters of this view include Westcott (1902), Stott (1964) and, more tentatively, Bultmann (1973). Against it may be argued the unreliability of patristic sources for Cerinthus's views; the fact that 1 John does not attack the idea that 'Christ' or the Spirit departed from Jesus at his death (if the insistence that Jesus 'came by blood' refers to this, then the allusion is quite opaque); and the absence of any references to Cerinthus's other reported teachings, for example, the idea that Jesus was the son of a

Demiurge (an inferior creator-god). There is also no evidence that Cerinthus suffered from the ethical faults attributed to 1 John's opponents. For these reasons Schnackenburg (1992), Marshall (1978) and others are probably right to reject the idea of Cerinthus as the principal adversary.

Docetists

Other scholars prefer to dub the opponents more loosely 'Docetists', without specific reference to Cerinthus (so, most recently, Schnelle 1992). Docetism (from Greek *dokeō*, 'I seem') was a tendency in the early church rather than a systematically argued doctrine (the name first appears in the writings of Serapion of Antioch, c. 190–203, but the tendency itself is probably earlier). Docetists considered the humanity and sufferings of Jesus to be apparent rather than real; some of them suggested Simon of Cyrene took Jesus' place on the cross. Important evidence comes from Ignatius of Antioch, who in his *Letter to the Smyrnaeans* gives thanks that his readers are firmly persuaded that Jesus was truly the Son of David *after the flesh*; he was truly nailed (to the cross) *in the flesh*, truly suffered, and was *in the flesh* after the resurrection (*Smyrn.* 1-3). In the same letter (*Smyrn.* 5.2) he speaks explicitly of him as 'flesh-bearer' (*sarkophoros*). In both this letter and that to the Trallians he denounces those who claim that Jesus only *appeared* (*dokeō*) to suffer (*Trall.* 9-10). Some of the christological passages we have cited (esp. 1 Jn 4.2; 5.6; and 2 Jn 7) *could* refer to such beliefs; for example, 5.6, with its affirmation that Jesus came by water and blood, might refer to his real baptism and death. But if our author is seeking to refute Docetism, he seems to be doing it very obscurely. One would have expected much more explicit references to Jesus' birth, death and resurrection, such as are found in Ignatius. There is also no evidence from 1 John that those attacked indulged in the 'judaizing' practices denounced by Ignatius as followed by the Docetists.

'Gnostics'

Gnosticism (from Greek *gnōsis*, 'knowledge') is a syncretistic way of thought, combining Jewish and Christian ideas with elements drawn from pagan philosophy (especially popular Platonism and Stoicism). A striking feature is its pervasive dualism in which the created world and material things generally are perceived as evil. Flesh is contrasted with spirit, and only some human beings are deemed to have the divine 'seed' or 'spark' which might bring redemption through knowledge. Among those who believe that the polemic of 1 John is directed against some form of Gnosticism are Dodd, Kümmel, and Bogart. Dodd (1946) saw 1 John as reacting against what he called the 'higher paganism' or 'Hellenistic mysticism' of the Hermetic tracts (cf. above, Chapter 3 §5). Kümmel thought some kind of Jewish Gnosticism was at stake (1975, pp. 225, 442), while Bogart argued 1 John was combating a gnostic perfectionist sect (1977, esp. pp. 115-22). The main problem in tackling such theories is the varying ways in which the authors use this elusive term 'Gnosticism'. There are also difficulties over chronology. The Nag Hammadi codices (one of the main sources for Gnosticism) belong to the third to fifth centuries CE, and so postdate 1 John. Even if we suppose that their texts were originally composed in the second century CE, this is still later than any probable date for 1 John. The Hermetic texts used by Dodd and the testimonies of the Church Fathers on gnostic beliefs likewise postdate the Johannines. All this means that rather than talking about 'Gnosticism' as such, it would be better to speak of 'incipient Gnosticism' (or 'gnosis', as some scholars prefer).

The real difficulty with assuming that the author of 1 John is reacting *against* incipient Gnosticism is that some of his thought seems to be in harmony with it. His basic approach is dualistic and he sees the *kosmos* as evil, telling his readers not to love the world or the things of the world; he uses terms like *sperma* and *chrisma*, which are known to have been favoured by Gnostics, as if he were happy with them; he stresses the importance of knowledge; he actually teaches some kind of perfectionism. Those who wish to defend the author's orthodoxy claim that he means something different by these terms; they also argue that he believes firmly in the incarnation. But he is treading a tightrope, and the suspicion cannot be entirely allayed that he has gnostic leanings (cf. Vouga 1988, pp. 380-81). He cannot be attacking fully-fledged Gnosticism, for this does not yet exist; if he is attacking some kind of incipient Gnosticism, he goes about it in a strange way.

5. *Some Alternative Views*

The difficulties in identifying a single set of opponents have led to the idea that more than one group may be involved. Thus Smalley suggests that the Johannine community was split into three distinct groups: (a) Johannine Christians committed to the 'apostolic gospel'; (b) 'heretically inclined members from a Jewish background'; (c) 'heterodox followers from a Hellenistic (and/or pagan) background' (1984, p. xxiv). He sees 1 John as responding at times to one group, at times to another. The main problems with Smalley's view are lack of evidence for the heretically inclined Jewish group; too sharp a differentiation between 'Palestinian' and 'Hellenistic' Judaism; and too ready an attribution to this period of the categories 'orthodox' and 'heterodox'/'heretical'. Smalley is aware of the problems in using these labels, but this does not stop him employing them.

Brown sees 1 John's community as divided into just two groups: the epistolary author's adherents and his opponents (1982, p. 69). He believes 1 John was written, at a time of schism, to counter the opponents' misinterpretation of the Gospel. He argues that these opponents denied the importance of Jesus compared with the Spirit; that they refused to acknowledge that he was the 'Christ come in the flesh'; they failed to emphasize moral behaviour, claiming a perfectionist freedom from sin, and they did not love their fellow Christians (1982, pp. 47-68). Others who have argued that 1 John was written as a defence of the Gospel of John include Houlden (1973) and Wengst (1976). The strength of Brown's thesis is that it uses the text itself to determine the views of the 'opponents' rather than making them conform to groups known from outside sources. Its weakness lies in its over-ambitious reconstruction of their teaching, taking every possible statement as polemical, and the very hypothetical reconstruction of the history of the Johannine community. His theory also depends the chronological priority of the Gospel of John (which may be right; cf. Chapter 4 §4) and on the assumption that 1 John is polemical ethically as well as christologically (which this chapter challenges).

6. A Fresh Approach

All this suggests that perhaps the polemical character of 1 John has been exaggerated. Judith Lieu points out that there are no references to any 'schismatics' until 2.18, and that what 1 John says about them in no way proves that they are claiming superior 'spiritual' gifts (1981, 1991). She argues strongly that 1 John's primary concern is not to expose 'heresy' but to encourage readers and help them build up spiritual discernment. She believes it is methodologically unsound to conflate the moral antitheses with the christological confessions to provide the 'opponents' with a coherent ideology. While recognizing that there is polemic in 1 John, she does not believe it controls its thought. Pheme Perkins similarly advocates a 'less polemicized reading' of 1–3 John, arguing that critics have misread the situation when they see the Johannine community as violently torn apart. Our author's educational climate encouraged a rhetorical style which fostered antithetical and hostile language 'quite unlike anything we are used to. Personal attack, boasting, and challenges were all part of the on-going fabric of life' (1979, pp. xxi-xxii). She believes that there is no evidence that the 'schismatics' had set up an opposition church. The most thorough-going non-polemical reading of 1 John is that of Dietmar Neufeld (1994). In a detailed analysis he argues that 1 John's purpose is to 'transform the readers' expectations, speech and conduct' (p. 133). 'The words of the text do not simply describe the author's or community's theological position, but enact belief' (p. 135).

What then are the beliefs about Jesus which our author is seeking to 'enact' or instil? First of all, he affirms Jesus as the Christ, the Son of God. But he means more than just that Jesus is the messiah. He is *uniquely* God's Son, in a way that other pious people are not (4.9). As Dunn (1989) has aptly recognized, the 'Son of God' confession in 1 John, as in the Gospel of John, is more 'highly rated' than in other New Testament texts. It implies a unique oneness with the Father. We note the repeated parallelism, effectively putting the Father and Son on a level of equality: 'Whoever confesses that Jesus is the Son of God, *God* remains in them and they in God' (4.15). 'Our fellowship is with the Father and with his Son Jesus Christ' (1.3). Those who deny Jesus Christ also deny the Father (2.22). God himself bears witness concerning his Son: 'And this is the witness, that God has given us eternal life, and this life is in his Son. Whoever has the Son has life; whoever does not have the Son does not have life' (5.11-12). The Son gives life through his sacrificial death: his 'blood' is the means of the forgiveness of sins (1.7). This atonement is not just for the Johannine community, but for the sins of the whole world (2.2). Jesus' coming manifests God's love (4.9) and destroys the works of the devil (3.8). Those who trust that Jesus is God's Son conquer the world (5.5).

An important christological affirmation comes at the end of 1 John: 'We know that the Son of God has come, and has given us discernment, that we might know the True One; and we are in the True One, in his Son Jesus Christ. This is the true God and eternal life' (5.20). There has been much debate about the referent for 'this' in the last sentence. Some think it refers to God the Father (so Westcott 1902; Brooke 1912; Stott 1964), but this would be rather tautologous. Some believe it refers to all that 1 John has been affirming (so Dodd 1946), but this would be an odd use of the masculine pronoun. Most naturally 'this' is taken as referring to its immediate grammatical antecedent, namely Jesus Christ (so Bultmann 1973; Schnackenburg 1992; Brown 1982). If it is Jesus Christ who is described as 'true God and eternal life', then we have an explicit affirmation of Jesus' divinity. Against this Grayston has argued 'it would be surprising if the writer...were now to ascribe full deity to him in a throw-away line' (1984, p. 147). But is this a 'throw-away line'? It reads more like a christological climax, as suggested by the solemn opening 'we know', echoing two previous assurances beginning with this same word. Grayston believes that the end of 1 John reveals signs of 'improvisation and rhetorical haste'. But while it does not equal the splendid perorations of classical oratory, the end is hardly the 'ragbag' some have suggested. The author proclaims his purpose (v. 13): to let his audience know (*eidete*, from the same verb as *oidamen*) that they have life in the Son. He clarifies points which he feels he should have tackled; and reaffirms ideas previously enunciated, strengthening the confidence of his audience by the repeated *oidamen*, 'we know' (twice in v. 15, as well as in 18, 19 and 20). What more fitting climax than to conclude by affirming directly what he had hinted at in veiled manner, namely the divinity of Jesus (cf. Marshall 1978)? It is frustrating that the ambiguity of the text makes this interpretation uncertain.

7. Conclusions

Attempts have been made to identify 1 John's 'opponents' as charismatics, Jews, Jewish Christians, Cerinthians, Docetists and Gnostics; but none of these identifications is fully convincing. This does not mean that 'opponents' did not exist, but only that the precise historical situation is not now recoverable. Methodologically, conflating all possibly polemical statements into a whole to reconstruct the adversaries' ideology is suspect, as the author may be aiming at more than one group; yet the more complicated the hypothesis, the less chance of its being right. The strongest case for polemics can be made for the christological 'confessions' and 'denials', together with the references to 'antichrists' and 'false prophets'. In his ethical teaching on love, obedience and the avoidance of sin, it is more likely the author of 1 John is directing his thoughts to his own community rather than outsiders or particular adversaries. It is true that 2 John includes warnings, apparently aimed at a dissident missionary group, but 1 John is probably less polemical than often assumed (3 John contains no theological polemic). It therefore seems desirable to keep an open mind in approaching this text. The next chapter will seek to let 1 John speak in its own right, without any presuppositions about 'opponents', authorship or specific relationship to the Gospel of John.

FURTHER READING

Commentaries by Brooke (1912), Brown (1982), Bultmann (1973), Dodd (1946), Grayston (1984), Houlden (1973), Marshall (1978), Perkins (1979), Schnackenburg (1992), Smalley (1984), Stott (1964), Westcott (1902).

J. Bogart, *Orthodox and Heretical Perfectionism in the Johannine* Community (Missoula, MT: Scholars Press, 1977).

P. Bonnard, *Les épîtres johanniques* (Geneva: Labor et Fides, 1983).

R.E. Brown, *The Community of the Beloved Disciple* (New York: Paulist Press, 1979).

J.D.G. Dunn, *Christology in the Making* (London: SCM Press, 2nd edn, 1989), esp. pp. 56-60.

W.G. Kümmel, *Introduction to the New Testament* (ET; London: SCM Press, 1975).

J. Lieu, 'Authority to Become Children of God', *NovT* 23 (1981), pp. 210-28.

—*The Theology of the Johannine Epistles* (Cambridge: Cambridge University Press, 1991).

J.C. O'Neill, *The Puzzle of 1 John* (London: SPCK, 1966).

D. Neufeld, *Reconceiving Texts as Speech-Acts* (Leiden: E.J. Brill, 1994).

J. Painter, 'The "Opponents" in 1 John', *NTS* 32 (1986), pp. 48-71.

J.A.T. Robinson, 'The Destination and Purpose of the Johannine Epistles', *NTS* 7 (1960–61), 56-65. Argues for a Jewish Christian background.

U. Schnelle, *Antidocetic Christology in the Gospel of John* (Minneapolis: Fortress Press, 1992).

F. Vouga, 'The Johannine School', *Bib* 69 (1988), pp. 371-85.

K. Wengst, *Häresie und Orthodoxie in Spiegel des ersten Johannesbriefes* (Gütersloh: Mohn, 1976).

R.A. Whitacre, *Johannine Polemic* (Chico: Scholars Press, 1982).

Chapter Six

1 JOHN: LEADING THEOLOGICAL IDEAS

In this chapter we study some of the leading theological ideas of
1 John, paying attention to their context and their potential rhetorical
and pastoral purposes. The ideas will be examined in the order in
which they are presented by the author, following the outline given
earlier (Chapter 3 §2).

1. *Prooemium or Opening Statement (1.1-4)*

1 John begins with an elaborate Prooemium or Preface, quite unlike
the usual greeting at the start of a letter. Comprising a single sentence,
with 15 separate clauses, it is structurally different from the simple
paratactic style of the rest of the Epistle, suggesting that it may have
been added to the text to give it weight and authority. The accumula-
tion of five clauses all beginning with the same word (*ho*, 'that which')
is designed to be impressive, while frequent use of verbs of perception—hearing, seeing, even touching—serves to reassure and instil
confidence. The Prooemium is couched in the first person plural. Some
have suggested that this is merely a literary convention—an editorial
'we', or even a 'plural of majesty'. More likely it is a genuine plural to
denote a group distinct from the readers, for example, eye-witnesses
or tradition-bearers who speak for the Johannine school. Grayston
writes: 'A Christian group addresses a group of readers in formal
language: they claim to possess an original disclosure and experience
and intend to communicate what they possess' (1984, p. 33). The verbs
'we bear witness'...'we proclaim' have a performative character, and
Neufeld (1994) rightly sees this Preface as a 'speech act'. The vivid
language also reveals the depth of feeling.

But for all its impressiveness, the text is obscure. As Houlden
remarks, 'Intensity of soul does not mean clarity of mind' (1973,
p. 46). What is meant by 'from the beginning' (*ap' archēs*)? Is it the
beginning of creation (so Jn 8.44; cf. *en archē[i]*: Gen. 1.1; Jn 1.1), or of
Jesus' ministry (cf. Jn 15.27; Lk. 1.2), or of the church (cf. Acts 11.15)?

Are the verbs relating to perception to be taken literally or meta-phorically? And is the 'word of life' (*ho logos tēs zoēs*) to be understood as the pre-incarnate and incarnate Word (cf. Jn 1.1, 14), or the life-bringing message of, and about, Jesus (cf. Jn 6.68; Phil. 2.16)? Much depends on whether the Prooemium draws on the Gospel's Prologue. If it does, then a reference to Jesus as the eternal Logos might be possible; but it is hard to see why anyone should change the simple clarity of the Prologue into 1 John's rhetorical obscurity. If, however, we interpret the Prooemium from the rest of 1 John, the sense 'life-bringing message' for 'word of life' becomes more likely. For nowhere else in 1 John is *logos* personified; it is always used in the sense of preached (or spoken) word.

This encourages us to consider whether 'that which was from the beginning' might also refer to the preached word. Of the seven other examples of *ap' archēs* in 1 John, only one must signify the beginning of creation (3.8), though a further two might do so (2.13, 14). The remaining four (2.7; 24 *bis*; 3.11), together with the two examples in 2 John (vv. 5, 6), seem to refer to the beginning of the Gospel procla-mation, though it is ambiguous whether the preaching of Jesus or that of the community is intended. The verbs of hearing readily apply to the Gospel message; those of seeing and touching less easily so—though a metaphorical sense is not impossible. The phrase 'the life was made manifest' (v. 3, with *phaneroomai*) might refer to the incar-nation, but it could equally denote the revelation of eternal life in the preaching of Jesus. Possibly the passage is deliberately ambiguous (for a full discussion see Brown 1982, pp. 154-70).

The Prooemium also introduces the important theme of *koinōnia*, usually translated 'fellowship' or 'communion'. This word means 'participation' or 'sharing': it can be used of a business partnership (cf. Lk. 5.10); of sharing material goods (Rom. 15.26; 2 Cor. 8.4); or reli-gious sharing, in faith, salvation, preaching, suffering, or sacrament (Phlm 6; Phil. 1.5; 3.10; 1 Cor. 10.16; Acts 2.42; cf. Rev. 1.9). J.P. Samp-ley (1980) has argued that it is also used in Paul as a technical term for a missionary partnership whereby a group offer material support to Paul in return for a share in the fruits of his endeavours, but *pace* Perkins (1983) that is not the meaning here. In 1 John's Prooemium the emphasis is on the 'community' which believers share with God the Father and Jesus Christ. The community which they share with one another is dependent on this, and upon their remaining in fellow-ship with God by being forgiven of their sins and 'walking in the light' (1.7). The concept of *koinōnia* or fellowship is striking, and con-trasts sharply with the thought of the pagan philosopher Epictetus, who asks where could one ever find someone who thought they could have *koinōnia* with Zeus (*Discourses* 2.19.27). Although the language is different, the thought is not far distant from John's Gospel where Jesus speaks of himself as the Vine and his followers as the branches, urging them to remain in him and his love by keeping his commandments (Jn 15.1-10). In the Gospel, as in 1 John, union with Jesus means union also with God the Father (Jn 17.20-21).

The Prooemium ends with the hope that 'our' (or 'your') joy may be made complete (the MSS vary). Grayston (1984) sees these words as 'polite convention' (cf. 2 Jn 4; 3 Jn 4); but one suspects they are more than this. The concept of a faith that brings joy is common to John's Gospel (e.g. 15.11), the gnostic writings and Paul. Probably the mutual joy of author(s) and readers is intended; the warm associations of the words 'fellowship' and 'joy' serve to foster goodwill among the audience.

2. *Main Body*

Walking in the Light as a Sign of Fellowship with God (1.5–2.11)
(a) 1.5-10. The author declares his central theological premise: 'God is light and in him there is no darkness at all' (v. 5). The same thought is enunciated both positively and negatively (a stylistic trait common to 1 John and the Gospel of John). While 'light' has many connotations in Jewish and Christian thought (e.g. glory, knowledge, revelation), it is evident from the context that God's holiness or goodness is intended. God is totally good, and the corollary is that those who would have fellowship with God must have nothing to do with 'darkness', that is, sin. But if they do sin, then they can receive forgiveness through Jesus Christ. These are key verses for showing the author's protreptic purpose—to warn his audience of the seriousness of sin.

(b) 2.1-6. A vivid vocative, 'little children', alerts readers to the importance of what follows. The author writes so that they may not sin; but if they do, he says, 'we have an Advocate with the Father, Jesus Christ the righteous'. This subsection develops a theme already flagged in 1.7, where the addressees were told that the blood of Jesus cleanses them from sin. Now in 2.1 they are further reassured: Jesus is their advocate and an atoning sacrifice. Watson (1993) has argued that the author is employing the classical rhetorical technique of 'amplification', which serves both to invest its subject with dignity and to stress specific ideas by the use of strong, evocative words. He may be over-emphasizing the subtlety of our author's style, but the repetition certainly reinforces the message.

This subsection also contains the first of several tests for having fellowship with God (cf. above Chapter 3 §3). The author says: 'By this we know that we have known him, if we keep his commandments' (2.3). This introduces another recurrent theme—knowledge of God (cf. the emphatic statement in Jn 17.3, 'This is eternal life, that they should know you, the only true God...'). But what is meant by 'know'? Dodd argues that it denotes neither intellectual knowledge nor mystical experience (though it might include these); rather it harks back to concepts familiar from the Hebrew Bible (e.g. Jer. 9.3; 31.34), whereby knowledge of God involves being aware of God's saving actions for people, and of the need to respond with obedience (1946, pp. 29-31). Thus it is not the same as the secret knowledge communicated to 'Gnostics': it implies ethical behaviour. That 1 John intends something like this is shown in v. 5: 'Whoever keeps his word, truly God's love is perfected in that person. By this we know that we are in him'. The ideas of 'knowing God' (2.3, 4), 'being in God' (2.5), and 'abiding in him' (2.6) are closely related; the term 'abiding' carries the connotation of perseverance (cf. Malatesta 1978; Strecker 1996, pp. 44-45). The purpose of 2.1-6 is then to encourage addressees and spur them to right conduct.

(c) 2.7-11. The address 'beloved' affirms community and affection between author and audience. It also heralds another of 1 John's great themes: the love of God. The author reminds addressees of the old commandment which they had 'from the beginning' (here unambiguously the beginning of the Gospel proclamation). He is so sure that they know what this commandment is that he does not need to quote it: he must be either citing common oral tradition or alluding to the Gospel of John (cf. 13.34; 15.12, 17). The term 'old' would have positive associations in a culture taught to value what was well established. But the author realizes the commandment is also new, because it was given in a new way by Jesus. So he partially corrects himself, adding a fresh idea: the commandment is also 'true' (*alēthēs*).

The concept of truth (*alētheia*) appeared already at 1.6, where it was said that those who claim fellowship with God while not 'walking in the light' lie and do not 'do the truth' (cf. 2.4). 'Doing the truth' corresponds to the Hebrew phrase *ʿāsah ʾemeth*, meaning 'to act loyally', and hence to act according to God's will: it occurs in the Hebrew Bible (e.g. Isa. 26.10), the Qumran texts (e.g. 1 QS I.5), and in semitizing Greek (e.g. Gen. 32.11 LXX; Tob. 4.10; *T. Reub.* 6.9); it occurs only once elsewhere in the New Testament (Jn 3.21). 'Truth' in this sense has connotations of genuineness, reliability and integrity. The concept is prominent in John's Gospel, where truth is manifested through Jesus, and is even identified with him (Jn 1.17; 14.6 etc). In 1 John the two pairs of opposites—truth and falsehood, light and darkness—are frequently associated. Jesus' reliable new commandment is given because the darkness is passing away and the true light is appearing (cf. Jn 1.5). Cosmic and ethical dualism are thus combined. The section finishes with an antithesis: anyone who claims to be in the light but hates their 'brother', is still in the darkness (2.11). Specific individuals may be in mind, but more probably this is a general warning, aimed at inculcating consistency between what people claim and how they live. 'Doing the truth' means loving one's fellows.

Admonitions and Warning (2.12-17)
(a) 2.12-14. Six admonitions follow addressed respectively to 'children', 'fathers' and 'young men'. Brown has suggested that these might refer to different classes of church members, with 'children' as the newly-baptized, 'fathers' as senior church leaders, and 'young men' as junior church officers; but evidence is lacking for such a technical understanding. From a modern viewpoint it is problematic that two of the three groups are addressed in exclusively masculine terms (attempts to show that 'fathers' and 'young men' are sexually inclusive have been unsuccessful). Watson's proposal (1993) that the 'children' are the Johannine community as a whole, and the 'fathers' and 'young men' two constitutive classes, has much to commend it, though we need not go all the way with his elaborate analysis. But even if 'children' denotes all church members, the references to 'fathers' and 'young men' (with no mention of 'mothers' and 'young women') is still androcentric. The address perpetuates the Jewish tradition that men constitute the religious assembly or at least its leadership. The church today does not have to follow the same practice.

(b) 2.15-17. The admonitions serve as a transition to the next theme—not to love the world. 'The world' (*ho kosmos*), is a favourite Johannine term, occurring 24 times in 1–3 John, 78 times in John's Gospel, representing c. 57 per cent of the New Testament occurrences (in c. 15 per cent of the corpus). It is here used pejoratively (cf. Cassem 1972–73, pp. 84, 88-89, stressing the tension between God's love of the world and denunciations against Christians loving it). Readers are also warned against the 'lust of the flesh' (with *sarx* used in a bad sense.) The dualistic contrast is strongly pointed between the world, which is passing away (like the darkness in 2.8), and those who do the will of God, who abide for ever.

The 'Last Hour' and True Confession or Denial of Christ (2.18-27)

The transitoriness of the world triggers the thought that it is now the 'last hour', and the expected Antichrist has come in the shape of those who departed from the community. They are called 'liars' and 'deceivers' because they deny that Jesus is the Christ. Perkins's claim (1979, pp. xxi-xxii) that such strong language is typical of ancient oral literature should not blind us to the seriousness of the charge. 'Antichrist' here stands for the archetypal spiritual enemy of God. Though the name first occurs here, the concept is found in earlier Jewish and Christian literature (e.g. Dan. 11.36-37; 2 Thess. 2.3-8; Rev. 13; cf. Brooke 1912, pp. 69-79; Schnackenburg 1992, pp. 135-39; Jenks 1991). In our text a mythological concept has been historicized: human teachers with whom the author disagrees are identified with God's eschatological enemy. This is the language of polemic. These 'deceivers' are contrasted with the author's addressees, who are told they need no teacher, because they have an 'anointing from the Holy One' (probably here meaning God), giving them knowledge of everything (2.27).

The word *chrisma* here translated 'anointing' is puzzling. It derives from the verb *chriō*, meaning 'anoint', the same root as in 'Christ' and 'Antichrist', giving a play on words. *Chrisma* appears only here in the New Testament. In secular Greek it is a concrete noun meaning 'ointment' or 'unguent'. In the LXX it is used in the phrase 'oil of anointing' in the consecration of priests, prophets and kings. The Church Fathers used it for the oil with which baptismal candidates were anointed, as well as for the act of anointing itself. Some have thought that in 1 John it denotes a sacramental act, possibly part of a baptismal rite (such as was practised by both Gnostics and orthodox Fathers). More probably *chrisma* is used metaphorically. We may compare the New Testament references to God's 'anointing' of Jesus with the Spirit (Lk. 4.18; Acts 4.27, 10.38). If that is the case, *chrisma* might be a distinctive image for the Spirit's work as teacher of truth (cf. the Paraclete in the Gospel of John). It may seem illogical for the author to say that his addressees need no teacher when he himself is teaching them, but probably he saw his own teaching as part of the 'anointing'. The idea that his pupils have all knowledge may link up with the thought that they are living in the 'last days' when God had promised that he would write his laws in his people's hearts and they would all know him (Jer. 33.33-34; cf. also Isa. 54.13; Jn 6.45).

The Children of God and the Children of the Devil (2.28–3.24)

(a) 2.28–3.3. Mention of the 'last hour' reminds our author of the parousia (Second Coming). Earnestly addressing his readers as 'little children' (cf. 2.1), he urges them to abide faithfully in Christ, so that they may have confidence when he appears. They know that he is just, and everyone who acts justly is born of him. This leads to the idea of the spiritual birth of Christians. He exclaims in wonder at God's great love that we should be called his children. Linking up with the theme of the parousia, he says it has not yet been manifested what we shall be. But when he (God or Christ) is manifested, we shall be like him (3.2). The thought is awesome. Therefore we must purify ourselves, as he is pure.

(b) 3.4-10. Thus eschatology has been linked to ethics, and the author returns to a well-worn theme—human sinfulness. Jesus was 'manifested' to take away sins (3.5), being sinless himself. Similar ideas were expressed earlier (1.7, 9; 2.1-2). Curiously, the same Greek word *phaneroomai* ('be manifested') is used in 3.2-5 with three different meanings: 'appear' (of the parousia), 'be made clear' (of the future state of Christians), and 'become visible' (of Christ's birth and ministry). The author now insists: nobody who abides in Jesus sins. Earnestly he warns his readers: those who commit sin are of the devil. Thus the familiar dualism is hammered home, but the theme is amplified with a new thought: those born of God *cannot* sin because God's *sperma*, 'seed', is in them. The meaning of 'seed' is problematic: some refer it to Jesus, as the 'seed' or offspring of God; some to the preached Gospel ('sown' as the word); others see it as a designation of the Holy Spirit (as in some gnostic texts). This last suggestion seems most likely. The author provides no explanation, but presses on with his antithesis: such people cannot sin because they are born of God (see further Chapter 8). By this the children of God and the children of the devil are manifested. Those who do not act righteously are not 'of God', nor those who does not love their 'brother' (3.10). The last phrase reads like an afterthought, but it is the catchphrase which leads into the next subsection—on love.

(c) 3.11-18. A solemn opening introduces the passage: 'This is the message which you heard from the beginning, that we love one another', amplified by the new thought, 'not as Cain who murdered his brother'. The reference to Cain is often said to be the only specific Old Testament allusion in 1 John (so Marshall 1978, p. 189); in fact, as Lieu (1993) has shown, Old Testament language and thought permeate our text. Cain's wickedness was a well-known theme in early Judaism (e.g. *T. Benj.* 7.5). In the gnostic *Valentinian Exposition* (11.38, NHL 440) Cain and Abel stand for all humanity, divided into evil and good. In 1 John, Cain's murderous hatred illustrates the hatred of 'the world' towards the Johannine community. Readers are warned not to marvel if the world hates them (cf. Jn 15.18). Is this a sign of a beleaguered and sectarian community (so Segovia 1981)? Our author encourages his readers with the thought, 'We know that we have passed from death into life, because we love the "brothers"' (3.14). The language is that of 'realized eschatology' (cf. Jn 5.24): the true believers have already moved from the realm of death to that of life (cf. 1 Pet. 2.9; Rom. 6.1-11 etc.). Distinctive to 1 John is the idea that mutual love is proof of this passing from death to life. It leads the author on to the example of Jesus' sacrificial love: 'By this we know love, because he laid down his life for us' (3.16; cf. Jn 15.13). So readers are urged to love in action and truth. The teaching is illustrated by a telling example (3.17; cf. Jas 1.27; 2.14-17).

(d) 3.19-24. Returning to the theme of judgment the author speaks of confidence even if our heart condemns us. Is he thinking of people who know they have lapsed from his high ideal of love? He assures readers that God is greater than their hearts, and speaks of the power of prayer. But the logical sequence of thought is obscure. We are given a fresh definition of Christ's commandment: to believe in his Name and love one another. In our author's thought love and obedience are inextricably bound up together. But another new idea is quickly added: those who keep Christ's command abide in him, and he in them. By this we know that he abides in us, from the Spirit which he has given us (note the 'test formula').

The Two Kinds of Spirits (4.1-6)
Mention of the Spirit leads to the thought that not all who claim to speak from the Holy Spirit in fact do so. The author warns his beloved pupils not to trust every spirit but to test them, because 'many false prophets have gone out into the world' (4.1). The concept of false prophets is familiar from the Hebrew Bible and elsewhere in the New Testament; but this must allude to a contemporary situation in the Johannine community. Using the 'test formula' once again, the author says 'By this you know the Spirit of God: every spirit which confesses Jesus Christ come in the flesh is from God, and every spirit which does not confess Jesus is not from God'. This, he says, is the spirit of the Antichrist. But he reminds his 'children' that they are of God and have conquered these opponents (4.4). As a further test he adds: 'Those who know God listen to us, and those who are not of God do not listen to us. By this we know the Spirit of Truth and the Spirit of Deceit'. Once more those who are of God and those who are not are

polarized (cf. Jn 8.43-47); the author is confident that he is on the right side. There is also a new idea—that of the two Spirits.

The Nature and the Demands of Love (4.7-21)

No catchword leads to the next section, though the affectionate 'beloved' may prepare readers for the injunction to love one another. There follows the profoundest and most moving part of this text where the nature of love is expounded (to be discussed in Chapter 7). This section culminates with the lapidary saying: 'We have this commandment from him, that those who love God love their brother also'.

Victory and Testimony (5.1-12)

Previously discussed themes are brought together and those of victory, divine begetting, and witness are developed. Everyone born of God is said to have conquered the world (cf. Jn 16.33; 1 Jn 2.13, 14). In an abrupt transition Jesus is said to be the one who came through water and blood, and 'the Spirit, Water and Blood bear witness'. The theme of witness has not appeared since the Prooemium. Some Latin manuscripts, and some Latin Church Fathers, read at this point (5.8) a Trinitarian reference to the witness of the Father, the Word and the Holy Spirit. This is the famous Johannine 'comma', which for centuries was used as a proof-text for the Trinity. But the words are not found in the Greek manuscripts, and are demonstrably not original (hence their omission in virtually all modern texts and translations). They are an early gloss which caught the imagination of the Latin Church because of its doctrinal usefulness. The witness does not just belong to God: it is also said to be within the believer (v. 10; the Greek is obscure). The section ends with a favourite Johannine theme, eternal life, and the stark antithesis: 'Those who have the Son have eternal life; those who do not have the Son of God do not have eternal life' (5.12). The language is strongly reminiscent of John's Gospel (cf. esp. 3.36).

3. Conclusion, Postscripts and Re-affirmation (5.13-21)

(a) 5.13. Some scholars believe that 1 John originally ended here. 5.13 certainly reads like a conclusion on the purpose of the Epistle: 'I have written these things to you that you may know you have eternal life', with the loosely added explanatory phrase 'to those who believe in the Name of the Son of God'. We are reminded of Jn 20.31: 'These things are written so that you may believe that Jesus is the Christ, the

Son of God' with a similar tacked-on phrase 'and so that believing you may have life in his Name' (often thought to be the original end of John's Gospel). But there is a subtle difference: the Gospel is written so that people *may believe and have life*; 1 John so that believers may *know* they have eternal life.

(b) 5.14-17. Surprisingly, at this point, a new theme is introduced: prayer. 'And this is the confidence (*parrhēsia*) that we have before him, that if we pray according to his will, he hears us' (5.14). This is not a doxology (as in Paul's letters), but rather an exhortation (cf. the end of James). It reads like a postscript. A further afterthought follows, dealing with a special case of intercessory prayer. In their final sections both 1 John and James (5.19-20) mention prayer for a 'brother' who sins, but their teaching is different: James says that if a brother wanders (*planaomai*) from the truth, one should know that whoever turns a sinner from his wandering will save a life from death and 'cover' a multitude of sins. 1 John's message is more sombre: one should pray for such a person unless their sin is 'unto death' (5.16-17). If it is, the author does not encourage intercession (see further Chapter 8).

(c) 5.18-21. A brief conclusion follows: the author stresses that nobody born of God sins, and repeats his pessimistic belief that the whole world lies in the power of the Evil One; but he utters the encouraging thought that the Son of God has come and given us the ability to distinguish the True One. Attention has already been drawn to the ambiguity of the affirmation that follows: 'We are in the True One, in his Son Jesus Christ. This (or 'he') is the true God and eternal life.' (cf. Chapter 5 §6). The theme of eternal life makes an *inclusio* with the Prooemium. The final verse is a sharp warning: 'Little children, guard yourselves from idols'. While some scholars have taken this literally, most believe that 'idols' should be understood metaphorically of false teaching (cf. Chapter 3 §5 on Qumranic usage). Thus 1 John ends on the dualistic note with which the main text began: the contrast between the real God and falsehood.

4. *Conclusions*

We earlier quoted Houlden's words about 1 John insisting inflexibly upon a small number of points. This study rather suggests a rich mine of theological ideas, sometimes expressed in metaphorical and tantalizingly imprecise language. 1 John affirms God's nature as 'light', and the incompatibility of good and evil; it stresses the importance of a right Christology; it calls for love and obedience, and consistency between one's religious profession and practical conduct. Future judgment is expected, and the author believes that he is living in the end-time. The concepts of 'community', 'abiding', and 'being in' God or Christ all stress the close relationship of believers with the Father and the Son. The use of the terms *chrisma* and *sperma* suggests a vital role for the Spirit. The seriousness of sin, and Jesus' sacrificial and intercessory roles are major themes, as is the teaching on love. The Epistle combines encouragement, warning and polemic. In spite of its obscurities, one suspects it would have been effective in achieving its purposes.

FURTHER READING

Commentaries by Brooke (1912), Brown (1982), Houlden (1973), Marshall (1978), Perkins (1979), Schnackenburg (1992), Strecker (1996).

N.H. Cassem, 'A Grammatical and Contextual Inventory of the Use of *kosmos* in the Johannine Corpus with Some Implications for a Johannine Cosmic Theology', *NTS* 19 (1972–73), pp. 81-91.

H. Conzelmann, 'Was von Anfang war', in *idem*, *Theologie als Schriftauslegung* (Beiträge zur evangelischen Theologie, 65; Munich: Chr. Kaiser Verlag, 1974), pp. 207-14. First published in W. Eltester (ed.), *Neutestamentliche Studien für Rudolf Bultmann zu seinem siebzigste Geburtstag* (Beihefte zur ZNW, 21; Berlin: de Gruyter, 1954), pp. 194-201.

C.C. Jenks, *The Origins and Early Development of the Antichrist Myth* (Beihefte zur ZNW, 59; Berlin: de Gruyter, 1991).

J. Lieu, 'What Was from the Beginning', *NTS* 39 (1993), pp. 458-77.

E. Malatesta, *Interiority and Covenant* (Rome: Biblical Institute, 1978). On 'being in' and 'abiding in'.

D. Neufeld, *Reconceiving Text as Speech Acts: An Analysis of 1 John* (Leiden: E.J. Brill, 1994).

P. Perkins, 'Koinōnia in 1 John 1.3-7', *CBQ* 45 (1983), pp. 631-41.

J.P. Sampley, *Pauline Partnership in Christ* (Philadelphia: Fortress Press, 1980).

F. Segovia, 'Love and Hatred of Jesus and Johannine Sectarianism', *CBQ* 43 (1981), pp. 259-72.

D.F. Watson, 'Amplification Techniques in 1 John: The Interaction of Rhetorical Style and Invention', *JSNT* 51 (1993), pp. 99-123.

Chapter Seven

GOD'S LOVE AND THE HUMAN RESPONSE

1. *Divine Love and Human Love*

Their teaching on love is one of the Johannines' most attractive features. The theme is prominent in 1 John. First appearing in 2.5, it recurs in 2.7-11, 15-17; 3.1-3, 10-18, 21-23, and 5.1-3. The fullest treatment is 4.7-21, the so-called 'Hymn of Love' (so Klauck 1991), seen by many as the heart of the writing. The theme also appears briefly in 2–3 John. Drawing on these materials one can construct a fairly coherent 'theology' of love; at the same time, we must be aware that the texts are written for particular situations, and are not intended as a systematic doctrinal exposition. There are ambiguities in the phrase 'love of God' (e.g. 2.5), which can be either an objective genitive, love for God, or subjective, God's own love. Some passages are seriously obscure: for example, 5.1 might mean 'whoever loves the Father loves Christ' or 'whoever loves the Father loves their fellow Christian', or even, more generally, 'whoever loves the parent loves the child'. These and other obscurities mean that our assessment of the Epistles' theology must sometimes be provisional.

The author speaks of two kinds of love—God's for humanity, and human love for God; but these cannot be rigidly separated. Probably the most famous text in the whole Bible is 'God is love'—'the most comprehensive and sublime of all biblical affirmations about God's being' (Stott 1964, p. 160), which occurs twice in 1 John (4.8, 16), being unique to it. 1 John, like Paul (Rom. 5.8), stresses that God loved us first (4.10, 19), and showed this love in sending his Son to die, so that we might have life (4.9; cf. Jn 3.16). We know love through Jesus' laying down his life for us; in response we are called to lay down our lives for the 'brothers' (1 Jn 3.16). God's love is especially shown in the fact that believers are called his children (3.1; 4.7).

In the Johannines the proper response to God's love is love for others: sometimes this response is expressed by the use of 'we' with 'one another': 'Beloved, if God so loved us, we must love one another' (1 Jn

4.11-12; 2 Jn 5; cf. Jn 13.34; 15.12, 17), sometimes by the term 'brother' (*adelphos*): 'This is the commandment that we have from him, that those who love God should love their brother also' (4.21). The meaning of 'brother' has been much discussed. Does it denote 'fellow human being', with the idea of the community of all humanity? Or does it mean Christian 'brother'? And if the latter, is 'brother' used generically to include Christian women, or does the author have in mind Christian men? We shall return to these questions later.

The response to God's love involves obedience to his commands (1 Jn 5.2; cf. 2 Jn 6). Similar ideas are found in the Gospel's Supper Discourses (Jn 14.15, 21; 15.10-12). But what are God's commands? In 1 John it is clear that there is a double command to *faith* and *mutual love*: 'This is his command that we believe in the Name of his Son Jesus Christ and that we love one another' (3.23; this is probably true of the Gospel also: von Wahlde 1990). Faith is not so much intellectual assent (which one cannot produce at will) as trust, commitment and 'a receptive attitude' (so Schlatter 1982). The second command, to love, is, as Schnackenburg (1992, p. 190) says, secondary to the first and a necessary consequence of it. Such love, 1 John insists, must be real, and not just verbal: 'Little children, let us not love in word or tongue, but in deed and truth' (3.18). The phrase 'in truth' does not mean just 'in fact'; it rather suggests love in accord with reality (so Marshall 1978, p. 196; cf. Chapter 6 §2 on 'truth'). The very practical nature of this 'brotherly' love is illustrated by a moving example: 'If anyone has the necessities of life and sees their "brother" in need and shuts up their compassion from him, how does God's love abide in that person?' (3.17). This last saying also shows that the human response to God's love must involve love for others. One may compare 4.21: 'We have this command from him, that those who love God should love their "brother" also'.

Love for God excludes love for 'the world' and 'the things in the world'. These are described as 'the desire of the flesh, the desire of the eyes, and the boastfulness of life' (2.16). The use of such emotive terms as *epithymia* and *alazoneia* suggests that the author has in mind sensual cravings, ruthless greed, and the pretentiousness of material success, rather than the physical world in general. But he may also be thinking of the transitoriness of created things (2.17). The thought is close to Jas 4.4: 'Friendship with the world is enmity towards God'.

1 John also speaks, in striking language, of the *results* of mutual love: 'We know that we have crossed out of death into life, because we love the "brothers"' (3.14); conversely anyone who hates a 'brother' is a 'murderer' (*anthrōpoktonos*, a strong and rare word used for

special emphasis); such people have no life in them (3.15). But those who stand firm in their love, have God's abiding presence. They have confidence in judgment, because 'perfect love casts out fear' (4.18).

2. *The Language of Love*

Before proceeding further it is worth considering in more detail what is meant by the word 'love'. For modern readers it suggests an emotion. We use it for strong affection for parents, children, brothers and sisters; for the powerful and abiding love of wife and husband; for the mutual attraction of a man and a woman; for some people it may include intensely felt same-sex relationships. In English, the word 'love' can convey any of these ideas, and often the meaning has to be indicated by an epithet, such as 'sexual', 'marital', or 'parental'. Greek has a wide range of words to express the concept of love: *erōs*, used mostly for sexual love; *philia*, usually affection and friendship; *storgē*, a more neutral word for natural affection; *pothos* and *himeros*, meaning yearning and longing; and *agapē*, used by New Testament writers preeminently for Christian love, including both God's love for humanity and human love for God. In 1–3 John the idea of 'love' is expressed exclusively by *agapē* (21 times) and its cognate verb *agapaō* (31 times) and adjective *agapētos*, 'beloved' (10 times). In 1 John two-thirds of the occurrences of these words occur in the section 4.7–5.3 (John's Gospel uses both *agapaō* and *phileō*, apparently as synonyms).

Much has been written on the word *agapē*. Nygren (1932–39) and Spicq (1958–59) each devoted a three-volume work to it. It has sometimes been claimed that the noun is a Christian creation, or at the very least part of the specialized vocabulary of early Christian literature— 'the last stronghold of the old conception of a special biblical Greek' (Tarelli 1950, p. 64). Thus Thayer's 1890 *Lexicon* describes *agapē* as 'a purely biblical and ecclesiastical word' (so too Souter in his *Pocket Lexicon* [1920]). Often a sharp distinction is drawn between Christian *agapē* and pagan *erōs* (cf. Nygren 1932, pp. 23-27). Serious objections may be made to these ideas. First, *agapē* is not an exclusively Christian word: it appears, with its cognate *agapēsis*, not infrequently in the LXX and other Jewish writings (e.g. Aristeas, Philo, *Testaments of the Twelve Patriarchs*). It is true that Deissmann's reading (1923) of *Agapē* as a title of Isis (Oxyrhynchus Papyri 1380) has been disputed (see Stauffer 1954); but in two important studies Ceresa-Gastaldo (1951-2; 1953) has shown that there are at least four other certain, and several further possible, examples of *agapē* in secular papyri uninfluenced by the Bible. It is used for love of one's country; kindness or favour; marital love; and as a female proper name.

Secondly, the use of the abstract noun *agapē* cannot be separated from that of the cognate verb *agapaō*. This occurs already in the earliest Greek literature (Homer) with the meaning 'welcome with affection' (cf. *agapazō*). *Agapaō* is used throughout the classical age covering a wide semantic field, including 'to love one's children', 'to show affection for the dead', and 'to be pleased, contented, or fond of'. Beginning in the fourth century BCE, as Joly (1968) has ably shown, *agapaō* gradually replaced *phileō* as a general verb expressing affection. One factor may have been a shift of meaning in *phileō*, which takes on the sense of 'kiss', as in Modern Greek. Schnackenburg's assertion (1992, p. 213) that *agapaō* 'was hardly ever used for human love in Greek' is inaccurate. (Joly 1968 cites multiple examples from Demosthenes, Isocrates, Aristotle, Polybius, Plutarch *et al.*)

Thirdly, as Barr (1961) has stressed, one must be wary of assuming that words always carry the same connotations. It is just not true that *agapē* always denotes affectionate love with no sexual overtones. In the LXX it is used for Amnon's incestuous lust for Tamar (2 Kgdms [= 2 Sam.] 13.15); for erotic heterosexual love in the Song of Songs (e.g. 2.4-5; 5.8); for David's love for Jonathan; and metaphorically for Yahweh's love for Israel as his 'wife' (Jer. 2.2). The cognate noun *agapēsis* is used both for prostitution (Jer. 2.23) and for God's eternal love (Jer. 38.3 LXX = 31.3 MT; cf. Hos. 11.4). Ceresa-Gastaldo (1951–52) has suggested that the bridge between this wide-ranging LXX usage and the narrower New Testament use is Hellenistic-Jewish literature. The *Letter of Aristeas*, which uses a purported dialogue between the Egyptian king and the translators of the LXX as a means of moral instruction, speaks of love (*agapē*) as a gift from God (229; cf. 1 Jn 4.7). The Book of Wisdom (6.17-18) states: 'The beginning of wisdom is the truest desire for instruction; concern for instruction is love (*agapē*) [of wisdom]; love is the keeping of her laws; attention to [her] laws is assurance of immortality; immortality brings one near to God'. This is an example of an ancient rhetorical figure known as a sorites, in which different concepts are equated with one another in a chain until a climax is reached. Though much longer and more loosely structured, 1 John's 'Hymn' (4.7-21) contains a similar series of interrelated statements beginning and ending with the theme of mutual love. 1 John and Wisdom share common themes in their linking of love and obedience, and the idea that obedient love brings one near to God.

In commenting on *Aristeas*, Meecham argued that Alexandrian Hellenistic writers 'purged' *agapē* from its 'carnal associations' and thus paved the way for New Testament usage (1935, p. 63). One should, however, be wary of the word 'purge': *agapaō* continued to be used in an erotic sense in secular literature. Curiously, *erōs* and its cognates followed a similar development; from connoting passionate sexual love, they came to be used of the love of wisdom (e.g. Plato, *Phaedo* 66e; Wis. 8.2) and, in the Church Fathers, of Christian mutual love— and even of God's love. The evidence thus suggests that *agapaō* and cognates were accessible to New Testament authors as part of the regular vocabulary of Hellenistic Greek, both secular and religious-philosophical.

3. *God is Love*

The heart of 1 John's teaching is that 'precious gem' (Loader 1992, p. xvii), 'God is love' (1 Jn 4.8, 16). This has been the theme of so much exposition and preaching that it is hard to discuss. It has been seen as making a definitive statement about God's nature and as a 'high peak' of divine revelation in Scripture. Dodd writes: 'To say "God is love" implies that all His activity is loving activity. If He creates, He creates in love; if He rules, He rules in love; if He judges, He judges in love. All that He does is an expression of His nature, which is—to love' (1946, p. 110).

Dodd's words are profoundly moving; but can we deduce all this from the text? The statement 'God is love' parallels two other Johannine sayings—'God is light' (1 Jn 1.5), and 'God is spirit' (Jn 4.24). Marshall (1978, p. 212) has pointed out that there is nothing in the nature of the love saying to suggest that it is 'superior' to other New Testament sayings about God's nature. It is paralleled by the stern statement in Heb. 12.29 (cf. Deut. 4.24: 'our God is a consuming fire'), which the author uses to induce reverent awe and to warn against apostasy. 1 John's statements about God's nature also have affinities with the 'I am' sayings of John's Gospel and Revelation, where similarly we have a subject (the pronoun 'I'), the verb to be, and an abstract noun as complement, for example, 'I am the resurrection and the life' (Jn 11.25). The noun may also be a concrete one (e.g. bread, vine) used metaphorically. We can no more deduce from the statement 'God is love' that every single activity of God is done in love than we can deduce from 'I am the bread of life' that every activity of Jesus is concerned with feeding.

We have to recognize that the Johannine authors were fond of vivid metaphorical and abstract formulations, such as are indeed found in pagan and gnostic literature, e.g. the Hermetic, 'I am that light, *Nous,* your God' (*CH* 1.6 cited above, Chapter 3 §5). But our author is not engaging in philosophical speculation or Hellenistic mysticism. The Johannine statements are different from the abstruse speculations of developed Gnosticism. 'God is love' in 1 Jn 4.8 is immediately followed by a reference to God's action: 'In this the love of God was manifested among us, that God sent his only Son into the world, so that we might live through him' (4.9). Similarly, 'God is love' in 4.16 leads into an affirmation of God's abiding presence with those who love.

The Johannine predications about God are inseparable from their implications for human behaviour. Thus 'God is light' (1.5) entails the need for God's people to behave in accordance with God's nature; 'God is spirit' (Jn 4.24) leads into the need to worship 'in spirit and in truth'. The assurance 'God is love' brings with it the imperative that those who would be God's children must love one another. Thus, while Dodd may be going beyond 1 John's thought in asserting that all God's activity is carried out in love, he is right that Divine love manifests itself in action.

In this belief our author is true to his Jewish roots. It is popularly assumed that the idea of God as love is a special 'New Testament' insight, whereas the 'Old Testament' teaches of God's wrath. This is not the case. The writers of the Hebrew Bible regularly speak of God's love, sometimes using abstract nouns (e.g. ʾahªbah; ḥesed; raḥªmim), sometimes by describing his beneficent actions (e.g. in rescuing Israel from Egypt). People sometimes fail to appreciate how often the Hebrew Bible refers to God's love because they search English concordances under the word 'love', without realizing that God's loving nature is also depicted by such terms as 'mercy', kindness', 'goodness' (cf. Snaith 1944: 94-142). In the Hebrew Bible God's love is especially shown in the Covenant, which requires a response from God's people: 'Know that the Lord your God is God, the faithful God who keeps covenant and steadfast love with those who love him and keep his commandments...' (Deut. 7.9). Though the term 'covenant' is absent from 1 John, the idea of mutual obligation is not. As Malatesta (1978) has strongly argued, the concept of a new covenant in people's hearts underlies much of 1 John's speech about God's indwelling presence in those who love him, and their response of obedience.

4. *Mutual Love as a Response to God's Love*

The demand for a response to God's love is expressed in many different ways in 1 John (see 2.15-17; 3.11-18, 23; 4.7-21; 5.1-3). An important text shaping its thought is the Deuteronomic *shema* (Deut. 6.4-5): 'Hear, O Israel: the Lord our God is one Lord; and you shall love the Lord your God with all your heart, and with all your soul, and with all your might' (Deut. 6.4-5). Here the affirmation 'God is one' defines how God may be known and calls for a response (cf. Grayston 1984, p. 124). The Levitical command to love one's neighbour is likewise rooted in God's character: 'You shall love your neighbour as yourself: I am the Lord' (Lev. 19.18; cited some eight times in the Hebrew Bible). It is often thought that 'neighbour' in this text denotes only 'fellow Jew', but one should read on to v. 34. 'The alien who resides with you shall be to you as a citizen among you; you shall love the alien as yourself; for you were aliens in Egypt. I am the Lord your God'. We note again the grounding of the command in God's nature and saving activity.

An even more important antecedent to 1 John's teaching on love is Jesus' summary of the Law in the double 'love command' (Mk 12.28-34; Mt. 22.34-40; Lk. 10.25-28). Jesus is not unique here—there are parallels in the *Testaments of the Twelve Patriarchs* (e.g. *T. Iss.* 5.2; 7.6), but it is virtually certain that 1 John's teaching derives from the Gospel tradition. However, it may not stem directly from Jesus himself. It is more probable that our author draws on Jesus' teaching as mediated through the Johannine 'school'. We observe the reformulation of the second part of the 'love command' from love of *neighbour* to love of *one another* (cf. Jn 13.35 etc) or to love of *the brothers* (see further Furnish 1972; Perkins 1982). Yet the language with which 1 John speaks of love is closely similar to that of the Gospel of John: note especially the unusual phrase (*psychēn tithenai*, 'lay down' (lit. 'place') one's life (3.16; cf. Jn 15.13). Either our author was familiar with the teaching on love in the Supper Discourses (so Brown 1982), or he had access to a tradition very close to them.

5. *Problems with 'Brotherly' Love*

From the time of Augustine 1 John's teaching on love has been regarded as the Epistle's supreme contribution to Christian theology. It has rightly been compared to Paul's great 'hymn' (1 Cor. 13), and has been used as a foundation by those seeking to write a biblical theology of love (cf. Nygren 1932–39; Spicq 1958–59; Outka 1972). But it is not without its problems. Many people have seen in it a *restriction* of Jesus' love command. In the Synoptic tradition Jesus teaches that 'neighbour' is not confined to fellow Jew, but includes even a hated Samaritan (Lk. 10.29-37). The Sermon on the Mount specifically enjoins love of enemies (Mt. 5.43-48; cf. Lk. 6.27-31). Jesus' whole life exemplifies love of the loveless. But nowhere in the Johannine literature is there a reference to love for enemies, or even strangers. The 'brothers' so frequently mentioned appear to be members of the Johannine community who are in accord with the author's own teaching. The most extreme critic is J.T. Sanders, who sees Johannine ethics as weak and morally bankrupt. A Johannine Christian, he says, on seeing a wounded traveller would ask 'Are you saved, brother?', instead of giving aid (1986, p. 100).

Too much should not be made of the change from the Synoptic 'neighbour' to Johannine 'brother' or 'one another': these terms are often used as synonyms in Jewish and Christian Greek (e.g. Gal. 5.13-15). It is possible, as Robinson (1985) and others have argued, that in the Johannine 'brother' and 'one another' may include fellow human beings. But even if we follow the majority of scholars who think they mean primarily 'fellow Christians', we still must reply to Sanders that the Johannines nowhere suggest that a Johannine Christian would neglect a dying stranger. Such a basic duty of Jewish and Christian piety would have been taken for granted. 1–3 John are not concerned with enunciating a complete Gospel, but rather dealing with particular situations. Their community is divided and failing in certain basic areas of faith and practice; the texts focus on the most urgent need—mutual love among the committed.

What of attitudes to dissentients? In the modern climate of ecumenism and inter-faith dialogue the Johannine Epistles may seem intolerant and uncharitable. In interpreting them, we have to understand the importance for their author(s) of a right understanding of Jesus' person, and the indissoluble connection between right belief and right conduct. The secessionists (if such they be) were seen as the equivalent of idolaters. To offer them friendship was to affirm their false beliefs. To share a meal with them was to participate in their sin (2 Jn 11; cf. 1 Cor. 10.20; 2 Cor. 6.14). This may help explain the strange teaching at the end of 1 John that it is not worth praying for somebody who has sinned 'unto death'. We shall reserve till our last Chapter how such ideas might be interpreted today.

6. *Sexism in the Johannine Epistles?*

Throughout this discussion we have referred to 'brother' and 'the brothers'—a literal rendering of Greek words used. But does 'brothers' include 'sisters'? The Greek noun *adelphos* is used for a blood-brother, for a fellow member of a community, or occasionally for a fellow human being (e.g. Gen. 9.5). In the plural it can be inclusive, denoting siblings (cf. German *Geschwister*). The NRSV renders it throughout as 'brothers and sisters', but this unduly stresses the supposed presence of women. There is no way of telling whether or not the author(s) had them in mind when writing. Masculine terminology predominates in the admonitions of 1 Jn 2.12-14 (though 'children' could be inclusive). Ancient philosophical schools sometimes included women, but not always. There were women among Jesus' disciples, but the Twelve were all men and some of his teaching appears to be given exclusively to them. Some Pauline letters and 1 Peter contain injunctions directly addressed to women, but Galatians with all its references to circumcision seems to be primarily aimed at men (I owe this point to Judith Lieu). If the Johannine authors had wanted to include women specifically they could have done so: compare James's reference to a 'brother or a sister' (*adelphos ē adelphē*) in need (Jas 2.15) and Jesus' saying in Mark (3.35) that whoever does the will of God is his 'brother and sister and mother'. In contrast, 1–3 John nowhere explicitly mention women (unless 2 John's 'elect lady' and her 'sister' are real women). We must therefore conclude that, by modern standards, the formulation of 1–3 John's teaching is androcentric in that males are perceived as the norm, though it is probably too much to call it 'sexist'. One hopes that the author(s), if pressed, would agree that all that is said about love, faith, and obedience applies also to Christian women.

7. Conclusion

Their teaching on love is indeed one of the most important contributions that the Johannines can make to Christian theology and ethics. Their insight that Christian love is grounded in Divine love is fundamental. The recognition that love is inconsistent with fear is a valuable testimony in the face of many religions which build precisely on fear. Their insistence that those who claim to love God must also show love to their fellows is a clarion call against hypocrisy; and even if 'brother' is understood in a narrow sense, this does not preclude a wider application (cf. 1 Thess. 3.12; 5.15; Gal. 6.10).

FURTHER READING

Commentaries by Brown (1982), Dodd (1946), Grayston (1984), Klauck (1991), Loader (1992), Marshall (1978), Schnackenburg (1992), Stott (1964), Strecker (1996), esp. pp. 144-48.

J. Barr, *The Semantics of Biblical Language* (London: SCM Press; Philadelphia: Trinity Press International, 1961), ch. 8.

A. Ceresa-Gastaldo, '*Agapē* in Documents Earlier than the NT', *Aegyptus* 31 (1951–52), pp. 269-306.

—'*Agapē* in Documents outside Biblical Influence', *Rivista di Filologia Classica* 31 (1953), pp. 347-56. Both are in Italian.

A. Deissmann, *Light from the Ancient East* (ET; London: Hodder & Stoughton, 4th edn, 1927; Grand Rapids, MI: Baker Book House, 4th edn, repr. 1978 [orig. German edn, 1923]. See esp. p. 75 n. 3.

V.P. Furnish, *The Love Command in the New Testament* (Nashville: Abingdon Press, 1972).

W. Harrelson, 'The Idea of Agape in the NT', *Journal of Religion* 31 (1951), pp. 169-82. Criticizes Nygren.

R. Joly, *Le vocabulaire chrétien de l'amour est-il original?* (Brussels: Presses Universitaires, 1968). Criticizes Spicq.

E. Malatesta, *Interiority and Covenant* (Rome: Biblical Institute, 1978).

H.G. Meecham, *The Letter of Aristeas* (Manchester: Manchester University Press, 1935).

J. Moffatt, *Love in the New Testament* (London: Hodder, 1929).

A. Nygren, *Agape and Eros* (3 vols.; London: SPCK, 1932–39), esp. I.

G. Outka, *Agape* (Yale: Yale University Press, 1972).

P. Perkins, *Love Commands in the New Testament* (New York: Paulist Press, 1982).

J.A.T. Robinson, *The Priority of John* (London: SCM Press, 1985), esp. pp. 329-33.

J.T. Sanders, *Ethics in the New Testament* (Philadelphia: Fortress Press, 1975; London: SCM Press, 2nd edn, 1986).

A. Schlatter, *Der Glaube* (Stuttgart: Calwer Verlag, 6th edn, 1982), esp. p. 218.

M. Silva, *Biblical Words and their Meaning* (Grand Rapids: Zondervan, 1983), esp. p. 96.

N.H. Snaith, *Distinctive Ideas of the Old Testament* (London: Epworth, 1944), esp. pp. 94-130.

A. Souter, *A Pocket Lexicon to the Greek New Testament* (Oxford: Clarendon Press, 1920).

C. Spicq, *Agapè dans le Nouveau Testament* (3 vols.; Paris: Gabalda, 1958–59), esp. III on 1–3 John.

—*Notes de lexicographie néotestamentaire*, I (Göttingen: Vandenhoeck & Ruprecht, 1987), pp. 16-30.

E. Stauffer, '*Agapaō, agapē, agapētos*', in *TDNT*, I, pp. 21-55, esp. p. 38.

C.C. Tarelli, '*Agapē*', *JTS* 51 (1950), pp. 64-67.

J.H. Thayer, *Grimm's Greek–English Lexicon of the New Testament* (Edinburgh: T. & T. Clark, rev. edn, 1890).

U. von Wahlde, *The Johannine Commandments* (New York: Paulist Press, 1990).

Chapter Eight

SIN, FORGIVENESS, JUDGMENT AND ESCHATOLOGY

1. *Introduction*

If we had only the first two chapters of 1 John, its teaching on sin
might seem fairly straightforward. God is 'light', i.e. perfect goodness
(cf. Chapter 6 §2); those who are God's children must 'walk in the
light', that is, behave in conformity with God's demands. If they fail,
they must confess their sins and God will forgive them. This forgiveness is effected through the death of Jesus (1.7-9). He is their champion (*paraklētos*) with the Father and atones for the sins of the whole
world (2.1-2). However, even these apparently simple statements raise
questions. How can Jesus' death enable God to forgive sins? Was
there no means of forgiveness before his self-sacrifice? Did he die as
our representative or our substitute? And how can he expiate the sins
of the whole world, if the whole world does not repent? To understand 1 John's thought we need to investigate the Jewish background.

2. *Sacrifice and Forgiveness*

Ancient Judaism had an elaborate system of sacrifices which could be
offered in thanksgiving or fulfilment of vows, as an earnest of repentance and reparation for sin, as a sign of self-dedication or as a means
of reconciliation with God (see Carpenter 1988). Such sacrifices often
involved shedding animal blood (a symbol of their life). There was
also the special rite of the Day of Atonement when the High Priest
entered the Holy of Holies and made sacrifice for his own sins and the
unwitting sins of the people by sprinkling blood on the *hilastērion*
('mercy-seat'). Very early, the Christian church saw the death of Jesus
an atonement, replacing this complex system of Jewish rituals (cf. Mk
10.45; Rom. 3.25; 1 Cor. 11.25; 1 Pet. 1.18-19); the theology is worked
out in most detail in Hebrews 7–10.

The author of 1 John works within this frame of understanding.
Jesus' *blood* cleanses from sin (1.7); he was manifested (*phaneroomai*) to

'take away' sins (3.5); and is an atoning sacrifice (*hilasmos*) (2.2; 4.10). There has been a long and arid controversy over whether *hilasmos* (together with the related term *hilastērion* in Rom. 3.24) means 'propitiation' (rendering God favourable) or 'expiation' (wiping out sins and their effects) (see the standard dictionaries and commentaries). The main point is that 1 John, in common with most of the rest of the New Testament authors, perceives the need for an objective sacrifice to be made in order for God to forgive sins—in this case the death of Jesus.

But Jesus is not only the sacrificial victim; he is also the one who intercedes with the Father. In 2.1 he is called an 'advocate' or 'champion' (*paraklētos*), a term found only in John's Gospel and 1 John among New Testament writings (see further Grayston 1981). One might wonder why such intercession is necessary if Jesus' death constitutes a 'full, perfect and sufficient sacrifice' (*Book of Common Prayer*, 1662); but the idea seems to be that since human beings regularly sin—even those who have been converted, put their trust in Christ, and become God's children—a heavenly intercessor is needed to continue to plead for them. In John's Gospel the 'paraclete' is the Holy Spirit (Spirit of Truth) who serves as Jesus' successor after his departure from earth, guiding his disciples (14.16-17; 15.26; 16.7-15); in 1 John 'paraclete' refers to Jesus himself. The Gospel's image of the Spirit as 'advocate' is close to that of Paul in Rom. 8.26, when he speaks of the Spirit interceding 'with sighs too deep for words', while 1 John's thought is closer to that of Hebrews (e.g. 7.25; cf. Rom. 8.34), where Jesus is intercessor. The tension between the two Johannine writings may not be so great as sometimes supposed, because the idea of Jesus as 'paraclete' may be implied in the Gospel reference to the Spirit as 'another paraclete' (14.16); and John's Gospel does, in fact, depict Jesus as intercessor, notably in the 'high-priestly' prayer of ch. 17. On the other hand, 1 John displays no knowledge of the Gospel's developed doctrine of the Spirit as a personal being. It is a matter of radical concern how this teaching about sacrifice and intercession may be understood and applied in the modern world.

3. *Future Judgment*

In early Christian thought Jesus is not only the sacrifice for sin; he is also the one appointed by God as future judge (Jn 5.28-29; Acts 10.42 etc.); the Synoptic Gospels and other New Testament writings see this as taking place at his parousia (literally, 'presence' or 'arrival') in power and glory to gather his Elect (Mk 13.26-27; Mt. 24.30-31; 2 Thess. 2.1-12 etc.). Do the Johannines also have this expectation? The evidence is not completely clear. 2 John 7 speaks of deceivers who do not 'acknowledge Jesus Christ coming in the flesh'. If the present participle *erchomenon*, 'coming', is given its normal grammatical force this must either refer to the present time (which makes no sense) or be used futuristically (a common usage). In that case the author is referring to a future coming of Jesus. Such a view is taken, among others, by Strecker (1996). But since there is no other evidence that a 'fleshly' second coming was controversial at this time, most commentators assume that the author intended to say 'having come', with reference to the incarnation (cf. 1 Jn 4.2; Polycarp, *Phil.* 7.1—both using past tenses). If that is his meaning, 'our author is not skilled in the niceties of Greek idiom' (Dodd 1946, p. 149).

A future coming is more frequently seen in 1 Jn 2.28–3.3, referring to 'his' parousia and future manifestation. Unfortunately all the key phrases are ambiguous: the author has just spoken of the *chrisma* which teaches his protégés, and bids them 'abide in it/him', so that if (or 'when') it/he is manifested they may have confidence and not be ashamed. The vocabulary is that of judgment; the problem is that the subject of 'be manifested' (*phaneroomai*) is obscure. It could be either neuter or masculine. Grammatically it ought to refer to the *chrisma* (neuter); but even if the 'anointing' has rightly been identified with the Holy Spirit, it is difficult to believe that the author intended an eschatological manifestation of the Spirit in this way. From what follows, the subject of *phaneroomai* must be God or Christ—but which?

Further ambiguities arise in the next verses: according to the commonly accepted text, the author says, 'Beloved, we are now children of God, and it has not yet been manifested (*phaneroomai*) what we shall be. We know that if (or 'when') he is manifested, we shall be like him, because we shall see him as he is' (3.2). It is uncertain in both 2.28 and 3.2 whether *ean* has its usual meaning of 'if ' (implying a contingency), or whether it should be rendered 'when' (implying certainty). Grammatically 'he' in v. 2 ought to refer to God (the last noun named), but since our author is not distinguished for his good Greek, many commentators think he must be referring to Jesus' 'second coming' (cf. Mt. 24.3; 1 Cor. 15.23).

Against this Grayston has argued, on theological grounds, that God is intended. He sees Christ's 'disclosure' (a term he prefers to 'manifestation') as occurring through his incarnation and preaching, which effectively judges people as they accept or reject him. Believers have already passed from death to life (1 Jn 3.14). There is no need for any further parousia of Jesus. Final judgment, in his view, belongs to

God, whose future parousia in judgment is well attested in the Hebrew Bible and Judaism (Grayston 1984, pp. 95-97; cf. O'Neill 1966, pp. 32-36). The view has merits in that it saves Jesus being victim, intercessor and judge; it relieves the tension of the 'realized' and 'final' eschatology; it also avoids the awkwardness of 2.29, which speaks of those who act righteously being born 'from him', where the only antecedent is the one who may appear. If this is Jesus, we have an idea not otherwise attested in the New Testament that believers are born from Jesus; whereas if God is the source of the birth, this harmonizes with a widespread New Testament concept (cf. 1 Pet. 1.3; Jas 1.18), occurring frequently in 1 John (cf. also Jn 1.13). However, it must be admitted that the whole section is fraught with difficulty, and small changes to an insecure punctuation could alter the meaning radically (see Synge 1952).

These matters have been treated at length to illustrate the difficulties in discovering 1 John's precise meaning. Similar problems occur with many other passages: in 3.19-20, for example, it is not clear whether the author is assuring readers that God is less accusing than their hearts, or warning them that God is more severe. However, the main burden of 1 John's thought seems to be this: there will be future judgment (whether by God or Jesus); believers should have confidence in the face of this; God (or Jesus) is reliable and just, and will forgive them their sins, as long as they confess them. Meanwhile they should love one another, keep God's (or Jesus') commandments, and purify themselves as 'he' is pure: when they see 'him' they will be transformed to be like 'him'. This last idea has often been thought to derive from Hellenistic mysticism, but is found also in Judaism.

4. *Sin and Sinlessness*

In the first half of 1 John (1.5–3.3) the author's basic meaning was fairly clear, though some details remained obscure. In the second part (3.4–5.12) things get more complicated. The main purpose seems to be to stress the seriousness of sin. 'Whoever commits sin (*hamartia*) also commits lawlessness' (3.4). 'Lawlessness' (*anomia*) may be regarded as more heinous than 'sin', being a sign of the spiritual rebelliousness characteristic of the end-time (cf. 2 Thess. 2.3-7; Mt. 24.11-12). In Jewish thought a sharp contrast is often drawn between 'lawless' and ungodly sinners and the righteous (cf. Ps. 1.1; *Ps. Sol.* 3; *1 En.* 1.1 etc.). It is presumably this climate of thought which led our author to the bold statement: 'Nobody who remains in him sins: nobody who sins has seen or known him' (3.6); 'nobody born of God sins, because his seed (*sperma*) remains in them; such people cannot sin, because they are born of God' (3.9). The same idea is echoed towards the end of the Epistle: 'We know that nobody born (perfect participle) from God sins; but the one born (aorist participle, possibly referring to Jesus) from God keeps them and the Evil One does not touch them' (5.18).

Every commentator wrestles with the tension—not to say downright contradiction—between these strong statements about sinlessness and the author's earlier claims that 'if we say we have no sin we deceive ourselves' (1.8), that 'if we say that we have not sinned we make him a liar' (1.10), and 'if anyone sins, we have an Advocate with the Father' (2.1). Four main approaches may be distinguished, based on: (a) Greek grammar; (b) polemical citation; (c) theological paradox; (d) rhetorical purpose.

a. *Greek Grammar*

Many have sought an explanation in the subtleties of Greek grammatical usage. The statements about the sinlessness of God's children are expressed in the present tense—'nobody who remains in him sins' (3.6, 9) etc.—whereas in 2.1, 'If anyone sins...', the verb is in the aorist. Now in ancient Greek, as in certain other languages, the different tenses may signify not only different references to time (past, present or future) but also differences of 'aspect' or 'kinds of action'. The present stem may be used to indicate a continuous state or repeated action, while the aorist stem can indicate a momentary or 'one-off' action. So a number of scholars have suggested that what 1 John means is this: if anyone commits a particular act of sin, Jesus Christ pleads for them. But nobody born of God 'habitually' sins. Sin is not characteristic of God's children (see for example Dodd 1946 and Stott 1964 on 3.6).

But is this fine distinction what the author was really intending to express? There are several reasons for thinking that it was not. First of all, in Hellenistic Greek distinctions of 'aspect' were by no means universally observed, and one often finds present and aorist tenses side by side without distinction in meaning (e.g. Mk 1.3; Mt. 8.9). Secondly, the grammatical constructions in the two 1 John passages are not the same: in 3.6 and 3.9 the verbs that mean 'does not sin' are in the present indicative, as is appropriate for a main verb in a general statement. However, in 2.1 the verbs meaning 'sin' are not main verbs but belong to subordinate ('so that' and 'if ' clauses). They are aorist subjunctives, such as are commonly used by New Testament writers in constructions of this type. The aorist was evidently preferred to the present here not for any special 'aspectual' significance it might once have carried, but because its forms had become familiar through usage. Third, if the author had wanted to stress in 3.6, 3.9 and 5.18 that he was talking about *habitual sin* there are plenty of ways he could have done it more clearly. In any case 3.9 states categorically that those born from God *cannot sin*. Grammar alone is not enough to get us out of this conundrum.

b. *Polemical Citation*

H.C. Swadling (1982) has put forward an ingenious proposal: noting that *sperma* in the sense of 'divine seed' is a 'gnostic commonplace', he argues that 3.6 and 3.9 are quotations from the slogans of 'gnostic' opponents (cf. also Klauck 1991, pp. 197-98). Since quotation marks are not shown in Greek manuscripts, this section could be paraphrased as follows (proposed slogans are italicized):

> (v. 5) You know that the role of Christ is to remove sins—he committed no sin at all.
> (v. 6) *Anyone who remains in him is sinless—and anyone who sins has not seen him and does not know him.*
> (vv. 7-8) Little children, let no one mislead you. It is those who act righteously who are righteous, just as Christ is righteous (etc.),
> (v. 9) *All those who are born of God do not sin, because the divine seed remains in them; they cannot sin because they are born of God.*
> (v. 10) The way to distinguish the children of God and the children of the devil is this: those who do not act rightly are not of God, nor those who do not love their brother.

Swadling sees the author as 'demystifying' the concept of birth from divine 'seed', because opponents had claimed it brought an automatic state of sinlessness. Rather, he suggests, the reborn need to keep themselves safe (a variant reading in 5.18) and preserve themselves from habitual sin.

At a stroke, it seems, Swadling has cut the Gordian knot. But has he? There is no doubt that ancient authors did sometimes quote opponents' slogans without acknowledgment; but is this really what is happening here? The resultant sequence is jerky in thought; if recited orally a good speaker might indicate the meaning by tone of voice; in a written text one wonders whether readers could have grasped what was happening. It is ironical that the very verses which Swadling assigns to the 'opponents' are attributed by both Bogart (1977) and Brown (1982) to the author himself. They see the claims of 3.6 and 3.9 as representing 'orthodox' perfectionism, and statements in 1.6, 8, 10 as directed against 'heretical' perfectionism. A final problem for Swadling's view is 5.18, where he has to slip in the word 'habitual' to make his case work. If it can be supplied in 5.18, why not in 3.6 and 9? In fact, 3.4-10 hang together as a consistent unit, and vv. 7, 8 with their reference to those who 'do righteousness' (a Semitism), being righteous like God, and those who 'do sin' being of the devil, far from countering 3.6 and 3.9, reinforce it. The whole passage harmonizes with our author's basic theology that righteousness and sin belong to two different 'worlds' and just do not mix.

c. *Theological Paradox*

Another approach is to explain the tension on grounds of theological paradox. It is not uncommon in biblical study to come across concepts which seem mutually incompatible: the Kingdom has arrived, but it is not yet here; 'those who are not with me are against me' (Mt. 12.30), but 'whoever is not against us is for us' (Mk 9.40); Christians are justified by faith, yet God will judge everyone according to their deeds; the believer is righteous and a sinner both at once—'simul justus et peccator' (Luther). So the tension in 1 John has been explained by the idea that the Christian as sinner lives under forgiveness, and precisely as one already sharing in salvation overcomes individual acts of sin (Braun 1951: 277). But this is a desperate playing with words. Perhaps nearer the mark is the idea that the sinlessness of those who have become God's children is an ideal, as yet imperfectly realized (so Marshall 1978; Smalley 1984 etc.). This leads us to our final possibility.

d. *Rhetorical Purpose*

Many problems have arisen because commentators have taken 1 John too literally, without looking at its rhetorical purpose. Most people make extreme utterances occasionally in particular contexts, and it is not unusual to find logically inconsistent statements within the same political speech or religious address. The framework of 1 John's discourse is ethical dualism. In the first part (1.5–3.3) the author sets out the need for consistency between what one claims and how one behaves, assuring readers that sins can be forgiven, but exhorting them to 'walk in the light' and not to 'love the world' (equated with darkness). They are living in the difficult last days when sin and deceit are manifest (exemplified in the antichrists); but they are protected by the *chrisma* and the fact that they are God's children.

In his second part (3.4–5.12) he heightens his contrast between God's children who do not sin, and sinners, the children of the devil, for the destruction of whose works Jesus was manifested (3.8). In Judaism it was widely thought that in the end-time there would be no more sin among the Elect (*Ps. Sol.* 17.32; *1 En.* 5.8; *Jub.* 5.12; cf. Jer.

31.33-34). Our author sees his pupils as God's children, beloved and presumably Elect; they are living at the 'last hour' (2.11). In the eschatological conflict they are already conquerors (4.4), because the One that is with them (God) is stronger than 'the one who is in the world' (Devil/Antichrist). Surely they should be sinless, as befits the Elect.

Assertions like 'nobody born of God sins', though grammatically statements of fact in the indicative, serve the function of exhortation: 'Nobody born of God ought to sin' (cf. our English usage 'Nobody does that' to dissuade someone from what we believe to be wrong). In hyperbolic language the pastor seeks to promote right belief and right conduct. He does not believe that those under instruction are actually perfect; but sinlessness is what is expected of God's children; compare Deut. 18.13, 'You shall be perfect with the Lord your God'; Mt. 5.48, 'You shall be perfect as your heavenly Father is perfect' (on 'perfectionist tendencies' in Jewish and Christian literature see further Bogart 1977, ch. 4).

5. *Sin unto Death?*

A particularly thorny problem arises from our author's last discussion of sin, namely 5.16-17, literally: 'If anyone sees his "brother" sinning a sin not unto death, he will pray, and he [probably signifying God] will grant him (masc. sing.) life, to those (masc. plur.) sinning not unto death. There is a sin unto death (*hamartia pros thanaton*). I do not say that one should pray about that [sin]. Every unrighteousness is sin, and there is a sin unto death.' What is meant by this difficult passage?

It looks as if the author is following a Jewish distinction between different kinds of sin. Parts of the Hebrew Bible distinguish sharply between unconscious, inadvertent sins which could be atoned for by sacrifice (e.g. Lev. 4–7), and deliberate, wilful 'sins of a high hand', so terrible that they could never be forgiven (cf. Num. 15.30-31; Isa. 22.14; Ps. 19.13). Levitical legislation punished such sins with death, a final cutting off from the religious community (see Lev. 20.1-22; cf. Num. 18.22). At Qumran, in one section of the *Community Rule* (1 QS VIII.1–IX.2; Vermes 1998, p. 110) members of the 'Council of Holiness' who deliberately sin are to be permanently expelled, while those who sin inadvertently must do penance for two years (on this and related texts see further Knibb 1998). Other extra-biblical Jewish texts speak of certain sins leading to death, using phraseology very similar to 1 John (note esp. *T. Iss.* 7.1 [*hamartia eis thanaton*] and *Jub.* 33.13, 18).

Now it is most unlikely that the author of 1 John is speaking of physical death, but he may well intend a spiritual death—the opposite of 'eternal life'. One way of understanding the text would be to assume a division of sins into two classes: mortal sins (leading to eternal death) and venial or pardonable ones. It is unlikely that only accidental sin could be seen as venial, for believers all too often sin deliberately. Tertullian suggests a classification of sins into petty ones like breaking engagements and 'heavy, deadly offences' like murder, idolatry, adultery, blasphemy and denying Christ: 'for these', he says, 'Christ will no longer plead' (cited in Westcott 1902, p. 211). To this day the Roman Catholic Church distinguishes between venial and mortal sins on these lines. But if this is the author's meaning, he fails to make it clear. No other passage in the New Testament suggests such a distinction, which effectively limits the atoning efficacy of Jesus' death. And can one repent of a 'mortal' sin? If one can, why does the author say such a person should not be prayed for?

A more likely interpretation is that there is one particular sin which may lead to spiritual death; if a member of the community has committed this, there is no point in praying for him or her. Only one sin can fit this bill, and that is apostasy (cf. Dodd 1946; Brooke 1912). Apostasy—deliberate rejection of Christ once one had been converted—was viewed with the utmost seriousness in the early church. There is reason to believe that this is the sin for which Hebrews says there is no repentance (6.4-6; 10.26). It may well be the sin against which Jesus solemnly warns in the Gospels: 'Whoever denies me before people I also will deny before my Father in heaven' (Mt. 10.32-33; cf. Lk. 9.26; 12.8-9).

Does the author think it possible that his own addressees should commit this terrible sin, or does he see it only as a possibility for his 'opponents'? It has been pointed out that 1 John speaks of seeing a *'brother'* committing a sin 'not unto death', but does not specify who might be committing a deadly sin. Scholer (1975) therefore argues that it is not possible for members of the believing community to commit the 'sin unto death'. He suggests that it is a sin of outsiders or unbelievers—notably 1 John's opponents who had denied Christ. But he is probably reading the text too subtly. It seems more likely that 5.16-17 is a solemn warning also to the addressees that they should take care not to commit this ultimate sin. They must stand firm in their faith, obedience and love. Apostasy, that is, falling back into pagan ways in the face of persecution, was a real possibility in the early Church (cf. Edwards 1989). So too was falling away from the right understanding of the faith. Many scholars believe that vv. 16-18 are an addition to the original text, since their teaching is not presupposed earlier. But interpreted as we have suggested, they harmonize well with 1 John's final note of warning, 'Little children, guard yourselves from "idols" [i.e. false beliefs and practices]' (5.21). One should, however, be wary of too rigid an interpretation of these disturbing verses: Origen has a wise comment: 'What kind of sins are sins to death, what not to death but to loss, cannot, I think, easily be determined by anyone' (cited in Westcott 1902, p. 211).

6. *Conclusion*

1 John's teaching on sin and forgiveness has proved more difficult than a simple summary might suggest. It is clear that the author regards sin with the greatest abhorrence, seeing it as incompatible with God's character and with the status of believers as God's children. In the interests of paraenesis he has articulated his concern in the sharpest possible language, using Jewish categories of thought; at the same time he affirms that sins may be forgiven through the atoning death of Jesus. The philosophical and theological problems raised by this belief lie beyond his scope.

FURTHER READING

Commentaries by Brooke (1912), Brown (1982), Dodd (1946), Grayston (1984), Klauck (1991), Marshall (1978), Smalley (1984), Stott (1964), Strecker (1996), Westcott (1902).

J. Bogart, *Orthodox and Heretical Perfectionism in the Johannine Community* (Missoula, MT: Scholars Press, 1977).

I. Bradley, *The Power of Sacrifice* (London: Darton, Longman & Todd, 1995).

H. Braun, 'Literar-Analyse und theologische Schichtung im ersten Johannesbrief', *ZTK* 48 (1951), pp. 262-91.

E.E. Carpenter, 'Sacrifices and Offerings in the Old Testament', in *ISBE*, IV, pp. 260-73.

M.J. Edwards, 'Martyrdom and the First Epistle of John', *NovT* 31 (1989), pp. 164-71.

K. Grayston, 'The Meaning of PARAKLĒTOS', *JSNT* 13 (1981), pp. 67-82.

M.A. Knibb, *The Qumran Cummunity* (Cambridge Commentaries on the Writings of the Jewish and Christian World 200 BC to AD 200, 2; Cambridge: Cambridge University Press, 1998), esp. pp. 122-37.

J. Lieu, *The Theology of the Johannine Epistles* (Cambridge: Cambridge University Press, 1991), esp. pp. 58-65.

S. Lyonnet and L. Sabourin, *Sin, Redemption and Sacrifice* (Rome: Biblical Institute, 1970), esp. pp. 42-45.

F. García Martínez, *The Dead Sea Scrolls Translated: The Qumran Texts in English* (ET; Leiden: E.J. Brill; Grand Rapids: Eerdmans, 2nd edn, 1996), esp. pp. 122-37.

J.C. O'Neill, *The Puzzle of 1 John* (London: SPCK, 1966).

D.M. Scholer, 'Sins Within and Sins Without', in G.F. Hawthorne (ed.), *Current Issues in Biblical and Patristic Interpretation* (Grand Rapids: Eerdmans, 1975), pp. 230-46.

H.C. Swadling, 'Sin and Sinlessness in 1 John', *SJT* 35 (1982), pp. 205-11.

F.C. Synge, '1 John 3,2', *JTS* NS 3 (1952), p. 79.

G. Vermes, *The Complete Dead Sea Scrolls in English* (London: Penguin, 1998; New York: Allen Lane, 1997).

Chapter Nine

CONCLUSIONS

The introduction to this book identified some key issues concerning
the Johannine Epistles. Questions were raised about their composition
and authorship, genre and milieu. We noted their alleged dualism,
sectarianism, and polarization of attitudes, and asked how far these
were consistent with their teaching on love. Problems were found
with their understanding of sin. An important issue is whether these
writings have any message for today. We now draw together the
threads of this study and seek to assess the theological strengths and
weaknesses of these intriguing writings.

1. *Literary and Historical Character of the Epistles*

The literary form of 2 and 3 John is that of letter. 3 John comes closest
to the pattern of the simple, informal papyrus letter. It deals with specific issues—hospitality to travelling missionaries, the pretensions of a
local church leader Diotrephes, and the commendation of Demetrius
(probably 3 John's bearer). 2 John seems to be a more artificial creation, probably dependent on both 3 John and 1 John. The 'Elect Lady'
to whom it is addressed is usually interpreted as a personification of a
church, though she may be a real woman (cf. above Chapter 2 §3).
Unless either *eklektē* or *kyria* is a personal name, this is the only New
Testament writing to contain no proper names (other than Jesus).
2 John urges love, obedience and adherence to the truth. It also deals
with the problem of 'deceivers', who may be either the same group as
those denounced in 1 John, or possibly others with similar views who,
the author feels, need castigation in similar language. These letters
may or may not be by the same man, but they apparently come from
the same Johannine 'circle' or community.

The genre of 1 John remains enigmatic. In its present form it is not a
letter (whether literary or otherwise). Its general character is hortatory
and paraenetic, setting out a kind of 'Two Ways' theology marked by
stark antitheses (cf. the Sermon on the Mount). Like 2 and 3 John it is

consciously a written document (cf. 1.4; 2.12-14; 2.26; 5.13), but at the same time it probably incorporates oral material of a catechetical kind. There is much to be said for the view that it is an *encheiridion* or handbook compiled from both oral and written sources (cf. Chapter 3 §6). It refers to deceivers, who are denounced as 'antichrists', but their identity remains obscure. There is no statement of their teachings or detailed refutation of them, but they are countered by christological challenges, for example, 'Who is the liar, but the one who denies that Jesus is the Christ?' (2.22). In spite of this material, I do not see the primary purpose of 1 John as polemical. Its main purpose is to strengthen Christian faith. Indeed, if I am right in my hypothesis that it is some kind of instruction book, references to opponents may already have lost their topical relevance, being retained out of reverence for the master's teaching or because of their wider applicability. The intended audience for 1 John is unknown. There is no mention of Gentiles or Jewish–Gentile controversies. The theological content reveals a strong debt to Judaism, and there is much to be said for the view that it was intended for a Jewish-Christian audience, probably in the Diaspora.

The relationship of 1–3 John to John's Gospel is uncertain. Similarities of language and thought suggest that they stem from the same community, though not necessarily the same author, for there are theological differences. Although some of 1 John's ideas seem more 'primitive' than those of the Gospel of John (e.g. its teaching on atonement and eschatology), apparent allusions to the Gospel support the view that it was written after it. The evidence is insufficient to demonstrate that it was written specifically in *defence* of it. Stylistically 1 John has a strong Jewish and Semitic flavour (there are Semitisms also in 2–3 John). Its author has some natural rhetorical skill, but his Greek is marked by obscurities and ambiguities, and there are many places where his meaning is unclear. The internal evidence does not corroborate ancient traditions that the Johannines were written by the Apostle John or the shadowy 'John the Elder', known from Papias and Eusebius. But it is likely their author(s) were by origin Jewish. The basic thought-world is that of the Hebrew Bible; 1 John in particular has affinities with other Jewish writings, including the Qumran texts, *Jubilees* and the *Testaments of the Twelve Patriarchs*; it also shows some familiarity with incipient Gnosticism. However, one should not forget that 1–3 John are *Christian* writings, with many points of contact with the religious thought of other New Testament epistles and, indeed, the Gospels. The author(s) write because they are inspired by faith in Jesus Christ, as messiah, and from a sense of the love, holiness and faithfulness of God. The date of the Johannines cannot be precisely determined, but they were probably written towards the end of the first century CE.

2. *Sectarianism and Dualism*

We turn now to problems concerning the social and religious understanding of 1–3 John. Raymond Brown considers the question of sectarianism a 'burning issue'. He asks bluntly: 'Has the association of Johannine Christians become a sect?' (1979: 14). A number of scholars, with varying degrees of confidence or hesitancy, have answered in the affirmative, among them Meeks (1972), Smith (1975), Culpepper (1975), Bogart (1977) and Segovia (1981). Much depends on what is meant by 'sect'. In popular English usage this term is usually employed for a denomination or similar religious grouping with distinctive beliefs whose members are, of their own choice, separated from the mainstream or institutional church. In North America 'sect' is more often used as a sociological term for an exclusive community who see themselves as separated from the surrounding society and who hold negative views of 'the world' (cf. Meeks 1972). Were the Johannine Christians a 'sect' in either of these senses?

The first point to be made is that the existence of a 'Johannine community' separated from other New Testament communities is itself a conjecture. It is true that John's Gospel and 1–3 John share a common fund of ideas emphasizing such concepts as mutual love, truth, and light–dark dualism. But the notion that these stem from a separate ecclesial community is a hypothesis, not a fact. We do not know how 'Johannine' Christians related to the Pauline churches, the 'great church' at Jerusalem, or other early Christian communities. For a group to be called a 'sect' in the religious sense one would expect it to have distinctive doctrines and/or distinctive forms of worship. The *Concise Oxford Dictionary* defines a sect as a 'body of persons agreed upon religious doctrines usually different from those of an established or orthodox Church from which they have separated and usually having distinctive common worship'. But we know practically nothing about the worship of Johannine Christians, not even for certain whether they practised baptism or celebrated the Lord's Supper (1–3 John say nothing about these sacraments, and John's Gospel only alludes to them indirectly). As for church government, there is no reason to think it was very different from that found in the rest of the New Testament. Like the Pauline congregations, the Johannine churches seem to have had a 'charismatic' element with an emphasis on reception of the Spirit, accompanied by strong leadership on the part of individuals, such as Diotrephes and the Elder of 2–3 John. Although some scholars have thought the Gospel of John's portrayal of Peter implies polemic against the Petrine or 'great' church (discussed in Quast 1989, pp. 7-16), this is speculative, and there is no hint of such hostility in the Epistles.

Turning to religious beliefs, we must stress that the doctrinal ideas of 1–3 John (and John's Gospel) are essentially those of mainstream New Testament Christianity—the goodness and holiness of God; God's loving fatherhood and Jesus' divine sonship; human sinfulness and the need for forgiveness; the atoning death of Jesus; the gift of the Spirit; future judgment and hope of glory. The resurrection is not mentioned in 1–3 John, but Jesus' exaltation to heaven may be presupposed by his role as intercessor. 1 John does contain peculiar features, notably the terms *chrisma, sperma* and 'antichrist', and the idea of the impeccability (sinlessness) of God's children; also the concept of 'sin unto death'. But are these distinctive ideas more numerous or peculiar than those found uniquely in other New Testament documents (e.g. baptism for the dead in 1 Corinthians)? The ideal of eschatological sinlessness is, in any case, implied by many texts (e.g. 1 Thess. 5.23; Jude 24).

The problem with using the category of sectarianism (in the religious sense) is that it presupposes a clear-cut 'orthodoxy' or normative form of Christianity against which other manifestations of the faith can be measured. In practice, the New Testament documents exhibit a range of christologies and soteriologies. The alternative is to regard Johannine Christianity as sectarian in contradistinction to Judaism (rather than the rest of early Christianity). If this makes it a 'sect', so too are all the other New Testament churches.

What of the broader, more sociological understanding of 'sect', applied to inward-looking groups with 'world-denying' tendencies? The Johannine Epistles certainly presuppose a tightly-knit group who love one another, expressing their cohesiveness through such terms as 'brothers', 'beloved' and 'community' (*koinōnia*). They are hostile towards 'the world' and expect to be hated by it. They use vigorous, pejorative language for those with whom they disagree theologically, and seek to dissociate themselves from them. These features suggest a tendency towards sectarianism in the sociological sense. But are the Johannine Epistles any more 'sectarian' than other New Testament writings?

Ethical 'dualism', or a polarity between light and dark, good and evil, belief and unbelief, runs through the New Testament as a whole.

Paul tells believers not to be 'mismated' with unbelievers, 'For what fellowship has light with darkness? Or what accord has Christ with Belial?' (2 Cor. 6.14-15). Christians are told to 'walk as children of light', taking no part in 'the unfruitful works of darkness' (Eph. 5.8, 11). They are to set their minds 'on things above, not on things on the earth' (Col. 3.2). The Epistle of James decries friendship with 'the world', holding up the ideal of keeping oneself 'unspotted' from it (1.27). Jesus himself demands a whole-hearted, 'otherworldly' discipleship, bidding his followers not to lay up treasures on earth: 'no one can serve two masters…you cannot serve God and Mammon' (Mt. 6.24). In Mark 'the cares of the world and the deceit of wealth and the desires for other things' prevent the word bearing fruit (Mk 4.19). The main purpose of such ethical 'dualism' is to inculcate selfless, holy conduct. We have to face the fact that if the Johannines are 'sectarian' for expressing these views, so too is much of the rest of the New Testament.

As for attitudes to opponents, we have already commented on ancient conventions which permitted much more colourful language than is customary today. In fact, the language of the Johannines is in some respects mild compared with 2 Peter, where opponents are reviled as 'bold and wilful…like irrational animals…blots and blemishes…accursed children', for whom nether darkness has been reserved (2.10-17). In Acts, Paul castigates one opponent as 'a complete fraud and imposter, son of the devil, enemy of righteousness' (13.10); and in his letters he is not afraid to dub those with whom he differs theologically as 'pseudo-apostles and confidence tricksters' (2 Cor. 11.13). Matthew's Gospel denounces the scribes and Pharisees as hypocrites, blind guides, fools and children of Hell (Mt. 23.13-29). This does not make the Johannine attitudes any better, but it helps us understand them. Perhaps it was hoped by such language to shock people into repentance. At the very least such terms served as a warning to readers.

We conclude, then, that there is a sense in which 1–2 John are sectarian (there is not enough material to make a judgment on 3 John). But, as we have seen, they share this characteristic with many other New Testament writings. Their hyperbolic language serves to reinforce their ethical and christological purpose. It is another question whether it is right or helpful to use such language today.

3. *Love and Ethical Conduct*

The teaching of 1 John on love is so moving that it is hard to understand why it has come under attack in recent years. The main problems arise from a reading which presupposes that a full theology of love is being given; this is then criticized as inadequate. The teaching should be seen in its social and rhetorical context. 1 John is concerned with the fundamentals of the Christian life. The author seeks to promote love of God and mutual love among members. We can compare 1 Peter, probably also incorporating catechetical material, which sets out basics of the faith: redemption and new birth through Jesus Christ; the call to holiness and obedience, and *philadelphia*—brotherly (and sisterly) love. 'Having purified your souls in obedience to the truth so that you have genuine mutual love, *love one another* from a pure heart fervently, having been born again, not from perishable seed, but from imperishable, through the living and abiding word of God' (1 Pet. 1.22-23). Romans (12.10), 1 Thessalonians (4.9), Hebrews (13.1), and even 2 Peter (1.7) similarly urge mutual love. Some of these texts (Rom. 12.14; Heb. 13.2) also enjoin love of enemies or hospitality to strangers; but one cannot expect every Christian writing to urge every Christian duty (or touch on every Christian doctrine). 1 John is not concerned with relations with non-Christians, but with inter-Christian relationships and the believer's relationship with God.

1 John's injunction to love is rooted in its understanding of God's nature as love. The logical corollary of the great affirmation 'God is love' is that Christian love should also be universal. The author wants Christian love to be practical, including concern for both physical and spiritual needs (3.17; 5.16). He is adamant that one cannot love God without loving fellow Christians: 'Those who say "I love God" and hate their brothers [and sisters] are liars; for how can those who do not love a brother [or sister] whom they have seen love God whom they have not seen?' (4.20). We might add, 'How can those who do not love their fellow Christians whom they have seen love strangers whom they have not seen?' It seems to be a case of 'charity begins at home'.

Unlike many other New Testament texts, 1 John does not list rules for proper Christian conduct. There are no *Haustafeln* (tables of household rules) governing behaviour of wives and husbands, slaves and masters, such as we find in Colossians, Ephesians and 1 Peter. Though obedience to God's (or Christ's) commands is frequently enjoined, it is never spelt out what these commands are: the only one mentioned is the command to love. This is both a strength and a weakness of Johannine ethics.

4. *Doctrine and Religious Experience*

For some the great strength of 1 John is its championing of doctrinal orthodoxy against the threat of 'heresy'. The reality of Christ's 'coming in the flesh' is strongly upheld, and a firm stance taken against any who would deny it. Yet it is precisely this insistence on a particular understanding of Jesus' sonship and messiahship which others see as a weakness. 1 John has been characterized as 'reactionary' and 'inflexible', with its harking back to what was 'from the beginning', and sometimes contrasted adversely with the Gospel of John, which is seen as theologically 'creative'. One must reply that the church and world need both conservative and progressive (or radical) theologians—progressive to explore and break new ground; conservative to preserve what is good. In any case 1 John is not lacking more speculative elements, for example, when it speaks of the indescribable transformation awaiting believers (3.2). Similarly, the language of 'eternal life', 'chrism', 'seed', 'having God' and 'being' or 'abiding' in God is capable of creative, mystical interpretation. This is not cut-and-dried dogmatic theology, but the language of religious experience.

One problem for modern readers is that some of the language does not correspond to their own religious experience. Some are unhappy with its androcentric language. Many are ill-at-ease with its 'black-and-white' outlook, dividing humanity into 'children of God' and 'children of the devil'. The Johannine polarization seems too sharp. What are we to make, in a modern, scientific age, of references to the 'antichrist' and the devil? Do we take these terms literally, or do we 'demythologize' them? In a sense our author may have already started demythologizing by identifying the end-time 'antichrist' with contemporary human beings. But one would hardly wish to imitate the mediaeval thinkers or Protestant Reformers who described their religious opponents (emperors and popes) as God's archetypal spiritual enemy. Even if 'antichrist' is demythologized, the author still believes in an imminent parousia. And what about the devil? Can we believe in spiritual conflict at a cosmic level? Does the whole world lie in the power of the 'Evil One' (1 Jn 5.19)? While some Christians are content to accept this world-view, many feel that it is unduly pessimistic, that it denies the true victory of the Cross, and that it takes picture-language too literally. We no longer believe in demons as the cause of epilepsy, or mental illness or sudden disaster; we believe in our own responsibility for our actions; why bring in the devil, except as a last resort to explain the problem of evil? Even then, the hypothesis does not really account for the presence of evil in the world; for Scripture leaves unexplained how the 'devil' ('Satan', or 'the Evil One') came into being, or how a God who is all-powerful, as well as all-just and all-good, can tolerate the activities of a spiritual being that lures men and women to sin.

1 John's teaching on sin and atonement also causes difficulties for some readers. While many have found hope and encouragement in its assurances of forgiveness, especially 2.1, enshrined in the 'Comfortable Words' of the *Book of Common Prayer* (1662), people are disturbed by its reference to a 'sin unto death' (5.16-17), and puzzled (or worried) by the assertion that God's children cannot sin, which runs contrary to Christian experience as well as formally contradicting what was said earlier in this writing. Some are put off by the language of 'blood' and sacrifice. How can Jesus' death remove sin? Once again we are dealing with a mode of thought alien to the modern world of computers and astrophysics. Yet here, as with the devil, 1 John's concepts are those of the rest of the Bible. He writes as heir to a long tradition of Jewish thought, in the context of other ancient faiths which made use of rituals of sacrifice and appeasement. Such concepts and rituals still have power to move and motivate (cf. Bradley 1995). Perhaps we need a radical rethinking of how Biblical ideas of sacrifice and atonement can be re-expressed in ways meaningful for a modern world. In this respect the Johannine Epistles provide stimulus for ongoing theological enquiry.

5. Conclusion

Biblical texts may serve as warnings as well as examples. Even a 'sectarian' reading of 1–3 John can teach something of the dangers of belonging to a closed group who hold to rigid doctrinal lines. At the same time we get a glimpse into the values of a community where mutual love and obedience to God's commands are taken seriously. Whatever our reading of the text, the Johannines speak to us of a God who is just and loving, and of a Saviour who gave his life for all humanity. They set before us ideals of righteousness, love and purity of conduct. They offer hope for the future and assure us of the possibility of forgiveness. However great the problems caused by their obscurity of expression or 'mythological' modes of thought, they have a message for us today. 'Trust in God's Son Jesus Christ and love one another' (1 Jn 3.23). 'Beloved, let us love one another, for love is of God' (4.7).

FURTHER READING

On sectarianism and relation to mainstream Christianity:

J. Bogart, *Orthodox and Heretical Perfectionism in the Johannine Community* (SBLDS, 33: Missoula, MT, 1977).

R.E. Brown, *The Community of the Beloved Disciple* (New York: Paulist Press, 1979).

R.A. Culpepper, *The Johannine School* (SBLDS, 26; Missoula, MT: Scholars Press, 1975).

W.A. Meeks, 'The Man from Heaven in Johannine Sectarianism', *JBL* 91 (1972), pp. 44-72.

K. Quast, *Peter and the Beloved Disciple* (Sheffield: JSOT Press, 1989).

F. Segovia, 'The Love and Hatred of Jesus in Johannine Sectarianism', *CBQ* 43 (1981), pp. 258-72, esp. 258.

D.M. Smith, 'Johannine Christianity', *NTS* 21 (1975), pp. 222-48, esp. 224.

On the devil and theodicy:

Loader 1992, pp. 36-37.

J. Hick, *Evil and the God of Love* (London: Macmillan, 1966).

On the atonement:

D.M. Bailey, *God Was in Christ* (London: Faber & Faber, 1948), chs. 7-8. A classic work.

I. Bradley, *The Power of Sacrifice* (London: Darton, Longman & Todd, 1995).

Part III

REVELATION
John M. Court

COMMENTARIES ON AND STUDIES OF THE BOOK OF REVELATION

Commentaries on the book of Revelation:

Two massive commentaries have been published recently which provide great opportunities for exploration:

David Aune, *Revelation* (WBC, 52 A, B and C, 3 vols.; Waco, TX: Thomas Nelson, 1997, 1998).

G.K. Beale, *The Book of Revelation* (NIGTC, Grand Rapids, MI: Eerdmans; Carlisle: Paternoster Press, 1999).

It is wise never to rely on a single commentary, but rather to use several interactively. Among numerous earlier commentaries these are particularly worth consulting:

G.B. Caird, *The Revelation of St John the Divine* (Black's New Testament Commentaries; London: A. & C. Black, 1966).

R.H. Charles, *A Critical and Exegetical Commentary on the Revelation of St John* (2 vols.; ICC; Edinburgh: T. & T. Clark, 1920).

Austin Farrer, *The Revelation of St John the Divine: A Commentary on the English Text* (Oxford: Oxford University Press, 1964).

A.J.P. Garrow, *Revelation* (New Testament Readings; London and New York: Routledge, 1997).

J.P.M. Sweet, *Revelation* (SCM Pelican Commentaries; London: SCM Press, 1979).

Studies of the book of Revelation:

Richard Bauckham, *The Theology of the Book of Revelation* (New Testament Theology Series, Cambridge: Cambridge University Press 1993). An admirably succinct treatment of the book's great theological importance.

A. Yarbro Collins, *Crisis and Catharsis: The Power of the Apocalypse* (Philadelphia: Westminster Press 1984). Essentially a sociological analysis of the book.

John M. Court, *Myth and History in the Book of Revelation* (Atlanta: John Knox Press; London: SPCK 1979). Authors should not recommend their own books, but this will serve to emphasize the interplay between inherited traditions and actual historical situations.

—*The Book of Revelation and the Johannine Apocalyptic Tradition* (JSNTSup, 190; Sheffield: Sheffield Academic Press, 2000).

Colin J. Hemer, *The Letters to the Seven Churches of Asia in their Local Setting* (JSNTSup, 11; Sheffield: JSOT Press, 1986). A splendid book combining firsthand fieldwork in Asia Minor with a survey of ancient sources and inscriptions.

E. Schüssler Fiorenza, *The Book of Revelation: Justice and Judgment* (Philadelphia: Fortress Press 1985). A compilation from articles over an extended period, holding together issues of literary structure and historical-rhetorical situation.

Works in this list are cited in the following chapters by author's name and date only.

Chapter One

INTRODUCTION: REVELATION REVISITED

I have written this chapter as an explanation of those factors which have influenced me in my approach to the writing of this book. As is often the case with academic introductions that discuss methods of study, it might well be preferable to read the primary text of the book of Revelation first, together with the thematic guide provided by Chapter 2. The reader can then come back to the 'Introduction' last of all, or study it in conjunction with the literary, historical and theological chapters of this part of the book.

The act of study is a personal matter. Each of us makes the text her or his own. So I begin with my own personal reactions to the book of Revelation. In particular I would draw some contrasts between the way I looked at the text in the mid-1960s and the way I perceive it now at the start of the new century. But this is not just a personal matter. The contrasts I draw do also reflect some shifts in the wider academic perspectives on biblical literature over the last 30 years, and the effects that these have on Revelation in particular.

In an earlier book, which I wrote in 1979, I emphasized the importance of understanding the historical context in which Revelation was originally written. Imagery, symbolism and mythology, such as is found in Revelation, can have an almost limitless life-span, and may seem innately volatile. But within a specific religious tradition, such as Jewish and Judaeo-Christian apocalyptic, we can see the same imagery and myth being repackaged and controlled in ways that relate very closely to the political circumstances and religious needs of a particular moment of history, the time of writing of the latest version. This sets before us a quest for the details of ancient history (that is no longer the exclusive preserve of the classicist) and for the history of early Christianity. In recent years this quest has also been directed to social as well as political history, in a desire to reconstruct what it felt like to live in the world of the New Testament.

There is an irony in the fact that historical interpretation of the book of Revelation, in the sense of concern with the contemporary history of the time when the book was written, arose rather late in the day, when much of the data for it was already lost. Such historical inter-pretation of Revelation was motivated in the sixteenth and seven-teenth centuries largely as a reaction against those fantastic construc-tions of world history, cyclical patterns, epochs, or concern for the Millennium, which had dominated exegesis of the Apocalypse in the Middle Ages. But there were some new sources of information to come in the nineteenth and twentieth centuries from archaeology or from the interaction with classical history. These can be seen, for example, when Sir William Ramsay studied the seven letters against their settings in Asia Minor, and Stanislas Giet compared the events of Revelation with the Jewish Revolt and War (66–70 CE), as described by Josephus. But there is an obvious danger, when the evidence is severely limited, that a researcher with special interests will find what he or she wishes to see; historical parallels or coincidences may be identified too easily.

I may already have given the impression, from my personalized approach to the study of Revelation, that I am going to say, 'I used to think as a historian, but now I have changed my mind!' It is true that methods of interpretation seem like changes of fashion, and are usu-ally thought to be mutually exclusive. This has appeared to be espe-cially the case with the historical method, that it seemed incompatible with other options, such as allegorical readings, literary reconstruc-tions, and the comparative studies of religion. But my approach was and is determinedly against such exclusivity. I have wanted to show that we need to take the traditions of mythology seriously, to appreci-ate the similarities with other religions, the literary manner in which they are presented, and the allegories of theological truth. But like other theological activity, for the author and readers of Revelation these myths were time-bound. We need the historical method to demonstrate how these ideas were particularly related to their con-temporary circumstances.

So in what ways have my own perspectives been altered by New Testament scholarship over the last 30 years? I have observed the fol-lowing areas of change, which I would argue are highly significant, and not just for my personal interpretation of the book of Revelation:

1. The modern relevance of the ideas of apocalyptic
2. The computerization of criticism
3. Sociological interpretations
4. Images of empire
5. Literary genres and symbolic structures

1. *The Modern Relevance of the Ideas of Apocalyptic*

H.H. Rowley (*The Relevance of Apocalyptic* [London: Lutterworth Press, 1944]) and his English-language associates fought a lonely battle to make the apocalyptic literature seem relevant to Christian theology. Only with the 'rediscovery of Apocalyptic' (e.g. Klaus Koch's book of that title, published in Germany in 1970 [ET, London: SCM Press, 1972]) did German-speaking scholars come to share with their English counterparts a general appreciation of its relevance as a significantly radical strand of Judaism, which had fed into Christian thought. The bizarre world of the Apocalypse might still be dismissed by some as the delusions of a sick nature, but, with the new literary and historical understanding, it would at least be appreciated that the apocalyptist was no psychosomatic case, but had actually been made sick by the evil realities that he was forced to suffer. The Apocalypse thus belongs to the literature of protest and revolt. Or at least that is the emphasis that has spoken most clearly in recent years.

For comparison, we can look back at C.S. Lewis, preaching a sermon and writing in *The Guardian* in 1942. He is describing the dominance of materialism as the popular creed of Western Europe:

> For let us make no mistake. If the end of the world appeared in all the literal trappings of the Apocalypse, if the modern materialist saw with his own eyes the heavens rolled up and the great white throne appearing, if he had the sensation of being himself hurled into the Lake of Fire, he would continue forever, in that lake itself, to regard his experience as an illusion and to find the explanation of it in psycho-analysis, or cerebral pathology. Experience by itself proves nothing.

In recent decades there has been a much greater willingness to consider such 'experiences' positively, with a more sympathetic understanding of their context. The book that used to be regarded as useful only as the script for a horror film came to be seen as applicable to the Marxist/Socialist view of the twentieth century. In the words of the historian E.J. Hobsbawm, 'We have been taught by the experience of our century to live in the expectation of apocalypse'. And, as Raymond Williams, the literary critic, expressed it,

> All the big things, just now, are against us, but within what is not only a very powerful but also an exceptionally unstable social and cultural order there are forces moving of which nobody can depict the outcome.

Since the bombing of Hiroshima, the nuclear threat has been dominant, and often visualized in terms such as Rev. 16.17-21:

> a violent earthquake, such as had not occurred since people were upon the earth, so violent was that earthquake. The great city was split into three parts, and the cities of the nations fell... And every island fled away and no mountains were to be found.

As Sallie McFague writes, 'the threat of a nuclear holocaust... [epitomizes] the genuinely novel context in which all constructive work in our time, including theology, must take place' (*Models of God: Theology for an Ecological, Nuclear Age* [London: SCM Press, 1987], p. ix). In recent years other kinds of cosmic pollution and other abuses of environmental resources have been recognized as equally life-threatening in the end. 'Green' campaigners use a mixture of scientific and apocalyptic language in what Jürgen Moltmann called 'the beginning of a life and death struggle for creation on the earth' (1985, p. xi).

The Christian Apocalypse consoles those who glimpse what hell can be, and encourages those who would build a new Jerusalem. Sects (such as Jezreel's Trumpeters) have built Jerusalem to Revelation's ground plan before; what is different now is the scale of the threat and the wider recognition of society's vulnerability. As on the placards proclaiming the end of the world, the text of Revelation is often taken literally, especially by influential fundamentalist groups in the United States of America. The year 1993 saw a most extreme example of this in the Branch Davidian sect, the group led by David Koresh, which immolated itself at the 'Ranch Apocalypse' at Waco in Texas. More positively, in South Africa, Archbishop Desmond Tutu has testified to the power of the vision of Rev. 7.9-12 to uphold him, in the fight against apartheid. And Chinese Christians used the Apocalypse in the days before Tiananmen Square. Such readings of the text (by literal or allegorical means) are analysing world conditions by reference to Scripture, not prophesying directly from Scripture like a confident mediaeval exegete. As in the case of nuclear apocalyptic, comparisons may be simplistic, and may mistake the broadly similar theme for the exactly identical situation; but the text functions as an immediately relevant handling of the issues, not an esoteric code or the fantasies of a disordered brain.

2. *The Computerization of Criticism*

Literary criticism has been rejuvenated by computer technology. Research projects of a much larger scale, in concordances and analyses of language, grammar and style, can be conceived and carried through without the risk of madness which assailed Alexander Cruden, the pioneer concordance-compiler. Among these new possibilities are the statistical studies of literary style that may assist in the attribution of authorship (e.g. are some or all of the works in the Johannine corpus by the same author?) or the estimate of a single work's integrity (in Revelation only ch. 12 was identified as possibly from a different source, because the statistics were so wildly discrepant). Anthony Kenny set out the principles clearly (in a *THES* article summarizing his book):

> The use of stylometry in authorship attribution studies depends on the hypothesis that there are quantifiable features of style which are characteristic of particular authors. Ideally, a stylometric test of authorship should be a feature which is characteristic of all the known works of a particular author and which is unique to his works. Features which are to be found in all and only the works of a particular author turn out to be frustratingly difficult to come by. Authorship attribution problems are easier to deal with when they can be cast into the following form: in respect of the measured features, does the doubtful work resemble the work of candidate author A more than it resembles the work of candidate author B?

Studies of language, just as much as studies of an author's style, can benefit from the enlarged scope and mathematical precision of computer applications. It was a highlight of an earlier generation of literary criticism when R.H. Charles attempted to demonstrate the regularities in the apparently barbaric Greek of the Apocalypse (see pp. cxvii-clix of the introduction to his ICC commentary on Revelation [1920]). Essentially the author wrote in Greek but thought in Hebrew. In contrast, G.K. Beale has recently described the 'stylistic use of the Old Testament' in Revelation as 'intentional solecisms' designed 'to create a "biblical" effect in the hearer' ('Revelation', in *It is Written: Scripture Citing Scripture: Essays in Honour of Barnabas Lindars* [ed. D.A. Carson and H.M.G. Williamson, Cambridge: Cambridge University Press, 1988], p. 332).

Nowadays critics are agreed about very little, beyond the extent of the general influence of the prophetic literature of the Old Testament (especially Ezekiel, Isaiah, Jeremiah and Daniel) upon the author of the Apocalypse. The question to resolve is one of means: whether that influence is mediated through classical Hebrew texts, a Greek version (the Septuagint), or a living language of Aramaic (so that the Semitic idioms are bilingual with the Greek). This looks like one exemplification, in the particular text of the Apocalypse, of a much broader issue, the analysis of the actual nature of 'Biblical Greek' (the term used for the impact of the Old Testament tradition upon Koine Greek). The great need here is for sharper definition (what do we mean by a 'Semitism'? is it clearly distinct from a 'Septuagintalism'?). Wide-ranging relationships of language must be identified and charted, not simply covered by 'umbrella' terms. What the computer offers is the facility to classify and compare examples of grammatical structures, idioms and vocabulary in a precise way in relation to a vast and potentially exhaustive database.

3. *Sociological Interpretations*

Sociological methods have been employed to interpret available data on the community that produced Revelation. The model frequently employed is that of a sectarian group, marginalized by the attitudes of society. The group is under severe stress, not necessarily overt persecution, but certainly ostracism and social contempt. They feel threatened and insecure, and must also contend with religious stress. Such stress is produced not only by the externally enforced worship of the Roman Emperor, with economic sanctions for non-conformists, but also by some internal conflicts, symbolized in the text of Revelation by the Nicolaitans (2.6, 15) and the synagogue of Satan (2.9). But to speak of sects is not to concentrate entirely on the negative aspects. As Bryan Wilson says, in *The Social Dimensions of Sectarianism: Sects and New Religious Movements in Contemporary Society* (Oxford: Clarendon Press, 1990):

> Sects make a strong reassertion of certain abiding human values, and all of them provide specific grounds for hope in an uncertain world, and offer the occasion for service and self-expression.

For the sociologist of religion, sects are a particularly appropriate and convenient field of research. They are small, clearly defined, self-enclosed communities with relatively fixed belief systems. In the modern world such deviant groups constitute the sharpest of challenges to secularized society, even more than they do to the established religion, from which they are a splinter-group. Care is necessary in transposing this model to the ancient world. In the case of the varied movements of early Christianity, which are the representatives of orthodoxy and of heresy, in the years before the religion is 'established' in any meaningful sense? On the other hand the inherent tension between sects and society may be as applicable to the churches in relation to the Roman Empire as it is in modern secular-ism; but the analogy needs to be defended, with careful analysis of the issues.

4. *Images of Empire*

The title is that of a collection of essays, published in 1991, and of the conference organized by Loveday Alexander in Sheffield in March 1990, at which the material was first presented as papers. I use it as a very effective symbol of the broadly interdisciplinary treatment of the theme of Empire, which is essential if the sociological model of the sect is to be sustained.

The programme of the conference was:

> to explore the conflicting images generated by the Roman Empire and their afterlife. With the wealth of Roman, Jewish and Christian literature at our disposal we have an unparalleled opportunity to explore a variety of attitudes to an empire, both 'from above' and 'from below'...the wider issues raised by the investigation of any well-documented political system from the past, and the living force of the images generated in that past society. Both the positive and the negative images of the Roman Empire have had an influence right through to the twentieth century; and successive generations of believers have had to wrestle... with the meaning of texts (written under the Romans) for a community facing the diverse political realities of the twentieth century.

One of the images in the background is that of the four World Empires found in Daniel and the traditions of Jewish Apocalyptic. Against this one would set Rome's own self-generated ideology, which persists to the present day in the overworked phrase 'the grandeur that was Rome' (borrowed from Edgar Allan Poe). The basis of this lay in the political acts and writing of Augustus himself, the promotion of the imperial cult from the eastern provinces, the histories of Livy, and the rhetoric of such as Aelius Aristides. But the view of Rome from within is not entirely harmonious, as can be documented from the writings of Tacitus. The essential contrast between the views of Rome from inside and outside, from above and below, is forcibly presented in the book by Klaus Wengst, *Pax Romana and the Peace of Jesus Christ* (1987). His may well be a partisan view; there are certainly other ways of construing some of the texts that Wengst uses. We also need to consider the views of other provincials (e.g. in Asia Minor) and the attitudes of the lowest classes of Roman society (including the slaves) as well as the unusual features of relationships between Rome, the Jews and eventually the Christians.

The tensions between images of Rome persist in the writings of

Church Fathers, such as Tertullian and Augustine (particularly in *City of God*). In turn the twentieth century made its own use of the images of Babylon and the Evil Empire, debated the political appropriateness of Romans 13, and related Apocalyptic hopes to liberation theology. A further instance is provided by Rainer Stahl, who teaches Old Testament at Leipzig, in *Von Weltengagement zu Weltüberwindung: Theologische Positionen im Danielbuch* (Kampen: Kok Pharos, 1993). He used the underlying image of 'World Empire' from Daniel to interpret modern situations. 'The Russian empire is broken to pieces and has set free Eastern Germany. What can we say about it, having Daniel in mind?'

5. *Literary Genres and Symbolic Structures*

The method known as genre criticism is a significant part of the new literary approaches to the text. The beginnings of genre identification were in form criticism with its recognition of formulae (e.g. warnings, macarisms) and of formulaic structures appropriate to particular purposes such as letter-writing. But the study of larger-scale literary genres has now progressed much further, as can be seen in volume 14 of the experimental journal *Semeia*, published in 1979 and dedicated to explore the morphology of the genre of apocalypse. The declared aims (see pp. iii-iv) were:

> to provide a comprehensive survey of all the texts which might be or have been classified as apocalypses and can be dated with any plausibility in the period 250 BCE—250 CE, with the purpose of establishing how far they can purposefully be regarded as members of one genre...

> to lend perspective to the view of apocalypses [which in the past was based on a few works that were used as the basis for broad generalizations] by showing the extent and the limits of the similarities which are found throughout the apocalyptic corpus...

> to provide perspective on the individual works by which both the typical and the distinctive elements can be more fully appreciated.

It is a study of the phenomena of the genre, although some implications for the history of the genre are bound to emerge.

It has long been recognized that the book of Revelation is an amalgam of literary types, even allowing for a single authorship of the final work. In the past the variety has been used by critics in order to discriminate, for example favouring the letters to the seven churches in chs. 2 and 3, but despising their apocalyptic packaging. Recent study of the component parts of Revelation may not be so partisan, but has often resulted in a battle between the genres. Is the dominant type that of the letters, or are they merely an epistolary frame for communications that more closely resemble imperial edicts? Given such an imperial perspective, with its political dimension so important in modern interpretation, is the setting of chs. 4 and 5 modelled on the Emperor's audience chamber? The dominant genre is then Roman imperial court ceremonial which is here so effectively parodied. Does this mean we must reject the influential interpretation in terms of a heavenly liturgy, which itself is a projection of the liturgical forms and practice of the early church? (See Gregory Dix, *The Shape of the Liturgy* [London: A. & C. Black, 2nd edn, 1945], p. 28). Or is the character of Revelation essentially dramatic, as a literary form 'meant to be read aloud', indeed to be performed as a combination of liturgical and theatrical experience? Recognition of such a genre would entail that we picture the twenty-four elders in the heavenly transformation of a Greek theatre, with God's throne and Christ as the Lamb on stage.

There is equal diversity among the schools of literary structuralism, which sought to explain, from the organizational principles and apparently self-conscious structures of the text, the nature of the symbolic universe that was constructed or reflected in this book. If one can speak of this 'universe' in terms of Realism, then it can be conceived as a response to their social world, made by the group to which the author belongs, a group that may well be on the margins. One can hardly expect any single diagram on a printed page to do justice to the structure of this text, let alone this universe. One needs to think in terms of interlocking facets in a three-dimensional figure. Structuralism invites some reconsideration of traditional interpretations, such as the theories of recapitulation. It should not be assumed that the order of Revelation is chronological, rather than thematically and theologically conceived. The combination of linear narrative with repetitions and celebrations in the form of hymns can reveal a deliberate intention to set up tensions in the structure, for rhetorical effect. The resulting overall shape of this chiastic work has been likened to the geometric figure of a conic spiral by Elizabeth Schüssler Fiorenza (*The Book of Revelation: Justice and Judgment* [1985]).

6. *Readers and the Range of their Response*

To talk exclusively of author's intention (even if collectively expressed of the author's community) would be regarded as unforgivably one-sided in terms of the modern approach to a literary text. There is need to leave room for all that happens to a text after it leaves the author's hands. In the case of the biblical tradition there is an extremely rich vein of interpretation, up to and including modern preaching, apologetic, and literary reading. Even in the historical context in which the text was first produced there is room to consider the earliest stages of audience interaction with the text. What impression did the author hope to make? Can we tell if he succeeded in whole or in part? Even without regarding it as a theatrical script for performance, are there signs that a text has been modified by audience participation?

In the opening vision of Revelation 1, there is a call narrative which underlines the authority of the writer and legitimates the activity of this Christian prophet. To see how vital is this initial emphasis, one can ask what would be lost if the Apocalypse began, as it obviously could, with 1.9. The text has undeniable importance in a struggle for power. The Christian prophet is asserting the dominion of Jesus as king over against the blasphemous pretensions of the emperor to set himself up as God (in his imperial edicts). But might the power struggle also be internal as well as external to this Christian community? The book begins as it does because the author knows that the voice of his prophecy has been and will be contested by other Christians. Against this threat to his authority John attests his own direct commissioning and deliberately allows his narrative voice to merge with the words of angels and of Christ himself.

A larger literary structure than any discussed so far is the ultimate canon of Scripture of the Old and New Testaments which concludes with the book of Revelation. Defining the limits of canon so as to include Revelation, after protracted disputes about it in the church, is an example of large-scale reader response that needs to be discussed in historical terms. But exponents of canonical criticism insist that the sweep of material 'from Moses to Patmos' should be evaluated in literary and theological terms. How may we best describe the climax to the canon which this last book represents? But if the literary model of the Old Testament 'canon' is at all influential in the arrangement of the New Testament, we may have to conclude that Revelation, like Daniel and the works of the Chronicler among the 'Writings', is more appendix than climax.

7. Conclusions: Wider Acceptance of Pluralism in Method

The contrast between the older and newer approaches is most marked as Revelation is applied to Christian preaching. Not so long ago typical selections for sermons were the glimpses of early Christian behaviour in the seven letters, and the comforting passages used at funerals. Now the focus is on political, social and environmental threats, and the themes of responsibility, justice, judgment and vengeance. The book becomes a study of power, also raising ethical issues about responses to power at a time of crisis. Revelation functions as a warning to the complacent within society, or has a cathartic effect on the community by arousing intense feelings of inflammatory aggressiveness. Or it may be a moral lesson on the victim's desire for vengeance. How can one decide which function is most appropriate, most true to the original situation of the writer?

Some refuse to see the book as relative to any one situation in particular, but rather as timeless and therefore valid for all times. Just as allegorical exegesis emphasizes the moment of interpretation as much as, if not more than, the moment of writing, so a modern hermeneutic theory insists that the meaning of a work is primarily what it means to the reader. Pluralism of method can turn into an ideological pluralism in which there are no objectively correct answers, only a range of subjective responses. There may be a heady sense of freedom about such interpretation, but it is difficult to pose questions of original or ultimate truth. The contributions of the author and of his situation to what is said—and the ways in which this handles, and is handled by, the continuity of traditions—must still retain some significance, if not decisive control, in questions of meaning.

Revelation is a relevant text for many crises. But the intoxication of a theme like Justice and Judgment should not blind one to the balance of other issues in the book. Literature rich in imagery and symbolism deserves to be studied as a work of art, in the light of the great works of art (e.g. paintings) that it has inspired. And Revelation's vision of an alternative world derives power from the actual contrast with the socio-political realities that gave it birth. For literary tensions and theological dialectic to be understood fully, historical questions must remain part of the interpreter's task. To appreciate the apocalyptic traditions that feed into the book, and the theological, sectarian and monastic traditions that are fed by it, Revelation's place in the story must be located and illuminated. The 'new look' at Revelation produced by both structural and sociological analyses is welcome, precisely because it contributes to a fuller reading of the book and of the circumstances that produced it. The real need is for a total view, to interrelate methods and results and demonstrate Revelation's lasting contribution to the Christian tradition.

FURTHER READING

Loveday Alexander (ed.), *Images of Empire* (Sheffield: JSOT Press, 1991).

David E. Aune, 'The Form and the Function of Proclamations to the Seven Churches (Rev 2–3)', *NTS* 36.2 (April 1990), pp. 182-204.

John M. Court, *Myth and History in the Book of Revelation* (Atlanta: John Knox Press; London: SPCK, 1979).

Paul D. Hanson, *Visionaries and their Apocalypses* (Issues in Religion and Theology, 2; Philadelphia: Fortress Press; London: SPCK, 1983).

Anthony Kenny, *A Stylometric Study of the New Testament* (Oxford: Oxford University Press, 1986).

Jürgen Moltmann, *God in Creation: An Ecological Doctrine of Creation* (The Gifford Lectures 1984–85; London: SCM Press, 1985).

Daryl D. Schmidt, 'Semitisms and Septuagintalisms in the Book of Revelation', *NTS* 37.4 (October 1991), pp. 592-603.

Klaus Wengst, *The Pax Romana and the Peace of Jesus Christ* (London: SCM Press, 1987).

Chapter Two

READING REVELATION BY THEMES

Outline Chart of the Book of Revelation

1.1-3   Introduction as to an apocalyptic work

1.4-8   Introduction as to a circular letter to the Asian churches

1.9-20   John's heavenly vision of Christ as the Son of Man

2, 3   Seven particular letters to seven existing churches (associated with the author) in Asia Minor

4, 5   John's vision of worship in the royal throne-room of heaven; Christ as the Lamb receives the sealed book of prophecy

6   Christ opens six of the seven seals: the realities of the present and of recent history (e.g. war and famine) are interpreted as symbols of prophecy

7   Heavenly interlude:
         the sealing of those who are to be spared
         the worship by those called to be saints

8, 9   The seventh seal:
         silence and liturgy
         six of the seven trumpet blasts portending disasters

10   Interlude:
         the mighty angel
         the seven thunders are suppressed
         the prophet John receives (and inwardly digests) a scroll

11   The contents of this scroll (a flash-back, to interpret past history):
         the fall of Jerusalem to the Romans (67–70 CE)

the model provided by Peter and Paul of apostolic witness to Christ (64–67 CE)

The seventh trumpet sounds amid heavenly worship

12, 13 The seventh trumpet heralds the disastrous arrival on earth of the two beasts (13.1, 11)

The portent of the woman with the child (12) supplies the context: the diabolical beasts are on earth because the devil was expelled from heaven (12.9); and this expulsion was a consequence of Christ's incarnation and resurrection. So the church on earth is persecuted (12.17)

14 The song of the saints in heaven

Angelic proclamations of judgment on earth

Harvest and winepress as symbols of God's judgment

15 Heavenly interlude, as the seven bowls of wrath are introduced

16 The bowls contain plagues (like the plagues of Egypt at the time of the Exodus) which are the judgment of God's wrath upon the earth (and what the beasts have brought about there)

17 The Roman Empire (particularly the blasphemy of worshipping the Emperor as divine) is to be destroyed in God's judgment

18 Warnings of the fall of imperial Rome, and the lamentations of those (merchants and clients) affected by her fall

19 Song of triumph in heaven

Anticipation of the marriage of Christ, the Lamb

Christ rides forth victorious to the last battle

20 The Millennium (the thousand-year reign of Christ and the saints)

The final resurgence of the powers of evil

The Last Judgment

21.1–22.5 The vision of the heavenly city, New Jerusalem (the church in heaven as the bride of Christ)

The new created order—the paradise garden

22.6-20 Final guarantees and solemn warnings, appropriate to an apocalyptic work (see 1.1-3)

Christ's Second Coming is imminent

22.21 Ending appropriate to a letter (see 1.4-8)

Introduction

According to Etienne Charpentier (1982, p. 105), 'the Book of Revelation, the Apocalypse, is a book of fire and blood in the image of our world'. This view suggests a sense of realism and of urgent relevance, just as some people have found that experience of wartime or of nuclear catastrophe sends them back to these words of prophecy. A few readers are confident, in an almost proprietorial way, about the meaning of the book and how it relates to them in their present situation. Most people are much less sure and may not even know where to begin (or whether they want to begin!). Some readers may even doubt whether this book deserves to be in the New Testament at all.

In such circumstances the most important question is how one should read the book. There are three main things to consider:

1. We must be aware of the situation in which the book came into being: in a small Christian group, politically vulnerable and persecuted for its faith.

2. It must be read imaginatively, in a way that is responsive to the writer's images and use of symbolism: this means enjoying the sound of the words themselves and relating the verbal pictures to the reader's memory of the Old Testament and of Christian art.

3. Perhaps most importantly, we must recognize the author's theological priorities: the relationships of this world to the world to come, and of the church to the crucified and risen Lord, and of the Son to the Father who is the world's creator—all these are vital connections in the structure of the Apocalypse.

I suggest we study a selection of passages, arranged thematically into five sequences, which pick up these theological priorities. In this way it is possible to see a relationship between sequence A, Visions of God; sequence B, Visions of the Church in the World; sequence C, Visions of Creation and the End of the Universe; sequence D, Visions of Rival Powers; and sequence E, Visions of Future Hope. This is not to stop your reading the book of Revelation straight through from start to finish. But perhaps this can best be done subsequently, following the outline chart of the book that precedes this chapter, and in the light of the thematic perspectives which I am now going to indicate.

A. *Visions of God*

A.1. *Revelation 1.12-16: The Son of Man*

Many are the faces of Christ in Christian art through the centuries and in different parts of the world. Even in a single time and place there may be contrasting features. In the dominant image of Christ as 'all powerful' in the Byzantine cathedrals, some representations are of a fierce judge, others are benevolent, with hand lifted in blessing.

Christ as the Son of Man in heavenly glory—this is the face of Christ that John sees in his first vision. We know that the heavenly Son of Man was an important image of Christ for the early Christians. The gospels refer to the Son of Man in three different ways. He has power on earth, with authority to forgive sins (Mk 2.10) and as Lord of the Sabbath (Mk 2.28). He is the one who is destined to suffer rejection and betrayal and to be condemned to death (Mk 8.31; 9.31; 10.33-34). And it is the Son of Man, prophesied at a time of trial, who is 'seated at the right hand of the Power, and "coming with the clouds of heaven"' (Mk 14.62). The early Christians were familiar with the picture in Dan. 7.13-14 ('I saw one like a son of man coming with the clouds of heaven. And he came to the Ancient of Days and was presented before him. To him was given dominion and glory and kingship'). They saw this prophecy fulfilled in Jesus who had shared their earthly conditions and sufferings and was vindicated through resurrection after a cruel death. The relationship of suffering to triumph, demonstrated in Jesus, was a source of great encouragement to Christians experiencing hardship.

In John's vision of the heavenly Son of Man there is a mixture of elements from Old Testament pictures (Ezek. 1, Dan. 7, and Moses in Exod. 34). It is an image of great power and glory, both judgmental (the 'sharp, two-edged sword') and intensely reassuring (1.17). The author is commissioned to write what he sees for the benefit of the Christian churches. They are the seven stars and lampstands and so they are already part of the picture. This vision of the glorious figure of Christ is for their benefit. And when the individual churches are addressed in the letters, particular features of the description of the Son of Man are directly called to mind (e.g. 1.16 in 2.12).

A.2. *Revelation 1.17-20: Death and Life*

Stephen, the first Christian martyr, according to Acts 7, has a vision of heaven before he is stoned to death.

But filled with the Holy Spirit, he gazed into heaven and saw the glory
of God and Jesus standing at the right hand of God. 'Look,' he said, 'I
see the heavens opened and the Son of Man standing at the right hand
of God!' (7.55-56).

The most distinctive feature of Stephen's vision is that the Son of Man
is *standing*, rather than traditionally sitting at the right hand of God.
What effect does this have? It emphasizes the immediacy of the contact between Jesus and this man who is to die for the name of Christ.
Christ stands ready to come, ready for his triumphal second coming,
at the point of Stephen's death.

In Revelation we have seen the close connection between the
churches and the heavenly vision. The Christian communities are in
difficulties and the vision of Christ the Son of Man in glory will sustain them. But this works for isolated individuals as well as for
beleaguered groups and churches. To the church in Laodicea, the
risen Christ is described as 'the Amen, the faithful and true witness,
the origin of God's creation' (3.14). This is a marvellous description,
combining the depth of understanding of the person of Christ (as in
Col. 1.15-20 and Jn 1) with the richness of early Christian worship and
the beginnings of the liturgy. But the centrepiece is Christ as the faithful *witness* (*martus* is the Greek word which starts by meaning 'witness' and, as a consequence of the persecutions of early Christianity,
finishes by meaning 'martyr' as well).

Stephen, the martyr, faced a death in the image of Christ's death.
For Christ is the true witness who experienced death in obedience to
God. The individual Christian in the seven churches is in the same
position. There is a particular example referred to in the church at
Pergamum: 'Antipas my witness, my faithful one, who was killed
among you, where Satan lives' (2.13). We know nothing of the circumstances of this death. But we know that it was early Christian
belief that by such a death a disciple perfectly followed his or her
Lord. And earthly disciple and heavenly Lord were united in this
moment.

A.3. *Revelation 4.1-8: The Throne of God*

Before the main hall was an ante-room where those waiting sat on
raised stone benches along the walls. There was a stone basin in the
centre, which contained water for washing the hands (a symbolic purifi-
cation of the whole body). From this room there was access to the audience chamber itself, where the king received visitors, flanked by his
counsellors and priests on more raised benches. In the centre of the
northern wall is the superb throne made of gypsum on which the king

himself sat. On the wall above and on each side of the throne is a fresco
representing griffins (with head of eagle and body of lion) symbolizing
the earthly and heavenly powers of the king.

This is a description of the palace of King Minos at Knossos on Crete,
claimed to be the oldest throne and audience chamber in the world.
But for representative symbols of power it can be matched by the
palace of the Persian kings at Persepolis, by the Peacock throne in the
Hall of Private Audience (Diwan-i-Khas) in the Red Fort at Delhi, or
even by the chair of St Augustine at the east end of Canterbury
Cathedral. John's vision in Revelation stands between the symbols of
ancient political power in the East and their reinterpretation as spiritual power in the great liturgies and architecture of the Christian
church. David E. Aune has argued for a more particular relationship:
'John's description of the heavenly ceremonial practiced in the throne
room of God bears such a striking resemblance to the ceremonial of
the [Roman] imperial court and cult that the latter can only be a parody of the former' ('The Influence of Roman Imperial Court Ceremonial on the Apocalypse of John', *Papers of the Chicago Society of Biblical
Research* 27 [1983], p. 5).

It is certainly important to see John's description within an ongoing
tradition. The threefold acclamation of holiness (4.8) goes back to
Isaiah's vision in the temple (Isa. 6.3) and leads on to the *Trishagion* or
Sanctus ('Holy, Holy, Holy') in the Christian liturgy (cf. 1 Clem. 34.6).
The wording in Revelation is actually closer to later liturgies than to
the Septuagint translation of Isaiah. The four living creatures around
the throne (4.6) reflect the vision of God in Ezek. 1.5-28 and in turn are
the basis for the much later Christian symbols for the Four Evangelists
(lion, ox, man, eagle). And the 24 elders, seated like the presbyters
round the bishop, or the advisers beside the monarch—do they
represent for John the angelic host, or the Christian saints, or the
patriarchs and other worthy figures of the Old Testament? Like the
statues at Chartres Cathedral, the figures of both Old and New Testaments come together, flanking the centrepiece of the vision, the
inexpressible majesty of almighty God.

A.4. *Revelation 5.1-6: The Lamb of God*
There is a vivid Flemish painting by the brothers Hubert and Jan van
Eyck, an altarpiece completed in 1432 and now in the cathedral
church of St Bavon in Ghent, Belgium. The inscription reads, 'Hubert
van Eyck, the most famous painter ever known, started this work of
art...his brother Jan, who was the second in art, finished the momentous commission... Admire now what they have done for you.' The

Lamb of God is the main subject of the painting, sometimes referred to as *The Adoration of the Mystic Lamb*. The setting is a landscape, the paradise garden seen in northern European terms. A host of worshippers—burghers, ladies, friars and ecclesiastics—come from all four corners of the picture. In the centre a ring of angels surrounds an altar with a red frontal on which stands the figure of the Lamb. The glory of God radiates over the landscape from a light source in which the dove as the spirit of God is represented, and out of a fountain in the foreground come the streams of the water of life.

It should be with some surprise that the Lamb of God is first seen in John's vision of the continuing heavenly worship around God's throne. A legally sealed and witnessed document contains a statement of what is to happen to the world. But nobody is found worthy to open the document, except Jesus Christ himself. The Seer affirms that Christ is the descendant of David, whose kingdom in Judaea traced its origins back to the sons of Jacob. Jacob called Judah his son 'a lion's whelp' (Gen. 49.9). So the Messiah, the son of David, can be called the Lion of the tribe of Judah. But when the Christ, who is found worthy, is seen, he appears not as a lion but as a lamb.

Christ is the 'Lamb standing, as though it had been slain'. He bears the marks of his suffering and death, though he stands by the throne of God in his risen glory. It is in his death that his victory is achieved; as conqueror he can reveal the future, for he sees with the spiritual eyes of God into all parts of the earth (5.6). These ideas are represented also in the van Eyck altarpiece. The spiritual light of God pervades every part of the picture. And the Lamb stands on the altar alongside a chalice of his blood; the altar frontal is red, the liturgical colour for martyrdom. From this comes the confidence that 'the Lamb will conquer them, for he is Lord of lords and King of kings' (17.14).

A.5. *Revelation 5.7-14: The Lamb of God*
John stressed the uniqueness of Christ in an unfamiliar way. He alone has been found worthy to open the scroll. When Paul describes the uniqueness of Christ, it is in relation to universal sinfulness ('There is no one who is righteous, not even one', Rom. 3.10). Jesus Christ is the sole righteous person, suffering innocently in his death. For Paul the death of Christ deals with sin and enables Christians, baptized into his death, to be united with Christ in resurrected life (Rom. 6.3-11). John uses very different words, but his concentration on the uniqueness of Christ's sacrificial death is essentially complementary to that of Paul.

The Lamb of God is clearly an image of sacrifice, reminiscent of the lamb which is sacrificed at the Jewish Passover (Exod. 12). In later years each Jewish family sacrificed a lamb at the temple. So Paul could recall this in describing the death of Jesus as a Passover sacrifice (1 Cor. 5.7). And, according to John's Gospel, John the Baptist draws attention to Jesus as 'the Lamb of God who takes away the sin of the world' (Jn 1.29). But this idea of sacrifice does not work purely in terms of Jewish practice, because neither the Passover lamb nor the lamb of the daily burnt offering was intended to atone for sins. Perhaps we need to refer to the Suffering Servant, in Isa. 53.7, 12 described as 'a lamb that is led to the slaughter' who 'bore the sins of many'. But the most important part of the definition of the Lamb as an image of sacrifice is the action of Christ himself in dying on the cross; the rest is interpretation.

The great paradox is that the victim (the Lamb) functions as the leader (the Lion and the Shepherd) in Rev. 5.5 and 14.1-7. There may be a precedent for this in the Jewish apocalyptic *Book of Enoch* where David is represented as a lamb who becomes the ram and leader of the flock (89.46). In the next chapter one of the sheep sprouts a great horn, and he becomes the victorious bell-wether of God's flock, as does the messianic figure in *Testament of Joseph* 19.8. Possibly this ram was already a familiar idea in apocalyptic circles. But let us not forget that the power of John's statement lies in the paradoxical combination of strength and weakness. 'The Lamb bore the marks of slaughter...with his life-blood he had ransomed for God men from every tribe, tongue, people and race. The Lamb is the symbol of self-sacrificing and redemptive love' (Caird 1966, p. 74).

A.6. *Revelation 15.2-8: The Old Testament Vision of God*
With this vision we are taken back into the audience chamber or sanctuary of heaven; it is both the palace of God and the temple for his worshippers. Among the furnishings of the throne room, which we have seen before, the focus of attention is on 'a sea of glass, like crystal' (4.6). Its origins are probably in the 'sea' of cast bronze in Solomon's temple (1 Kgs 7.23), a symbol of the cosmos (the ocean of chaos transformed by God in creation mythology). Now the cosmos reflects a fiery red, whether the fire of the judgment which is coming, or the colour of blood, shed in the sacrifice of Christ's martyrs who now worship in the presence of God. For the congregation has increased beyond the 4 living creatures and the 24 elders. It now comprises the 144 thousand servants of God who were selected and sealed (7.4-8) and have now been resurrected from the earth (14.1-5), to sing God's praise to the accompaniment of harp music.

The song of praise is ascribed first to Moses. It is striking how much of the chapter's symbolism recalls the Exodus: the plagues of Egypt (Exod. 7–11); the way through the Red Sea (Exod. 14); the song which Moses and the Israelites sing (Exod. 15); the tent of meeting and the cloud of smoke which prevents entry (Exod. 40.35; cf. the smoke in Isa. 6.4). The conquerors celebrate their victory just as the Israelites celebrated their crossing of the sea. The crossing of the Red Sea stands for the martyrdom of the victors and their crossing over into God's presence through death. And yet the song of praise is also ascribed to the Lamb, because those victories were only achieved through Christ and his sacrifice. The words of the song are a skilful amalgam of Old Testament quotations. It sums up the Old Testament vision of God, as the King to whom all nations come (Mic. 4.1-3). This could be regarded by Israel in a rather nationalistic way (Isa. 49.22-23; 60.10-16). But in Revelation the martyrs express a confidence in *universal* salvation, of which they are the 'first fruits'.

The rest of the chapter reminds the reader of two essentially com-plementary aspects: the God of justice for Israel and the world is the God of wrath, who executes his judgment with righteous anger and authorizes the plagues with power. Again the comparison is with Moses and the plagues on Egypt. This is no doctrine of God as a petty tyrant, but rather of God as ultimately in control of all creation. As G.B. Caird wrote: 'The proof of God's ultimate sovereignty is that he can use even the powers of evil to be the means of their own destruc-tion' (1966, p. 197).

A.7. *Revelation 19.11-16: The Rider on the White Horse*

Everybody knows of the four horsemen of the Apocalypse, the riders on white, red, black and pale horses (Rev. 6.2-8; see also sequence D.1 below). They represent major threats to the first-century Mediter-ranean world: death and destruction from warfare, famine and pesti-lence. It is likely that the first rider, the warlike figure on the white horse, represents the conquering power of one of the new religious movements (mystery religions). Mithraism (the cult of Mithras) spread from Persia throughout the Roman empire. It was associated with the armed forces of Parthia and the Roman legions and it spread rapidly wherever those armies went. While everybody knows the symbols of four horsemen, comparatively few are aware of the much more powerful figure, the bloodstained rider of ch. 19.

We have already seen how John achieves a dramatic effect by con-trast and paradox, in the figure of the Lamb of God. This rider is another image of Christ, as the bloodstained robe, the title 'the Word of God' (19.13), and the acclamation 'Faithful and True' (19.11 recall-ing 3.14), all make clear. Other features such as 'eyes...like a flame of fire' and 'from his mouth...a sharp sword', recall the vision of the heavenly Son of Man in Revelation 1. The accompanying armies of heaven, dressed in pure white linen and also riding white horses, are those who have conquered with Christ (7.14) and follow the leader-ship of the Lamb (14.1-7). Their celibacy recalls the ideals of the Qum-ran community.

This vision is set in deliberate contrast to that of the first rider. The way of Christ is declared superior to the way of Mithras and the mystery cults and more powerful than the might of the Roman legions. On Christ's head are 'many diadems' (19.12), in contrast to the limited number of crowned heads among the adverse powers of the beast and the dragon. The title of Christ's victory is inscribed where his sword of judgment would normally hang (19.16) and also on his blood-soaked garment. With the same kind of artistic contrast in mind, Franz Marc and Wassily Kandinsky coined the term 'Blue Rider' in 1911 for their new movement in modern art, based on exu-berant colour and profound emotions. Blue is associated with the other-worldly and spiritual, because it is rarely found in nature except as the colour of the sky. In contrast to the Horsemen of the Apoca-lypse, bearers of devastation and death, the paradoxical formula of the Blue Rider stands for spiritual renewal pitted against spiritual despair. While Kandinsky in an earlier phase had depicted Cossack riders, Marc now painted a group of heroic horses in the imagery of paradise. The desired result was a positive programme of spiritual harmony; he said in the prospectus for the 1912 *Almanac*: 'we stand before the new pictures as in a dream and we hear the apocalyptic [revelatory] horsemen in the air'.

One other feature of the context of Revelation 19 deserves more attention than it is usually given. A marriage is announced at 19.7, 9; but it does not take place until the arrival of the bride at 21.2. This theme of wedding celebration absorbs the Old Testament idea of a great feast at the end of time symbolizing God's kingdom (e.g. Isa. 25.6). The same connection is made in some of the Royal Psalms in the Psalter, especially Psalm 45 (the Royal Wedding Psalm), where the joy of the celebration and the beauty of the royal bride are depicted, and the bridegroom is introduced:

> You are the most handsome of men... Gird your sword on your thigh, O mighty one, in your glory and majesty. In your majesty ride on victori-ously for the cause of truth and to defend the right; let your right hand teach you dread deeds.

Here is a prototype of Revelation's imagery: the wedding of the war-
rior-king who rides in triumph. If this wedding is announced in ch. 19
and solemnized in ch. 21, it could mean that the intervening ch. 20 is
concerned with who will, and who will not, receive wedding invita-
tions (see sequence D.7 below)

Summary of Sequence A: Visions of God

John sees visions and is commissioned to communicate them to the
churches. Are they real visions, or artistic creations, or a mixture of
the two? John's writing faithfully reflects the range of thought of early
Christians about the majesty of God the Creator of the world, and
about the person of Jesus Christ,

> the Son of Man
> the faithful witness to God
> the Lamb of God
> now vindicated and victorious.

We must not underestimate the depth of theological awareness that
underlies these dramatic visions. For Christian believers, to see Christ
in this way generates a tremendous confidence and trust in God's salvation, whatever the future may hold.

B. *Visions of The Church in the World*

B.1. *Revelation 1.1-11: The Lord's Day*
After the prologue (vv. 1-3), which describes the nature of the Revelation, the book begins all over again in the form of a letter. The opening
greetings exactly follow the standard pattern with which we are
familiar from the letters of Paul. We know a great deal about the early
church from those letters which Paul addressed to particular named
churches. It is possible to imagine how each letter, when it arrived,
would be read aloud to the congregation at its regular meeting (cf.
1 Thess. 5.27; Col. 4.16). In this way the writer could speak quite
directly to the whole local church gathered in the context of worship.

It is reasonable to suppose that John saw his first vision as if in a
local meeting of the church community. 'I was in the Spirit on the
Lord's day' (1.10). If John was not actually in the meeting, because of
the circumstances of solitary exile on Patmos, then he imagined himself back with one of the church communities on the Asian mainland.
We can hardly exclude the possibility of an actual ecstatic experience
of physical translation (see Ezek. 3.12; 2 Cor. 12.2). For the suggestion

of Christian meetings on the first day of the week, Revelation should be compared with Jn 20.19, 26; Acts 20.7 and 1 Cor. 16.2 (see also *Did.* 14.1; Ignatius, *Magn.* 9.1. 'Of Jewish origin…is the seven-day week, and the weekly day of worship which the Church soon transferred from the sabbath to Sunday, the day of the Resurrection' (T. Klauser, *A Short History of the Western Liturgy* [Oxford: Oxford University Press, 2nd edn, 1979] p. 6). By the time of Justin Martyr in the mid-second century CE, the Sunday assembly for word and sacrament had become conventional (see *1 Apology* 65–67). It is worth noting that while the Jewish sabbath (Saturday) was kept as a day of rest, and many people now regard Saturday and Sunday alike as the 'weekend', the innovative Christian choice of Sunday to celebrate the Resurrection ('the Lord's day') meant gathering for the eucharist at a very early hour on a normal working day.

The influence of Sunday worship is strong in the Apocalypse. We have little hard evidence about any standard patterns in the earliest Christian worship. But it is an attractive speculation that in the many hymns of Revelation, the heavenly songs of praise, worship and thanksgiving, we can trace the instincts of the early Christian community. If so, then certainly the human words are transfigured into the glorious songs of the angels and saints in heaven. These words then came to be used in the later Christian liturgies, thus completing the circle. According to Revelation the worship of earth and heaven is drawn together in unanimous paeans of praise.

> To the one seated on the throne and to the Lamb be blessing and honour and glory and might for ever and ever! (Rev. 5.13)

B.2. *Revelation 2.1-7: The Church in Ephesus*

In the foundations of Rochester Cathedral in Kent the crypt, constructed in Early English style, is arranged in seven aisles, originally housing seven chapels, to symbolize the seven churches of the Apocalypse. The original seven churches were actual centres of Christianity in Asia Minor—not the only seven, of course, for that would be to disregard other centres visited by St Paul. These seven in Revelation are chosen for practical reasons: they were probably centres of the Johannine mission field—perhaps the only churches acknowledging John—and they are also linked, for purposes of communication, by the imperial post road that circumscribes the west-central region of the province of Asia. But they are also the first of the book's symbolic sequences of sevens, symbols of the whole church, foundations of Christendom, and as such figure, with their guardian angels, as the stars and lampstands of the opening vision (1.12-20). In the Early

Church references to angels are intriguing, but angelology is not an exact science. As Stuart G. Hall writes, 'Jesus Christ's own self-manifestation to a prophet may be called an angel' (*Doctrine and Practice in the Early Church* [London: SPCK, 1991], p. 55)

The message to Ephesus stands first and foremost among the seven dictated letters and the seven churches. Ephesus was the port of entry, regularly used by the Roman governor arriving in the province; it was the commercial centre and chief city of Roman Asia. (Only Sardis, the ancient capital of Lydia, has a similar status symbol in the opening reference of its letter.) The allusions to the opening vision (2.1; 3.1; 1.12-13, 16) are not random selections, but symbols appropriate to the location. For the Seer, the true church is centred on Christ himself; theologically this is far more significant than the representative character or political pretensions of the local 'centre'. The threat to 'remove your lampstand' (2.5) is both a symbol of this judgment and an allusion to the history of Ephesus as one of movement. The site of the city had to be changed (c. 550 and again c. 287 BCE) because the navigability of its harbour was threatened by the silting up of the river Cayster. Theological threats and promises thus can be seen to satirize the local environment of the church. Both 'tree' and 'paradise' (2.7) are echoes of Genesis 2–3, but also parodies of the tree-shrine of Artemis (Diana) at Ephesus and of its sacred enclosure which offered asylum.

There are indications of clear religious opposition in Ephesus (false apostles—2.2; Nicolaitans—2.6) but their identities are far from clear. We have already noted the likelihood of internal religious tensions, as well as external 'persecution' in these churches. The Johannine communities may still sustain a prophetic type of ministry, just as the Seer himself is a Christian prophet with ecstatic experiences (1.10). If so, the church organization would differ radically from that which is known elsewhere in Asia Minor. And there could be rival prophets to John, such as 'Balaam' and 'Jezebel' (2.15, 20), just as the prophets of ancient Israel experienced contradiction (cf. 1 Kgs 22). But care is needed because there is little evidence on which to identify these local opponents, or even associate them together. Perhaps it is most plausible that they should be pro-government collaborators (like Israel's false prophets) rather than other apocalyptic prophets more radical than John himself. The irony is that Balaam originally represented the kind of prophet who could not be bought (Num. 22–24; ctr. 31.16).

B.3. *Revelation 3.14-22: The Church in Laodicea*
Laodicea is the last of the seven representative churches to be addressed. It serves as a particular example of how all the unsatisfactory
features of a local church situation are vividly depicted. As we saw in
the previous sequence the church is addressed by the risen Christ,
here named as 'the Amen, the faithful and true witness' (3.14). This is
the standard by which the local Christians can and should be
measuring themselves.

Laodicea does not emerge as conspicuously faithful. The description suggests a resourceful, successful and perhaps rather self-satis-
fied community which lacks spiritual depth. John's picture contains
references to the local features of this city in the Lycus valley, neighbour to Colossae and Hierapolis. He uses the local references to make
a telling spiritual commentary on the church. The quality of the local
water supply was a famous joke; it was brought five miles by aque-
duct, warmed up by the sun. Colossae had cold pure water and Hierapolis hot medicinal springs. Laodicea is actually criticized for its
ineffectiveness, with water no use for anything—not for being half-
hearted, which is the usual sense in which the proverbial lukewarm-
ness is understood today. The city stood at the crossroads, controlling
the trade routes. This makes the door or gate (3.20) especially significant. Laodicea went in for an ostentatious building programme after
the earthquake in 60 CE, with a monumental triple gate to the city. As
a trading city it was the centre for banking. One local speciality was
cloth woven from the raven-black wool of local sheep. The medical
school was renowned for its eye-specialists; a 'Phrygian powder' (an
eyesalve made from alum) was widely used.

All these features are combined in a symbolic description of the
church as measured by its risen Lord. It may have appeared notably
successful to others, but was itself blind to its own spiritual ineffectiveness. The emphasis in the conclusion is upon the individual and
voluntary action. As Colin J. Hemer wrote, the Christian needs

> the fellowship of Christ in the present as the antidote to the self-suffi-
> ciency of a Christless church. Christ would not abuse and exploit hospi-
> tality as Roman potentates did. Only with the personal presence of
> Christ would [the Christian] conquer (1986, p. 207).

B.4. *Revelation 1.5-6; 5.9-10: The Priesthood*
These two texts are often taken out of Revelation as proofs of the idea
of the priesthood of the whole people of God, the priesthood of all
believers. They are combined with 1 Pet. 2.9: 'But you are a chosen
race, a royal priesthood, a holy nation, God's own people, in order

that you may proclaim the mighty acts of him who called you out of darkness into his marvelous light'. These texts are applying to the church language from the Old Testament about the people of Israel (see Exod. 19.5-6). Of course historic Israel had a quite narrowly defined and institutional priesthood, and a charismatic experience of individual prophecy that could on occasion condemn the priesthood, as well as this wider vision of national vocation and purpose.

I have already referred to theories about the nature of ministry (prophetic or priestly) implied in Revelation. What is clear from the context of this quotation in the Apocalypse is that, for the Seer, the priestly function of the people of God depends upon the self-sacrificial act of Christ. God's people are ransomed for God, freed from their sins, by the blood of Christ. Kenneth Mason writes:

> All the New Testament ideas about priesthood are rooted in an inchoate but vivid intuition of natural and universal human priesthood—a potential priesthood of every man and woman... The institutional priesthoods which society develops have to be seen as an admission of failure. It is as though the consecration of human life has to be acted out in show because it is not achieved in reality. If that is so then the various references in the New Testament to priesthood can be read as claims to the restoration of that reality through the work of Christ... Revelation had shown that priesthood and sacrifice found their fulness in Christ crucified (*Priesthood and Society* [Norwich: Canterbury Press, 1992], pp. 39, 55).

We can conclude that for believers any kind of Christian ministry or sacrificial act depends ultimately upon the action of Christ as priest and victim, even if the precise nature of the sacramental theology varies with situation and time.

But there is a further dimension that Revelation emphasizes. As a 1986 Church of England report on the ordained priesthood has said:

> The final chapters of the Revelation to John present a picture of the fulfilment of all things in which the whole company of the redeemed serve God face to face. Part of this picture is that there will be no more temple (Revelation 21.22): God will be immediately present to his people. In other words, there will be no more need for sacraments or priests to mediate God's presence. Thus, whereas those who are redeemed by Christ will be kings and priests for ever, the priesthood of the ordained ministry belongs to the realm which is passing away (*The Priesthood of the Ordained Ministry* [Board for Mission and Unity, London: Church House Publishing, 1986, p. 101).

This sense of the future is important to bear in mind as one thinks of ongoing controversies among Christians on the qualifications for priesthood. As T.F. Torrance observed many years ago, church worship must have a future dimension and reflect world-wide perspectives.

> Liturgy must allow the perfect pattern of the Kingdom of God to do battle with the artificial patterns of our worship, in order that through crucifixion with Christ they may be rent wide open, to make room for the Advent presence of the Risen and Ascended Lord (*Church Service Society Annual* of the Church of Scotland [May 1954], pp. 17-18).

B.5. *Revelation 6.9-17; 7.1-4: Suffering and being Sealed*

For Christians the church in the world is not, and cannot be, immune to the world's problems. If the world suffers, the church suffers. The Christian communities may find themselves driven into a kind of ghetto by the world's persecution, but this does not justify escapism and other-worldly retreat. Some people assume (wrongly) that Revelation was produced by an escapist sectarian group. Nothing could be further from the truth. The book has a universal perspective and a sense of world-wide mission and interaction with the world.

In sequence A.4. we have seen how the Lamb of God was found worthy to open the sealed document (5.5). As the seals are opened the four horsemen appear, symbols of death and destruction, warfare, famine and pestilence (see sequence D.1.). The cities of Asia Minor suffered severely in the first century from such destructive forces, and also from major earthquakes (the sixth seal—6.12). The Christians suffered with their communities; in addition they suffered as they were singled out, treated as scapegoats and persecuted (just as the Emperor Nero selected the Christians and blamed them for the fire in Rome). These are the souls beneath the altar 'slaughtered for the word of God and for the testimony they had given' (6.9). Not surprisingly, they cry out with the urgency of those who have suffered enough, who feel that the world cannot endure much more, and who themselves are waiting, like 'midnight's children', for their new birth.

God's punishment of evildoers, traditionally conceived in Old Testament terms as the day of God's wrath, comes from the four corners of the earth and will affect all creation progressively. The suggested fractions are a tenth, a quarter and a third. In no way are the Christians spared from earthquake and plague, but they are sealed by God so that they may witness effectively. Remember that the seals on the document are the guarantees of the witnesses; so the seal on the forehead is a guarantee of witness! And the number of those sealed (144,000) is not the maximum number of the elect. Like Israel in the Old Testament it is a representative sign to the nations (Isa. 49.6), a symbolic number in relation to the infinite possibilities of universal mission.

Adela Yarbro Collins has written about the significance of holy war traditions in Revelation. The present scenario is one of passive resistance, rather than the violent revolution attempted by the Zealots. But it is important to notice that the role of the elect, those who are sealed to be the 'first-fruits', is not entirely passive. They do not merely wait around for someone else's victory.

> The elect are not purely passive because the deaths suffered by members of the community are thought to play a role in bringing about the turning point, the eschatological battle… The faithful are to suffer persecution and death in the present. They expect a violent resolution of the conflict in which heavenly forces will defeat their adversaries. Their contribution to this outcome may be made in the form of a martyr's death, which hastens the end, because a fixed number of martyrs must die before the eschatological battle (*JBL* 96.2 [1977], pp. 255-56).

B.6. *Revelation 11.1-3: The Two Witnesses*

The two witnesses are symbols of the mission of the church in these difficult days. There is an attractive and, I think, compelling interpretation that identifies these witnesses with the saints Peter and Paul, both of whom, according to tradition, met their deaths in Rome during the emperor Nero's persecution. Paul was beheaded and Peter was crucified. Clement of Rome describes both apostles as leading examples of those who 'contended to the point of death' (The sporting imagery is Paul's own in 1 Cor. 9.24-27). The Roman historian Tacitus sets the scene for this general persecution of Christians (*Annals* 15.44):

> Mockery of every sort was added to their deaths. Covered with the skins of beasts, they were torn by dogs and perished, or were nailed to crosses, or were doomed to the flames and burnt, to serve as a nightly illumination when daylight had expired. Nero offered his gardens for the spectacle.

Peter and Paul, as depicted in the Acts of the Apostles, are both the pioneers and major representatives of the church's mission. Luke sees their work as parallel and symbolic. Paul himself explains, in Gal. 2.7-8, how it could be said that Peter and Paul had divided the world between them in God's service:

> I had been entrusted with the gospel for the uncircumcised, just as Peter had been entrusted with the gospel for the circumcised (for he who worked through Peter making him an apostle to the circumcised also worked through me in sending me to the Gentiles).

The critical period of activity of the two witnesses is the same duration as the trampling of the holy city. Forty-two months, or one thousand two hundred and sixty days, is three and a half years, which is
the duration of crisis in the traditional calculations of time in apocalyptic vision (see Dan. 7.25). But it is also the time-span of the Jewish
War and the siege of Jerusalem (from Spring 67 until 29 August 70
CE), the dramatic sequel to Nero's persecution. While apocalyptic
prophecies conventionally work by modifying traditional symbols, it
may not be a superficial coincidence if they can point to particular
events with uncanny precision. We are dealing with a theological
reinterpretation of a sequence of momentous events, rather than simply the prediction of the world's end, which may well prove to be
mistaken.

B.7. *Revelation 11.4-13: Olive Trees and Lampstands*
As a result of the experience of the church in Nero's day, and in the
following years, the ideas contained in the word 'witness' must
include the readiness to die for one's faith. Witness means facing up
to death. It is not only evidence that one possesses and hangs on to; it
is also something that a believer is prepared to communicate to others
in the spirit of prophecy, and it is something for which one is ready to
give up all, in the surrender of life itself.

Witness is a prophetic activity, consistent with the tradition of Old
Testament prophecy. The Christian experience of hardship and rejection is strictly comparable with Elijah's. Those who rejoice at the
death of the witnesses do so 'because these two prophets had been a
torment to the inhabitants of the earth' (11.10). The reasons and reactions are the same as those which greeted the prophetic troublers of
Israel (see 1 Kgs 18.17). And the prophetic activity is authoritative,
powerful in a way that compares with that of Moses and Elijah (11.5-
6). And it is a preaching of repentance, because the sackcloth the
prophets wear (11.3) is a symbol to encourage penitence. The witnesses are also identified with the esoteric imagery of Zech. 4.1-14.
This means that they see things God's way. They share his universal
perspective as 'eyes of the Lord which range through the whole earth'
(seven lamps on a lampstand) and are anointed agents of God's purpose (two olive trees).

For the Seer, Christian witness follows the path of Christ from suffering to glory. In their deaths the martyrs are symbolically associated
with Christ's crucifixion (11.8). Like Christ also they have their Easter
Day (11.11) and their day of ascension (11.12). God's kingdom is universal, but works through human agencies and representatives such

as these. It is a situation of cosmic confrontation, because the powers of evil ranged against God's purpose for the world are no mere phantoms. The prophetic figure presents the gospel to the world and offers the occasion for repentance. The prophet may be an isolated individual or representative of the church, but as witness he or she speaks with God-given authority, accompanied by actions which are a powerful symbol and testimony.

Summary of Section B:
Visions of the Church in the World

> Let anyone who has an ear listen to what the Spirit is saying to the churches

This expression is repeated in all seven of the letters to John's churches in Asia Minor. It is rarely studied because it is assumed to be a catchphrase associated with these coded secret messages. But the reverse is the case, as Anne-Marit Enroth demonstrates (in *NTS* 36.4 [1990], pp. 598-608):

> The Hearing Formula is an invitation and an encouragement to hear. It underlines what should be heard and how it should be heard, and what follows from hearing aright… It is openly directed towards the communities mentioned in the letters, who in fact represent the whole church… The Hearing Formula is positive, for it does not contain the idea of judgement or of hardening. On the contrary, it underlines the promise and possibility of salvation.

Every aspect of these extracts which describe the church—worship and witness, being Christ-centred and coping with fierce opposition, showing a spiritual effectiveness, working out one's ministry in terms of priesthood and prophecy—is capable of a direct translation into the situation of today's church in the modern world. Revelation offers significant and positive ideas for those with ears to hear. On these grounds the beleaguered apocalyptic community cannot be dismissed as an outdated, self-conscious irrelevance.

If anyone had been tempted to think differently, a visit to Canterbury Cathedral on the morning of Sunday 9 December 1984 would have put them right. There is the site of Thomas à Becket's martyrdom, there is the chapel of the Modern (twentieth-century) Martyrs, and there in the pulpit was Bishop (now Archbishop) Desmond Tutu, preaching a most impressive sermon about the power of God expressed through the witness of individual Christians, and proclaiming his Christian confidence in words from Rev. 7.9-12:

> After this I looked and there was a great multitude that no one could count, from every nation, from all tribes and peoples and languages, standing before the throne and before the Lamb, robed in white, with palm branches in their hands. They cried out in a loud voice, saying, 'Salvation belongs to our God who is seated on the throne, and to the Lamb!... Amen! Blessing and glory and wisdom and thanksgiving and honor and power and might be to our God forever and ever! Amen.'

(See further on this text §2 in sequence E: Visions of the Future)

C. *Visions of Creation*

C.1. *Revelation 4.8-11: Hymn of Praise to the Creator*

In sequence B we were reflecting upon the experiences of the Christian community in the social world in which it lives. But what of the physical world, the natural environment for all human beings? did John's religious community have views about that, which might be mirrored in his visions?

The Judaeo-Christian tradition has been fairly consistent in affirming a view of the world as created by the activity and command of God; at least this is the teaching in the account of the seven days of Creation in Gen. 1.1–2.4 which is a primary reference point in the biblical tradition. The world is God's world and fundamentally good. Such a positive view of Creation is affirmed in the Apocalypse by the 24 elders (representative figures of the heavenly council) in a song of praise: 'you created all things, and by your will they existed and were created' (4.11). It is reasonable to assume that the hymn would be echoed by every creature (as in 5.13), and more particularly by John's church at worship 'on the Lord's day' (1.10).

Such harmony cannot be quite complete. Creation is good, but what of the matter from which it is created? The doctrine of 'Creation from Nothing' was an attempt to avoid the dualism between good creation and evil matter which preoccupied Gnostics and Manichees. Dualism was there in the Babylonian account of creation from which the writers of Genesis borrowed; the god Marduk brought order out of chaos, but the battle had to be renewed each year as the rivers of Mesopotamia overflowed. The biblical writers were more confident of God the Creator's omnipotence. But in Revelation the hymn to the Creator follows the Trisagion (4.8); the reaffirmed holiness of God cannot ultimately tolerate the presence of evil (see Isa. 6.5-7). Some aspects of the good Creation have become corrupted and must be reformed or purged. But for the moment the Seer is content to be enveloped in the heavenly liturgy.

A poem by R.S. Thomas, entitled 'Alive', offers a modern statement of this positive theology of creation:

> It is alive. It is you, God. Looking out I
> can see no death. The earth moves, the
> sea moves, the wind goes on its exuberant
> journeys. Many creatures reflect you, the flowers
> your colour, the tides the precision of your
> calculations. There is nothing too ample,
> for you to overflow, nothing so small that your
> workmanship is not revealed. I listen
> and it is you speaking. I find the place where you lay
> warm. At night, if I waken, there are the sleepless
> conurbations of the stars. The darkness
> is the deepening shadow of your presence; the silence a
> process in the metabolism of the being of love.

C.2. *Revelation 6.12-17: The Great Earthquake*

We have already paused at these verses (in sequence B.5). Then the emphasis was on the 'sealing'—the protective care of God for his saints and martyrs; now we turn to the event that follows the opening of the sixth seal, when all—especially 'the rich and powerful' (6.15)—cower before what they interpret as the judgment of God. What is happening here? Is it a natural disaster, as when Mount Etna erupts and a productive area of Sicily is buried beneath a lava flow? Is it what insurance assessors call an 'act of God', when there is nobody else to blame?

Several of John's seven cities had recent direct experience of destruction by earthquake (e.g. Sardis, Philadelphia and Laodicea). This region was particularly vulnerable to tremors, as parts of Turkey are today. John can relate to this direct experience and further intensify it, using traditional symbolism, to make of it a solemn warning, an anticipatory 'sign of the end'. The world is destined to experience a catastrophe, magnified many times beyond recent 'acts of God'. John uses most immediately the apocalyptic material from Mk 13.8/Lk. 21.11 (several earthquakes become a 'great' one) and Lk. 23.30 ('say to the mountains, "Fall on us" '). Already the 'larger than life' or cosmic dimension is apparent in an event that affects 'every mountain and island' (6.14) as well as sun, moon and stars (6.12-13). The further ingredients are derived from several descriptions in the Old Testament of the ultimate Day of Yahweh: the blood-red moon from Joel 2.31; the rolling up of the sky like a scroll from Isa. 34.4; from Hos. 10.8 the destruction of Samaria which provokes a call for the mountains to cover the shame; and the question 'Who is able to stand?' from Mal. 3.2.

This extract offers a first, admonitory glimpse of that nightmare scenario—the natural world dislocated and crashing to its doom. Perhaps the most terrifying aspect is that it occurs in the midst of present social and political realities (the facts of the first-century CE Roman Empire as depicted by the four horsemen—see sequence D.1 below). Artists have often striven to depict such a nightmare. In the aftermath of the Napoleonic Wars Francis Danby (1793–1861) painted in the grand apocalyptic manner. His picture *The Deluge* hangs in the Tate Gallery, London. Ten years previously in 1828 he had painted *An Attempt to Illustrate the Opening of the Sixth Seal*. A comparable symbol, but much less realistic in manner, is Vincent van Gogh's *The Starry Night* painted at the asylum at Saint-Rémy in June 1889 and described as 'a lyrical delirium without precedent'. Philip Callow writes:

> High over the sleeping town of Saint-Rémy, birthplace of Nostradamus, nocturnal prophecies stream through the firmament... Flame-like cypresses thrust the eye upward. The whole sky sizzling with volts is a great field, a playground, the land beneath it reduced and subjected. Here is the grand attempt to merge night and day, to combine sun and orange moon in one glittering vastness. Below the writhing of 11 exploded stars creep the stiff lines and angles of a town busily complete in itself and insulated against revelations, with a thin church spire looking strangely northern as it pokes up to prick the horizon (*Vincent van Gogh: A Life* [London: Allison & Busby, 1991]).

C.3. *Revelation 8.6-13: Ecological Crisis*

The apocalyptic narrative gathers momentum as we move from the seven seals to the seven trumpets. The sixth seal, indeed, has given advance warning of the nightmare scenario, but the other seals are concerned with present realities. It is bad enough that Death already affects 'a fourth of the earth, to kill with sword, famine and pestilence, and by the wild animals of the earth' (6.8); but the target of the new sequence of trumpets is a third, not a quarter. The consequences of the first four trumpet blasts attack the earth, salt and fresh water, heavenly bodies and the atmosphere. At this stage the 'Green' reading of Revelation, with its projections of environmental disasters, sounds very compelling. What Jürgen Moltmann (1985, p. xi) called 'a life and death struggle for creation on this earth' has begun.

The ecological crisis is shown in pollutions of air, earth and water as well as in the over-use or misuse of finite natural resources. As Jonathan Clatworthy writes, Western society in particular seems convinced

> that all natural phenomena (i.e. those not produced by human interference) are undeveloped and therefore valueless. Mountains of ice in Antarctica, Brazilian rain forests and the bottoms of oceans, while undeveloped, do not contribute to any economic activity and are therefore of no value until they are brought within the orbit of human development (*Theology in Green* 2 [1992], p. 8).

What is needed is a world-view that challenges both the basic concept of economic development, with its associated value-systems, and the reading of Gen. 1.28 to which it might appeal as a proof-text.

> According to the Bible, man's lordship over the world is justified because he is made in the image of God. According to Bacon and Descartes, it is man's rule over the world that substantiates his divinity (Jürgen Moltmann, *The Future of Creation* [London: SCM Press 1979], p. 128).

An 'environmentally friendly' interpretation of the extract from Revelation would show how the earth, seas and rivers, the ozone layer and the solar system have all been polluted and seriously damaged by human ambition and greed. To replace a pervasive economic system with a 'Green Theology', that is, to respect God's role and purpose in the universe he created, and to value natural creation as good, appears to be a way of heeding the angels' trumpets before it is too late. That it is an issue for scientists as well as the religious community is shown by the 1990 appeal, *Preserving and Cherishing the Earth* (see *Christianity and Crisis* 14 [May 1990]), which notes that we

> are now threatened by self-inflicted, swiftly moving environmental alterations about whose long-term biological and ecological consequences we are still painfully ignorant... Mindful of our common responsibility, we scientists urgently appeal to the world religious community to commit itself, in word and deed, and as boldly as is required, to preserve the environment of the Earth. As scientists, many of us have had profound experiences of awe and reverence before the universe. We understand that what is regarded as sacred is more likely to be treated with care and respect. Our planetary home should be so regarded. Efforts to safeguard and cherish the environment need to be infused with a vision of the sacred.

C.4. *Revelation* 10.1-11: *No Further Delay!*
Again, it is clear that time has moved on in the Seer's narrative. While the opening of the sixth seal revealed a nightmare-vision which anticipated the end of the world (6.12-17, see C.2. above), and the fifth seal produced the imploring cry from the martyr-souls, 'How long will it be before you judge and avenge our blood?' (6.10, see B.5. above), now the critical period has arrived and 'there will be no more delay'

(10.6). The 'mighty angel' who confirms this with an oath (10.5) is a direct messenger from God, a cosmic figure who wears about him fourfold signs of God's presence in the universe (cloud, rainbow, sun and fire—10.1). So he swears by God as Creator (10.6) that the schedule of God's plan is now to be implemented. John found the prototype of this angelic figure in 'the man clothed in linen' who, when asked 'How long?' swears in a similar oath that 'it would be for a time, two times and half a time' (Dan. 12.6-7). As it is revealed to John, this same apocalyptic time-scale of three and a half years (or its equivalent in months or days) is about to start (11.2-3).

Thus the period of the last days is implemented, without further delay. As G.B. Caird argued, the message from a further sequence of seven, 'the seven thunders', is not recorded (10.4); the sealing-up amounts to suppression rather than the traditional idea of preservation for a later date (compare Dan. 12.9). So God short-circuits further delay; in mercy

> God has cancelled the doom of which they [the thunders] were the symbol... John is told to break in upon the sordid cavalcade of human sin and its ineluctable nemesis, because this is precisely what God himself has done. Humanity must be stopped forthwith from endlessly producing the means of its own torment and destruction. 'If the Lord had not cut short the time, not a living creature could have escaped' (Mark xiii. 20) (Caird 1966, pp. 126-27).

John's communication from the mighty angel is a sworn declaration about the 'mystery of God' (10.7), or the plans of God, previously prophesied but until now shrouded in mystery. The communication is also symbolized by the 'little scroll' (10.9) which the Christian prophet duly receives and absorbs. The bitter/sweet scroll is a vivid and accurate image for the nature of the prophetic experience—a glorious vocation from God which must be agony to pursue ('it will turn your stomach sour', NEB). It is not just a matter of prophesying blessing for the faithful and a curse for the faithless. Certainly this traumatic yet transcendent destiny was the regular experience of the Old Testament prophets. The prototype for John's scroll is to be found in Ezek. 2.8–3.3. Revelation 10.11 indicates not only the wide application of the Seer's message, but also the compulsion that a prophet feels to discharge the commission God has given. As Amos 3.8 expressed the idea proverbially, 'the lion has roared; who will not fear? The Lord God has spoken; who can but prophesy?' The actual content of the scroll, which made John's stomach bitter, is the subject matter of ch. 11 (see sequences B.6 and 7 above).

C.5. *Revelation 11.15-19: The Kingdom of God*
In the 'apocalyptic' chapter of Luke's Gospel (Lk. 21, compare Mk 13),
it is said:

> There will be signs in the sun, the moon, and the stars, and on the earth
> distress among nations confused by the roaring of the sea and the
> waves. People will faint from fear and foreboding of what is coming
> upon the world, for the powers of the heavens will be shaken... Look at
> the fig tree [see Rev. 6.13] and all the trees; as soon as they sprout leaves
> you can see for yourselves and know that summer is already near. *So
> also, when you see these things taking place, you know that the kingdom of God
> is near* (21.25-26, 29-31).

Luke uses a description of turmoil in nature in much the same way as
John does for his nightmare scenario following the opening of the
sixth seal (see C.2. above). Luke's 'unnatural' imagery is associated in
some way with the historical event of the fall of Jerusalem at the end
of the Jewish War (Lk. 21.20). This hardly appears to be the most aus-
picious moment to look for the realization of God's kingdom. In Revelation 11, John has been describing the fate of the 'two witnesses',
probably the historical events of the martyrdoms of Peter and Paul in
Rome. Because these martyrs are united with their Lord in death, resurrection and ascension, Rome is merged symbolically with Jerusalem
(11.8). The moment of martyrdom (and consequent setback for the
church) again does not seem to be a good occasion for God's kingdom. But it is precisely at this moment that the dramatic juxtaposition
is made, as the seventh—and last—trumpet sounds:

> The kingdom of the world has become the kingdom of our Lord and of
> his Messiah, and he will reign forever and ever...
> We give you thanks, Lord God Almighty...for you have taken your
> great power and begun to reign (11.15, 17).

Psychologically it could not be a better moment to realize the nearness
of God's power. But it seems that John wants to say that the world is
actually changing for the good, and not just that the reader's way of
perceiving the world is changing and should change. The Old Testament tradition, especially in the Psalms, frequently speaks of the reality of God's kingly power and of the decisive moment of God's
enthronement in Jerusalem (Mount Zion), perhaps through the coro-
nation of an earthly monarch as God's agent (messiah). Psalm 2 is a
good example of these ideas, not least because of the way it is applied
by John in ch. 11 and elsewhere (see 2.27; compare Acts 4.25-26).
When human rebellion against God has achieved its self-destructive
worst—whether in political or in ecological terms—then God will

seize power and reign. The underlying reality (that God is ultimately in control) will become a total reality, dramatically and explicitly revealed to all. An illustration from a modern hymn is apt here:

> 'The kingdom is upon you!'
> the voice of Jesus cries,
> fulfilling with its message
> the wisdom of the wise;
> it lightens with fresh insight
> the striving human mind,
> creating new dimensions
> of purpose for mankind.
> (Robert Willis)

Gustav Dalman wrote:

> There can be no doubt whatever that in the Old Testament and in Jewish literature the word *malkut* when applied to God always means 'kingly rule' and never means 'kingdom', as if to suggest the territory ruled by him (*The Words of Jesus* [Edinburgh: T. & T. Clark, 1902], p. 94).

This is a dangerous observation because it suggests that any talk of God's lordship is only in terms of a spiritual abstraction. This is not true of Israel's religious nationalism (ultimately a theocracy) in the Old Testament and is no more true of those parts of the New Testament (e.g. Luke–Acts and Revelation) where the kingdom of God must engage with other political realities. Ultimately Revelation is saying that the political dominance of Rome (with its religious, social and economic implications) must yield to God's government, while Luke–Acts declares that Christianity and Roman citizenship are quite compatible.

C.6. *Revelation 14.6-7, 14-20: The Harvest of the Earth*

For British readers 'harvest' may recall Harvest Festival, with churches decorated with golden corn, fruit, hops and a harvest loaf. But such a liturgical celebration of harvest can only be traced back to Robert Stephen Hawker of Morwenstow in north Cornwall, who on the first Sunday of October 1843 urged his parishioners to 'gather together in the chancel of our church...and there receive, in the bread of the new corn, that blessed sacrament which was ordained to strengthen and refresh our souls'. In part this was a revival of the Lammas Day (1 August) celebrations that were popular in the Middle Ages. But the Harvest of the Earth (both grain and grape) in Revelation is something quite different.

In the Old Testament tradition both harvest and vintage symbolize divine judgment, with the effect of purifying Israel and eradicating its enemies. The closest parallel to Revelation 14 comes in Joel 3.9-17, where there is again a double harvest of grain and grape. The context is that of the final battle and of eschatological judgment, as all the nations gather outside Jerusalem in 'the valley of Jehoshaphat'. In Joel 3.13 the imagery corresponds exactly to Rev. 14.15, 18-19:

> Put in the sickle, for the harvest is ripe.
> Go in, tread, for the wine press is full.
> The vats overflow, for their wickedness is great.

The winepress is a natural symbol for bloody vengeance, with grape juice the colour of blood. The question for the reader is, whose blood?

R.H. Preston and R.T. Hanson pointed to a modern analogy (in their Torch Commentary, *The Revelation of Saint John the Divine* [London: SCM Press, 1949], pp. 104-105):

> We may be horrified at the picture of blood up to the horses' bridles, but, after the experience of two world wars in one generation, many thinking people are much more ready to admit that the root cause behind this terrible effusion of blood is not ignorance, or social conditions, but sin, the breaking of God's fundamental laws. They have seen in the history of the last twenty-five years the wine-press of the wrath of God.

But should not we recoil not only at the scale of the slaughter but also at the idea of slaughter as punishment by a just (and loving?) God? The rider on the white horse in Revelation 19 (see sequence A, above) is a figure of the last judgment; 'he will tread the winepress of the fury of the wrath of God the Almighty' (19.15). His robe is blood-stained; but is this like Isa. 63.1-2, or does John intend it to be the blood of his own self-sacrifice?

'The wine press was trodden *outside the city*' (14.20). This is associated both with the place of crucifixion and with the theology of the writer to the Hebrews: 'Jesus also suffered outside the city gate in order to sanctify the people by his own blood. Let us then go to him outside the camp and bear the abuse he endured' (13.12-13). Reference could then be made to the martyrdom of the saints, as the 'first fruits' described in 14.4. Certainly harvest and vintage stand together as parallel symbols in the structure of ch. 14. The context is the ultimate judgment of the earth which is now ordered. The analogy is the natural—and liturgical—process which begins with the offering of the first fruits (Exod. 22.29), continues with the grain harvest of Pentecost (Weeks), and ends with the grape harvest at Tabernacles. It is important to remember that harvest in Revelation has at least as much to do with rescuing and preserving the crop as with destroying the rampant weeds. The model is then the gospel parable of the weeds (Mt. 13.24-30, 36-43).

C.7. *Revelation 18.21-24: The End of the Known World*
The quartet by Olivier Messiaen, *Quatuor pour la fin du temps*, is known to have been inspired by John's apocalyptic vision of the end of the world. The music was written for fellow captives, after France had fallen and while the composer was a prisoner of war. The first performance took place in 1941 in Stalag VIIIA, Silesia, before an audience of 5000. A string on the cello was missing and the piano keys stuck. But the work remains one of the most horrifying and desolate in the repertory of chamber music. There is mystery, despair and agony in the long-drawn-out solos of the clarinet in the third movement and of the cello in the fifth; there is bitter stridency in the angular rhythms and melodies, deathly colours and sublime resignation. It is a lament for the loss not only of civilization but of life itself.

The destruction of Babylon was announced by the second flying angel:

> Fallen, fallen is Babylon the great! She has made all nations drink of the wine of the wrath of her fornication. (14.8)

The theme is developed throughout ch. 18 with authoritative utterance and symbolic action from angels and heavenly voices, and in between come the laments of kings, merchants and shipmasters. The issue is the predicted end of a political, social and economic system which seems to span the known world—the end of the Roman Empire and all that it represents. This momentous event is what Thomas R. Edgar calls

> the destruction of a system of international economic or commercial interests that has its headquarters in a major city. This economic entity has exercised influence or control over all the political rulers and governments of the earth (*JETS* 25.3 [1982], p. 341).

The analogy could be with the sudden end of the British Raj in India, the termination of any colonialist power, the end of Communism and the USSR, or the collapse of United States hegemony.

Karl Marx was attracted to use the imagery of the beasts in Revelation to convey the realities of historical capitalism. Recently the theory of the World System, propounded by Immanuel Wallerstein in 1974, to the effect that historical capitalism is the unifying process of world history, has been related to this apocalyptic paradigm by Kenneth Durkin, in an unpublished article:

> It is a social system in which those who operate by its rules have such a great impact that they create the conditions which force others to conform to the patterns or suffer the consequences [see Rev.13.16-17]... The world-system of historical capitalism is the shape of the one social system which has evolved in order to transform the natural world into utilizable form. Unfortunately it is a system where part of the process, the accumulation of capital, has become the ultimate objective of the system, utilizing the human social capacity to transform the world for this end.

Whichever system (e.g. the ancient Roman Empire or historical capitalism) one prefers to see as the subject of the lamentations and divine judgment of Revelation 18, this imagery emphasizes both the human pretentions and the ultimate fragility of the system. Human beings and divine creation are exploited in ways that are contrary to the ultimate purpose of the Creator. God's judgment is decisive and comprehensive. For us who are within the system it is the end of the world as we know it.

Summary of Section C: Visions of Creation

For the present, the glorious celebration of the world around us and of its Creator has given way to a scenario of nightmare, a realization of the extent of the ecological crisis, and a sense of the fragility of an apparently self-sufficient social and economic system. The time of God's harvest is at hand, when he will call all producers to account, and rescue the good produce from the weeds. Harvest is a time of judgment; it is also a time for triumphant celebration, as the God of Creation is enthroned in glory and the reality of his ultimate power is fully acknowledged. For the Christian community which suffers in the world—and cares desperately for the redemption of the world— John's message is that the fear and foreboding are held in tension with the hope and joy expressed in the anticipatory hymns of heaven. Here on earth there are still other powers with which the church must reckon, powers that rival God and seem set to destroy, with their self-destructive impulses, not only goodness but the whole creation.

D. *Visions of Rival Powers*

D.1. *Revelation 6.1-8: The Four Horsemen of the Apocalypse*
Rex Ingram made the silent epic *The Four Horsemen of the Apocalypse* for screening in 1921; it is often regarded as the first 'modern' film

because of its techniques in cutting and production. In a memorable scene, Rudolph Valentino as a French soldier is on night reconnaissance during World War I, moving stealthily through the downpour. A German officer, who happens to be his cousin, creeps towards him. They meet in no-man's land, recognizing each other by the light of a starshell. A moment later they are engulfed in a massive explosion. The battle scenes are amazing, as are the sight of the four supernatural figures of horsemen riding out of the storm clouds, and a sea of crosses covering the landscape at the end. The film is based on a Spanish novel indicting German behaviour in the war and trying to persuade Spain to join the Allied side. There are no sympathetic Germans in this typical example of a film which 'hates the Hun'.

Similarly it was a 'world at war' about which the author of Revelation wrote, for the benefit of his Christian communities. It was equally vital for him to differentiate sharply between the 'good' and the 'bad' in his story. But the contrasts could be even more effective on occasion by means of parody. We have seen this already in sequence A, at the point where John set up a superficial resemblance between the first of the four horsemen and the rider on the white horse in Revelation 19, in order that he might dramatize the differences. The image of the victorious warrior Christ succeeds, both by contrast with the Roman army's use of Mithras and in continuity with the Old Testament picture of the royal agent of Yahweh. The present sequence of 'Rival Powers' will be concerned with other contrasts of this kind, as the Seer identifies the evil forces who are in opposition to God in his world.

The four horsemen are best seen as caricatures, much as political factors and personalities might be depicted by a modern cartoonist. Traditional interpretation in the Ethiopian Orthodox Church has identified them as a collection chosen at random rather than a historical sequence of Roman emperors (1. Augustus–Tiberius–Constantine; 2. Vespasian–Titus; 3. Claudius; 4. Diocletian—also Mohammed!). In Europe in the late Middle Ages, faced with the need to explain great disasters such as the Black Death, the imagery of the four horsemen provided a personification of Death, merging with the activities of God himself, to be the ultimate cause of such events. But in the first century CE the horsemen are most likely to symbolize more 'down to earth' political factors in the Roman Empire (e.g. the cult of Mithras, international warfare, famine and plague). They are cast as parodies of the coloured horses to be found in Zech. 1.8-11 and 6.1-8, which symbolize God's control of 'all the earth'. But they have become caricature figures, heavy with symbolism; their functions are explained in three ways: by the colour of the horse, by the symbol (bow, sword, scales, name) that is carried, and by the interpretation of their activity. They appear as present realities, powers hostile to the earth, four of the first sequence of plagues. Although released as part of God's plan, the existence of such destructive forces must put God's ultimate control at risk.

The four horsemen represented menacing features in the contemporary political situation of the Roman Empire. For this reason, to interpret one of the horsemen now as Saddam Hussein of Iraq, as Philip Wilby did in his 1992 BBC video composition *The Cry of Iona*, would be entirely consistent with the original author's intention.

D.2. *Revelation 9.1-11: The Destroyer*

As the fifth trumpet is blown, the earth experiences the first of three 'events' called 'woes'. The sequences of numbers in the Apocalypse are complicated to understand, not least because they overlap. There are three explicit series of seven plagues, heralded respectively by the opening of seals, the sounding of trumpets and the emptying of bowls. Even though some of the same symbols recur (particularly variations upon the Egyptian plagues of Exodus), commentators are by no means agreed that the second and third series are replays of the first. The plagues are directed at different recipients, and the scale of their effect is progressive. It is thus possible to trace through the series either a narrative moving to a climax, or a symbolic pattern reaching completion. A.M. Farrer drew attention in his commentary to the weighting given to the larger or smaller 'halves' of the series of seven (the four horsemen or the three woes). But the three 'woes' may also be a larger pattern (it extends beyond 11.14-15 and may encompass the sequence of bowls also). In origin 'woe' is simply an exclamation of despair (as 8.13) but it becomes the umbrella term for an apocalyptic sequence of disasters. H.B. Swete (Commentary, *The Apocalypse of St John* [London: Macmillan, 1906]) made them into figures from Greek tragedy when he personalized them as avenging Furies. This would certainly suit the locust scorpions of the first 'woe'. But it is possible that such a larger pattern of three is derived from the traditional apocalyptic sequence of birth-pains, afflictions and the end (as described in Mk 13.7-23, 24-25, 26-27).

The 'star' (9.1) is a fallen angel, an evil power permitted by God to act. Stars are identified as angels in Revelation (see 1.20); but this Satanic figure should be contrasted with the angel 'from heaven' in 20.1 who imprisons the evil forces again in 'the bottomless pit'. This star may be the same as that called 'Wormwood' in 8.11 (see Jer. 9.15;

23.15 for the name). John has taken the myth of the fallen star (see Isa. 14.12-21) and combined it with features of a prophecy of Babylon's doom (Jer. 51) and an account of the Egyptian plague of locusts (Exod. 10.12-15) enriched by the prophetic interpretation of Joel. Thus the author of Revelation can describe the evil empire of Rome being destroyed (and destroying itself) in terms of the fate of both Egypt and Babylon.

The prophecy of Joel begins from a dramatic description of the natural disaster of a locust plague, like the devastation caused by a grassland fire (1.19). Within the book itself, however, and even more in rabbinic interpretation, the locust becomes a symbol first of invading armies (2.4-7) and then—as composite creatures—of supernatural agencies of destruction at the end of time. What for Joel is a portent of the eschatological Day of the Lord (2.30-31), God's army of judgment destroying until the people repent, becomes in Revelation an interim stage towards the climax, a period of 'torture' strictly limited to 'five months' with a similar but vain hope for repentance (9.20-21). Destruction is the name of the exercise, and so the fallen angel is given such a name, doubly emphasized by being given in Hebrew and Greek. 'Abaddon' (Destruction) is a synonym for Sheol, the waiting-room of death. 'Apollyon' (Destroyer) may refer to the Greek god Apollo (certainly the Greek playwright Aeschylus suggested that Apollo meant—and therefore was—a destroyer) and may even allude to the emperor Domitian's identification of himself with Apollo.

D.3. *Revelation 12.18—13.8: The Beast from the Sea*

The beast arises from the sea as a direct response to the Satanic summons (12.18). This is in turn a consequence of the dragon's fall from heaven (12.9—see E.3 and 4 below). So the beast represents a wide-ranging power in this world and, according to the Christian prophet, is motivated by Satan. To discover more, we need to investigate the background to Revelation's imagery. The Old Testament used such mythology to illustrate the belief that 'the dominant world powers which threatened Israel and opposed God were reassertions of the primeval chaos subdued at the Creation' (Kenneth Durkin in an unpublished article). The seas (as the original waters of chaos) had been put in their proper place at Creation (Gen. 1.9), but their assertiveness would need to be conquered again—as in the crossing of the Red Sea at the Exodus (see Isa. 51.9), so also in the last days (see Isa. 27.1). The work of John Day (*God's Conflict with the Dragon and the Sea in the Old Testament: Echoes of a Canaanite Myth* [Cambridge: Cambridge University Press, 1985]) should be consulted on the theme.

Revelation's beast combines most of the features from the four beasts (world empires) of Daniel 7. John J. Collins (*The Apocalyptic Vision of the Book of Daniel* [Missoula: Scholars Press, 1977], pp. 114-15) makes clear that we are dealing with potent symbolism and not just breaking a code:

> The four kings/kingdoms are presented in Daniel 7 as manifestations of the ancient chaos monster. It should be quite clear that we are not dealing here with a code which can be discarded when it is deciphered. We cannot say that the statement in Dan. 7.3 is adequately paraphrased in Dan. 7.17... The interpretation...is not intended to replace the vision or to provide an adequate substitute for it. It tells us only enough to make clear that Daniel was not witnessing a mythical drama unrelated to particular earthly events but an interpretation of contemporary history. That interpretation is provided by showing that the events in question conform to a mythic pattern.

In Revelation also the potency of the myth empowers the judgment against a contemporary reality of world politics. The beast expresses 'the magnitude and inter-relation of the developed human rebellion against God' (Kenneth Durkin). This rebellion is focused for the present in the international affairs of the Roman Empire. Because in the first century CE no more comprehensive social system can be conceived than the Roman Empire, the potential of political catastrophe for the world is maximized.

But it may well be that the Empire contains a seed of its own destruction, or at least of its own mortality (13.3). The 'death-blow' which 'had been healed' is to the author's mind a blasphemous parody of the saving death of Christ ('a Lamb standing as if it had been slaughtered', Rev. 5.6). But, like other amazing things associated with the beast, the 'mortal wound' appears to enhance its authority. For those who know their mythology, however, this is a true sign of mortality/vulnerability, as in the judgment of God on the serpent and Eve in the garden of Eden (Gen. 3.15); like serpent/dragon (Rev. 12.9), like beast. According to the immediate application of this imagery, in the Roman Empire there were widespread fears that the emperor Nero, though dead by his own hand, would return 'redivivus' at the head of troops from Parthia; this could be taken as striking evidence of Rome's blasphemous arrogance and ultimate fallibility. So the ten 'horns' of the beast (13.1) will eventually destroy 'Babylon' (17.16-17). The Seer believes that political forces within the Empire will undermine its economic, social and religious stability.

D.4. *Revelation 13.11-18: The Second Beast*

Third in the line of authority from the dragon—Satan in Revelation 12—and the Beast from the sea, comes the Beast from the earth. This hierarchy of authority appears as a grotesque parody of the sequence of communication in Rev. 1.1-2. From the point of view of the Beast from the sea, every successful public performer (like a comedian or magician) needs a straight man or an assistant. And the second beast (otherwise known as 'the false prophet', 16.13; 19.20) fills this role. Daniel supplies the prototypes, in the he-goat of ch. 8 and in the story of the statue in 3.1-7. But in the context of Revelation this beast, with Satanic powers of speech and magical skills, sustains the first beast in its parody of Christ the Lamb.

If the first beast represents the cult of the Emperor, with the full weight of Roman central authority, then the second beast stands for the personnel concerned with the cult at a local level. Earthly origins (13.11) point to the local setting; the second beast derives its authority from the first (13.12); and the second beast forces the population to make an image of the first beast and worship it (13.14-15). The Asiarchs (see also Acts 19.31) or members of the *koinon/commune*, or provincial council, could be charged with such responsibilities, and even function as priests of the imperial cult. They are less likely to have been professional magicians, to work the miraculous signs indicated in 13.13-15. This part of the description of the second beast remains problematic; it could be a mythological elaboration of Mk 13.22: 'false prophets will appear and produce signs and omens, to lead astray, if possible, the elect'. This was all part of the traditional expectations, fostered by apocalyptic writings (see also 2 Thess. 2.9-10).

There may have been corresponding realities, however, in the way the cult of the emperors was manipulated. Credulity and religious susceptibilities were exploited in a very eclectic system that made the most of local opportunities. Wonders were stage-managed, if not to the extent that Lucian described when writing of Alexander of Abonuteichos in the second century CE (*Alex* 12ff., 26). Suetonius tells how 'the statue of Jupiter at Olympia which' the emperor Caligula 'had ordered taken to pieces and moved to Rome, suddenly uttered such a peal of laughter that the scaffolding collapsed and the workmen took to their heels' (*Gaius* 57.1). Heron of Alexandria describes the mechanics of a statue of Dionysus which automatically squirts milk as well as pouring out wine (*Druckwerke* 13.1). The sign of fire (13.13) is reminiscent of Elijah (1 Kgs 18.38—see also Rev. 11.5); but in the different context of the imperial cult it may refer to thunder and lightning. In one of Martial's epigrams (9.86) the emperor Domitian is called 'Thunderer of the Palatine' just as Jupiter is the 'Thunderer of the Tarpeian'. Dio Cassius relates that the emperor Caligula had a mechanical contrivance 'by which he gave answering peals when it thundered and sent return flashes when it lightened' (*Roman History* 59.28.6). Emperors made effective use of quite advanced technology, as Suetonius reveals in his description of Nero's Golden House (Domus Aurea) with its revolving ceilings (*Nero* 31.2).

Much obsessive ingenuity has been spent on decoding the 'number of the Beast' (13.18) which the second beast applies in a branding process. If 13 is a number of ill-omen, who would work in room 666? More apposite could be the concern about computerized banking and supermarket bar codes involving 6-6-6 as a way of taking over the world! For it is clear that 13.17 refers to some kind of economic sanction, restricting trade.

As A.M. Farrer (1964, p. 159) pointed out, the number 666 is achieved mathematically by taking the square of 6 (= 36) and then triangulating it, that is, adding together all the numbers up to and including 36. If the root number 6 is associated with the mythology of Creation (which earlier proved so useful in elucidating the imagery of the beast—see D.3), then the sixth day is when humankind was created (Gen. 1.26-31). The mathematics could then symbolize pushing human ambition to its furthest limits—away from God. Certainly the 'week' of Creation is widely influential in Revelation, with seven as completeness and eight as 'the week + 1' (Resurrection on the first day of the next week, or its blasphemous parody in Rev. 17.11, where the pretentious head really 'belongs to the seven').

Gematria is the calculation of totals from the numerical equivalents of the letters in a word; it sounds like a game, but it was played with great seriousness in the ancient world to tell fortunes or convey cryptic messages, usually in Hebrew or Greek. There is an alternative reading (616 for 666) in 13.18 which shows all the signs of making a text fit a desired solution—the name of the emperor Nero in Latin. In the context where the arrogance of Rome and the blasphemy of the imperial cult are condemned, several possible solutions of 666 are relevant: Nero's name in Hebrew, or the emperors Titus or Domitian in Greek.

D.5. *Revelation 16.12-16: Armageddon*

Hal Lindsay's *The Late Great Planet Earth* (Grand Rapids 1970) is one of the best-selling religious books of the twentieth century, with 28 million copies in print by 1990. It has been immensely influential in the Bible Belt and in the Christian political right of the United States of America. The book is a popularization of the apocalyptic passages in the widely used *Reference Bible* of C.I. Scofield. All the ancient prophecies are being fulfilled, so history must be moving to its climax. The Jews have come back to their Promised Land; soon the Temple will be rebuilt. When that happens the day of Armageddon is near and the world will plunge to ruin in nuclear and environmental catastophe. A terrible dictator (worse than Hitler, Stalin or Chairman Mao) will arise to be the Antichrist. (While Mikhail Gorbachev was in power—and his famous birth-mark could be seen as the mark of the Beast—it was a Soviet Antichrist. His departure caused the scenarios to be rewritten, and Saddam Hussein, the rebuilder of ancient Babylon—cf. Revelation 17, 18—became a candidate during the Gulf War). Most of the world will obey the Antichrist, and he will turn on the Jews; at the same time 144,000 Jews will convert to Christianity and start a crusade to evangelize the world. Then a decisive pitched battle will be fought with nuclear weapons in Palestine.

If Lindsay's scenario for Armageddon fails to convince as a modern application of the Apocalypse, it is still a fair question why this final battle (prepared for by the pouring of the sixth bowl's contents—16.12) should be associated with a place in Israel called Armageddon (16.16). The place-name 'in Hebrew' (strictly 'Har/magedon') would denote Mount Megiddo. But Megiddo is a city on the plain (see Zech. 12.11) not a mountain, and the range of hills, at least seven miles away, is usually called Carmel. Megiddo was, however, a famous battle-ground—the scene of a defeat of the Canaanites by Barak and Deborah (Judg. 5), and where King Josiah was defeated and met his death (2 Kgs 23.29-30; 2 Chron. 35.22-23). But how relevant are such significant but remote events of Old Testament history?

Perhaps we should ask why the place-name is given 'in Hebrew' when it would be just as intelligible as a Greek name from the Septuagint? An attractive explanation is that we have an approximation in Greek to the Hebrew term 'mount of assembly' which is used in Isa. 14.13. There it referred to the (mythological) mountain in the far north—'Zaphon'—on which the gods are believed to assemble, and which the presumptuous king of Babylon seeks to climb in blasphemous pride. This pagan tradition was adopted by the Hebrews in the poetry of Ps. 48.1-2: 'His holy mountain, beautiful in elevation, is the joy of all the earth, Mount Zion, in the far north, the city of the great King'. The ideal of all mountains (even including pagan hopes) is applied by the Psalmist to the actual Mount Zion on which the Temple stood. In this case Rev. 16.16 is saying that the final conflict will take place around Jerusalem (the 'mount of assembly'). The outcome is now predictable, because the battle-ground is chosen by God, who in the biblical tradition has already subsumed the power of all other citadels to himself. Can we say that the nature of the battle is more to do with the power-struggle between spiritual forces than with an actual conflict of World War III?

D.6. *Revelation 17.1-18: Babylon the Great*

Talk of a trade war between Europe and the United States of America hits the headlines. There is much emotive language about fair competition in the marketplace and the iniquities of tariff barriers for importers on the one side and of large government subsidies to producers on the other. Trade is the lifeblood of world economies; it is what makes the world go round! But vital though this is, one should perhaps recall that the trade discussed is between developed nations, for the real benefit of the multinational corporations. The countries of the Third World are helplessly manipulated; their prospects for life, and not only their economic development, are the real casualties of the monetarist system.

We have already seen (in C.7 and D.4, above) how the 'mark...of the beast' is concerned with economic sanctions and trade restrictions (13.17). Further, the lament over Babylon, which extends through ch. 18, has much to do with trade, and the grief of the merchants at Babylon's fall (18.11-19). So it is important that Babylon as a 'woman sitting on a scarlet beast' (17.3) should have an economic aspect to her interpretation. Analogies between ancient and modern theories of economics are precarious, but it is clear that the Roman Empire opened up vast trading possibilities, and these contributed greatly to its well-being and stability. Imperial religion and the cult of Roma, the goddess of Rome linked with the imperial cult (and attested for at least five of the seven cities of Asia), would have both direct and indirect economic aspects. But some producers then (as now in the Third World) disadvantaged by shortages and trading restriction, would face crippling debt and commercial ruin. They would be justified in yearning for the demise of Rome, its blasphemous religion and its economic cartels.

As J.-P. Ruiz shows (*Ezekiel in the Apocalypse* [Frankfurt: Peter Lang, 1989]), Revelation used themes from Old Testament prophecy (Ezekiel as well as Daniel and Jeremiah) to denounce those hated features for which the Roman Empire stands—an example unique to the New Testament of the classic oracle against a foreign nation. The Old Testament regularly used prostitution as a symbol for idolatry (sacral prostitution) and lack of faith in the true God (e.g. Jer. 2–3 and Hosea; see the ironic judgment in Isa. 23.17-18). On that basis it could then be applied more widely to include laxity in sexual morals and even commercial exploitation. John had earlier used the symbol with reference to the woman Jezebel and the trade-guilds of Thyatira (2.20-23); now he takes three motifs (the beast and the city of Babylon as well as the prostitute) from his prophetic sources and blends them into a metaphoric unity. In his vision this woman, animal and city must yield to another woman (the church as the Bride of Christ) and another city (the New Jerusalem), through the agency of another animal (the Lamb that was slaughtered). In literary terms this is a splendid example of biblical intertextuality (interpretation within the Bible's own traditions). But it is clearly something else as well: an apocalyptic text which uses metaphors to confront real issues in a contemporary crisis.

D.7. *Revelation 20.1-10: The Millennium*
It is calculated that about 40 per cent of the United States population are 'Born Again' Christians. Many may look for the end of the world in terms of a Rapture of the Saved 'to meet the Lord in the air' (1 Thess. 5.17) and a Millennium (to reign with Christ for a thousand years). There will be 'high management openings for can-do Christians'. Jesus 'needs saints who develop success patterns in this present real-life testing ground... Many leaders will be needed to reign over cities, nations, territories and millennium projects'. In this new era 'strikes by workers and oppression by employers will be unknown', and Jesus will be 'committed to the instant destruction of the insubordinate or rebellious'. 'He will not permit the practice or propagation of false religion in any form.' 'At the Last Judgment no oral evidence will be required as in human courts; from the recesses of the individual's own memory the whole story will be revealed and flashed instantaneously before His mind' (citations from Paul Boyer's *When Time Shall Be No More* [Harvard: Harvard University Press, 1992).

Chapter 20 of Revelation is the biblical text that set the programme for a wide range of such literal expectations about the millennial kingdom, and the much larger sociological phenomenon of millenarian sects. Although a thousand years is undoubtedly a long time, it is conceived in the Apocalypse as only an interim during which Satan is imprisoned and those who share Christ's resurrection also fulfil a priestly ministry (20.6, see also 1.5-6; 5.9-10 in sequence B). The Millennium resembles an earthly triumph and vindication of the deaths of Christ and the martyrs. In the traditional doctrines of Roman Catholicism it has been regarded as an error to concentrate on the literal period of one thousand years for this earthly kingdom, rather than see it as a symbol for the prolonged but indefinite time of the church (between the resurrection of Christ and the Last Judgment).

Two points are important: to keep the Millennium in proportion, as only a small part of Revelation's programme, and to study this section in the literary context of the book as a whole (see J. Webb Mealy, *After the Thousand Years* [Sheffield: JSOT Press, 1992]). Apparent inconsistencies between the visions of the end have given literary critics opportunity for much speculative rearrangement. It is hardly surprising if historically there has been disagreement on the literal nature of the Millennium and on its relation to the second coming of Christ. For some who closely follow the actual order of Revelation the Second Coming (19.11-16) precedes the Millennium and these last events are established by divine cataclysm. For others who associate the Second Coming with the last judgment (20.11-15), the Millennium must come first; then the earthly reign of Christian saints is the climax, and yet the natural outcome, of a gradual but sustained activity of the church in the world. Both of these ways of interpreting Revelation have been widely influential through the Christian centuries. They may be labelled Pre-millennialist and Post-millennialist respectively, with reference to the timing of the Second Coming.

Essentially Christians have taken over the structure of the Jewish dream in Daniel 7, a dream of two ages (this age and the age to come) which fall either side of the coming of a son of man, and the saints' receiving the kingdom (Dan. 7.18). So the Millennium faces both ways: it is a divine vindication demonstrated on earth, and an earthly anticipation of heavenly conditions. In Daniel it would seem that the kingdom of the saints is God's final word, and not an interim event. But in Revelation God appears to be equally involved in the trial of humanity, the just sentencing, the new opportunity offered by resurrection for the Millennium, and the ultimate annihilation in 'the second death' of those rival powers opposed to God. In an exegetical 'tour de force' J. Webb Mealy combines the different and possibly inconsistent aspects of the text in a theological reflection upon resurrection and judgment. Modern sensitivities may take him further than Revelation:

> According to John, the millennium is the length of the just jail sentence that will be served by those who reject God in this life. And for him the last judgment is a picture of the gracious release granted to those who have served out that sentence... The negative mystery is that those who

have rejected God's grace in their mortal lives will never allow themselves to be reconciled to him, even though in his mercy they are
granted the gift of resurrection itself... The positive mystery is...that
God's patience towards the human race, his grace, and his willingness
to give opportunity for repentance never expire, come self-deception,
come rebellion, come murder, come suicide. To the very end, and to the
very final proof, enter them or not, the doors to his kingdom remain
open (Rev. 21.25) (pp. 247-48).

E. *Visions of the Future*

E.1. *Revelation 3.7-13: Pillars in the Temple of God*

Revelation attaches particular significance to doors (cf. 4.1); they are
what a modern idiom might call 'windows of opportunity'. The
opportunity before the church at Philadelphia (its 'open door') was
for outgoing missionary activity (cf. similar language used by Paul in
1 Cor. 16.9 and 2 Cor. 2.12). The city was well placed for communications with Phrygia, from its position on the route from Smyrna and
Lydia. Ignatius later recognized this aspect, in his letter to the Phil.
9.1. But in John's message the church seems to be facing the prospect
of disaster; the best that can be hoped for is survival and holding the
ground. The real security then rests in a transcendent vision of 'the
new Jerusalem that comes down from my God out of heaven' (3.12).
With this major theme the sixth letter anticipates the climactic vision
of John's book.

By association of ideas, talk of open doors leads to shutting and
keys. The reference to 'the synagogue of Satan' (3.9) might allude to
the shutting out of Christians, excommunicated by the Jews. But the
conflict is more likely to be an internal Christian matter, similar to the
issue with the Nicolaitans at Ephesus (2.6). Samuel Sandmel was
equally opposed to the theory of official Jewish excommunication and
suggested 'that the intent is to say that *true* Jews would not oppose
Christianity, and therefore those Jews who oppose it are not true
Jews' (*Anti-Semitism in the New Testament* [Philadelphia: Fortress
Press, 1978], p. 123). The struggling Christian community looks up to
the authority of the key-holder who has opened their door so that
none can shut it (3.7). The risen Christ is here depicted, in terms of the
prophecy of Isa. 22.22, as the prime minister, second only in authority
to the king himself in the Kingdom of God. Isaiah prophesied that
Eliakim would replace Shebna (22.15-19); his new authority and
duties are described (22.21-24); but 21.25 seems to suggest an eventual
removal from office. Isaiah's idea of 'a peg in a secure place' becomes
in Rev. 3.12 'a pillar in the temple of my God'. Pillars remain standing

when all else falls, and so they are an image of stability in a volcanic region like Philadelphia's, under constant threat of earthquake. These are powerful metaphors of transcendence for a city that is slow to recover and a church that looks disaster in the face.

The pillar is inscribed with the name of God and belongs to the future city, the new Jerusalem (3.12). An inscribed 'new name' is also found on a 'white stone' in the letter to Pergamum (2.17). After recent archaeological excavations in London have revealed burials with white pebbles in the mouth, one might speculate that it was a concrete sign of a Christian in the rite of passage to the future life. But in any case Philadelphia is no stranger to new names; the city had assumed new names as a vote of thanks to the Roman emperor (under Tiberius it became Neocaesarea, and from Vespasian to Domitian it bore the name Flavia Philadelphia). Once again we read the signs of a power struggle between Rome and the authority of Christ in the Kingdom of God. Perhaps some enthusiasts in Philadelphia sought to anticipate the new situation of the Kingdom. Colin J. Hemer has observed that the later town (Alasehir) on the site of Philadelphia makes a visual impact today that is strikingly 'foursquare' (see 21.16); its groundplan reveals a 'square enclosure and chess-board street pattern untypical of Turkish towns' (1986, p. 174). Possibly the local town was trying to live up to the ideal of symmetry and make the promise its own, by converting it into an actual possession. Sir William Calder (*BJRL* 7 [1923], pp. 309-54) also believed that the prophetic movement of the heresy known as Montanism originated in the district of Philadelphia. Predictions of a physical descent of the new Jerusalem to earth were a vital part of Montanism, seeking to turn expectation into new reality.

E.2. *Revelation 7.9-17: Naught for your Comfort?*

> I tell you naught for your comfort,
> Yea, naught for your desire
> Save that the sky grows darker yet
> And the sea rises higher.

These words from G.K. Chesterton's poem 'Ballad of the White Horse' were used by Trevor Huddleston to focus attention on the plight of the non-Whites in South Africa as long ago as 1956. Alan Paton, another famous name from the same generation of the struggle in South Africa, wrote in his autobiography *Towards the Mountain* ([New York: Charles Scribner's Sons, 1980], p. 12) about the vision of John on Patmos, of that world where there shall be no more death, neither sorrow, nor crying, neither shall there be any more pain. The visions are ineffable, of a world that will never be seen, but towards which we journey nevertheless.

Huddleston sees the symbol of the storm clouds; Paton the power of an ideal, however unrealistic. In contrast Desmond Tutu seems to take the words of Revelation at their face value (see above, in the summary of sequence B). Like the author of Revelation himself, he acknowledges the spiritual encouragement achieved by combining the images of suffering and of hope. Again and again John speaks of the harshness of the world's sufferings and the heavenly peace of those who have overcome in the power of faith. It is no accident that the vision of 7.9-17 follows rapidly on the breaking open of the seals and the protective sealing of God's servants. In the same way the triumph and thanksgiving of 11.15-18 are the immediate sequel to the account of the two representative witnesses in 11.3-13.

> True security will come when all of us, Black and White, know we count as of equal worth in the land of our birth, which we love with a passionate love. White South Africa, please know that... Blacks will be free whatever you do or don't do. That is not in question. Don't let the *when* and the *how* be in doubt. Don't delay our freedom, which is your freedom as well. Revelation 7.9-12 is the vision that upholds me. May it come true for our land (Desmond Tutu, *Hope and Suffering* [London: Collins, 1984], pp. 101-102).

E.3. *Revelation 12.1-12: The Woman Clothed with the Sun*
Morris West's novel *The Clowns of God* (London 1981) takes as its themes the world of apocalyptic and the ways that church and society react to the idea of the second coming of Christ. The novel is a compelling piece of storytelling with a serious purpose. If you have read it, you will have your own estimate of how satisfactory the conclusion is. If you have not, I do not wish to spoil the ending for you, but perhaps I can say that it has to do with a special celebration and recollection of the birth of Christ, in unusual surroundings.

Chapter 12 of Revelation starts with a representation of the birth of Christ. But the imagery and the theological emphases are so different from the stories in Matthew and Luke that you may not recognize it at first. The Gospels lay stress on the ministry and teaching of Jesus as well as his death and resurrection. And the meaning of all these events in the whole life was read back by Luke and Matthew and built into their telling of the infancy stories as well. But Revelation starts by depicting a woman in heavenly dress (Israel? Eve? Mary?) and then moves rapidly from the birthpangs to the threatened life of the child (the innocent who dies on the cross) and to the purposes of God who takes Christ to himself (in resurrection and ascension).

In Col. 2.14-15 Paul speaks of the consequences of Christ's death on the cross and the cancellation of the bond of sin: 'he set this aside, nailing it to the cross. He disarmed the rulers and authorities and made a public example of them, triumphing over them in it.' These same consequences are represented in even more dramatic pictures in Revelation. There is civil war in heaven between the hosts of angels, led by the archangel (and champion of Israel) Michael, and the powers of Satan. In Old Testament texts such as Job 1, Satan is a member of the heavenly council; but in subsequent Jewish and Christian interpretation he has changed roles from devil's advocate to devil. The heavenly triumph of Christ achieves a decisive realignment: the Satanic powers are expelled from heaven, for the earthly forces of the Christian church to contend with. The church's witnesses are well-equipped for the struggle. They are sustained by the victory that Christ has won (12.11) and the knowledge that God's consummation is near (12.12).

It has been argued forcibly by Adela Yarbro Collins (*The Combat Myth in the Book of Revelation* [Missoula: Scholars Press, 1976]) that most of Revelation is influenced by a traditional structure known as combat myth, and this is seen especially clearly in 12.1-12. This typical pattern of combat derives from Near Eastern mythology, and it may be glimpsed in the Old Testament (e.g. Isa. 27.1; 51.9-10 and many Psalms). Essentially there are three phases: a rebellion of evil forces, often symbolized as monsters; the temporary dominance of the powers of chaos; and final victory for the forces of good. The contest, graphically described, is often linked to the ordering of creation, or to eschatological expectation. Revelation clearly uses such traditional resources of pictorial language, and the interrelation of suffering, punishment and victory is vital to the expression of the author's hopes. But John does not simply reproduce a standard pattern, either once or several times. And the narrative of ch. 12 is not complete at v. 12. The story goes on...

E.4. *Revelation 12.13-17: The Pursuit*

Of increasing importance in early Christian art is the representation of the mother of Christ, often central in the group of disciples and symbolic of the church as a whole. A good example is the picture of Pentecost in the Rabbula Gospels, a manuscript of the Gospels produced in 586 CE in eastern Syria. The twelve apostles are gathered with Mary, distinctively dressed in red-brown and black, in the centre of the picture. The Holy Spirit descends as a dove over Mary, and there are tongues of fire above all thirteen figures.

In Revelation 12 the mother of Christ is pursued by the dragon, now that he is cast down to earth. She is preserved from this persecution (in circumstances that may allude to the flight of the Christians from Jerusalem to Pella at the time of the Jewish War). The dragon in his anger transfers the attack to the rest of the woman's offspring, that is the brothers and sisters of Christ, in the broadest sense of members of the Christian church.

This woman has a kaleidoscopic character in John's vision, embracing the sweep of salvation history, from the Old Testament to the current persecution of the Christians, from the daughter of Zion to the mother of believers. Even more significant is the deliberate contrast being made by John between this glorious figure and another woman, the personification of evil and blasphemy in the harlot of Revelation 17 (see D6 above in the sequence of Visions of Rival Powers). Again the author makes a deliberate association between the mother of Christ in Revelation 12 and the bride of Christ in Revelation 21.

There is another tradition in Christian art that makes out a major contrast between two women, the one blindfolded and carrying stone tablets who represents the Jewish synagogue, and the other tall and graceful in power who is the Christian church triumphant. We should observe that there is no basis whatsoever for this anti-Semitic contrast in Revelation 12. Rather, John's kaleidoscope shows a continuity between Israel and the church. This corresponds with the suggestion made above concerning 3.9 (see E.1.).

E.5. *Revelation 21.1-21: The New Jerusalem*
Until its demolition in 1961, there stood for three-quarters of a century at the top of Chatham Hill in Kent a massive building called Jezreel's Tower. It was not far short of a perfect cube with the dimension of 144 feet, built as an assembly room and headquarters for the Southcottian sect called the New and Latter House of Israel. In the long history of millennial movements and sects this is a striking example of trying to force God's hand by a literal implementation of prophecy. It is a fanatical attempt to build the new Jerusalem on earth according to the blueprint of John's vision.

Of course, the builders of the mediaeval cathedrals, like Abbot Suger of St Denis, were also concerned to reflect the symbolism of Revelation in their buildings. So there are twelve bays with vaulting to represent the fact that the church of God is built upon the twelve apostles. As we have noted before, Revelation expresses in more visionary language truths found elsewhere in the New Testament. So here Rev. 21.14 corresponds to the building metaphor in Eph. 2.19-22 where the apostles are the foundation and Christ himself is corner-stone (or alternatively key-stone).

Just as the builders of the late mediaeval cathedrals created a revolution in architectural terms, so John's vision of the new Jerusalem has a major difference from any earlier visions of heaven in Jewish apocalyptic. This holy city is seen in the act of coming down from heaven (21.2). In this new creation the gulf is bridged between earth and heaven. Jewish mystics and Greek thinkers alike imagined correspondences between earth and heaven. But on the basis of the gospel, Christians can speak with confidence of the Incarnation and of God's dwelling with his people in the transfigured conditions of this world. Rev. 21.3 is possible because of Jn 1.14 and 3.13.

E.6. *Revelation 21.22—22.5: City and Garden*

A wealth of images are jostling for position in John's vision of the new (or renewed) creation. There is the holy city and also the paradise garden (as it was before the Fall). We should look at each individual insight and resist the temptation to tidy it all into a single landscape. The new city of Jerusalem is here surveyed because of the symbolism of numbers and precious stones, and even more because this measurement is the counterpart of the measuring and the trampling of old Jerusalem in the Jewish War (Rev. 11.1-2). The garden and the source of water (so prominent in the van Eyck altarpiece mentioned in the sequence A.4) themselves correspond to the imagery of Gen. 2.9 and Ezek. 47.1.

'Those who conquer will inherit these things, and I will be their God and they will be my children' (21.7). It is striking that we find the heavenly city and paradise garden described in terms that fulfil the promises made to those who conquer in the seven cities of Asia Minor (Rev. 2, 3). The heavenly Jerusalem, according to Colin J. Hemer (1986, p. 16),

> is set in implicit contrast with the imperfections of the seven actual earthly cities. The parallels are not...obtrusive or systematic; there are repeated echoes of the same images, promises developed in a larger context, particular opponents overcome and disabilities reversed.

As we saw in sequence B.2, in the letter to Ephesus (Rev. 2.7) the promise was made 'to eat from the tree of life, that is in the paradise of God' (see 22.2). And the reference to God's throne in the Laodicean letter (3.21) is resumed in 22.3. It was to the church in Philadelphia that special mention was made of 'the new Jerusalem that comes down from my God out of heaven' (3.12, see E.1 above).

In John's vision the actual cities were scrutinized by the risen Christ, and were to face a period of severe trial. We observed in sequences A and B how features of the Son of Man vision are made fundamental texts in all the messages to the seven churches. Those messages also point forward, in a less structured way, to the hope of New Jerusalem. Where there is an inheritance promised to the victors in the church, these promises are fulfilled in the climactic vision ('Those who conquer will inherit these things', 21.7). The vision of hope that is set before them could be understood in terms of spiritual development and blessing for the individual believer. But it also clearly relates to an eschatological fulfilment and vindication that will be closely linked to the earthly facts of daily life in the churches.

E.7. *Revelation 22.6-21: The Risks of Prophecy*

Revelation is a work of Christian prophecy, as this conclusion makes clear. There is a general impression (not necessarily historically accurate) that the voice of prophecy had been silenced for centuries since the prophets of the Old Testament. New religious movements, including Christianity, brought an upsurge of prophetic activity in the first century, and a recurrence of the practical problem: how do you test a prophet and know that he or she speaks the truth? The twentieth century experiences similar difficulties with the rise of charismatic movements in some churches.

The early Christians had their guidelines for testing prophets. Confidence tricksters were exposed by the amount of free board and lodging they claimed. There were also elements of a credal test of basic beliefs (how they measured up to the earliest gospel tradition, or the prototype creeds) in order to judge the truth of what they said. Immediate prophecy (22.10)—that is, not sealed up for the distant future, after the pattern of Dan. 12.9—could be vulnerable to corrupting interpretation and interpolation. A threat (22.18-19), which itself rests on the power of prophetic symbolism, might be adequate to discourage tampering.

John's is a burning personal faith that the Son of Man, whom he has glimpsed in glory, will be coming soon. For him Christ is the faithful and true witness who provides a direct link for the believer to the Father of all. The words of John's prophecy participate in this trustworthiness and truth (22.6). Like others in the early church (and in subsequent crises) he prays earnestly the Aramaic prayer *marana tha*— Come, Lord Jesus (22.20). Despite one's personal faith (or because of it) one yearns for the world to be confronted by the Risen Lord. In that way, perhaps, the unbelievers will be convinced and the souls of the believers and martyrs will be relieved from their duties of witness. Meanwhile the saints need the grace of Christ (22.21).

Summary of Section E: Visions of the Future

Samuel Wesley's well-known hymn 'Aurelia', with words by S.J. Stone, might be used to sum up Revelation's perspective of the church, the promises made in the present and the vision of their future fulfilment:

> The Church's one foundation
> Is Jesus Christ her Lord...
> She waits the consummation
> Of peace for evermore;
> Till with the vision glorious
> Her longing eyes are blest,
> And the great Church victorious
> Shall be the Church at rest.

Some theological reflections by Jürgen Moltmann on 'The Consummation of Creation', in which he applies texts from Revelation 21, provide us with an underlying rationale for visionary material of this kind:

> In the prophetic and apocalyptic visions we find two formal principles: first, the negation of the negative and, secondly, the [positive] fulfilment of anticipations. In this double form the visions remain both realistic and futuristic. The negation of what is negative—'death shall be no more, neither shall there be mourning nor crying nor pain any more' (Rev. 21.4)—defines the space that is open for the positive reality that is to come. The vision of 'the classless society' also follows this method of describing the future by means of a negation of the negative. But the mere negation of what is negative does not necessarily lead to a definition of the positive. Consequently eschatology too cannot be developed merely as negative theology...
>
> The victory of Christ over the forces of this world which are hostile to God would make it possible for Christians again to live in the cosmos, once more understood as creation. The expressions used to visualize the future and the new being of man do not go back to some presupposed primal condition; they explain the 'new thing' of the raising of the crucified Jesus by promising his lordship over everything, the dead and the living: 'The city has no need of sun or moon to shine upon it, for the glory of God is its light, and its lamp is the Lamb' (Rev. 21.23) (*The Future of Creation* [London: SCM Press, 1979], pp. 124-25, 169).

Conclusions from These Five Sequences of Readings through Revelation

The five sequences have provided a schematic framework within which we may organize blocks of material from Revelation, in order to understand it better. We have seen how certain fundamental statements were made about the being of God, and the death and saving activity of Christ. The primary context of the book, in which these theological claims were made, was the present existence of a cluster of Christian communities in Asia Minor, who were shown their responsibilities to bear witness to their faith and to die for it, if necessary. The larger context of thought was the whole world around them, which was in origin the good creation of God. But its future was threatened in terrifying ways. The positive side to this fear was the ultimate destruction of all those contrary forces and insidious movements of distortion which were dominating the world. John maintains that from the ashes of this destruction would come the restoration of creation as it should be, and the uniting of earth and heaven in the eternal worship of God.

However strange and multicoloured the language of Revelation may appear to be, it expresses a number of ideas very clearly:

1. The transcendent power of God as creator and of Christ as redeemer;
2. The relationship of believers through Christ to God in the Spirit;
3. The interaction of worship and witness for the church in the world;
4. The transitory nature of this age (even in its religious dimensions);
5. The element of self-sacrifice inherent in Christian witness;
6. The political implications of Christian living;
7. The power of a vision of hope in a context of suffering.

FURTHER READING

G.B. Caird, *The Revelation of St John the Divine* (Black's New Testament Commentaries: London: A. & C. Black 1966).

Etienne Charpentier, *How to Read the New Testament* (London: SCM Press, 1982).

Austin Farrer, *The Revelation of St John the Divine: A Commentary on the English Text* (Oxford: Oxford University Press 1964).

C.H. Giblin, *The Book of Revelation: The Open Book of Prophecy* (Collegeville, MN: Michael Glazier, Liturgical Press 1991).

Sophie Laws, *In the Light of the Lamb: Imagery, Parody and Theology in the Apocalypse of John* (Good News Studies, 31, Wilmington DE: Michael Glazier 1988).

John A.T. Robinson, 'Interpreting the Book of Revelation', in *idem*, *Where Three Ways Meet* (London: SCM Press 1987), pp. 35-75.

J.P.M. Sweet, *Revelation* (SCM Pelican Commentaries, London: SCM Press 1979).

My thanks are due to the Bible Reading Fellowship for their kindness in allowing me to reuse and develop material from the Guidelines treatment of Revelation in this chapter.

Chapter Three

WHAT KIND OF BOOK? THE LITERARY CHARACTER
OF THE BOOK OF REVELATION

Is Revelation Distinctive?

Should the book of Revelation be considered on its own, as a unique work? Some would maintain that Daniel in the Old Testament and Revelation in the New Testament stand alone as the only works of the literary type of 'apocalypse' in the biblical canon. But even this statement invites some form of comparison between them. It would be even more profitable to compare Revelation with other apocalyptic works, both Jewish and Christian, outside the limits of the Bible. There are approximately 15 Jewish apocalypses dating from the intertestamental period and 24 early Christian examples. The comparison helps one to understand this type of writing, and the conventions associated with it—what the first readers of such a work would have taken as read.

> Generally speaking, apocalyptic is understood to mean a complex of writings and ideas which were widespread about the turn of the era in Palestine, in the Israelite diaspora and in early Christian circles; but which can also appear in similar form in other religious situations and mental climates... A second and narrower use of the word [is] the title of literary compositions which resemble the book of Revelation, i.e. secret divine disclosures about the end of the world and the heavenly state. The word apocalypse has become the usual term for this type of book. It is also applied to books and parts of books to which the ancient church did not as yet give this title—for example the synoptic apocalypse of Mark 13 (Koch 1972, pp. 13, 18).

Some Christian commentators have wanted to say that Revelation is distinctive in early Christianity because it is a prophetic rather than an apocalyptic book (cf. Chapter 2, sequence E.7 above). It symbolizes the rebirth of prophecy in the early Christian church, after years in which Jewish theology was seen in terms of Law rather than Prophecy, that is, as scribal exposition focused on the Torah (the Pentateuch or five books of the Law of Moses). Revelation as prophecy should therefore be compared directly with the oracles of Hebrew prophets contained in the books of the Old Testament such as Isaiah, Jeremiah and especially Ezekiel, and the scrolls of the Minor Prophets (particularly Joel, Zephaniah and Zechariah).

But it is not easy to sustain the description of Revelation as prophecy, if that is understood as a statement about literary form (but also see below for observations about interpreting tradition and on dramatic performance). The text does not resemble consistently either the spoken or the subsequently written (anthologized) oracles of the prophets. Revelation as composition is a literary mixture of materials, only some of which are oral in character: narratives of visionary experience, letters, hymns, traditional mythology and bizarre imagery, coded references to the sequence of historical events, stylized threats of judgment and accompanying lamentations, symbols of number and colour, projections of the future in terms of a new (or renewed) order of creation. I suspect that Christian writers describe Revelation as prophecy not because some of its characteristic features are prophetic, but because they wish, for apologetic purposes, to reclaim the work as Christian prophecy and, therefore, as inspired Christian preaching. But I think we can appreciate the value of Revelation as a Christian work within the context of the early church without misrepresenting its essential character in this way.

Definition of Apocalypse as a Literary Genre

What is the definition of the term 'apocalypse'? It denotes a form or genre of literature. To say that the name derives from a Greek word meaning 'that which is uncovered or revealed' is only part of the definition, because that takes no account of the technical senses in which the Greek word is now used by scholars. As a modern term of classification of ancient literatures it does not include all ancient works that have 'apocalypse' in their title (e.g. *Apocalypse of Moses*), but it does include other texts or parts of texts that did not carry that label (e.g. *Testament of Abraham*).

We can trace the development of thought in the growing complexity of definitions of the genre 'apocalypse'. First comes Klaus Koch's *Rediscovery of Apocalyptic*, justifying serious academic attention to the subject, in the words already quoted. Then we have John J. Collins on p. 9 of the introduction to *Semeia* 14 (1979), based on the constant elements in the paradigm established by the SBL project:

'Apocalypse' is a genre of revelatory literature with a narrative frame-work, in which a revelation is mediated by an otherworldly being to a human recipient, disclosing a transcendent reality which is both tempo-ral, insofar as it envisages eschatological salvation, and spatial, insofar as it involves another, supernatural world.

Thirdly there is a threefold definition by David E. Aune (*Semeia* 36, [1986], pp. 65-96) which incorporates both a critical appraisal of Collins' definition and some insights from David Hellholm and the International Colloquium on Apocalypticism at Uppsala in 1979:

The definition should be formulated in terms of form, content and function... The proposed definition of the apocalyptic genre, with spe-cial reference to the Apocalypse of John, is as follows:
1) Form: an apocalypse is a prose narrative, in autobiographical form, of revelatory visions experienced by the author, so structured that the cen-tral revelatory message constitutes a literary climax, and framed by a narrative of the circumstances surrounding the revelatory experience(s).
2) Content: the communication of a transcendent, often eschatological, perspective on human experience.
3) Function: (a) to legitimate the transcendent authorization of the mes-sage, (b) by mediating a new actualization of the original revelatory experience through literary devices, structures and imagery, which function to 'conceal' the message which the text 'reveals', so that (c) the recipients of the message will be encouraged to modify their cognitive and behavioral stance in conformity with transcendent perspectives.

The Collins/SBL definition was subsequently expanded to include some reference to function, in the light of comments such as those of Aune and Hellholm. Collins had originally classified the range of extant apocalypses under two main types and further sub-categories. The book of Revelation was assigned to category Ib—Apocalypses with Cosmic and/or Political Eschatology (which have neither histor-ical review nor otherworldly journey). This typology shows its subjec-tive aspect: not all scholars would agree that Revelation has no review of history, even if its otherworldly journey is very limited in compari-son with some apocalypses. There is real danger in trying to build too much into an essentially generic definition—the simpler it is, the more useful it can be. The enlarged range of literary questions opened up by genre criticism are highly significant, but it may be better to treat them under headings other than 'definition' later in this chapter. Genre criticism is also important, perhaps more important, for what it can reveal about divergency and variations, and not just for classify-ing standard 'types'.

For practical purposes there is a range of questions that need to be asked about the form, content and function of any apocalypse:

Form	Who reveals?
	to whom?
	How (under what circumstances)?
Content	What is revealed?
	What is the declared purpose of the revelation?
Function	For what purpose is the literary text designed?
	Are there indications of early response to the text?

These are the aspects of the definitions of apocalyptic writing that seem to me most important for Revelation. It is essentially revelatory, and that revelation is made through a framework of narrative. It is unlike the oracle of a prophet because the revelation comes through a mediator who is out of this world (the risen Christ or angelic figures) but who communicates directly to a human recipient (John). What is disclosed is transcendent, beyond this world; a kind of heavenly storeroom is opened up to John, the earthly visitor, so that he can see things which (although still in heaven) have a direct bearing on human affairs. The perspective is either a time sequence (such as linear history), so that at the appropriate moment these realities will appear on earth and so transform events as to bring about a final salvation. Or the perspective is of a spatial dimension concerned with the connection between worlds: the new vision is of a key relationship between local happenings and cosmic realities, so that the one is perceived through the other. Such visionary perspectives are born in a situation of crisis, so as to encourage or console the 'righteous' community in its sufferings. But an apocalypse is relevant not only to a time of crisis; in less stressful circumstances it goes on being used in other ways (e.g. to teach moral lessons by extreme example).

Additional Note on Apocalyptic and Apocalypticism

As we have seen already, 'apocalyptic' can be used strictly of the essential ideas of the literary genre, or (much more loosely) of a fashion of thinking and writing, characterized by a heightened sense of eschatology, or imminent expectation of the end-time. The problem of communication begins with this variability in the use of the word. It is possible to construct a synthesis, or identify a fairly coherent body of ancient thought, which starts from, but extends beyond, the literary apocalypses. But if one then relates this 'Apocalyptic', by comparative methods, to modern movements associated with political, social and environmental disaster, it is imperative to use strict criteria for this enlarged, comparative usage. Does the modern thinker, understandably scared of the nuclear holocaust, really express the same ideas in a similar context to John in the first century CE?

David Aune commends

> the three-fold distinction between 'apocalypses' (as literature), 'apocalyptic eschatology' (as a world view) and 'apocalypticism' (as a socio-religious movement) proposed recently by a number of scholars [as] an important step forward in the discussion... It can no longer be assumed that apocalypses were produced by apocalyptic groups who espoused a distinctive type of apocalyptic eschatology (1986: p. 67).

But it is probably safer to restrict the use of 'apocalyptic' to denote the literary genre as the source of such ideas, and to use terms like 'heightened eschatology' for looser references to the ideas in general, and 'millennial' or 'millenarian' to refer to the socio-religious movements.

We should try to safeguard 'apocalyptic' and 'apocalypticism' as terms related to a literary genre. Certainly, as J.Z. Smith observed ('Wisdom and Apocalyptic', in P.D. Hanson (ed.), *Visionaries and their Apocalypses* [London: SPCK, 1983], pp. 101-20), apocalyptic/ism is a 'scribal phenomenon', essentially 'bookish' in the methods of handling the message by writing it down rather than communicating prophetically through the spoken word. Of course such attitudes to texts as cryptic or revelatory will outlast the period when the original literary genre flourished.

The Literary Components of the Apocalypse of John

The exotic richness of Revelation lies in a diversity of literary sub-forms that do not belong automatically to the genre of apocalypse. These include:

Autobiographical narratives of visions (from 1.9 onwards)
Commissioning of a Prophet (1.17-19; 10.8–11.2)
Prophetic oracles (1.7, 8; 13.9-10; 14.12-13; 16.15; 19.9-10; 21.5-8)
Oaths (10.5-7)
Plague sequences (chs. 6, 8 and 9, 16)
Liturgical hymns (4.11; 5.9-14; 7.10-12, 15-17; 11.15-18; 12.10-12; 15.3-4; 16.5-7; 19.1-8) (There is also the possibility of longer liturgical structures underlying chs. 1, 4 and 5, 7 and 19)
Lamentations and dirges (18.2-24)
Woes (8.13)

Lists of virtues and vices (9.20-21; 14.4-5; 21.8, 27; 22.14-15) (Such
lists, used for moral exhortation, technically known as catalog-
ical paraenesis, are frequent in the Pauline letters—see 1 Thess.
4.1-12; Col. 3.5-17; Eph. 4.2-3, 17-24)

Letters (Cf. both the formal structures of the short letters in chs. 2
and 3 and the overall epistolary framework in chs. 1 and 22,
with its opening and closing formulae [1.4-6; 22.21] and authority claims [1.1-3; 22.6-12, 16-20])

Lyle D. Vander Broek writes (in collaboration with James L. Bailey—
Literary Forms in the New Testament [London: SPCK, 1992], p. 203),

> The exegete is called upon to recognise the uniqueness of these [literary
> sub-]forms in Revelation and to understand how they relate to the
> apocalyptic genre.

This unique relationship is easier to assert than to expound. To see the
problem, one only has to consider the question, Which came first, the
letter or the vision? The letter form provides the framework, but even
the letters are given in a vision. But any commentator has a duty to
hazard a guess as to why John employed this particular combination
of literary materials.

The Integrity of the Work and its Structure

Among the older skills of literary criticism, the examination of sources
and style in the Book of Revelation reached a peak with the two-
volume commentary by R.H. Charles in the International Critical
Commentary series (1920). Twenty-five years of work produced a
minute dissection of language and text, with the final chapters
reordered and reconstructed, and many other passages assigned to an
uncomprehending editor as later interpolations or meaningless sur-
vivals. In contrast, the second half of this century has seen a growing
tendency to acknowledge the work's literary unity, while of course
allowing for incongruities.

The modern reader notices a variety of structural devices which the
author has employed to secure the literary unity of the work. The
most important of these features are:

(a)   The sequences controlled by a significant number (such as
seven or three). This principle of organization, repeated on
three occasions in the sequences of plagues, allows for an element of recapitulation, while ensuring the progressive nature
of the narrative. (Theories of total recapitulation overlook the
distinctive character and purpose of each sequence, as well

as the changing proportion of the world affected by the plagues.)

(b) The deliberate interlocking of elements, with a sequence of three woes within the seven trumpets (chs. 8–11), or a bridging device (8.1-5) which relates seals and trumpets together.

(c) The emphatic juxtapositions of triumph and tragedy, sequences of plagues and liturgical orders of praise (e.g. ch. 12). The deliberate contrast heightens the effect of both elements, while striving to preserve Christian hope in the darkest hour. From the perspectives of analytical psychology, this device may also relate to what Jung called 'coniunctio oppositorum', or the creation of a dialectical unity of opposites.

It is also important to investigate the possibilities of larger patterns of structural organization for the whole book. Perhaps one of the most useful and significant is a chiastic arrangement, such as is suggested by Elisabeth Schüssler Fiorenza (1985, ch. 6):

A	1.1-8
B	1.9–3.22
C	4.1–9.21 + 11.15-19
D	10.1–11.14; 12.1–14.20 + 15.2-4
C′	15.1; 15.5–19.10
B′	19.11–22.9
A′	22.10-21

The positive effect of such a chiastic structure, where the sections with the same letters correspond to one another, is the focus given to the central section of the book (D) around which the rest is orientated. But for others the disadvantage inherent in this analysis is the obligation felt to chop up the text and reallocate sections, in order to make them fit the pattern. This can destroy some of the effective juxtapositions to which attention was drawn above.

But the real advantage rests in the principle underlying Elisabeth Schüssler Fiorenza's discussion of the literary structure.

> The early Christian apocalyptic tension between the now of the community and the eschatological future, between the 'already and not-yet' of the end-time, is expressed in the literary-structural tension between the forward-movement of the narrative, cyclic repetitions, and hymnic proclamations. The dramatic narrative of Revelation can best be envisioned as a conic spiral moving from the present to the eschatological future. It could also be likened to a dramatic motion-picture whose individual scenes portray the persons or actions every time from a different angle, while at the same time adding some new light or color to the whole (p. 7).

The principle involved is that a literary pattern can resemble a three-dimensional geometric figure, and this conveys a sense of the depth and of the perspectives within the book. In the same way a computer projection in the round would give a more adequate account than the flat contrasts of a semiotic square, or the simpler two-dimensional arrangement in patterns of sevens. In the end what is most important is that the reader should attempt to draw a route-map (with contour lines, to show height and depth!), and to offer a personal description of the journey through the book. The outline provided above at the beginning of Chapter 2 might serve as a starting point.

The Character of Revelation's Language

Everybody agrees that the Greek language in Revelation is peculiar. But there is widespread disagreement about the reasons for this. These are the main explanations:

1. It is essentially Greek, but barbaric, with deviations explained as a sloppiness or lack of competence, a deliberate flouting of the rules of syntax, or mistakes made because it is a second language. Parallels to these errors are claimed in the workaday vernacular language of the papyri found in Egypt.
2. The original apocalypse was written in Aramaic; the translation deliberately strives to reflect the original inspiration.
3. According to a nineteenth-century theory, this is a unique form of the language known only to the Holy Ghost ('Holy Ghost Greek').
4. According to a more critical perspective, it is 'biblical Greek', which betrays Hebrew influences as well as a continuity with the Septuagint (Greek translation of the Hebrew Bible). But why is Revelation more peculiar than other parts of the New Testament that are also in biblical Greek?
5. It is a first-century CE Jewish dialect of Greek, as used in Palestine ('distinguishable dialect of spoken and written Jewish Greek'—Nigel Turner; 'while he writes in Greek, he thinks in Hebrew'—R.H. Charles; 'Greek language...little more than a membrane, stretched tightly over a Semitic framework'—S. Thompson).

It may prove impossible to decide between these theories; but sharper definition and more precise analysis of the types of Greek found in the New Testament should be forthcoming from the more intensive computerized studies of the biblical language. The interpreter of Revelation, however, must also consider some of the implications of this use of the language. Was John his own secretary, since scribal resources might be limited in his Patmos prison? Was the choice of words his own, or was he influenced by apocalyptic conventions or a basic structure of formulaic composition? He could be writing the first large-scale Christian work of the apocalyptic genre, but would he have modelled himself deliberately on earlier Jewish traditions? Would this entail the use of archaic (and appropriately arcane) language? The fact that John does not follow Daniel in adopting the convention of pseudonymity is not a decisive argument. The Christian revival of prophecy had transformed the situation in which the writer of Daniel had to use pseudonymity in order to key into the earlier Old Testament tradition of living prophecy. And John certainly does make use of Daniel for both his imagery and some of his literary sub-forms.

Author's Intention and Reader's Response

The modern emphasis is to examine a text from both perspectives, that is, to look not only at the way the author uses language, but also at the way that language would be understood. The need is to look for fruitful ways of describing the interaction between the author and the reader, and so to define the process of communication. We shall look at three possibilities that are not necessarily mutually exclusive.

1. As an Interpretation of Tradition (Intertextuality)

Austin Farrer emphasizes how important it is to understand John's book as a network of Old Testament exegesis:

> So far from reading like an attempt to communicate a previous visionary experience, the Revelation reads like a fresh and continuous scriptural meditation, conceived in the very words in which it is written down; as though, in fact, the author were thinking with his pen... He meditates into vision what he writes, and feels the presence of the mysteries he describes. But such vision can be achieved by a man working from words. The rabbis held that the most perilous technique of ecstasy was a meditation on the complicated text of Ezekiel's first chapter. St John takes the risk; in the fourth chapter of his Revelation he sees his way into heaven by the use of Ezekiel's and of several overlapping scriptural texts (1964, pp. 24, 26).

Readers (both ancient and modern) need to be attuned to a select area of Old Testament texts as living traditions, which author and reader have in common, and from which creative interpretations can readily be made. Some may feel that a commentator like Austin Farrer strains credulity by the varied and intricate patterns of scriptural allusions proposed. But it is important not to neglect the possibility of any textual allusions or adopted symbols, so long as they are treated as options for exegesis rather than eisegetical controls. This can apply not only to the Old Testament but also to the use of themes from earlier Christian texts. The question of relative dating can be difficult here, but texts such as the Little Apocalypse (Mark 13 and parallels) could well be influential, even if its independent existence as a text of the apocalyptic genre is unproven.

A good model to consider for such Intertextuality is that cited above from J.-P. Ruiz (*Ezekiel in the Apocalypse* [Frankfurt: Peter Lang, 1989]) in sequence D.6. in Chapter 2. He argues that John takes three motifs (prostitute, beast, city of Babylon) from his prophetic sources in Ezekiel, Daniel and Jeremiah. He blends them into a metaphoric unity in his vision, whereby this woman, animal and city must yield to another woman (the church as the Bride of Christ) and another city (New Jerusalem), through the agency of another animal (the Lamb that was slaughtered).

As Gabriel Josipovici writes in *The Book of God* (1988, p. 302):

> the biblical scribes worked within a living tradition, constantly transforming yet always remaining true to the spirit of the whole.

2. *As Dramatic Performance (Orality and the Text)*

This heading may be unexpected, given the emphasis of this chapter upon the literary character of the work. We can see how the act of writing is an important part of the book's authority. The command to 'write', for example, figures repeatedly in the literary sub-form of the prophetic oracle. And we have noted already that apocalyptic/ism is a 'scribal phenomenon', essentially 'bookish' in the methods of handling the message.

But with ancient texts we cannot exclude a spoken element on principle. Literature is linked to rhetoric by the fact that texts were often read aloud in the ancient world. With all the books in the New Testament it is likely that their written form is related to oral performance in public. This is not only to echo the results of Form Criticism about the kerygmatic function of the units in the Synoptic Gospels; we must also think of Paul's letters being read aloud to his churches, gathered for worship. And David Aune has drawn attention to the unique and innovative nature of Revelation (and the Shepherd of Hermas) among apocalypses, because, he claims, they were designed for dramatized performance:

Orality played an explicit role in the composition of the Apocalypse of John, for the entire document was written expressly for public performance (Rev. 1.3; 22.18), and each of the seven proclamations of Rev. 2–3 are presented as dictated by the author, as are many other segments of the book (cf. Rev. 21.5). The fact that both the Apocalypse of John and the *Shepherd of Hermas* were intended for oral performance before Christian congregations *constitutes a unique feature of these two apocalypses* (1986, p. 78).

Certainly we can say that the literary genre of apocalypse is modified significantly, even transformed, by the letter collection and the epistolary framework. The oral application of the author's message may then be the explanation we sought earlier for the unique combination of literary forms. This still may seem to us like a nice irony. But it is important to recognize the continuing work of literary criticism in studying the nature and the purpose of the interplay between oral and written forms. It may have begun with studies in the Old Testament prophets, or the early Christian prophetic revival, but it does not end there. In Rev. 1.3 and 22.18 we have clear evidence of essential parallelism between reading and hearing in the use of a text. As some modern film-making has shown, Revelation's symbols can be evoked with intense power in a dramatic oral presentation. But perhaps we should think of an ancient performance, with impersonal characteristics, like a Greek tragedy using masks for the actors.

3. *As Symbol and Allegory*

Dionysius of Alexandria fiercely contested Revelation's place in the New Testament canon, but he insisted that the book had a non-literal meaning (although one beyond his comprehension!). He employed the techniques of literary criticism on the Seer's language to show that the Apocalypse was not written by John the Apostle, like the Gospel and the first Epistle of John. For this reason there was no question of preferring the symbolic meaning of Revelation, as a 'higher' meaning; indeed it should not be as highly regarded as the more literal, but apostolic, sense of the Gospel.

Nowadays, although there are still problems and prejudices about the place of the Apocalypse in the Canon, higher criticism has made us less positive about apostolic authorship and its implications. Writings in the tradition (school of thought) of Paul or John are not denied worth as Scripture for that reason. And we do not share unquestioningly the criteria, established by Origen in the patristic period, for an almost hierarchical scale of values: from literal up to symbolic/ allegorical levels of moral and then spiritual meaning. A modern literary reading of the text may be attracted to the possibilities of allegory, but not because of any assumptions about the highest level of meaning.

But how is one to read apocalyptic images? Richard Bauckham ('The Figurae of John of Patmos', in A. Williams (ed.), *Prophecy and Millenarianism* [Harlow: Longman, 1980], p. 109) posed the question with this example:

> When we read in John's opening vision of the risen Christ that his head and his hair were white as white wool (Revelation 1.14) are we to visualize this feature as part of an attempt to share John's visual impression of the resplendent Son of Man? Or are we to treat it as a conventional item in literary descriptions of heavenly beings (cf. Apocalypse of Abraham II, of the archangel Jaoel)? Or are we to recall that in Daniel 7.9 this feature belongs not to the Son of Man but to the Ancient of Days, and so conclude that this reflects John's high Christology? Or should the white hair be allegorized as a symbol of Christ's eternal pre-existence? Such questions cannot be finally answered without fuller studies than we have of the apocalyptists' use of imagery and John's specific relation to the apocalyptic tradition in this respect.

It should be obvious from a reading of Revelation that the author's imagery and symbolism are not all of a single kind. The differences are further indicated by the way John handles them. Some of the symbols are followed immediately by an interpretation which 'breaks the code' (see 1.20; 7.13-14; 12.9); but sometimes the solution may appear as cryptic as the problem (see 13.18; 17.9-18). Other symbols are more recognizable, traditional figures, perhaps even stereotypes (such as Babylon, Egypt, Jerusalem, Sodom); the reader brings prior familiarity with such echoes to assist in identification. Yet other symbols may capitalize on a certain familiarity in order to surprise and shock; they are used by the author, being deliberately stimulating and provocative, in a creative expansion of ideas (see the Lamb contrasted with the expected Lion in 5.5-6; and the relationship of parody between the riders of white horses at 6.2 and 19.11-16). Finally, the author provides symbolic dream/visions of both heaven and the future, which may transcend all expectations (see chs. 4 and 21). And throughout the reader must remain open to the disconcerting possibilities that the same reality may be represented by more than one symbol, or that the same symbol may stand for more than a single reality.

It may be impossible to reach final conclusions on a particular symbol, as Richard Bauckham suggested above, through lack of data for comparison. But most commentators express personal preferences in their interpretations of the work as a whole. If there is a sliding scale—induced visionary experience; conventional but reworked allegorizing; traditional allegorical dream; remythologizing of imagery previously demythologized; symbolic vision—then most scholars would place John at the upper (and more creative) end of the scale. It is important not to underestimate the potency of symbolism. As Thomas Fawcett wrote in 1970 (before inclusive language was widely used):

> Man is confronted by a range of symbolic possibilities. The potential symbols in his experience determine the limits through which he can understand reality, and his receptiveness to these symbols determines his outlook. The history of man's use of symbols reflects his changing view of the universe and of his relationship to it. From this there emerges a most important characteristic of symbols, namely their power to direct our thinking and our orientation towards life (*The Symbolic Language of Religion* [London: SCM Press, 1970], p. 32).

A striking visual image is a conceptual breakthrough. Skilled use of visual images is a means not only of expressing spiritual understanding but indeed of thinking theologically, by means of reflection upon the image and by further elaboration of its implications. To understand John's work fully, we need to be able to describe his process of seeing and writing. It may be that interpretations of Revelation also need to be visual.

FURTHER READING

David E. Aune, 'The Apocalypse of John and the Problem of Genre', *Semeia* 36 (1986), pp. 65-96.

James L. Bailey and Lyle D. Vander Broek, *Literary Forms in the New Testament* (London: SPCK, 1992.)

David L. Barr, 'The Apocalypse of John as Oral Enactment', *Interpretation* 40.3 (July 1986), pp. 243-56.

A. Yarbro Collins, 'Reading the Book of Revelation in the Twentieth Century', *Interpretation* 40.3 (July 1986), pp. 229-42.

John J. Collins (ed.), *Apocalypse: The Morphology of a Genre* (1979).

Gabriel Josipovici, *The Book of God: A Response to the Bible. Semeia* 14 (New Haven: Yale University Press, 1988).

Frank Kermode, *The Sense of an Ending: Studies in the Theory of Fiction* (New York: Oxford University Press, 1967).

Klaus Koch, *The Rediscovery of Apocalyptic* (Studies in Biblical Theology, 2.22; London: SCM Press, 1972).

Gerard Mussies, 'The Greek of the Book of Revelation', in J. Lambrecht (ed.), *L'apocalypse johannique et l'apocalyptique dans le Nouveau Testament* (BETL, 53; Leuven: Leuven University Press, 1980), pp. 167-77.

Gerard Mussies, *The Morphology of Koine Greek as Used in the Apocalypse of St John: A Study in Bilingualism* (Leiden: E.J. Brill, 1971).

S.E. Porter, 'The Language of the Apocalypse in Recent Discussion', *NTS* 35 (1989), pp. 582-603.

E. Schüssler Fiorenza, *The Book of Revelation: Justice and Judgment* (Philadelphia: Fortress Press, 1985).

S. Thompson, *The Apocalypse and Semitic Syntax* (SNTS Monograph, 52; Cambridge: Cambridge University Press, 1985).

Chapter Four

FROM WHAT SETTING? THE HISTORICAL AND SOCIAL CONTEXT OF REVELATION'S COMMUNITY

From the beginnings of modern biblical criticism until recently, historical investigations have occupied a dominant position. Open any academic commentary on a book of the New Testament and you are likely to find an early and substantial part of the introduction concerned with questions of date of writing, authorship and historical setting. The balance has shifted within the last decade; questions of literary structure, ways of reading, and methods of interpretation are asserting themselves and pushing the more historical questions into the background. So in the present work Chapter 3 precedes Chapter 4!

The real issue, however, is not the subject matter of the questions but their presuppositions. Are you (the readers) concerned solely with your action of reading—as if there were no yesterday and no tomorrow? Or are you reading to discover the intentions of the book in front of you—because these will resemble the intentions of the author, like a reflection in a mirror? Or are we together studying the text and using our basic training in biblical criticism to provide a window—so that we can look in at the original setting of the text in history, and the historical situation can signal its message to us indirectly, for us to apply its message analogously in our different/modern circumstances? The first two approaches use techniques of literary criticism, modern (postmodern!) and not-so-modern. The third is the approach of historical criticism, and this can apply to the criticism of source material as much as to the setting of the finished text.

Historical criticism may seem old-fashioned, but it is an essential method if we are to appreciate one important aspect of any primary apocalyptic text. There is an interrelationship between the text and the situation of crisis that produced it. The state of emergency affecting the community produces the text as a coded response, a theological evaluation of the real issues. But the text itself may well fuel the crisis, as it functions within the community setting as inflammatory propaganda. We are dealing with a literature of protest and revolt. It may counsel revolution, passive resistance or religious quietism. Clearly, then, we need to know as much as we can discover about the mutual relationship of the particular crisis and response.

Apocalypticism has proved a powerful catalyst for certain aspects of religious belief. To understand their importance what is needed is a description of the social world of a community in which an apocalyptic text is produced. It is then possible to apply sociological methods and comparative insights from anthropology to the texts and other historical evidence. What circumstances and what kind of communities are inclined to develop apocalyptic ideas? Perhaps an even more significant question is this: are there any precise analogies between the situations that nurtured Jewish and early Christian apocalyptic and the modern contexts (the nuclear threat, environmental concerns and feminism) in which apocalyptic language is ardently employed?

Questions of Dating

As I have observed elsewhere:

> a book whose business is 'revelation' has revealed little of the circum-
> stances which produced it... *Revelation* comes from a situation of actual
> (or threatened) persecution of Christians by the local Roman imperial
> authorities in Asia Minor towards the end of the first century ('Revela-
> tion of John', in R.T. Coggins and J.L. Houlden (eds.), *A Dictionary of
> Biblical Interpretation* [London: SCM Press, 1990], p. 593).

As to dating, there are some clues, both external and internal to the book, which we should notice, before considering how to reconstruct the social setting of John's communities.

Can we Trust the External Evidence?

The traditional date for the Apocalypse of John is in the reign of the emperor Domitian (81–96 CE). The basis for this is a remark of Ire-naeus (*Adv. Haer.* 5.30.3):

> [the apocalyptic vision] was seen not such a long time ago, but almost in
> our generation, at the end of the reign of Domitian.

Other statements by Clement of Alexandria, Origen, Victorinus and Jerome are not necessarily independent of Irenaeus, and Eusebius quotes Irenaeus in his account of the Christian persecution under Domitian. Alternative datings, in the reigns of Trajan (98–117 CE), Nero (54–68 CE) or Claudius (41–54 CE), are late and may be based on misunderstandings.

> What Irenaeus says is straightforward, categorical, fairly precise and very credible. Domitian has always been remembered as a stereotypically bad emperor; a persecutor who insisted on emperor-worship.

But Robert B. Moberly, from whom this last quotation comes, is not for that reason convinced. He doubts that we should place such reliance on Irenaeus' memory of what he had heard second-hand. It is not a standard date, fixed at the time in an established chronology, but a date constructed retrospectively (perhaps by totalling the reigns of emperors) where it is easy to stretch or foreshorten a span of time.

> Irenaeus was writing in Gaul, during the AD 180s or late AD 170s, about when an apocalyptic vision had been seen in Patmos... He thinks that John saw it 80–95 sketchily charted years earlier—in other words 35 sketchily charted years, or so, before he (Irenaeus) was born. We would not normally regard so distant, belated and second-hand an opinion as, by itself, evidence... Such opinions in Irenaeus are not, to my mind, necessarily false—or true. He presumably said what he had heard, at Smyrna in his boyhood, in (say) AD c. 140' (Moberly 1992, pp. 376, 381).

This means that the dating question cannot be settled by the external 'evidence'. At best we are offered clues to set alongside indications from the book itself. These may point collectively towards the traditional date under Domitian, or alternatively to a Trajanic date for the completion of a work begun under the Neronian persecution (as proposed by Martin Hengel, *The Johannine Question* [1989], p. 81).

Internal Clues to the Dating

Revelation is preoccupied with the imminent collapse of the Roman Empire, the suffering and martyrdom of Christians as the result of persecution, and the problems of a blasphemous worship of the emperor. We cannot know whether any or all of these are present experiences or only realistic expectations at the time of writing. There are limited periods in the first century of the church's life in which these were realities, but not necessarily all at the same time. Otherwise we may be dealing with vivid, and credible, imaginings. What has already been said about the literary unity of the work, might cause hesitation before we argue for an apocalypse composed in stages. Only if literary and historical arguments combine is this more than a solution of last resort, or a sign of well-edited source materials. Here is a summary of the positive aspects in favour of four times (in reverse chronological order) when Christians experienced or feared persecution from Rome.

1. *The Reign of Trajan*

Only at this time is there clear evidence for the persecution of Christians in Asia Minor, documented in the exchange of letters between the younger Pliny and the emperor Trajan c. 112 CE (Pliny, *Ep.* X. 96-97). Pliny seems the complete caricature of a civil servant needing to consult the emperor on every decision; but we should be grateful because of the information he gives us about the issues involved.

> [Those who denied they were Christians] recited a prayer to the gods at my dictation, made supplication with incense and wine to your statue, which I had ordered to be brought into court for the purpose together with the images of the gods, and moreover cursed Christ—things which (so it is said) those who are really Christians cannot be made to do.
>
> [Those who ceased to be Christians] maintained, however, that the amount of their fault or error had been this, that it was their habit on a fixed day [cf. Rev. 1.10] to assemble before daylight and recite by turns a form of words to Christ as a god; and that they bound themselves with an oath [*sacramentum*]... After this was done, their custom was to depart, and to meet again to take food, but ordinary and harmless food.

Christianity has evidently spread rapidly in this part of Asia, so as to be a problem. There are anxieties about the effect on pagan cults, as well as emperor worship; the situation resembles that of Ephesus in Acts 19. All kinds of popular accusations against the Christians were current (such as arson, incest, ritual cannibalism). Counter-evidence is taken from two women deacons under torture (as happened with slaves' evidence under Roman law). The Christians held two meetings on a Sunday: the first an early service probably for the sacrament (Pliny misunderstands the term as taking an oath); the second is an 'Agape' or fellowship meal. The crucial test in these trials is the refusal of Christians to venerate pagan images, or even to demonstrate their loyalty by paying divine honours to the emperor. In reply Trajan cites no precedent to guide Pliny in knowing how far to pursue the Christians. Christianity is not yet an explicit offence on the statute book, but rather a matter for summary police action if a situation becomes dangerous. Tertullian later complained that Trajan's ruling was inconsistent: 'He says they must not be ferreted out, as though they were innocent; he orders them to be punished, as though they were guilty!'

The Apocalypse was completed or reworked early in the reign of Trajan, according to Martin Hengel in his discussion of *The Johannine Question*:

> The Apocalypse could be an earlier work, the nucleus of which was written in the time after the shock of the Neronian persecution, the

beginning of the Judaean war, the murder of Nero and the civil war; possibly it was reworked later, early in the reign of Trajan, by a pupil who depicted the elder as a recipient of apocalyptic revelation and a prophet (p. 81).

John the Elder was 'a real historical personality, a teacher and charismatic authority who worked in the Flavian period and early in the reign of Trajan in Ephesus and founded a school there'. Although the basis of the book was his experience in exile on Patmos, the final form of the work reflects later and different perspectives. The arguments for the later date have more to do with the total span of Hengel's theory than with any specific internal evidence. Time is needed for improvement in the Greek and change to a more conservative outlook (there are similarities between the seven letters and 1 John). Is it a pupil's viewpoint to depict John in Revelation as a Christian prophet, outside the group of twelve apostolic authorities of the past (see Rev. 21.14)? But the principal evidence for the time of Trajan is a working back through the Johannine tradition in Asia Minor, from Polycrates of Ephesus and Irenaeus, via Polycarp of Smyrna to Papias of Hierapolis, writing about a generation after John the Elder himself.

2. *The Reign of Domitian*

There is very little firm evidence for the persecution of Christians under Domitian, despite his notorious reputation. Dio Cassius and Suetonius both record the death of Flavius Clemens, among others in 96 CE. Dio says that Clemens and his wife Domitilla were accused of 'atheism' and 'Jewish customs'—which could mean Christianity, but is hardly conclusive. Clemens is not to be identified with Clement, bishop of Rome and author of *1 Clement* (often dated to Domitian's reign), which speaks of 'sudden and repeated misfortunes and calamities' and 'unexpected and repeated troubles' (1.1). Brian W. Jones (1992, pp. 114-15) writes,

> Just possibly, the phrases in question might refer to prominent Christian sympathizers denounced by informers late in the 90s: three or four executed or banished could well have represented a calamity to a comparatively small group.

It is all a question of scale and significance; but the fact remains that

> No pagan writer accused Domitian of persecuting Christians, though Nero's activities in this regard were recorded as was Domitian's determination to tax the Jews.

Christian tradition of Domitian as a persecutor grew quite rapidly. Eusebius quotes both Melito of Sardis (c. 170 CE) as saying that evil advisers persuaded Nero and Domitian to slander Christian teaching, and Tertullian as claiming a little later that Domitian 'almost equalled Nero in cruelty, but, because he had some commonsense, he soon stopped what he had begun and recalled those he had exiled' (*Hist. Eccl.* 3.20; 4.26). It is Eusebius who includes Domitian's banishment of John to Patmos in his *Chronicorum Canonum*. Domitilla is reckoned as a Christian, but instead of being the wife of Flavius Clemens and mother of his seven children, she has become his virgin niece; the second-century Christian catacomb in Rome named after Domitilla may reflect the growing tradition or merely the original ownership of the land.

Domitian's bad reputation certainly results from his enthusiasm for making the cult of the emperor compulsory, even in Rome and the West as well as in the East (cf. Rev. 13.11-17; 20.4). He revelled in his relationship to the newly deified emperors Vespasian and Titus. A Temple to Domitian and his deified relatives was dedicated at Ephesus in the year 89/90 CE, and S.R.F. Price (1984, pp. 197-98) believes this was the occasion that prompted John to write. Suetonius also tells the story of Domitian's dictating a circular letter to be used by the procurators beginning 'Our Lord and God commands this to be done' ('Dominus ac deus noster', cf. Jn 20.28). But in the end Domitian was assassinated and not deified.

3. *The Reign of Titus*

Although Suetonius called Titus 'the delight and darling of the human race' and recorded the spontaneous mourning and affection that greeted his early death in 81 CE, yet his accession in 79 CE on the death of his father, Vespasian, had been dreaded because of earlier glimpses he had given of his real character. His concessions to the Senate, and a policy of mild tolerance, failed to stop the spread of discontent, especially in the East. The Jews were ready to ascribe an agonizing end to the actual person who had destroyed the Temple in Jerusalem (cf. Rev. 11.2). According to Sulpicius Severus, Titus had reflected that to destroy the Temple

> would be an invaluable way of doing away with both the Christian and the Jewish religions, for, although mutually inimical, these two faiths had sprung from the same root...and, once the root was dug up, the stem would soon perish (*Chronicle* 2.30.6).

Dio Cassius records that a false Nero appeared in the reign of Titus; there may have been more than one of these impostors appearing at this time in Asia Minor, giving fresh impetus to the legend that Nero must return (*Redivivus*—after his suicide in 68 CE) at the head of a Parthian army to regain his throne (see Rev. 13.3; 17.8, 11). 'Nero Redivivus' rapidly becomes a symbol of renewed civil war for Rome and an eschatological omen. If Nero is appropriately the first of the sequence of seven heads (17.9), then the sixth who is now reigning (17.10) is Titus. Current expectations and fears centre upon Titus' brother Domitian who has been designated as the next emperor. Domitian must not reign long, if the church and Rome are to survive. For into the reign of the seventh emperor the diabolical eighth ('Nero Redivivus') will irrupt as a ghastly and catastrophic climax. If the riddle of the beast is correctly solved in this way, an amazingly precise date (within three years) has been achieved for this central focus of the Apocalypse, and therefore possibly for the whole book.

4. *The Year of the Four Emperors*

Robert B. Moberly (1992, pp. 376-93) is the most recent writer to make a case for Revelation (or its main vision) as a response to one particular year of crisis for the Roman empire. 69 CE was the year, following Nero's suicide, in which Galba, Otho and Vitellius struggled in turn to hold power, and from which Vespasian emerged victorious. Rome, personified as the goddess Roma and satirized as Babylon, is on the point of collapse from civil warfare. This does justice to the sense, throughout Rev. 16.17–19.2, of an imminent fall. Although Rome was in control of much of the world, this year was, in Tacitus' words, 'nearly the final year of the state'. With the fall of Otho, the number of Caesars who had died violently and bloodily (at their own or another's hand) could be calculated at five: Julius Caesar, Gaius (Caligula), Nero, Galba and Otho. The intervals between their deaths have become dramatically shorter. Vitellius is now the 'sixth' (see Rev. 17.10) reigning as emperor with help from the legions of Gaul, Upper and Lower Germany and Britain—four out of the (approximately) 'ten' armies of Rome (see 17.12). The other six acclaimed Vespasian in July 69, so that a final confrontation between Vitellius and Vespasian appeared imminent. It might be that Nero Redivivus would return from Parthia to play a part in Rome's downfall.

The recollection of the historical Nero is still vivid. The recent fact of Christian martyrdoms, in the ghastly public spectacle orchestrated by Nero (Tacitus, *Annals* 15.44—see sequence B.6 in Chapter 2 above), would help to explain Revelation's preoccupation with justice and vengeance (see 6.9-10). Depending on the date of the Neronian persecution (64, 65, or 66 CE), the interval between the first martyrdoms and the Year of the Four Emperors could be three and a half years (see

11.2; 12.6, 14; 13.5). If so, then the symbolic time has a very precise and literal reference. Also these were years in which (Moberly thinks) Jews and Christians shared a common grievance against Rome, and so interreligious animosity is not reflected in the main part of the Apocalypse. Certainly this dating comes between the Jewish revolt in 66 CE and the fall of Jerusalem in 70 CE; so the Temple is still standing and can be measured (see 11.1).

A case is therefore argued for an apocalyptic work conceived in rapid response to oral reports of the events in this year, as the garbled set of impressions reached Patmos before winter made travel impossible. It must be debated whether information of sufficient accuracy for the scenario in Revelation would have reached an isolated exile this quickly, and whether the author had the practical resources on the island to produce even a first draft of his work.

Are any of These Internal Indications Conclusive?

The evidence for any one of these four datings is cumulative but still not overwhelming. It may amount to no more than circumstantial evidence! It is an irony, frequently observed, that John's clues to the time of writing can afford to be so enigmatic, because his first recipients knew as well as he the situation for which he wrote. Only the first and last solutions offer firm evidence of persecution of Christians, because of the doubt about Domitian. The second has the benefit of external support from Irenaeus, if this can be trusted. The third, with its memories and fears about Titus, still makes good sense in a 'Jewish' apocalyptic milieu. But the earlier the date is set, the harder it is to allow for the highly developed use of traditional motifs in the book. In the late sixties or early seventies CE, it is more likely that Babylon stands for Jerusalem rather than Rome. But most commentators have difficulty with a proposal such as that of J.M. Ford (*Revelation* [AB, 38; New York: Doubleday, 1975])—a Jerusalem-orientated revelation to John the Baptist. The majority are convinced that Babylon is Rome or Roma.

If an early date still appeals, it would be better to consider the possibility of source materials and traditions, formulated in response to events, just as the material of Mark 13 may have been produced in Caligula's day, but then assimilated fairly thoroughly into a later work. So Christian thinking about the Roman Empire in, say, the last decade of the first century would be highly coloured by the experiences and attitudes of an earlier generation of Christians. Students of apocalyptic are very aware of how much material is recycled (perhaps repeatedly) from earlier contexts. One therefore looks at the material on two levels: (1) the traces of origins reflected in pieces of the text; and (2) the overall perspectives of the final version. This final version may have a literary (and dramatic) integrity, while indicating that some ingredients (e.g. chs. 11 and 12) belong to an earlier generation and have therefore now been given a retrospective character, presented as a 'flashback'.

Reconstructing the Social Setting of John's Community

There are two methods of approach to this task: to move from theory to practice, or vice versa. Most attempts have started from a social theory and sought to match the data of the Apocalypse to the theory. The danger is that a preferred model will simply be imposed. Alternatively to start from specific indications in Revelation runs the risk that evidence will point in several directions (as with the question of dating) and no single theory will result.

Engels, writing about 'Revelation' in 1883 within the Marx–Engels collaboration *On Religion*, popularized the work of German Protestant biblical scholars and argued that Revelation was the earliest extant text of Christianity. The Apocalypse gave an authentic picture of the primitive Christian community as a more or less revolutionary group (part of the revolution of the masses). The evidence was that John showed clear signs of class hatred, a vengeful attitude against Rome and against the ideology of the oppressive class. Clearly such an interpretation is indebted to the model of socialist movements, as much as to the biblical evidence.

More recent sociological theory frequently applies the model of the sect to apocalyptic writing in general. Revelation corresponds closely to the pattern of a Jewish and Christian literary genre and therefore should show a sectarian group, marginalized by the attitudes of mainstream society. To some extent this model is also a reading back from the experience of much more recent groups who have used Revelation, from the Puritans of New England, and Edward Irving, the hell-fire preacher and founder of the Catholic Apostolic Church, to the millenarian sects studied by contemporary anthropologists; because of this the results must be treated with caution. The theory of cognitive dissonance (beautifully illustrated in the novel by Alison Lurie, *Imaginary Friends* [London: Heineman, 1967; Abacus, 1987]) is often applied to such groups, to explain why they survive long after their original prophecies of the end have failed. Such disappointment, which might be expected to lead to the group's disintegration, is apparently overcome by a revised message, antinomianism, and increased missionary activity in compensation.

The dilemma of the social scientist, particularly with regard to religious movements in modern society, but also with their ancient parallels, is to know if the proliferation of sectarian movements indicates a revival of the religious spirit or a deterioration in the face of social pressures. Social scientists are primarily concerned with any religion's outward forms and structures; their criteria are quantitative rather than qualitative. And so their theoretical interpretations are unavoidably limited. If a dialogue between theological and sociological interpretation is possible, it is much more likely to produce comprehensive results.

Evidence from the Text of Revelation

John's community is clearly under severe stress, although not necessarily official persecution by the Roman authorities. Persecution in the first century, as we have seen, was localized and spasmodic, at the provocation of informers, rather than a regular process with an established legal base. But certainly the community faced ostracism and social contempt. They feel threatened and insecure, and must contend with religious as well as social stress. This stress is produced in the first place by the externally enforced worship of the Roman emperor, with social and economic sanctions applied against non-conformists. Ruler cults were a long-established and politically valuable principle in Asia Minor. In the Roman Empire, the East urged the familiar idea out of tribute and loyalty; the West reluctantly conformed when coerced by an enthusiastic emperor. But there is also some evidence in Revelation for another kind of religious stress which arises from internal religious conflicts. These are represented symbolically in the text by cryptic references to opponents of the churches, called the Nicolaitans (2.6, 15) and the synagogue of Satan (2.9)—possibly also by Balaam (2.14) and Jezebel (2.20) as alternative prophetic voices to the Seer's.

A comparison between the Gospel of John and the Apocalypse reveals a surprising difference in the nature of their religious communities. In the Gospel the group appears to be enclosed and inward-looking, a community of believers ultimately liberated from this world and its constraints (see Jn 17). But in Revelation the community is not closed like the stereotype of the apocalyptic sect. Instead it is a group with a very positive sense of mission to the world. It is possible to see this as one of the results of the process of cognitive dissonance (see above), on the assumption that the Gospel pre-dates Revelation in the same community. But a contrasting interpretation is more likely, given the depth of the positive attitude to mission throughout the traditions of Revelation. Revelation 7.2-4 does speak of 144,000 who are 'sealed' and protected like an elect; but it should be read as a symbolic number, modelled on Israel in the Old Testament, whose task it is to inspire and lead to salvation an infinitely larger number of people from the whole world (see 7.9-14; 5.9-10; 14.6). In ch. 15 the symbolic transition is at its most effective: the song of Moses (Old Testament) becomes the song of the Lamb (New Testament); and the 144,000 (15.2 = 14.1-2) become an infinite number with participation now open to the world (15.4).

A key idea for mission in Revelation is 'witness' (which is the same Greek word as 'martyrdom'). The visions of ch. 11, describing the fate of 'my two witnesses', indicate how this act of Christian 'witnessing' and mission is ultimately effective. 'Witness' is therefore defined as communicating the gospel message in the context of a fundamentally prophetic community. Witness is an activity undertaken in the closest relationship to Christ, on the path from suffering to glory (1.5; 11.8). God's reign is seen as being universal in scope, but working towards its fullest realization through human agencies and representative individuals. The prevailing situation in the world is such that acts of witness often entail the completion of Christian testimony by martyrdom.

The situation as depicted is that of cosmic confrontation; the powers of evil ranged against God's purposes for the world are no mere phantoms. The task of Christian prophecy, which in part inherits the mantle of the Old Testament prophets and the negative response they came to expect, is to present the gospel to the world and offer the occasion for repentance and change of heart. The prophetic figure and his or her community may feel isolated and vulnerable, but the witness can be confident of speaking with God-given authority. The way the group conducts itself is a powerful symbol and a testimony to the world.

'The Book of Revelation struggles to speak for the whole world; yet if it lost its minority status, it would lose its raison d'être.' Leonard L. Thompson seeks in this way a broader social base for the book at the end of his 'dramatic' presentation (*The Book of Revelation: Apocalypse and Empire* [1990]). He rightly resists the ideological tendency to find for Revelation a narrowly defined social location, determined solely by political or economic factors affecting a marginalized sect; this is to ignore the wider appeal of Revelation's language in ancient as in modern times. But it cannot speak for the public order of the status quo without ceasing to be an apocalypse. There is an 'ambivalent relationship with the larger order' so that the book can be accepted 'without relocating into a sect-type social base'. All that is required is for the larger order of society to be 'engaged as the enemy from a particular Christian perspective'.

> John and his audience can, however, be located in Roman society as a group of people who understand themselves as a minority that continuously encounters and attacks the larger Christian community and the even larger Roman social order. That communal self-understanding leads us back to the paradox of a 'cosmopolitan sectarianism'. The universal, cosmic vision of the Book of Revelation is grounded in first-century Asian life and necessarily entangles itself in all power structures in all dimensions of human society. But it entangles itself as opposition. It opposes the public order and enters the fray as other 'deviant' groups in the empire, not by joining rioters in the streets but by a literary vehicle, a written genre—in John's case, a genre offering revealed knowledge as an alternative to the knowledge derived from the public order (pp. 195-96).

Thompson emphasizes the importance of the communication of revealed knowledge as a basic clue to the book's social setting. But his broader approach must not be seen as emptying the Apocalypse of specific reference and allowing it to be 'all things to all people'. The epistolary framework of the book and, even more, the seven letters it contains are essential to the aim of 'direct communication'. Detailed symbolism in the letters links back to the vision of Christ who is the author of the communication, and forward to the vision of hope in the New Jerusalem. And these letters tell us specific facts about the local communities and what may be 'house churches' set up by John in these cities. The religious tensions with the Seer's opponents within the Christian churches are an important aspect of the social situation. As Martin Hengel suggests (1989), the issues and rivalries may be comparable with those reflected in the canonical letters—1–3 John. But the range of other social details needs to be studied, with Colin J. Hemer's *The Letters to the Seven Churches* as an informative guide. These seven letters afford valued glimpses of John's communities and show how the message of the Apocalypse is grounded in the historical realities of the churches.

FURTHER READING

A.A. Bell, 'The Date of the Apocalypse. The Evidence of some Roman Historians Reconsidered' *NTS* 25 (1979), pp. 93-102.

A. Yarbro Collins, 'Dating the Apocalypse of John', *Biblical Research* 26 (1981), pp. 33-45.

A. Yarbro Collins, *Crisis and Catharsis: The Power of the Apocalypse* (Philadelphia: Westminster Press, 1984).

Ian Hazlett (ed.), *Early Christianity: Origins and Evolution to AD 600* (Essays in honour of W.H.C. Frend; London: SPCK, 1991).

Colin J. Hemer, *The Letters to the Seven Churches of Asia in their Local Setting* (JSNTSup, 11; Sheffield: JSOT Press, 1986).

Martin Hengel, *The Johannine Question* (London: SCM Press, 1989).

Brian W. Jones, *The Emperor Domitian* (London: Routledge, 1992).

Robert B. Moberly, 'When was Revelation Conceived?', *Biblica* 73.3 (1992), pp. 376-93.

S.R.F. Price, *Rituals and Power: The Roman Imperial Cult in Asia Minor* (Cambridge: Cambridge University Press, 1984).

John A.T. Robinson, *Redating the New Testament* (London: SCM Press, 1976).

Leonard L. Thompson, *The Book of Revelation: Apocalypse and Empire* (New York: Oxford University Press, 1990).

Chapter Five

THE ABIDING THEOLOGICAL VALUES AND DOCTRINES OF REVELATION

How Jewish is the Theology of Revelation?

HOW THE RELATIONSHIP between Christianity and Judaism is reflected in the Apocalypse remains one of the most tantalizing of historical problems, while it is of the greatest theological significance. Most scholars are now much less confident about dating the so-called 'Parting of the Ways' to the last decades of the first century. It used to be thought that the additional formulation in the Eighteen Benedictions of Judaism—a curse upon the Minim, or heretics—applied solely to the Christians and showed how wide the gap had become. Even if this were so, it is not necessarily reflected in John's Gospel with its reference to excommunication from the synagogue at 9.22 and 12.42. The Apocalypse is related to the Gospel in a number of respects, some problematic, but its own relationship to Judaism shows little sign of the open confrontation found in the Gospel (e.g. Jn 8). It is not just that Revelation makes use of an originally Jewish literary genre (apocalypse). There also seems to be a positive role ascribed to Israel as the mother of the Messiah in Revelation 12—at least as positive as Paul's hopes for Israel in Romans 9–11. And there is no reason to suppose that remarks about 'a synagogue of Satan' (2.9; 3.9) are less symbolic, and therefore more anti-Semitic, than the denunciation of Jezebel the prophetess. Indeed, so Jewish has the Apocalypse appeared to be that Rudolf Bultmann, for example, could claim that the faith of Revelation was a Judaism which had only been slightly Christianized (*Theology of the New Testament* [2 vols.; London: SCM Press, 1975], II, p. 175).

Nevertheless the flight of the Jewish Christians to Pella, in the course of the Jewish War (which could be represented symbolically in Rev. 12.14-16), might well have been regarded by the Jews as an act of treachery, deserting their Jewish compatriots in the hour when solidarity was needed. This could have provoked the Jewish synagogue reaction after the War, culminating in the expulsion associated with the Birkat ha-Minim. But if earlier 'persecution' of Jewish Christians by Jews had been more intense (as may be reflected in 1 Thess. 2.14), then the practical boundaries had been drawn already, and the Christian withdrawal from Jerusalem was scarcely surprising.

Alan F. Segal in his comparison of Judaism and Christianity in the Roman world *Rebecca's Children* (1986, pp. 130-31) writes of the variety of responses among both Jewish and Christian groups to the historical fact of the fall of the Jerusalem Temple in 70 CE:

> Each different Christian community designed a response to the destruction of the Temple to fit its own interpretation of history. Within Christianity the Temple characteristically became either the body of Christ, the church, or the Christian community itself. Later Christianity used the passion of Jesus as justification for an end to the entire sacrificial cult. Jesus' sacrifice on the cross became the perfect sacrifice of the perfect priest on the perfect altar...[the Letter to the Hebrews]. In the Revelation of John...the new world envisioned at the end of time becomes a new Jerusalem but not a new Temple.

The key questions to ask, in response to Segal, are whether Revelation sees Christ's death fully in terms of the Jewish sacrificial system; and is the Temple missing from the New Jerusalem because it is superseded, or because its theological importance is realized in more spiritual terms (21.22), as was the case with the Pharisaic realization of Rabbinic Judaism after 70 CE?

Once again we are being offered not only such polarized alternatives in the interpretation of Revelation (independent-minded Christianity or a Jewish-Christian tradition) but also the possibility of a range of intermediate points on a sliding scale. We cannot resolve such matters in isolation, but we need to compare a whole range of theological issues. Not only are these important in determining the preponderance of theological concerns in Revelation, but they will also help us to establish how revolutionary the Apocalypse is in theological matters and therefore how provocative this book can be for future generations of readers, including ourselves. The topics we shall examine are these:

1. The person of Christ
2. The work of Christ
3. The doctrine of God
4. The work of the Holy Spirit

1. *The Person of Christ*

Margaret Barker's perspectives on Old Testament and inter-testamental theology are original, speculative and much debated by scholars.

But her discussion of evidence from Revelation for the picture of Christ as 'the Great Angel' helpfully focuses our attention on the key issues:

> The first Christians identified Jesus with the Great Angel not only in their reading of the Old Testament but also in their new writings… The prologue to Revelation is the earliest detailed recognition of Jesus as the Great Angel. Both the description and the setting are unmistakable. The Angel was a human figure with flaming eyes and feet like burnished bronze, appearing in the Temple. He was in the midst of the seven lampstands, meaning, surely, not that he stood among seven separate lamps but that he was the central stem of the sevenfold lamp, as Philo's Logos had been [*Rev. Div. Her*. 215]. He introduced himself as Yahweh: 'I am the first and the last and the living one' (Rev. 1.17), with which we should compare [Isa. 44.6; 48.12-13]… The Angel of John's vision was the one whom Isaiah had called Yahweh, the Redeemer of Israel (1992, pp. 200-201).

The figure is clearly Jesus, by virtue of the Resurrection (2.8). Yet, like Yahweh of the Old Testament, he permits people to eat from the tree of life (2.7), and he has the sword of judgment (2.12). The title 'Amen' in 3.14 might be a corruption of 'Amon' the heavenly master work-man (equivalent to Wisdom in Prov. 8.30). The Lamb in 5.6 has seven eyes, as the eyes of Yahweh in Zech. 4.10. The Christ figure rides from heaven as the warrior judge (19.11-14—see Deut. 32.43). He treads the winepress of wrath (19.15—see Isa. 63.3-6). Jerusalem was the bride of Yahweh (Isa. 54) and so is the bride of Christ (Rev. 21). For these and other reasons (especially the use of the Temple motifs as a setting) Margaret Barker concludes:

> There can be no doubt that for John the heavenly Christ was the ancient Yah-weh [emphasis hers]. Revelation had a Temple setting for the son of man/lamb/angel figure; the great judgement was a heavenly liturgy spilling over onto the earth (p. 203).

On this evidence the angel language of Revelation is either very sophisticated, with its resonances creating an advanced or 'exalted' Christology (on the way to Chalcedon), or it is a quite undeveloped and 'low' Christology, with Christ seen as an angel (a heavenly being functioning as a messenger or intermediary for God). Just possibly it is a mixture of both, as one particular tradition of Christianity searches for ways to express its faith. We must not conclude that the theology is undeveloped because the mode of expression is alien and sounds unsophisticated to us. To speak of Christ as an angel may not seem to be saying much about his relation to God. But this angelic figure at least controls and sends other angels (1.1; 22.16). Yet the

Christology of the Letter to the Hebrews, with its apparently strong Jewish colouring, asserts the superiority of Christ to any angel in the first chapter. Would the writer of Revelation have agreed?

The parallelism between the visions in Revelation 4 and 5 gives us the impression that the worship of heaven is jointly of God (as the one seated on the throne) and of the Lamb. This impression is maintained later in the book (e.g. 21.22; 22.1): the joint presence of God and the Lamb functions as the equivalent of the Temple (the symbol of God's presence) for the New Jerusalem. The Lamb is worshipped because of what he has done (victory achieved in some way by his death—see below on the work of Christ). He has already fulfilled the divine plan for salvation; the acclamation and ascription of divine honours to him now match the hymn to God himself (5.9; see 4.11). He now has the status deserving of worship; it is not said whether he had it before his victory. He is uniquely worthy to take the scroll from the right hand of God and reveal the future.

The Lamb first appears (at 5.6) 'between the throne and the four living creatures and among the elders'. If the four living creatures (in the tradition of Ezek. 1.5-14) are four fiery aspects of the glory of God, then the Lamb is included within the aura of the Godhead. But the Lamb is also 'among the elders' who are usually taken to be the patriarchal and apostolic representatives of the Old and New Testaments. If there is any precision in the choreography of this heavenly vision, then the Lamb's relationship to the elders could represent his function through the whole history of salvation, as God's link with humanity, rather than classifying the nature of the Lamb as human, not divine. To take the option of a more exalted Christology makes an attractive link with the later arguments of Irenaeus. He interpreted the four living creatures as 'images of the dispensation of the Son of God'. So God is revealed to the four corners of the world by means of the four canonical gospels. And so from this point it was appropriate to identify the four creatures as symbols of the four evangelists.

It is possible to defend a similar or stronger continuity within the writings of the Johannine circle from which both Revelation and the Gospel of John are claimed to originate. W. Grundmann (*Der Zeuge der Wahrheit* [Berlin: Evangelische Verlagsanstalt, 1985], pp. 59, 70) argued that two out of the four main features of the Fourth Gospel's view of Christ have their roots in Revelation. The structured sequence of seven 'I am' sayings has its starting point in Rev. 1.8, 17-18: 'I am the Alpha and the Omega... I am the first and the last, and the living one. I was dead, and see, I am alive forever and ever.' The 'I am' formula of Johannine theological statement begins as an oracular form of self-disclosure in the Apocalypse, where it functions 'to legitimate the revealer and the revelations which follow' (Aune 1986, p. 84). In the same way the theme of Christ as 'witness of Truth' originates with the testimony of 'Christ the faithful witness' (1.2, 5). (For more on this theme see below, under Holy Spirit).

2. *The Work of Christ*

Great care is needed, not only to describe the work of Christ in terms which Revelation uses, but also to allow for the thought-world where the imagery is used. Geza Vermes has observed:

> As anyone familiar with late Second Temple Jewish literature knows, warlike imagery is part of the apocalyptic style, but it does not necessarily entail violent political action, any more than the bloody metaphors in the description of the rider on the white horse (Rev. 19) would suggest that the early Church conceived of the returning Messiah as a cruel war-lord (*TLS*, 4 December 1992).

In the Apocalypse Christ performs (in past, present and future) a wide range of tasks, from communicating prophetic revelation (1.1-2, 5, 19) to riding on a white horse so as to judge and make war (19.11-13). But, in systematic theology, discussions of the work of Christ tend to focus on the purpose and results of the death of Christ. There are certainly a large number of references in the book to Christ, the Lamb's, act of dying. But we must be careful not to jump to conclusions about what they mean, like some commentators who fill up what is lacking in Revelation by echoes of Paul's language in Romans or elsewhere! This extract from Graeme Goldsworthy *The Gospel in Revelation* (1984, pp. 30, 47), commenting on 1.5-6; 5.5-6; 7.13-14, illustrates the danger:

> The Lion is the image of the glorified and reigning Christ. He alone can unlock the kingdom of God to us and make its reality known. But, like John, we can see the Lion only as he has come to us in the form of the slain Lamb. John points to the gospel-event; the living, dying and rising of Jesus Christ, as the key to the revelation of the kingdom. It is thus also the key to the Book of Revelation... When we speak of justification we are using a formal or technical way of referring to the gospel and its meaning. Through the life and death of Jesus the believer is accounted by God as free from the guilt of sin, and is thus accepted by God as his child. It is this message that permeates all that John is saying to us in Revelation. We note that it was the preaching of this gospel which led to the occasion for the writing of Revelation [Rev. 1.9].

Kenneth Grayston (1990) certainly avoids this pitfall. He has no wish to assimilate John's thought to the authentic views of Paul, his preferred interpreter of the death of Christ. He argues that the emphasis on the Lamb's dying is in Revelation for quite a different purpose, essentially as a call for vengeance and the means of achieving it:

> The author of Revelation is not embarrassed by the death of Christ and has no intention of excusing it, defending it, or explaining it away. Instead he uses it to attack the social and political structures of his day. The slain Lamb stands before the divine court and relentlessly accuses Roman society for its ill treatment of God's people and its radical disturbance of mankind and the world. The author of Revelation, in fact, adopts and revises an old perception of Christ's death, namely, as a protective device that turns away evil. The powers of evil cannot easily be restrained, and the saints must suffer as Christ had suffered; but they are not abandoned, they will not go unavenged, and their time of dominance will come. Shed blood calls for vengeance, and vengeance will soon fall upon those who are not written in the Lamb's book of life. In the great conflict between the creative powers of the heavenly world and the destructive powers of the abyss everything turns on the martyrdom of Christ—even when the author allows his imagination to run wild with bitter images of catastrophe and chaos. In the end, shed blood makes no further demands. The theme is life. There is new heaven and a new earth. The marriage of the Lamb to his bride is foreseen, and trees are planted for feeding and healing the nations (p. 358).

The message of Revelation about the death of Christ probably lies between these two extremes of interpretation. Even the language of 1.5-6 is not exactly what Paul would have said; it lacks the historical particularity of one sacrifice completely effected as a demonstration of God's love. On the other hand Kenneth Grayston's conclusion (summarized by one reviewer as 'the Apocalypse, despite the central image of the slaughtered Lamb, lapses into unselfcritical vindictiveness'!—John Muddiman in *Church Times*, 8 March 1991) scarcely does justice to the sympathetic appraisal of Revelation in his exegesis. The theme of the Passover lamb may be present in ch. 5, and we have no reason for devaluing the sacrificial language by describing it as merely traditional. The Lamb—'standing as if it had been slaughtered'—is 'intelligible if understood as indicating an unblemished male, wholly devoted in sacrifice to God (following the standard rules for choosing and offering the whole burnt offering)'. The 'sacrificial blood was an apotropaic rite [protective device] against the destructive forces unleashed by God' (Grayston 1990, p. 328). Even more significantly, 'John is asserting that the death of Christ is…a constitutive act for the created order and human history' (p. 332). It seems to me that it is the creative attempt to translate the death of Christ into a sacrifice of cosmic significance, supremely relevant to world problems as we know them, that is the distinctive contribution made by Revelation to understanding the work of Christ.

3. *The Doctrine of God*

The basis of Revelation's thought about God is given expression in the traditional language of the Old Testament prophets. So God is the holy and righteous judge whom the whole world should hold in awe. God's word can be heard, but God himself cannot be seen. As in Isaiah 6 what is seen, even in the holiest of this world's perspectives, the liturgical experience in the Temple, is only 'the hem of his robe', the point at which this world is touched by God's glorious otherness. It is therefore appropriate that the Seer often echoes the mystical language of Ezekiel, especially the esoteric symbolism of Ezekiel 1–3.

It is equally in the tradition of Daniel and other apocalyptic texts that Revelation has a dynamic concept of God as one who intervenes ultimately and decisively for both salvation and judgment. These apocalypses share with Old Testament prophecy a belief in the directness of divine intervention in human affairs; where they differ is in the sense of the scale required. For the apocalyptist, the world is in such desperate straits that only a cosmic intervention will save anyone. Although it is not referred to specifically in the text, the appropriate model would be the Great Flood of Genesis 6–9. The prime purpose is judgment, for the 'wickedness of humankind was great in the earth' (Gen. 6.5). But Noah and his family are rescued and blessed. In this saving act God establishes his 'covenant...that never again shall there be a flood to destroy the earth' (9.11). In the same way Revelation uses the Exodus plagues that devastated Egypt as prototypes for its own sequences of plagues (chs. 8, 9 and 16). The Exodus story is God's verdict on Egypt as well as Israel's deliverance. The twin aims of judgment and salvation are balanced finely.

Fundamentally, God is in control from first to last, from Creation to Paradise, as Creator of the world and as architect of its ultimate salvation, even if present appearances seem to deny it. That our world, as God's creation, is important for John, can be demonstrated statistically: out of 250 occurrences of the word 'earth' (*gē*) in the New Testament, 82 are in Revelation. God's power is righteous, uncompromising against evil in all its forms. Therefore the religious community— those who are striving to serve God, and so are enduring more than an equal share of suffering and martyrdom at the hands of this world's evil powers—trusts that God's power will avenge them. The situation is depicted in dualistic terms (God and Evil), because Evil is a force to be reckoned with by God's servants. But, as John's consoling vision reveals, the evil forces are essentially self-destructive, at war among themselves. The human participants are still scared to witless panic or despairing cry; it is not obvious that the story will have a happy ending. But from the heavenly perspective, although God's power is locked in a death or life struggle, God's triumph is already being celebrated. And the New Jerusalem will assuredly descend to earth.

M. Eugene Boring (1986, pp. 257, 260) analysed the theology of Revelation as a response to fundamental questions:

> Who, if anyone, rules in this world?
> What, if any, is the meaning of the tragic events which comprise our history?
> If there is a good God who is in control of things, why doesn't he do something about present evil?

The Apocalyptist's answer is: 'He *will*, for history is a unified story which is not over yet'. The reassurance is conveyed particularly in the hymns sung repeatedly in the worship of heaven. God has already acted. Christ is the Lord. God will go on acting consistently. The Kingdom of God is not a matter of uncertain speculation as to its coming. The coming of the Kingdom was combined with the Christological confession of Jesus' Lordship. God is Almighty (*pantocratōr*—see 1.8; 4.8; 11.17; 15.3; 16.7, 14; 19.6, 15; 21.22). The church is invited to join in the heavenly worship: 'Hallelujah! For the Lord our God the Almighty reigns' (19.6).

As we saw in our reading through Revelation, John's visionary experience began with a glorious celebration both of the divine Creator and of God's world. But in the present this gives way to a scenario of nightmare, a realization of the extent of the crisis (as we might see it for example in ecological and environmental issues). As in the Roman Empire of the first century, so again today there is a sense of how fragile are the apparently self-sufficient social and economic systems. The time of God's harvest is at hand, when he will call all producers to account, and rescue the good produce from the weeds. Harvest is a time of judgment; it is also a time for triumphant celebration, as the God of Creation is enthroned in glory and the reality of his ultimate power is fully acknowledged. For the Christian community which suffers in the world—and cares desperately for the redemption of the world—the fear and foreboding are held in tension with the hope and joy expressed in the anticipatory hymns of heaven. Here on earth there are still other powers with which the church must reckon, powers that appear to rival God and seem set to destroy, by means of their self-destructive impulses, not only goodness but the whole creation.

4. The Work of the Holy Spirit

> The charismatic movement has made the doctrine of the Spirit into something rather cosy, but the elemental biblical imagery of wind and fire is anything but that. The Holy Spirit is the Comforter, but also the one who leads us from conventional thinking into all truth, the inspirer of the prophets and *the speaker, in St. John's vision, of blasting words to the churches.*

This quotation is from Tony Grist writing in *The Guardian* 10 September 1990, but the emphasis is mine.

'Let anyone who has an ear listen to what the Spirit is saying to the churches.' This 'Hearing formula' is repeated in every one of the seven letters of chs. 2 and 3, and it is echoed at 13.9. The formula is thought to have originated with the early Christians; it is also found at Mk 4.9 and parallels, in the context of Synoptic Gospel parables. J. Roloff (*Die Offenbarung des Johannes* [Zürcher Bibelkommentare, 18; Zürich: Theologischer Verlag, 1984], p. 50) rightly sees the 'Hearing formula' as wider in application in Revelation than with the Synoptic parables. John's emphasis has moved away from esoteric ideas of grasping secrets (but see 13.18 for an intellectual variation). It becomes a prophetic warning and exhortation. The words are those of the Risen Lord speaking through inspired revelation. The Apocalypse has in this more localized way the sense of the continuity of the work of Jesus and the Holy Spirit that is established in the teaching on the Comforter in the Last Supper discourses of John's Gospel (see 14.16-17).

It is important to recollect how open are the ideas in Revelation about missionary outreach. Potentially anyone who responds to the prophetic warning, and then repents, can be rescued. There is no pre-destined total of the elect, only a symbolic inclusiveness (144,000)—based on tribes of Israel—which then merges with the incalculable multitude (7.9). And so the Spirit's words to the churches are not only addressed to the elect; potentially the prophetic warning and exhortation can be heard by anyone. Anne-Marit Enroth says:

> Characteristically the HF [Hearing Formula] is positive and open, for there is no connection with hardening and division of the hearers into two groups: those who do not hear and those who do (1990, p. 603).

The idea of hardening is prominent in the context of Mark 4 (see vv.

11-12; and compare Paul in Rom. 9.18; 11.7). This was a theological solution to the problem with which early Christians wrestled, as to why the gospel preaching was spurned. So it must be significant that, while the early church context for this formula includes hardening, 'this conception is absolutely lacking from the Book of Revelation' (p. 603).

The nature of prophetic Christian preaching, and the call to repentance, is indicated by 14.6-7:

> Then I saw another angel flying in midheaven, with an eternal gospel to proclaim to those who live on the earth—to every nation and tribe and language and people. He said in a loud voice, 'Fear God and give him glory, for the hour of his judgement has come; and worship him who made heaven and earth, the sea and the springs of water'.

Revelation by angels corresponds in apocalyptic imagery to inspired prophetic utterance. This preaching is repeatedly designated by two terms ('the word of God'/'the testimony [of Jesus]') which are bracketed together (see 1.9; 6.9; 20.4). The essence of prophecy is in bearing testimony to Jesus (19.10; 22.9), who is himself the 'faithful witness' (1.5). We should not forget that the genitive in the phrase 'testimony of Jesus' can be both subjective and objective. This emphasis on divinely inspired prophecy (not that Revelation itself should be called prophecy in distinction from apocalyptic—see above, Chapter 3) points to the significant role of prophets within the communities for which John wrote. Revelation helps us indirectly to understand the milieu of Christian prophecy.

Testimony/witness is a key idea in Revelation which leads actually (and etymologically) to martyrdom. The Greek words for it (*martus/ marturia*) evolve in meaning in the context of this New Testament book. It becomes a complex idea, as Elisabeth A. Castelli describes it, 'of martyrdom as death and as witness (a telling) and as victory (an inversion of contemporary power relations, repression becoming exaltation)' (*Imitating Paul: A Discourse of Power* [Louisville, KY: Westminster John Knox Press, 1991], p. 47). The visions of ch. 11 indicate how this witnessing is effective. Witness is an activity in the closest relation to Christ (Imitation of Christ) on the path from suffering to glory (see 1.5; 11.8). Revelation demonstrates a significant chain of witness from God, to Christ, to the angel, to the prophet, to the churches, to the world (see 1.1-2). God's reign is seen as universal in power, but it works towards its culmination through human agencies and representative individuals. Those who have the testimony are those who preserve Jesus' witness, declare it to the world, and suffer and die for it. What they declare is what Jesus himself reveals: the judgments and the sovereign authority of God.

Testimony/evidence is not simply what one has gained, like a detective, and holds onto as the vital clue. It is something that needs to be communicated because, like the prophet of old, one cannot keep it to oneself. But the role of Christian witness evolves from the original job description in the act of presenting the message to the world. As Jean-Pierre Jossua OP writes in *The Condition of the Witness* ([London: SCM Press, 1985], p. 64),

> Something of what one wants to bear witness to emerges only in the act
> of witnessing… The word of God is only grasped in its meaning for
> today…by expressing itself and acting as a word of salvation, of pity, of
> hope for specific human beings, at a given time.

Conclusions

This chapter is short on firm conclusions, but has tried to explore the range of theological issues that need to be considered. We must look at the text in its own terms, as well as observing its relationships with other texts. But we must not seek to homogenize Revelation into a single statement of Christian doctrine and thereby conflate the meanings of originally independent texts. That is to do a disservice by ignoring the possibility of distinctive points of view.

It is still possible to evaluate the work in its own terms, yet regard it as but one component of the larger context of biblical theology, not only in the New Testament but in the perspective of the Old Testament as well. Because of the Apocalypse's multiple points of contact, it can emerge very positively from the panoramic consideration 'from Moses to Patmos'. The recent work of Brevard Childs (*Biblical Theology of the Old and New Testaments* [1992]) deserves close, but not uncritical attention. His assessment of Revelation is as follows:

> The author has effected a profound alteration of the apocalyptic tradi-
> tion on the basis of his understanding of christology. The whole apoca-
> lyptic scenario which he inherited has now been interpreted as
> completed action. It does not lie in the future, but in every apocalyptic
> cycle described, God now rules his universe and the kingdom has come
> (7.10; 11.15; 19.6). Satan has been defeated by the Lamb and cast out of
> heaven. The Anti-Christ has been conquered and salvation realized
> (p. 321).

However, the writer of Revelation continues to use the apocalyptic vision to focus on the nature of the church's continuous struggle with evil, false prophets, and civil oppression. The biblical writer allows the eschatological tension between a heavenly and earthly reality to continue. Much like the Synoptics' use his attention turns to exhortation and a call for endurance even unto death (2.10).

FURTHER READING

David E. Aune, *Prophecy in Early Christianity and the Ancient Mediterranean World* (Grand Rapids, MI: Eerdmans, 1983).

Margaret Barker, *The Great Angel: A Study of Israel's Second God* (London: SPCK, 1992).

Richard Bauckham, *The Theology of the Book of Revelation* (New Testament Theology Series, Cambridge: Cambridge University Press, 1993).

M. Eugene Boring, *Sayings of the Risen Jesus: Christian Prophecy in the Synoptic Tradition* (SNTS Monographs, 46; Cambridge: Cambridge University Press, 1982).

M. Eugene Boring, 'The Theology of Revelation', *Interpretation* 40.3 (July 1986), pp. 257-69.

Maurice Casey, *From Jewish Prophet to Gentile God: The Origins and Development of New Testament Christology* (Cambridge: James Clarke, 1991).

Brevard S. Childs, *Biblical Theology of the Old and New Testaments* (London: SCM Press, 1992).

John M. Court, 'Risen, Ascended, Glorified', *Kings Theological Review* 6.2 (Autumn 1983), pp. 39-42.

J.D.G. Dunn, *The Partings of the Ways* (London: SCM Press, 1991).

Anne-Marit Enroth, 'The Hearing Formula in the Book of Revelation', *NTS* 36.4 (October 1990), pp. 598-608.

Paula Fredriksen, 'Apocalypse and Redemption in Early Christianity. From John of Patmos to Augustine of Hippo', *Vigiliae Christianae* 45.2 (June 1991), pp. 151-83.

Graeme Goldsworthy, *The Gospel in Revelation: Gospel and Apocalypse* (Exeter: Paternoster Press, 1984).

Kenneth Grayston, *Dying, We Live: A New Enquiry into the Death of Christ in the New Testament* (London: Darton, Longman & Todd, 1990).

Alan F. Segal, *Rebecca's Children: Judaism and Christianity in the Roman World* (Cambridge, MA: Harvard University Press, 1986).

INDEXES

INDEX OF REFERENCES

OLD TESTAMENT

New Testament

The Johannine Literature

INDEX OF AUTHORS